HONOURED
BY STRANGERS

HONOURED BY STRANGERS

The Life of
Captain Francis Cromie CB DSO RN
1882–1918

ROY BAINTON

Airlife
England

First published in the UK in 2002
by Airlife Publishing Ltd

British Library Cataloguing-in-Publication Data
A catalogue record for this book
is available from the British Library

ISBN 1 84037 196 X

This book contains some rare, early photographs and the publisher has made every endeavour to reproduce them to the highest quality. Some, however, have been technically impossible to reproduce to the standard that we normally demand, but have been included because of their rarity and interest value.

Typeset by Phoenix Typesetting, Ilkley, West Yorkshire.
Printed in England by Biddles Ltd., www.biddles.co.uk

For a complete list of all Airlife titles please contact:

Airlife Publishing Ltd

101 Longden Road, Shrewsbury, SY3 9EB England.
E-mail: airlife@airlifebooks.com
Website: www.airlifebooks.com

*This book is dedicated to
the memory of
W.L. 'Ben' Benson, submariner.*

Telegraphist W.L. Benson on the Russian depot ship *Dvina*.

By foreign hands thy dying eyes were closed,
By foreign hands thy decent limbs composed,
By foreign hands thy humble grave adorned,
By strangers, honoured, and by strangers, mourned!

'Elegy to the Memory of an Unfortunate Lady'
Alexander Pope
1688–1744

ACKNOWLEDGEMENTS

One thing I have discovered by rashly plunging into the deep end of history is that as the writer one is only a sheep dog, herding together a flock of facts, fantasies, rumours and memory. Without these, and without the interest, help and enthusiasm of those dozens of people who have consistently taken an interest in my efforts by repeatedly coming up with new revelations and information, this book would have never been written. So, my thanks go to the following:

To my good comrade, Mark Chamberlain, for inviting me to Sweden, and to his friend and mine, Björn Axel Johanssen, from whose study the first interest in HMS *E19* surfaced; to Margaret Bidmead at the Royal Navy Submarine Museum in Gosport for introducing me to the legend which is Cromie, and to Brian Head, whose personal help, interest and work in the RNSM's Baltic Archive continues to make every researcher's life much easier. To Paul Bach and Edna Tromans, Editor and Assistant Editor respectively, at *Saga* magazine, for their support, enthusiasm and assistance in recognising the potential of the Cromie story, for publishing not one but four features on the man, and for financing our trip to Russia at the same time as helping me to make a living. To the many readers of *Saga* magazine, Bill Dudley, Molly Williams, Jean Crisfield, the lovely Lilian Nield and her helpful son, Peter, and all the other readers who kept in touch. To Mr and Mrs David Kinna of Watford, for help and hospitality, and Lt-Col C.D. Darroch (Ret) of the Royal Hampshire Regiment Museum in Winchester.

Through the power of *Saga* came the most valuable contact – with Cromie's grandsons, Sean in Alabama, Tim van Rellim in Los Angeles, Chris in cyberspace, and the redoubtable Allen Wellesley-Miller and his enthusiastic wife, Margaret, in Dorset. To these family members I offer thanks for their assistance and patience, and apologies for the two years of intrusion into their privacy which this book necessitated.

To my friend Greg Harding, of Dallas, Texas, for giving up his time when in England to make a pilgrimage to Pembrokeshire. To Margaret and David London of the Manuscript Press in Southsea for their inestimable help and interest, and for their wonderful hospitality. To Michael J. Northeast whose interest turned up in the Baltic Flotilla's health records, and Edward Phillips, Head of Tasker Millward Lower School in Haverfordwest, which, in a previous incarnation as the Grammar School, was once Francis Cromie's seat of learning. To my agent, Malcolm Imrie, for staying the course and not giving up, and to

Peter Coles and Anne Walker at Airlife for having the courage to take this on against the rest of the publishing world's lack of interest.

Very special thanks and future gallons of ale go to Phil Thomaselli, of Swindon, for being so forthcoming with his vast knowledge of First World War espionage, for his help on his many trips to Kew, and for putting me in touch with one of the most crucial contacts of all, Professor Richard Spence at the University of Idaho, whose research whilst writing his new biography of Sidney Reilly turned up so many missing facts which had eluded me. And, without Richard Davies at Leeds University Russian Library, the aforementioned gentlemen would have remained strangers. To Steve McGlaughlin of California for his help in tracking down Russian naval officers.

Thanks also to my stalwart friend and saviour, photographer Graham Harrison. Our exotic adventure in Russia, where he saved me from a mugging by Gypsies, will stay with us both for ever. And in St Petersburg, a city of infinite beauty, for their friendship and hospitality, Eduard, Leonid and Svetlana Emdin, and Galena Varganova and her staff at the St Petersburg State University of Culture and Arts, and Prince Andrey Gagarin and his wife Princess Tina, for making our visit so much more memorable. To Trevor Langham, a member of those sons of fun, the Over the Hill Club, for arranging the tricky translation of Russian documents by Isobel Dodgson, whose help in this department was very important. And there was a minor character, Alexander Skalkin, officer with the Russian Customs Service, who saved my skin on the Estonian border and got me safely back to St Petersburg – a nice man. To my old friend Professor Theodor Siersdorfer, of Essen, in Germany, for his research into ships and for never failing to come up with obscure photographs. To H.O. 'Naz' Nazareth of Penumbra Productions for his enthusiasm, kindness and hospitality.

Finally, with much love for my wife Wendy, for suffering in penury whilst this book was being written, my son Martin for his utilisation of Hull University's Brynmor Jones Library on my behalf, and my daughter Sarah and her partner Ivan for their genuine support and enthusiasm. For those I've forgotten, it's not deliberate, you know who you are – thanks.

Roy Bainton

AUTHOR'S NOTE

Julian & Gregorian Calendars

Until February 1918 Russia had a different calendar in use from that of the West. The Julian (Old Style) calendar used by the Russians was 13 days behind the Western (Gregorian) calendar. In order to avoid confusion I have, wherever possible, used the Western calendar system, as this was in use with Cromie's flotilla and the Admiralty. However, if I am quoting direct from a Russian source, such as the Tsar's diary or letters, I have left the dates in the Old Style. As an illustration, a letter written by the Tsar on 3 March (old style) would actually be 16 March in the rest of Europe.

Russian/English Spellings

Translating Russian names into English for pronunciation appears to produce a wide variety of interpretation. Many of the sources consulted when researching this work appear to opt for various differences; e.g. Trotskii, Trotskiy, Trotsky; Milosevski, Miloshevsky, Milashovsky, etc. etc. I have reached my own consensus by taking the average spelling of each principal character's name across all the books consulted. Thus, out of 70 sources, as at least 50 spell 'Trotsky' – that's what I've used. The same process applies for place names, unless quoted within a letter or telegram, where the original writer's spelling is adhered to.

PREFACE

As I looked from the plane window the heavy iron-grey cloud suddenly cleared and there below us was Russia. I had last seen this coastline as a young merchant sailor in April 1959.

Back then, the murky fog of Stalinism had just begun to clear. Sputnik had in some odd way proved that the Union of Soviet Socialist Republics had a kind of prowess, at least in the arena of science and technology. It had offered a sympathetic Westerner something positive to look to after the four bitter decades of Russian struggle and social sacrifice since the October Revolution of 1917. Kruschev and the Politburo were a force to be reckoned with. Socialism, albeit a far cry from the pristine persuasion of Marx, Engels and their original Russian disciples, was still a powerful doctrine in the developing world. The Cuban crisis was yet to come. For all its monolithic greyness, the USSR was still a beacon of inspiration for a sixteen-year-old boy who had been brought up by a mother with a passion for the Communist way of life. Was it true that Russian plumbers and electricians could hum Mozart and quote Pushkin? Did women really dig the roads and work on the docks? Did the people own the banks? Did this USSR really have some of the finest doctors, physicians, writers, artists and musicians in the world? Were the armed forces of Communism still an implacable foe to the capitalist system? I believed so then. My mother always told me the truth.

And yet now it seemed obvious, forty-one years later, in the new millennium, as the plane moved closer to the ground below, that the cerebral promise of a proletarian Eldorado which drove Lenin and Trotsky on through those pre-Revolutionary decades of imprisonment and exile, appeared to have come to nought. There it was. The city with three names: noble St Petersburg; Petrograd; Leningrad. Cradle of the Revolution. A place to which a long-dead British naval officer had brought me.

Captain Francis Newton Allen Cromie had spent the last three difficult years of his life first along the coast of Estonia at Tallinn, then here; beginning as the patrician ally of Tsar Nicholas, then becoming an embarrassing Imperialist thorn in the side of the mighty, rumbling proletarian revolution, determined to wage the war he was paid to fight. His last meritorious months in 1918 were spent as a makeshift diplomat, trapped between the advancing Germans and the increasingly hostile Bolsheviks. As British Naval Attaché he could have thrown in the towel and gone home. No one would have blamed him. The military situation in Petrograd was a total mess. But Cromie, despite any faults he possessed, was a man of honour who obeyed orders. In the true sense of all *Boy's Own* heroes, he served his king and his country to the last. His reward was a bullet in the neck and eight decades of anonymity.

Cromie had seen this city when it was the focal point for a massive, unprecedented change in history. The experiment – Bolshevism, later to become Communism – outlasted all its original enemies and critics. And yet now it seemed as if it had never existed. What had happened to those seamless years of campaigns, meetings, debates and ultimately civil war that would send even the toughest of today's politicians gibbering into therapy? What had all the sacrifice, the bloodshed, the starvation, and the gulags been for?

Even at a height of several thousand feet I could see acre after acre of rusting, decrepit and abandoned factory sites. Crammed between these graveyards of heavy industry and looking from this distance for all the world like Gypsy camps were the houses of the sons and daughters of the Great Patriotic War. An air of depression dominated everything. I felt like an astronaut who had arrived in orbit over a neglected planet once colonised by Earth but now deserted. And yet there was life down there. The wide, busy highways away from the tightly packed social housing seemed as jammed as any British motorway. Here and there was a flash of neon; a shiny sports stadium, on some corners broad green public parks, and everywhere lots of trees.

Humanity was obviously still functioning with as much determination as elsewhere in the world.

As we swooped down over St Petersburg airport beneath the dull sky, I could see around the perimeter several old brick structures which must have been erected during the tragic siege of Leningrad in the Second World War. The runways appeared to be in bad need of repair. Lines of neglected, disused Aeroflot airliners offered silent testimony to a huge, state-run economy so recently passed into history.

In the baggage hall I waited with my colleague, the photographer Graham Harrison, as our luggage trundled into view on a carousel which seemed too small and inadequate for such a great destination point. We then had our first real taste of a Russia which existed before the revolution, and beyond: the queue.

In a country which has embraced the McDonald's culture, there was still a sinister air about the guards up in the gallery who looked down with suspicion upon the queuing foreigners below. Several booths awaited us; through them we would eventually proceed with our passports, visas and hopeful smiles. The process was reminiscent of a very slow sheep-dip. The young, uniformed passport-control lady eyed us up and down. Business or pleasure?

I wasn't sure, so opted for 'pleasure'.

At last, we were in Russia proper. The airport arrivals lounge seemed far too small for such an important place. It was heaving with Americans, Germans, the ubiquitous, camera-festooned Japanese. Having no idea how far it was to our hotel, the Pribaltiskaya, we braved the massed ranks of taxi hustlers until we found a price we thought sounded right: $50. I could feel Vladimir Ilyich Lenin squirming in his casket; to think that the almighty capitalist dollar would become Russia's currency – a perverse twist of fate indeed.

I looked back at the carved façade atop the airport building, and there he still was, looking down, surrounded by the Soviet flags of victory, the bald head, the jutting beard, the hammer and sickle above. Who knows; perhaps he'd have enjoyed the pleasures of Pizza Hut and Kentucky Fried Chicken, but somehow I doubt it.

The cab rumbled off and soon we were into St Petersburg's suburbs. Here, as in most of this city, the roads, many with tramlines running along the centre, are wide enough for four lanes of traffic. Yet owing to the frequent pot-holes, drivers take any route possible to forge ahead. Thus our trip took on all the aspects of a stock-car derby. I looked at Graham; he too was drop-jawed as we bumped, swerved and ground forwards, left, right, over the tram lines, right, left, screeching around buses. If you could drive like this in London you'd be home in a jiffy.

The pavements are wide, looked over by tall apartment buildings, many of them dating back to a more ornate period before the turn of the century, but others just simple, monolithic concrete boxes punctuated by rows of featureless windows. This was where the innocent citizens of Ronald Reagan's 'evil empire' had lived during those tense Cold War years. I was fascinated by St Petersburg's massive, broad drainpipes, at least 12 inches (30 cm) in diameter, their spouts feeding directly down onto the sidewalks. It is easy to forget how much snow falls here during the long Baltic winter; the resulting thaw in the spring must bring rivers of water down from those lofty roofs.

Occasionally, often obscured by trees, we could see Lenin's statue. There seemed to be two regular poses; one with his left hand clutching his open jacket, the right hand pointing upwards to some glorious future, the other with the same pointing hand, but the left clutching his folded cap. He must have had some sense of decorum during oratory; at least he took his hat off to make an important point, which is pretty generous considering the severity of the Russian winter. However, there weren't as many Lenins as I'd anticipated, and during the coming week we would discover why.

The Pribaltiskaya is a huge, Swedish-built hotel on Vasilievskiy Island over-looking the Baltic. We checked in and after a long day it felt good to take a shower, but a little unnerving having to remember not to drink the tap water or even clean one's teeth with it. In Russia, bottled water is a good business to be in.

Refreshed and changed I stood at the window. Although it was almost 8 p.m., the sun was still high. Mid-June is the time of St Petersburg's 'white nights', when the sun refuses to dip below the horizon until after midnight. This produces a kind of jet-lag effect for a British visitor; your head thinks it's tea time when actually your body tells you you're ready for cocoa and putting the cat out.

Gazing out over the steely blue Baltic my thoughts raced back to why I was here. Beneath that sparkling water Captain Francis Cromie had patrolled with his diligent, disciplined submariners eighty-five years ago. Without doubt, compared to the horrors and privations suffered by the soldiers on the Eastern and Western fronts, the Royal Navy's Baltic Flotilla, despite being challenged by war, revolution and the vicious winter ice, had a less fraught experience of the

Great War and one at least which most of them would live to recall. Now, after months of reading about all this, poring over documents in the Public Record Office, eagerly scanning long-neglected books in the British Library, I was here at last.

I thought of the days to come; how much of Cromie's revolutionary Petrograd would we still find out there, hidden behind the massed ranks of Stalin's tower blocks? Would we see the places where he had been, the rooftops over which he had escaped, the cemetery where he had been laid to rest?

Thomas Carlyle held a classic view of history. In *Heroes and Hero-Worship* he wrote, 'The history of the world is but the biography of great men.' It would be folly for a novice to challenge the might of a Carlyle, but one could argue that it is also the little men who help to make the talented ones great. Francis Newton Allen Cromie was certainly not one of history's 'little' men, yet in forgetting him, Britain has been slow to garland him with the epithet 'great'.

Francis Cromie had around him a large retinue of relatively minor characters, men such as his brave and able officers, his devoted ratings, and those Russians who, despite the raging, necessary fire of the Bolshevik revolution, and the contradiction of this Imperialist force in their midst, could still recognise a good, fair man when they saw one. It is through the scattered memories of many of these men who lived and fought with Cromie that we can begin to recognise and assemble his greatness – and thus be saddened by the cruel curtailment of his potential. Consider the subsequent careers of his officer colleagues in the Royal Navy's Baltic Project. The pioneer submariners who preceded Cromie by a year in the Baltic Campaign in October 1914, Lt-Cdrs Laurence, Nasmith and Horton, all became knights of the realm in later life. Max Horton, a great, colourful character, went on to become Commander-in-Chief of the Western Approaches in the Second World War – preceded in the post by Nasmith (who also received the VC) from 1939 to 1941 – and Laurence went on to command both the Submarine Service and the Navy's Aircraft Carrier Squadron. Their ability spoke volumes, and their potential was fulfilled admirably. All of this raises the poignant question: what might Francis Cromie have achieved had fate granted him another thirty years?

Cromie lived his life against a pageant of great events and old-fashioned heroism. His early adventures took place in the sunset of a traditional way of making war, where men faced men either hand to hand or across the decks of passing ships. The ragged banners of ten centuries of chivalry still fluttered from the mastheads of the world's navies when he was a young midshipman. If C.S. Forrester had set his great naval epics a century later, he would have had no finer model for his Hornblower than the subject of this book. Resourceful, dedicated, compassionate and brave: these are the qualities which set Cromie – and all great leaders – apart from those who simply climb the mundane ladder of promotion granted by privilege and class.

But this book concerns not only the epic adventures of the good captain; it is also an adventure for the author. It was not until a year had passed, twelve months of impatient, anguished searching for clues, verification and physical evidence, that I realised the true enormity of the task I had taken on. As the files swelled with legend, facts, hints and rumours and the shelves of my study began to sag, it slowly dawned on me that although I probably knew more about my subject that anyone alive, I was still faced with an enigma. Hopefully the inevitable areas of unfathomable mystery which still surround Captain Cromie's life will preserve that aura of mystique which surrounds all great men.

Had T.E. Lawrence not been such a brilliant writer, then apart from his deeds in Arabia we would perhaps still be totally baffled by his decision to abandon his life of fame and resort to the anonymity of false names and low ranks in the Tank Corps and the RAF. Yet even with a personality as promiment as Lawrence of Arabia, a thousand questions remain, leaving voids which have only been filled with speculation.

The story of Francis Cromie might well have remained hidden in the archives were it not for a series of chance encounters, all of which helped to fuel a growing curiosity. This book is the direct result of a late-night conversation after rather a lot to drink in a cosy apartment one bitterly cold night in Sweden.

Mark Chamberlain has been one of my closest friends for twenty years. We met through a mutual interest in traditional folk music and history. Mark is a graduate who has for many years taught English around Europe, and on one of his many trips over to the UK in 1995 I picked him up from Manchester airport. It was a bitterly cold, dark January afternoon and we drove for miles, looking for an open pub. We struck gold in Holmfirth, home of the TV series *Last of the Summer Wine*, where, over a great pint of Sheffield's finest, Ward's Bitter, Mark outlined a joint project for us: to write a screenplay based on the life of the seventeenth-century privateer, Captain William Kidd. Within weeks, with Mark back home in Sweden, where he was lecturing at Kalmar University, we had begun research into Kidd's life in earnest. The first draft took us a year to complete, and to our delight a London production company bought a one-year option on the script. Sadly, Hollywood and the director Ridley Scott beat us to the post – the tinsel-town writers of Los Angeles had already had the same idea.

With my background as a one-time merchant seaman and Mark's avid interest in all things nautical, however, it was not long before another subject came up. This time it was the brainchild of one of Mark's academic superiors at Kalmar, Björn Axel Johanssen. Björn is a committed marine historian, an accomplished author and expert on wrecks in the Baltic and Sweden's naval heritage. He was looking for a UK TV company to produce his magnum opus, *The Story of the Bell*, a history of marine salvage operations centred on the development of the diving bell.

In January 1999 I flew over to Kalmar and met both Mark and Björn. After a long, enjoyable dinner at the Chinese restaurant at Kalmar's railway station, Björn invited us back to his impressive study, where he began screening for us various videos filmed by his diving colleagues for TV documentaries. The footage was of wrecks of various cargo vessels, all in a marvellous state of preservation. After seeing four in a sequence, I asked Björn how they had been sunk.

'They were all sunk in one day in 1915', was his reply.

I was intrigued. 'An act of war?' It seemed a stupid question.

'Yes,' said Björn, 'a British submarine.' He brought a dossier from his desk. 'Here it is . . . the name was HMS *E19* . . .'

To my shame, I was unaware at that time that British submarines operated in the Baltic during the First World War.

'Was there a big loss of life?'

'No one died. All crews were saved and either put on to passing ships or set free in lifeboats . . .'

I jotted down 'E19' in my diary. A week later, back in Britain, I telephoned the Royal Naval Submarine Museum in Gosport and spoke to the Keeper of Archives, Margaret Bidmead. I asked her if she had a profile of HMS *E19*.

'Yes, we'll send you one. Would you like to see the service record of her commander?'

'Why,' I asked, 'is he interesting?'

'We like to think so . . .'

The next day I received four photocopied pages of A4; two gave a history of *E19*, but it was the two pages headed 'F.N.A. Cromie' which set my imagination on fire.

The rest is, as I hope we might say, history.

As a hand-to-mouth freelance feature writer on any subject which I think readers might find interesting, I failed to realise that my fascination with Captain Cromie was pushing me into an area of work usually populated by the literary greats. I stood back for a moment; this was going to be no easy project. Apart from the naval story, there was the immensely complicated subject of the Bolshevik revolution. The research alone might cost thousands. It would mean lots of travel; many trips to London. I would have to go to Russia at least. Perhaps this was just a good magazine article, after all. Then Mark Chamberlain called me from Sweden and I told him of my doubts. 'I'm not an academic. Maybe the reason no one knows much about Cromie is that there's very little to know . . .'

But Mark was adamant. 'Cromie deserves his own book . . . so if *you* don't do it, then who will?'

This is not a continuous circle without breaks and gaps. Much valuable personal domestic material on Cromie's private life has, as you will discover, been lost to us. The first half of this work has been a struggle because so little evidence of Cromie's life outside his naval career exists. Without the survival of his 1915–18 despatches to Commodore Hall and Admiral Phillimore, it is doubtful if I would have begun this work at all. There is a naval service record, some press cuttings, four grandsons scattered around the world with, except in one case, understandable reservations about talking too much – but no diaries, no letters. All have been destroyed. However, there are the notes and memoirs of those who knew Cromie – so with these, I can, I hope, make, if not a full portrait in oils, at least a good pencil sketch.

I am optimistic that what is presented here between the covers of this book, will serve in some way to place this colourful, brave and compassionate man where he truly belongs – standing tall amidst the ranks of the fallen sons and daughters of a calamitous episode of twentieth-century history.

When discussing this work in the early stages of research with Brian Head, the leader of the Royal Navy Submarine Museum's Baltic Project, one name figured prominently in the story of the Baltic Flotilla's plunge into war and revolution: Ben Benson. As leading telegraphist on HMS *E19*, Ben also became a kind of unofficial valet to Cromie, and kept a vibrant, often amusing diary of his days with his commander in the Baltic. After a long naval career, Ben went on to greater glories as a BBC radio engineer, but throughout his life he tried in every way possible to convince the Admiralty and anyone who would listen that Francis Cromie at least deserved a posthumous VC.

Needless to say, it never happened. Ben passed away in the 1980s after a full and fascinating life, and I only wish fate had granted me the chance to meet him, and that he had survived long enough to see this work. This book, then, is for you, Ben, and for all those brave Jack Tars in both world wars who put their lives on the line, above and below the waves.

CONTENTS

INTRODUCTION

There is properly no history; only biography.

Ralph Waldo Emerson, 1803–1882

I think Emerson got it the wrong way around.

It all seemed so easy. Sitting around with friends, telling them, in a condensed form, the story of the man who had become 'my hero'. Everyone would listen and agree, as friends do: 'What a great yarn – ought to make a great book – and a film . . .'

They were right, of course. But although I knew I had to write this book, I had little idea of how to go about it. Every morning I looked at the photograph of Captain Cromie facing me from alongside the year planner above my computer. The blank months of the year ahead seemed to align with his steady gaze – like a man pointing out to the sea, challenging me. Dare *you* go out there? This introduction is an attempt to illustrate the confusion which results from a writer's attempts to learn biography 'on the job'.

Like most self-taught modern scribes I started with the Internet. Although this valuable research tool improves daily, in 1999 all it gave me was a list of doctors, dentists and lawyers, mostly based in California. There were Cromies aplenty in Northern Ireland, especially in Armagh and County Down, but whatever contact I made resulted in no recognition of the Cromie family I was dealing with.

To a trained, graduate historian, such blundering through history would seem laughable; the correct methodology in such a search would have had a definite pattern. Looking for evidence of the captain was simply a private, obsessive hobby. As a hand-to-mouth magazine feature writer, always working within a 2,000-word limit, the absolute fine detail in a historical piece never required an expanded view. Birth date, place of birth, existing published cardinal points of interest in the subject's career, all held together with a loose mortar of stylistic description and narrative, the whole package rounded off with some decent pictures – such are the elements which pay a hack's mortgage. Having never been through the rigorous process of writing a history book or a detailed biography, I set out rather naively, imagining that I would eventually stumble across shelves of files and yellowing folders of news cuttings.

It only took a month to disabuse me of that notion. After (in retrospect) a rather stupid and fruitless search of the telephone books of the UK and writing to various military establishments, I was no further on. This book is therefore

1

the result of a steep learning curve for its author, a haphazard, educational journey of discovery which began in Sweden, then took me to Wales, Dorset, Gosport and London, and culminated, like Cromie's career, on the banks of the River Neva in St Petersburg.

For a century and a half, photography has given us a clearer picture of recent history. Beyond the 1840s we no longer have to rely on engravings, paintings and sketches to see what life was like in the Crimea, Victorian Britain or the American Civil War. We can see existence frozen in a long-past second; see the way people dressed, the true condition of their surroundings. As the nineteenth century ticked over into the twentieth, the way people looked, the invention of the car, and the spread of railways, gas and electricity, all combined in black and white images to create a false feeling of familiarity. The world of a man in a suit and tie, holding a pint of beer, in a 1920s photograph seems closer to our own. Perhaps if I could join him in that drink we would have much in common. Perhaps. These thoughts crossed my mind at first as I studied the many museum pictures of sailors and naval officers during the preparation of this book. But as one delves behind the photographs to study the mind-set of those who fill the archives of those times, we become aware that, cameras and clothing aside, our modern lives are vastly different in every possible way from theirs.

Francis Cromie stands, his medals proudly displayed in all their glory, his sensitive gaze aimed at a more different social horizon than we could ever imagine. His sideburns, his Hollywood good looks, his proud bearing, all these could be reproduced in a film studio today. Yet this would only represent a visual replica. When we look into the language of his peers, the docile nature, by today's liberal standards, of his subordinates, something crucial is revealed. This was an age of unquestioning service, when duty ruled. A century ago men and women 'knew their place', and to those that already had, only more would be given. To rise from his middle-class background, through the ranks of the Navy, and then be plunged, by fate, into a short career as a diplomat, speaks volumes for Francis Cromie's character. Here was a grammar-school boy who could not spell, yet he mastered the Russian language in a few months. He was a man who was torn: virtually begging the Admiralty to go home after three bitter winters in Russia, yet obsessed with his own hidden agenda for remaining behind. Reading his letters, it appears that he stoically accepted his new role as Naval Attaché, and with little idea of the level of duplicitous double-dealing of the hard, seasoned politicians around him, got on with the job as best he could. Without doubt the world he lived in may look vaguely familiar, but compared to the twenty-first century, it was a different planet altogether.

Francis Cromie's naval service record, stored on microfilm at the Public Record Office in Kew, tells us little about the man himself. It gives his date of birth as 30 January 1882, at Waterford, southern Ireland. An alternative record, at the Royal Navy Submarine Museum in Gosport, Hampshire, gives the same month and day, but the year is 1881. But what these records reveal is a full and vigorous life, albeit a short one. During two decades of naval service, he experienced some of the major conflicts in twentieth century history. In China, he witnessed the relief of Peking during the Boxer Rebellion. Although a valuable and talented young officer in what was referred to by Jack Tars as the 'Big Navy', i.e. the surface fleet, he volunteered for the unfathomed dangers of the fledgling submarine service at a time when it was far from popular with the Royal Navy's haughty, class-ridden hierarchy. And then came the Great War, with a massive, extra complication for Cromie – the Bolshevik Revolution, which took his life. So from the scratchy, copperplate handwriting on an old document, an enigma springs forth. What was it that made a talented, sensitive man like Francis Newton Allen Cromie make these choices?

My first port of call had to be the Royal Navy Submarine Museum (RNSM) in Gosport. There I struck up a valuable and lasting friendship with Brian Head, curator of the Baltic Section. Brian's own unpublished manuscript on the Baltic campaign has been a goldmine of information, saving many miles of travel and hours of additional research. To my delight I discovered that I could read copies of Cromie's letters to the Admiralty sent back from Russia to England between May 1916 and July 1918. And yet even this breakthrough threw up another mystery. Cromie's forty-two despatches from Russia, full of valuable insights into his world and his work, were addressed to Admiral Phillimore and Commodore Hall at the Admiralty, and, after 1917 to the head of Naval Intelligence, Admiral Reginald 'Blinker' Hall. But where were the replies? The answer at the RNSM was that their whereabouts was unknown. Admiral Phillimore's letters, which are stored at the Imperial War Museum, are in the main very intimate despatches addressed to his wife, with only a few references to his dealings with Cromie. Writing this book without Cromie's letters would have been too big a challenge, yet it seemed hard to gain a sense of balance in his relationship with his superiors without some official reaction to those despatches.

In the RNSM files I also found an article from the *Western Telegraph*, published in Haverfordwest in 1985. Headed 'Naval Hero of The Baltic "Forgotten" by Historians', from which I discovered that Cromie's mother was the daughter of Thomas Ince Webb-Bowen, the Chief Constable of Pembrokeshire. Young Francis was educated at the Fishguard Free School, and then transferred to Haverfordwest Grammar School, where his memory was still honoured.

The RNSM had much more material than I could absorb in that first day, but I was also steered in the direction of the unpublished diary of Cromie's telegraphist on board HMS *E19*, Ben Benson. With a photocopy of this and the Cromie letters in my bag, I had made a start. The *Telegraph* piece also referred to a book by Michael Wilson, himself an ex-submariner, *Baltic Assignment*. This apparently included an account of Cromie's war activities. After scouring the libraries of Nottinghamshire I finally found a copy. It was an exhilarating read, and included Cromie's Baltic exploits, extracts from his Admiralty despatches and the mystery of his death, and like Brian Head's own unpublished MSS on the Baltic campaign, was an invaluable reference source.

However, I still felt that there was a further, hidden dimension to this man. What were the real circumstances which had led to his death? Who pulled the trigger? It was time to visit the Public Record Office. I knew that Cromie's father had served with the British Army, so the Army records seemed a good place to begin. But when I finally found my man, his record was a blank page, with only his name, rank and place of birth at the top. Apparently, his original record may have been destroyed and this was simply a replacement page.

I was surprised to discover that Francis Cromie's father, Charles Francis Cromie, was born in Cincinatti, Ohio, USA. How the family, which appears to be of Irish origin, came to be in Cincinatti is unclear. Emigration from Ireland to America does, in the main, seem to be a constant east–west movement, but for some reason young Charles came back, and he enters the records in the service of Queen Victoria as a captain in the Hampshire Regiment in 1881, stationed at Fort Duncannon, a small hamlet on the northern banks of Waterford Harbour. At some time during the 1880s, he moved across the Irish Sea and settled in the port of Fishguard in Pembrokeshire.

At this point, it seemed I had enough to justify a trip to Wales. Thus, on a bright, sunny day in February 1999, out of insatiable curiosity, with only a few more pieces of this jigsaw and no lid to the box, I headed off with a friend, Greg Harding, for Wales. Our first evidence of Cromie appeared at the top of the memorial to the War Dead in Haverfordwest town centre. This being such a tall monument, crowned with a proud Welsh dragon, and the names inscribed alphabetically from the top, it was easy to see how his may have been overlooked. Yet a street map revealed further evidence: here was a Cromie Avenue, and around the corner, a Cromie Terrace. Out of interest I asked a lady in a house down Cromie Avenue if she knew who the thoroughfare had been named after. She shook her head. 'I think he might have been a councillor or something . . .'

I had telephoned ahead to arrange to visit what was once Haverfordwest's Grammar School. To my disappointment I discovered that the location, and the building, had long since changed. It was now a comprehensive, away from the town centre and renamed the Tasker Millward School. There we were met by the ebullient and helpful Head of the Lower School, Edward Phillips. To the school's credit, when the new buildings were occupied, the old Roll of Honour panel from the Grammar School and two plaques dedicated to Francis Cromie, DSO, RN, had been given pride of place in the assembly hall and the adjoining corridor repectively. Mr Phillips knew there was something special about these monuments, and was somewhat bemused by my interest, yet like most of the people I spoke to in Haverfordwest, was not aware of the breadth of Cromie's achievements. Hopefully, when the children of Tasker Millward see this book, it may alter their perception.

Thus far we had seen the physical memory of Cromie in the town of his childhood: a name on a memorial, an avenue, a terrace, and two walls in a school. We were also informed that there was, for many years, a Cromie House at the Grammar School, and as recently as the 1980s, the town's Barn Street County Primary School also had a Cromie House. It was vaguely exciting, but there had to be more. Where had he lived? Who were his family? We made a bee-line for the Public Library.

The first discovery there was an isolated press cutting from the *Pembrokeshire Telegraph*, dated 6 November 1924:

Late Capt Cromie

Memorial Service to Fishguard Officer in Russian Church

ROYALTY ATTEND THE SERVICE

A service in memory of Capt Francis Cromie, formerly of Fishguard, who was murdered at the British Embassy in Petrograd five years ago, was held recently at the Russian Church, Buckingham Palace Road, London.

The service was conducted by the Very Reverend John Selinkhin, assisted by the Rev. Constantine Versalovsky, and the Rev. Basil Thisthieff. It was preceded by a short address in Russian by the Rev. John Selinkhin who referred to the services the late Capt Cromie had rendered to his country for which he died so brutal a death.

There was a large congregation, among those present being Mrs Cromie (Capt Cromie's mother), Queen Olgof of the Hellenes and their daughters (Princess Elizabeth and Princess Marina), the Grand Duchess Zeria, Capt Masinth Dunbar (Representing the Admiralty), Mr C. Mabokoff (formerly Counsel of the Russian Embassy in London), Admiral Walkoff (formerly Naval Attaché at the Russian Embassy under the old Russian Government) and Mrs Walkoff and two daughters, Mr Duncan Fitzwilliams (formerly Consulting Surgeon in Russia and a native of Newcastle Emlyn), the Rev. B.S. Lombard (the late British Chaplain in Petrograd), General Holodovsky, Canon Ierwood and Captain Ierwood, Mrs Hurley, Mr Arthur Lang, Mrs T. Thornton, Mr Molchanoff and Mr & Mrs McNabb.

Capt Cromie will be remembered by many old Fishguardians. He was educated at the Fishguard National School and the Haverfordwest Grammar School and his name is inscribed on the shrine at St Mary's Church, Fishguard.

Floral tributes are regularly placed at this shrine in memory of the late Capt Cromie.

This was enticing. Royalty. The Russian Church. He seemed to have made much more of an impact than the existing record showed – and there was also the intriguing mention of his shrine in St Mary's Church, Fishguard. I had almost given up the search for further references when a second cutting appeared, this time from the letters page of the *Western Telegraph and News*, 27 August 1936:

'Cromie of The Baltic'
A Gallant Haverfordwest Sailor

Sir

A few weeks ago I stood beside the County War Memorial at Haverfordwest awaiting permission to undergo a minor operation in my throat. I looked up at the plate bearing the names of the fallen and recognised that of Captain Cromie.

I was one of the last Englishmen to see him alive and shake him by the hand. What grieves me is that I lived at Pembroke Dock for ten years without knowing of his Pembroke associations. I have told the story of the Russian revolution to many people, but I have never heard his name mentioned by anyone else, although one of Pembrokeshire's greatest sailors and a gentleman.

I served under him in Russia as I was a submarine sailor in those days. I remember one incident during the revolution when some of the Russian soldiers and sailors became very insulting. Captain Cromie turned to them and said, 'Remember – it is not me you insult, but the uniform I wear . . .' The Russians turned away, ashamed.

What stirring stories of those days I could tell – lying on the bottom of the ocean at the Baltic entrance to Kiel, waiting to capture a German ship which was due to come out, how we got into Riga harbour through the nets by following a small drifter, how we lay for two months at Panama, disabled, with no change of clothing, with very little food, only black bread made with straw.

I might mention that the main body of submarine ratings were sent home directly after the Revolution but 27 of us stayed there, till the last shell blew up everything.

We then came home disguised as Merchant Service Seamen. I have my passport now. It is some consolation to know that Captain Cromie died fighting on the grand stairway of the British embassy in Petrograd.
G. North Cade, late 3 Front Street, Pembroke Dock.
6 Picton Place, Altenborough, Notts.

As I ran my fingers over these old pieces of newsprint it dawned on me that it was probable that no one had bothered to read these cuttings for decades. After all, why should they? Could I expect others to share my recently acquired obsession? Of course not. I began to ponder over that list of mourners at the memorial service; it included Cromie's mother, but not his wife and daughter. This seemed odd. Had they died? Was he divorced? It would take me two years to reach the answer. I wondered who G. North Cade was; Altenborough was just down the road from my home. No doubt he would appear in Admiralty records somewhere, but that was yet to be discovered, and in any case, this letter had been written over sixty years earlier.

We then turned to the electoral registers. Maybe we could find an address for the Cromies. But the sun was creeping lower, and the records were arranged by wards, and not in alphabetical order. It was like looking for a needle in a haystack. The librarian suggested the Haverfordwest County Record Office, a short walk from the library. It was a worthwhile visit.

Here we discovered the roots of a family tree, but it was only an undated press cutting, outlining the families of various prominent Pembrokeshire dynasties. As Chief Constable of Pembrokeshire, Thomas Ince Webb-Bowen, represented a family with a long record of public service. The parish records of Camrose, Fishguard, revealed vicars with the name Webb-Bowen stretching back to the sixteenth century. Thomas was born on 22 September 1839. He married

Catherine Luther Anne Bowen Allen and they had two daughters, Nina Newtonia Webb-Bowen and Mary Grace Josephine Webb-Bowen. Mary Grace married Captain Charles Francis Cromie from Cincinatti, latterly of the Hampshire Regiment.

This was all the file in Haverfordwest's Record Office told us, but I now knew for sure who Cromie's parents were. Yet an index card showed a reference to a Dolores Anthea Cromie. The relevant file revealed a solicitor's letter from 1959, dealing with the will of a Gwladys Catherine Blunt. It appeared that she might be Francis Cromie's wife, and Dolores Anthea their daughter. Anthea's birth date, 11 April 1907, was perfect – Cromie would have been a young, married lieutenant aged 25. The letter went on to show that his mother, Mary, had at one time lived at a house called Glanmoy, in Goodwick, near Fishguard, and that Anthea had become Mrs D. A. Miller, of Upton, Poole, in Dorset. If she was still alive, then I had a trail to follow.

We searched for another hour, but darkness was already beginning to fall. It had been a very long drive to Haverfordwest – nearly 300 miles – for my friend Greg, who had come down from Grimsby, calling for me *en route* in Mansfield. I was worried about the long trek back. But Greg was as fascinated and curious as I was.

As we walked in the twilight to the car park, he said, 'Right – St Mary's Church, Fishguard, and let's see if that house, Glanmoy, is still standing . . .'

The Reverend Roger Griffiths, Vicar of the parishes of Fishguard, Llanchaer and Pontfaen, was not available when we reached the peaceful little church in Fishguard. We searched high and low for any evidence of a shrine to Captain Cromie, but there was nothing in the church and nothing of note in the grave-yard. A later communication from the vicar sadly confirmed that any memory of Francis Cromie had long since vanished from the church – and no one in the congregation recalled a shrine. Indeed, no one knew who the captain was.

It was dark when we drove off towards Goodwick. We had no idea if Cromie's mother's house, Glanmoy, still existed, but as we sped along I saw a sign: 'Glanmoy Country Hotel – turn right'. Greg swung the car around and we drove along a wooded lane, then suddenly, there it was: a fine, timbered house set on a hillside with a long lawn, bordered with a low stone wall. This was indeed the place, as we discovered from the current owners. Although they were unaware of Francis Cromie and his career, there was apparently a mention in the deeds of Mrs Cromie living there in the 1920s. The house, built entirely of pitch pine, was under a preservation order, and had been constructed in the Far East in sections, transported to Wales by sea and erected here on this impressive hillside. And yet, as we enjoyed the hospitality of our hosts in the small bar, I realised that this place held little significance for this story. By the time his mother moved here, Francis had been dead for several years. It was, however, an exciting coda to what had been a long day of incomplete discovery.

Over the ensuing days I set about trying to establish the existence of any Cromies in Dorset. But it had been four decades since Gwladys Blunt had died, and the search for Dolores Anthea seemed a dead end. I tried Dorset libraries, and phone books, and logged on to various genealogy web sites, all to no avail. Economy dictated that I could not afford at this time to make a fruitless journey to Dorset. If I could not get to any Cromie descendants, then maybe, somehow, I might get them to come to me. With what I had collected thus far – Cromie's service record, the material from Wales and that from the RNSM in Gosport – I at least had enough for what I thought would make a very good feature article. At this point I had become established as a fairly regular feature writer for *Saga* magazine. With *Saga*'s huge circulation and over-forty-five readership, this stirring story of a sadly neglected *Boy's Own* hero seemed right. Fortunately, the magazine's editor, Paul Bach, agreed. Like me, he began to view Francis Cromie as something bordering on another Lawrence of Arabia. As I outlined the captain's life, we both agreed that it was too much to fit in one feature, and Paul commissioned the story as a two-parter for 1999's June and July editions.

It was a good move – there were *Saga* readers who recognised the story. I soon had a flow of mail. The results of these contacts will all be outlined in greater detail in the following chapters, but briefly, here are some gems the postman continued to deliver.

To my delight I was contacted by Mr David Kinna of Watford. He informed me that his grandmother, who had lived in Reval (now Tallinn, in Estonia) during the Russian Revolution, was the woman to whom Cromie had gone for Russian lessons. This was a wonderful piece of news. Then came more information from Brian Head at the RNSM – was I aware that there was a lady in her nineties, still living in Manchester, Mrs Lilian Nield, who had been brought up in Narva during the Great War, and who had, as a little girl, met Cromie on various occasions when he had come to dinner at their house? To find someone alive who had a first-hand memory of the captain was beyond my wildest imagining. There was also a tablecloth, made by Lilian's mother, in the Russian Archive at Leeds University, which had been autographed by all the crew of Cromie's submarine, *E19*.

Then a letter arrived from a gentleman in Lyndhurst, Hampshire, Bill Dudley. Bill's father had served in Cromie's flotilla in the Baltic, aboard HMS *E1*. After falling for an Estonian girl in Reval he had requested permission to marry from Captain Cromie. Cromie agreed, and the marriage took place on board the flotilla's Russian accommodation ship, the *Dvina*. The issue of that marriage was William Dudley, who was christened a year later on the same vessel, using the ship's upturned bell as a font. This was followed by a fascinating parcel from Mrs Molly Williams of Hall Green in Birmingham. Her father, John Eastman, had also served in Russia with Cromie as seaman torpedoman on HMS *E8*. He seemed typical of his die-hard breed. After spending thirty-seven years in the Royal Navy, he had retired to Australia after the Second World War with the rank of lieutenant but minus his sight, yet had taken up the unusual hobby (for a person with no sight) of rug-making, at which he had won prizes. Even more exhilarating was a cassette recording of an Australian Broadcasting Corporation interview in the 1950s, of Lieutenant Eastman's first-hand account of the outbreak of the Russian Revolution.

Joe A. Rohan, an elderly gentleman from Shaldon in Devon telephoned. His grandmother had been Cromie's cousin. 'As children,' he said, 'we were always given Captain Cromie as an example in every crisis – a grazed knee, a fight, a dispute. It was always, "think of the captain – never say die!", even though I had no idea who he was . . .' Unfortunately, Joe had no knowledge of the whereabouts of the Cromies.

A lady from Edinburgh, Mrs Jean Crisfield, wrote to tell me she had the chart table from one of the E class submarines in her attic, and Michael Northeast of Hampshire, a retired port health officer, sent me fascinating pages from the naval surgeon's health records of Cromie's Baltic crews.

But all this was exciting and confusing in equal measure. Now that I had started something, and attempted to warn any potential competitors by announcing in *Saga* that my biography of Cromie 'would be published next year' I realised that I had to go on. Together with my agent, we put together what we thought was a pretty good proposal for this book. He was confident that we would soon have an offer from a major publishing house. It took a long six months of rejection before Airlife had the vision to recognise the potential of Francis Cromie's story, and here we are.

By August 1999 I had a tray full of anecdotes, sepia photographs, contacts and eager letters from potential readers of a biography. I travelled again to the RNSM, and came away with pages from the log-book of HMS *E19*. Yet like the Ince Webb-Bowens of Pembrokeshire, the Cromie family seemed to have vanished into history. But at the end of that month came a major breakthrough. I received a phone call from the *Saga* office informing me that they had received a fax from a lady in Louth in Lincolnshire. She was the ex-wife of a gentleman called Chris Wellesley-Miller, who was Francis Cromie's grandson. Like many divorcees, this lady was understandably reluctant to stir up the past too much, but somehow contact was made with her ex-husband and after eight months of wandering around in a fascinating, self-made wilderness, the trail was opening up before me. Chris sent me an e-mail. What it contained was so enthralling at first in its detail that it gave the prospective content of my book an added *frisson*. Chris is a history graduate, and had actually written a thesis in the 1970s on his grandfather, Captain Cromie. His opinions and conclusions concerning Cromie's work in Russia, his political leanings and the reasons for his death, were quite staggering. I read the e-mail again and again. Could Francis Cromie, a captain in the Royal Navy, thrice decorated by the Tsar, really have been a Bolshevik sympathiser? It has taken eighteen months to reach my own conclusions. Then came a telephone call from Allen Wellesley-Miller, another Cromie grandson. Allen has been pivotal in helping me to put this book together. And through Allen, I discovered yet more grandsons: Sean Wellesley, a businessman in Alabama, and Tim van Rellim (that's 'Miller', spelled backwards), who works as a film producer in Los Angeles.

Before long a dialogue had commenced. It began, after Chris's e-mail, with a visit to Dorset, where I spent a fascinating afternoon with Allen, who is an exceptionally skilled mechanical engineer, and his wife, Margaret. At last I began to feel much closer to my subject, as if the curtains had been opened to reveal the real man. To begin with, Allen produced Francis Cromie's ceremonial sword, souvenirs from his naval career, a writing case, a silver bowl presented to him after the Boxer Rebellion, his silver Navy rum measure – unused (Cromie was teetotal). But more exciting than any of these artefacts was the discovery that he was also a skilled watercolour artist. To my sheer delight I was allowed to borrow seven of his watercolours. They included fine miniatures of Japanese and British warships, including HMS *Barfleur*, in which he served as a midshipman during the Boxer Rebellion. There is also an accomplished study of a Thames river barge. All this revealed a completely new side to Cromie's character. Skilled seaman, gentleman, hero, and now, aesthete.

But despite the great leap forward that making contact with Cromie's blood-line undoubtedly was, I began to realise that I had to tread softly. Until my meeting with Allen, Cromie had been a myth, and myths can be speculated with. Now the speculation had to stop, and the diplomacy begin. I was in the midst of four members of the great man's family, and, in personality and individual outlook, four very different members at that. And there was a bitter disappointment to face up to.

There can come a point when a writer's eager research and investigation is regarded as prying. I had hit it off with Allen and Margaret pretty well, but Chris made it clear, after the initial exposure of his views on his grandfather's career and demise, that he wished to retreat back into cyberspace and not maintain contact. His feeling seemed to be: OK, so you're writing a book – I look forward to reading it. That was the gist of his departure. It was done politely, but my attempts to discover from him at which university and in what year he had written his Cromie thesis drew a blank. So I behaved rather shadily and wrote to his ex-wife to see if she could help me. After all, any thesis would still be available for a researcher to study at the relevant university. It would have given me quite a leg up and saved me months of research – the bibliography alone would have been solid gold at that stage. However, she politely refused to reveal anything. Allen, Tim and Sean confirmed that the thesis had been written, but could not recall which university Chris had been at, or in what year he had graduated. Thus I had two choices: make random searches and enquiries looking for a Cromie thesis at every university in the UK, or drop this line of enquiry. The latter made more sense. It was a sharp lesson: do your own research, and stop trying to cut corners.

I asked Allen about Cromie's personal life. Did any letters exist? I had seen a tantalising reference in the RNSM to a diary. I then received my first hints of a bitterness which had lasted down the years. I could not get a firm grip on the source of this without prying too much and appearing insensitive, but there seemed to be dark indications about Cromie's life and death which had caused both Gwladys Cromie and her daughter, Anthea (Allen's mother), lasting distress, beyond the tragedy of being widowed. Allen told me that there had been 'boxes of letters and documents' from the captain, but that his mother had burned them all in a display of remorse when Gwladys passed away. Hearing this was heartbreaking – what might those boxes have contained? But as my amateurish naivety began to evaporate, I realised that this kind of anguish must be common for time-served historians and biographers.

10

Top left: Francis Cromie's half-brother, Captain Henry Julian Cromie, aged 20,
    Hampshire Regiment. Killed in action on the Somme, 23 October 1916.
Top right: Francis Cromie's half-brother, Captain Maurice Francis Cromie, Hampshire
    Regiment. Killed in action at Gallipoli, 4 June 1915.
Above: Gwladys Cromie (Cromie's wife) in London, *circa* 1920.
(Photographs courtesy of Allen Wellesley-Miller and Sean Wellesley.)

So I decided that I would not outstay my welcome. If I was to get what information and anecdote there was from the family, then it would be drip-fed. It would have been boorish to expect anything else and, besides, I now had many new avenues opening up. The letters were still coming in. Press cuttings, telephone calls. Odd anomalies came to the surface. I had read, in the various accounts of Cromie's death, that his medals (which he always proudly wore) had been 'ripped away from him' as he died by the Red Guards. And thus I assumed that these valuable artefacts were lost to history. Yet speaking to Cromie's grandson, Tim, in Los Angeles, I discovered that he had the missing medals. The most tricky ground of all, however, was the intimation, gleaned from conversations with the family, that Captain Cromie had in some way been involved with another woman during his time in Russia. It was an avenue I hardly dared pursue, yet I had to know if it was true. I could scarcely write the man's life without including such an important detail. There were vague hints in Cromie's letters, and a mention of his female friends in the memoirs of the British intelligence agent Robert Bruce Lockhart, who worked closely with Cromie in those final hectic days in Petrograd.

The matter was taken out of my hands when yet another *Saga* reader, Mrs Masha Davies-Obolensky, faxed me. She was a friend of a Russian Prince, Andrey Gagarin (no relation to the cosmonaut), living in St Petersburg. I was told that Prince Gagarin had some valuable information regarding Cromie and his relationship with a member of his family, his father's sister, Sonia. Although we exchanged e-mails, Andrey was reluctant to impart his information until we could meet, face to face, in Russia.

But that was still to come. Within a few months I had also collected eleven different versions of Cromie's murder. The prospect of picking a path through these complex and differing reports in order to make an honest attempt at revealing the truth was daunting. But luck has been at my shoulder throughout. Richard Davies, in charge of the Russian Archives at Leeds University, had given my telephone number to another avid researcher into the murky world of First World War espionage, Phil Thomaselli of Swindon. Without Phil's generous and enthusiastic help, the final chapters of this book, dealing with the raid on the British Embassy in Petrograd, would have lacked much valuable information.

After a whole year of scattered snippets of information, erratic, ill-conceived journeying here and there, faxes, telephone conversations, letters and meetings, I looked at the shelf above my computer. What had begun with four sheets of paper from the RNSM was now packed with a 2 foot wide wedge of diverse information. From this random gathering of documentation a man was emerging. It was time to stop fooling around, and discover who he was.

CHAPTER 1

BORN TO SERVE

The reason for having diplomatic relations is not to confer a
compliment, but to secure a convenience.

Winston Churchill

Francis Newton Allen Cromie was born on 30 January 1882, at the start of a
turbulent decade in Victoria's long reign. It was a year of diverse happenings.
Gladstone had recently entered his second term as Prime Minister. British forces
were bombarding Alexandria, the French withdrew and thus Egypt became a
British colony. Wales beat Ireland in the first football international between the
two countries. Queen Victoria kindly gave Epping Forest to the nation. And
the previous year, something had happened which would stand him in good stead
twenty years later: flogging had been abolished in the Navy and the Army. In
Ireland, in the quiet little town of Fort Duncannon, Waterford, the British Army
kept watch as the Land Act, which finally recognised Irish demands for fair rents
and fixity of tenure, had come into force against a growing background of hatred
for all things English.

For the newly married, twenty-three-year-old Captain Charles Francis
Cromie, based at Fort Duncannon, these were anxious times. As Charles Stewart
Parnell continued to galvanise the Irish movement for home rule, the political
atmosphere became a tinderbox. The potential for violent confrontation was at
its peak. The Hampshire Regiment, like most British troops stationed on the
Emerald Isle, were not the most popular inhabitants in the town. Although not
at war, the Army was often regarded as a force of repression. In 1880, Captain
Charles Boycott (who was unwittingly about to add a new verb to the English
language), an estate manager for Lord Erne in County Mayo, had become the
first victim of Parnell's anti-eviction campaign. Irish peasantry, weary of their
repressive English landlords, had joined in solidarity. Even Boycott's servants
left him, and to harvest Lord Erne's crops, the ostracised estate manager had to
call upon a specially recruited workforce comprised of Catholicism's bitterest
enemy, the Orangemen. But worse than this, Boycott and his Protestant
labourers were protected by 1,000 troops.

Francis Cromie's father, Charles Francis Cromie, was born on 26 July 1858 in
Cincinatti, Ohio.[1] The reason for his journey back across the Atlantic, and the
date, remain a mystery. Perhaps his character was more suited to the powerful
British Empire than to the still undeveloped Mid-West of America. Yet here he

was, serving the Queen in the teeth of an Irish gale which would eventually develop into a hurricane for independence.

He was just nineteen on 30 January 1878, when he was commissioned as a second lieutenant in the Hampshire Regiment. However, before achieving this rank he already had almost four years of service with the regiment under his belt. We cannot judge by today's standards the tender ages of men of rank in the forces over a century ago. For the middle classes with some means, the Army was a good career choice for their offspring. Life expectancy in the late nineteenth century was still much shorter than it is today. Careers and responsibility came at an early age, and in controlling a vast empire, with all the potential of upheaval, for a military man they could be swiftly curtailed with the swipe of a sabre.

There is a coincidental resonance for his son's later career in the locations of Charles Cromie's regiment between 1874 and 1878: Gosport, Winchester and Devonport, where he was stationed at the time of his commission.[2] It would be three decades before Gosport and Devonport would sport flotillas of submarines in their harbours, but the Navy was already well established there. The Cromies were never far away from the sea. The year after his commission, 1879, found Charles in Wales, stationed at Pembroke Dock. With the lower status of his late teenage years in the Hampshire Regiment behind him, and his manhood achieved at twenty-one, this handsome, single young man, now with the rank of lieutenant, could afford to play the field. When the local constabulary held a prominent function, it would be natural to invite the officers of the Army. Nothing made a provincial society soirée more colourful than a smattering of splendid uniforms worn by the dashing soldiers of Victoria. And if the local Chief Constable was there, it is fair to speculate that his pretty daughters would attend.

Under what circumstances Charles met Mary, his bride-to-be, we do not know, but with both circulating in the same strata of Pembrokeshire society, there would have been ample opportunity for a romance to blossom. Charles had all the qualifications to impress a disciplined, organised public servant like Thomas Ince Webb-Bowen. His army career was in the ascendant; he was obviously, to judge by his later diplomatic career, quite capable of holding his own in good company. Perhaps the Chief Constable looked forward to this young man's rise through the ranks to much higher status, which would thus further enhance the Webb-Bowens' esteem.

By marrying Mary Grace Josephine Webb-Bowen, Captain Charles Cromie secured his place in the higher echelons of the middle class. Mary's father held a position of some importance in his native Wales. His career as Chief Constable spanned twenty-four years, and his marriage to Mary's mother, Catherine Luther Anne Bowen Allen, the youngest daughter of Charles Bowen Allen of Rickeston, Pembroke, had joined together two prominent Pembrokeshire families.[3] The Ince Webb-Bowens had been known for their service in Fishguard for centuries, both in the church and in civic service.

Within weeks of her marriage, Mary was to have her first real taste of life as an Army bride. There was trouble brewing across the water, and Charles's regiment was on the move again. As she sailed aboard the steamer from Pembroke Dock and watched the coastline of Wales vanish over the horizon, Mary cannot have imagined the adventure she was embarking upon. The couple's stay in their first port of call in Ireland, Cork, lasted only a few weeks. Wherever the army was needed, off they went. Next came Kilkenny, and then, in 1881, with Mary now pregnant with Francis, they braved the cold winter in Fort Duncannon, on Waterford Harbour.

Following the birth of Francis, their Irish travels continued for another year, until at last, after a brief spell back in England, stationed at Gosport, they finally returned to their beloved Wales to settle back in Fishguard. Charles's journeys were to continue through the coming years: Malta in 1884, India in 1886, Burma in 1888 and back to India for a year in 1891. But although his father continued to travel, young Francis was afforded some stability during this period as he grew up in Fishguard. Together with Pembroke Dock, a major centre for naval ship-building, this bustling little port had long been an entry point to Britain for the Irish, many of whom had settled in the area. For an adventurous young boy this beautiful, rocky coastline must have been heaven. There was an exciting inter-national atmosphere in these towns, where ships came and went, and foreign sailors and immigrants roamed the streets. It could be this proximity to the sea and all its mysteries, plus the fact that his father's enforced absences prevented him from influencing his son, that lay behind young Francis's later choice, not of an Army career like that of his father, but of a different life in the Royal Navy. Yet the reason for his entry into the Navy may be more prosaic: fault lines were already appearing in Charles and Mary's marriage, which were to have sad consequences later on.

Until the age of ten, Francis attended the Fishguard Free School. Here he got to grips with reading, writing and arithmetic. The daily regime was, by today's standards, a basic, Spartan existence. Education – or lack of it – in Wales during the 1880s had been a political football for some time. The Aberdare Committee, which reported in 1881, had argued for the establishment of secondary schools in Wales, but it was not until 1889 that its recommendations were acted upon under the Salisbury premiership, with the passing of the Welsh Intermediate Education Act. As to the Welsh element in Francis Cromie's character, Lloyd George's words on Welsh schooling, when speaking years later at Pengam in 1905, might well have summed up the adult Cromie: 'These schools would produce the higher type, the idea of a Welsh gentleman, not dependent on rank, wealth, birth or blood, but on character and attainments . . .'[4] From the basic mix of the 'three Rs' and a regular dose of religious instruction, it was time to move up the educational ladder. Schooling in the nineteenth century was largely segregated on class lines. Much secondary education beyond the age of ten could be costly, and many children were either at work by the age of twelve or, at the best, splitting their day with some basic education and a job to help out the family. But no doubt the Cromies' connections and their local prominence through the Ince Webb-Bowens would have been enough to move their boy on to something better.

Thus, in 1891 Francis Cromie moved to the Grammar School at Haverfordwest. The grammar schools, with their basic grounding in the classics, were a good educational compromise for the middle classes with their sights set on higher things. Haverfordwest Grammar had a notable foundation, and offered a worthy, broad curriculum. Sadly, since the school moved several decades ago to its new location in the town, to become the Tasker Millward School, the old records and log-books have been lost. It is therefore difficult to speculate upon Francis's performance, but judging by some of his spelling in his later correspondence, we can assume that this aspect of his training in English may not have been one of his stronger points in his three years at Haverfordwest, even though his letters and despatches are, fortunately, always well written and contain a fine eye for detail.

As his son's education progressed, Charles Cromie also gathered some military laurels by becoming a student at the Army's Staff College. This intense period of martial study set him above his peers – he was now able to display the letters S.C. after his name.[5] And yet, in some way, he failed to make his mark as a military man beyond this distinction. No doubt his increasingly unsettled home life and peripatetic existence was a distraction. After a career of almost nineteen years, during which he remained at the rank of captain, he returned from India in 1892 and left the Army. He now had his eyes set on a new career, as a diplomat in whichever far-flung corner of the Empire his Queen might offer.

This new life was not, however, one which he would be sharing with Mary and Francis. Here Francis Cromie's family tree grew another branch, and the way it grew and ended, in tragedy, is worth examining at some length for the uncanny similarity of the experiences his own family were to endure two decades later.

By 1894, at the age of thirty-six, Charles had a new woman in his life: Joan Angela Yonge of Otterbourne, near Winchester. He and Mary divorced, and Mary was left in Wales to order her affairs and bring up Francis. The split must have had embarrassing repercussions throughout the ranks of the Ince Webb-Bowens. Divorce over a century ago was not the common, almost routine way of dealing with marital differences that it is today; it was a subject of controversy.

Charles and Joan soon produced a brace of sons of their own. Now working for the Foreign Office, he held the post of Vice-Consul at Dar al Baida, in Morocco. Although Joan would join him abroad before long, Charles had moved his new wife to a more upmarket address at 70 Kensington Gardens Square in London. It was there that Joan gave birth to Maurice Francis Cromie on 7 July 1895. The following year, on 29 October, son number two, Henry Julian Cromie, came into the world. When the boys reached school age, it must have rankled with Mary back in Wales to learn that, unlike Francis, they would begin their long training for society life quite a few rungs further up the educational ladder than he had, with his free school and grammar school beginnings. Maurice and Henry, as befitted their place as sons of a diplomat, were despatched across the country to become boarders at Blundell's School, an ancient seat of learning founded in 1604 in far away Tiverton, Devon. For them only the best would do.

With the children out of the way, Joan could now see something of the world with Charles. After several terms at Blundell's, the boys entered the next stage of their education, and it seemed obvious that the Cromies already had their boys' careers planned for them. Dover College was one of the gentry's newer establishments. Only established in 1871, it had already earned a reputation as the school for sons of serving officers. In its short history, Dover College pupils had rushed to join the ranks of Army officers in droves to fight in the Afghan and Zulu wars of 1879, the Egyptian and Sudan campaigns of 1882 and 1884, and in Burma between 1885 and 1888. By the time Maurice and Henry arrived, the school already had a disciplined cadet force. This was all pointing in one inevitable direction – the Hampshire Regiment.

In the meantime, Charles's ex-wife, Mary, had moved away from Pembrokeshire. By 1905 she had taken up residence in London at 44 South Molton Street. She too had a new man in her life, who was soon to become Francis's stepfather. John Milner Lennard was a fifty-seven-year-old widower, and like his father before him, a successful ship owner and broker. John and Mary were practically neighbours in London, John living just off Baker Street at Montagu Mansions, with Mary just off Oxford Street, around the corner from Bond Street tube station, which had been opened only just over four years previously. The tradition being that the marriage would be solemnised in the nearest district to the bride's home, in this case St George, Hanover Square, the ceremony took place at the register office there on 16 December 1905.[6] Both Francis and his fiancée Gwladys attended, along with Mary's sister, Nina. It is possible that the non-attendance at the ceremony of Mary's father, Thomas Ince Webb-Bowen, could be put down to the rigours of travelling to London. He was sixty-six, a venerable age in 1905, and was to pass away just over a year later on 15 December 1906. It is interesting to note that he, too, had remarried by this time, his second wife being Ellen Benchley, the youngest daughter of Thomas Benchley of Wombwell, Kent.[7]

The rest of Charles and Joan Cromie's marriage warrants further inspection, if only for the comparisons which can be made between Charles's demise, far from home, and that of his first-born son, Francis, just over a decade later.

As their boys progressed with their education in Devon, Joan and Charles moved further afield. The summer of 1907 found them living in the fierce heat of Africa. After his spell at Dar al Baida, Charles had been moved on to act as Consul-General at Dakar, in Senegal. By September they had moved again, this time on a mission to the Congo Free State, many miles further down the coast, to the town of Boma, at the mouth of the Congo River. Charles had been unwell for some months with a severe bladder problem. On 23 September, the problem had increased to such an extent that he was no longer able to pass urine, and the only recourse to relieve his condition had to be surgery. In this he was lucky at first. The local doctor, Zubini, performed an operation, but the stricture could not be corrected. Not only was urine being retained, but a catheter could not be passed. Dr Zubini called for help. Anchored off the coast was HMS *Dwarf* of the Royal Navy. An urgent message was sent out to the vessel, and the ship's surgeon, W.L. Hawkins, came ashore. A second operation was performed, but after six days of intensive care, the wound would not heal and an abscess had formed. Zubini and Hawkins tried again, entering the abdomen, leaving an opening for drainage. For a few hours, it looked as if Charles Cromie might pull through, but at 10 a.m. on 30 September, after a long struggle, he died. He was forty-nine.[8]

When twenty-five-year-old Lieutenant Francis Cromie RN received the news of his distant father's death he was in command of submarine HMS *C5* at Sheerness. For his mother, Mary, despite her estrangement from Charles, there must have been a degree of shock and perhaps a slender, distant affinity with Joan Cromie. Now she, too, would know what it was like to bring up children with no husband.

But Joan's problems had only just begun. Stranded in the Congo, a colonial servant's widow, thousands of miles from home, she was now suddenly alone. After Charles's funeral in Boma, organised by the Belgian diplomatic community on 1 October 1907, the calamity of being married to a man without 'private means' came into sharp focus. Whilst Charles was alive and well, his salary, though meagre by the standards of much higher-ranked diplomats, was nevertheless adequate to keep a home in England and the boys at school. Although some of the countries he was stationed in were culturally unfamiliar and climatically uncomfortable, as a consul there was still the respect and status due to a representative of one of history's greatest empires. All the finesse of the British routine way of life travelled with these people; each posting had its servants, social functions, reasonable accommodation. If one could bear the heat and the long absences from England, then this was not too bad an existence. But now Joan, virtually penniless, had the lonely task of moving back to England, together with all the worldly effects which had travelled with them from consulate to consulate. His Britannic Majesty's Government was only interested in live consuls, not dead ones. She received plenty of sympathy, but that was not going to pay the bills. Without the selfless help of a Congo-based British businessman, independent of the servile work of His Majesty's minions, and the compassion of Boma's French community, Charles Cromie's demise would have posed even greater problems for his widow. When Joan first contacted the Foreign Office, she was dismayed to discover that her only immediate entitlement as a widow would be three months of her husband's salary, which would amount to a mere £225. By November she had arrived back in England, to stay with her parents at Kilm House in Otterbourne, near Winchester. From there, on 6 November 1907, she wrote to the Foreign Secretary, Sir Edward Grey:

Sir,
Owing to the sudden death of my husband, his having no private income of his own, I am left but with a small income of £125 in trust for my two small sons aged 11 and 12 years on which I shall have to educate and start them in life.

I am therefore writing to ask if it will be possible to obtain a grant at any rate to cover the costs and hospital expenses at Boma, and my passage home, these being over £350, a copy of which I could send you if required.

I should be grateful if you would try and obtain a grant for me, and as soon as possible.

I beg to remain,
Yours most respectfully,
Joan A. Cromie (Mrs. C. F. Cromie.)[9]

Similar letters setting out her problem were sent to anyone with influence who had known Charles Cromie. In one letter, also dated 6 November, to one of his old Army superiors, General Ewart, to request his influence at the Foreign Office, Joan puts the expenses at £400, adding, 'I do not care for myself in the least, but I want to give the boys a good start in life . . .'[10] and that her husband had 'only gone to Boma at special request . . .'. Eventually, the ponderous wheels of the FO ground slowly into motion, resulting in an internal letter, signed by W. Langley, to the Secretary of the Treasury on 13 November. It looks positive:

> Sir:
> I am directed by Secretary Sir Edward Grey to state that he has received an application from Mrs Cromie for some pecuniary assistance to meet the heavy expenses unexpectedly thrown upon her by the death at Boma of her husband, who was His Majesty's Consul-General at Dakar but who was recently called upon to proceed to Boma to take charge of His Majesty's Consulate there.
> Sir Edward Grey therefore wishes to recommend for the favourable consideration of the Lords Commissioners of His Majesty's Treasury Mrs Cromie's claim under the arrangements made with Their Lordships in October 1897 for a grant from public funds, and to propose as in similar cases that a gratuity of two hundred and twenty five pounds, or one quarter of the local allowance assigned to the late Captain Cromie should be issued to Mrs Cromie as a contribution towards the expenses of breaking up her establishment on the West Coast of Africa and removing the effects to this country.
>
> I am, Sir,
> Your most obedient, humble servant,
> (Signed) W. Langley.[11]

Governments never change. Anyone today, dealing with Whitehall bureaucracy will recognise the skilful circumlocution behind this official verbiage. In short, £400 or no £400, Joan Cromie was getting exactly what was due to her, and no more.

The higher echelons of the Diplomatic Corps were populated by the adorned sons of the landed gentry. To them, their meagre diplomatic salary was mere pin money – they had 'private means'. They had a choice in life: live out their days on the estate at home as squire or master of the hunt, work in the City in the family business, or take up one of the three ready-made vocations open to the privileged classes – Church, Army or Civil Service. When one had a private income regularly falling into your account at Coutts from the family coffers, even the embarrassment of sudden death held no financial fears. The nature of this well-heeled, high-class 'club' exposes the thoughtless expectations of Whitehall.

The following letter from the Liverpool trading company Cooksons, who, fortunately for the grandees of the Foreign Office, had an outpost in Boma, offers an illustration of how inventive minor diplomats had to be to keep the far corners of Edwardian Britain functioning, and gives an example of how any Briton of ability, qualified or not, in the absence of a designated representative of the Crown, would take up the reins of the Empire as an impromptu act of duty. Written in Boma, dated 14 October, it is addressed to Sir Edward Grey, Foreign Secretary:

Sir:

It is with deepest regret that I have to confirm my telegram of the 30th Sept., informing you of the death of Consul-General Captain Cromie, CMG which took place at the Croix Rouge Hospital here . . . It appears that he underwent an operation in Lagos last year, for the same sickness, but seems to have taken no steps to have the matter seen to when at home last year. On his arrival here it got gradually worse, and he only called in the doctor at the last moment.

HMS *Dwarf*, which had been on a visit here, had only left about two hours when he died – the end coming much quicker than was expected. His excellency, the Governor General, was kind enough to send a pigeon post to Banana [the *Dwarf*'s destination], informing the captain of his death, and the *Dwarf* returned the same night, arriving at midnight, the Consul was buried the next day, being carried to his grave by marines and sailors of HMS *Dwarf*. He was accorded full military honour by the State, the Governor General and all the officers of the State attending the funeral.

At the request of Captain Colin MacLean of HMS *Dwarf*, I took over charge of the Consulate until Mr Vice-Consul Michell arrived here yesterday, when I handed over to him.

I wired your Excellency on the 3rd inst. asking if I had authority to make disbursements of money to meet local current expenses, I did this as there was absolutely no cash at the Consulate, and the Consul was already indebted to me for over £100 which he had had for public and private accounts, and for which I hold his receipts. Moreover I had to pay for all telegrams, of course the Consul would have settled up with me at the end of the quarter, had he have lived, but as you are aware, I represent a business house here and am personally responsible for all monies paid out by me, and I should have liked to have some sort of guarantee for what I had paid out, as it would have looked more businesslike, anyhow I trust that your Excellency will see that the matter is so arranged that I am not the loser by having come to the aid of the Consulate in time of need.

I may mention that there is an amount of about £120 which the late Consul received from the Curator of Successions here, for the estate of the late Mr J. C. Killey, and which amount he remitted to his Bank, he intending, had he lived, to have remitted his cheque for this amount. There is also the sum of Frs.7,000 to 8,000 Frs. owing to the doctors for medical attendance, and Mrs Cromie has absolutely no money here. I have given my word that this money shall be paid, even if I have to pay it myself, but I trust your Excellency will see your way to give instructions that this amount is paid by the Government, as it would come very heavy on the widow if she has to pay it, moreover as Captain Cromie came down here at the request of the Foreign Office, and it was out of his district.

There are also various sums due to the State for expenses incurred by the Vice-Consuls on the upper river, and which the State are constantly asking me to pay, these really ought to be paid, as to a certain extent, they are for favours rendered to our Vice-Consuls, and it looks very bad if they are not paid, of course I shall be only too pleased to pay for them, for our own reputation, but not being a wealthy man, and being responsible to my Company, I must have some sort of guarantee.
Trusting to be favoured with an early reply
I have the honour to be Your Excellency's Most Obedient Servant
(Signed) A. Underwood.
P.S. Too much cannot be said for the very devoted way in which Mrs Cromie attended to her husband night and day for over a fortnight, and in a climate like this it means much, and I trust you will do all possible for the poor lady.[12]

Here was a man, Consul Charles Cromie, with his wife, travelling hundreds of miles in a jungle climate, in great physical pain, to collect intelligence for the Empire. He is a devoted servant of the British Government. He has to borrow money from a man outside the Government's employ, a man he has probably never met before, just to keep Whitehall's flag fluttering and clean. And when he is conquered by his illness and needs to resort to surgery, many thousands of miles from home, the expenses of medical attention have to come from his own pocket. Upon his death, his widow has to find the money to pay for a passage home. The Cromies, with their middle-class background, certainly had to earn their wages. A private income would have made all the difference. This shortage of money is a recurring theme when Francis gets to Russia. The Cromies seemed to have had the 'class', but never the cash to go with it. This scenario, with its pleading letters, would sadly repeat itself with significant similarity eleven years later for the other branch of the family.

Despite her problems, with this unhappy phase of her life behind her as Charles Cromie's death faded into history, Joan held house and home together and continued to bring up her boys successfully. As they completed their education at Dover College, their path into Army life continued without obstacle. Yet that much vaunted 'good start in life' to which she nobly clung for her boys over the years, was to be only that – a start. War arrived – not some far-flung colonial conflict but the biggest war ever, right on Britain's doorstep.

Maurice joined the Special Reserve of Officers on 11 August 1914, his occupation then being listed as 'schoolmaster'. Nine days later he was appointed to the 3rd Hampshire Regiment, a holding battalion, and as the Great War got into its bloody stride, he transferred to the 2nd Hants on 9 May 1915, and sailed with reinforcements to Gallipoli. Within a month, he was dead, killed in action at Gallipoli on 4 June 1915. He was just twenty years old. Henry was not far behind his doomed older brother. Also listed as 'occupation – schoolmaster' he had joined the 3rd Battalion of the Hampshires, and on 9 February 1915 he was posted to the 1st Battalion in France. Although still a teenager, he must have managed to fit in a little pleasant recreation in his new posting; he was admitted

to hospital ten days after arriving there with gonorrhoea. He was made a temporary captain on 2 July 1916. It was a short-lived promotion; he was killed in
action on the Somme on 23 October 1916, like his brother, just twenty years old.[13]

One might speculate what would have happened if Charles and Mary had not
divorced. Would Francis have been steered into the Hampshires? Would they
have had other children, too, as fodder for the cannon of the Somme and
Gallipoli? All that effort, travel and education snuffed out in seconds in the mud
and sand of two foreign lands. But during the two decades since Charles had
deserted Mary and his first-born son, a different story had been written on the
Welsh coast and beyond.

CHAPTER 2

MIDSHIPMAN CROMIE

The education of a man is never completed until he dies.

Robert E. Lee (1807–1870)

That Francis Cromie passed through the greater part of his childhood without the presence and influence of his father was probably to the boy's advantage. Unlike his half-brothers, who were to be installed in the traditional scholastic grandeur of Blundell's school, it might appear that he had more say in his own life, and thus would be spared the horrors of the Somme or Gallipoli. But Francis was already a fit and handsome teenager before the doomed Maurice and Julian were born.

With his time at Haverfordwest Grammar School drawing to a close, it was to the sea that a young Pembrokeshire boy looked for a career. No doubt Mary saw the Navy as the exact opposite of the Army. It was a different institution, with different traditions and more opportunities for a talented youth to fulfil his potential. Perhaps the thought of her son wearing the uniform of a regiment like the Hampshires would be too painful a reminder of the bitterness between her and Charles, which had culminated in divorce.

Entry into the Royal Navy for potential officer status first required a nomination on a boy's behalf from a suitably qualified member of society. This would be followed by a medical examination, then a competitive Civil Service entrance examination. Francis Cromie passed through these hurdles with no problems. After finishing at the Grammar School and spending the remainder of the summer at home in 1896, his papers came through for his first term of training. It was time for an exciting trip to London. There, Gieve, Matthews & Seagrove Ltd, the naval outfitters in Savile Row (today Gieves and Hawkes)[1] were the natural choice when choosing a uniform and a sea chest. In the second half of the nineteenth century, young boys who were destined to be naval officers received their nautical education on board former ships of the line, usually moored close to a prominent naval base. In the mid-nineteenth century cadets were quartered and educated on board the *Illustrious*, which was moored in Portsmouth Harbour, off Haslar Creek, a stretch of water which was to become synonymous with submarine warfare among sailors of the twentieth century. Under the stern command of their master, Captain Harris, the number of keen naval cadets increased until, after two years, a larger vessel was required. The *Britannia* replaced the *Illustrious* on 1 January 1852.[2]

From 1857 the ordinary sailor's uniform, presented to them on entry, consisted of a monkey jacket, double breasted and made of blue serge. This eventually led to sailors being referred to for decades as 'bluejackets'. The outfit was completed by bell-bottomed trousers in the same material and was topped off with a wide straw hat, around which was a ribbon bearing the ship's name. Queen Victoria always took a keen interest in her Navy. In 1869 she expressed a wish that beards should be worn in the Navy, but not moustaches. Her idea was that the Army had already cornered the market for moustaches. Therefore the officers and men had two simple choices: to be clean shaven or bearded – but not moustachioed.

In February 1862 *Britannia* was moved to Portland for a year, and finally found a permanent berth a half-mile upriver from Dartmouth in September 1863. Her new mooring, being away from the town, was considered to have less in the way of distractions for her 300 cadets. Their two years on board required intense concentration, and the proximity of a naval port, with all its attractions for a growing lad, was considered to be too much of a temptation. The junior-term boys slept on board another old two-decker, the *Hindostan*, which had been provided for extra accommodation in 1864. Moored ahead of the *Britannia*, a gangway connected the *Hindostan*'s stern to the *Britannia*'s bow.

The *Britannia* which was to be Francis Cromie's naval classroom for nearly two years was the fifth ship bearing that name. Much larger than the old ship, she was a 131-gun screw-and-sail vessel, originally launched as the *Prince of Wales* in 1860. She remained at her Dartmouth berth as a training ship for over forty years. Her masts and rigging were removed, with the exception of the fore-mast, which remained rigged for cadets to train on. The upper decks, which accommodated the officers, were covered in and also provided classroom space. Where the guns had once boomed from the triple tier of gun ports, the next gener-ation of naval officers now lived and slept, looking out at the river through glazed window frames which had once sported the polished black bulk of cannon.

Young Francis arrived in this Spartan environment on 15 January 1897, two weeks before his fifteenth birthday. This new existence was a world away from the warm cosiness of home in Pembrokeshire. With the rest of the first-term boys of that year, he had to take his sea chest (in which all boys were expected to keep their belongings) on board the old *Hindostan*. The cadets would spend their second year living on the *Britannia*. In the sharp cold of January 1897, it must have been quite a culture shock to be suddenly crammed in the old gun decks, where the boys had to struggle to come to terms with sleeping in a hammock for the first time. Here the discipline was rigorous, a far cry from the comparatively more genteel regime of the Grammar School. This was the breeding ground of captains, admirals and Sea Lords. In *Britannia*, whatever his family background, the status of his father and all the other points which went towards the epithet 'gentleman', a boy would pass through a catharsis designed solely to produce young men without fear, men who could think on their feet and take the initia-tive in any tight corner war might present. It was these rigorous two years which had produced Britain's Beattys and Jellicoes and a hundred other bold maritime leaders.

Francis Cromie's day on *Britannia* began with an icy swim in salt water.

Prayers were followed by inspection, then the hungry cadets were seated at the four long tables in the mess room for a breakfast of dry, stale bread, with very little butter, accompanied by weak tea. Lunch was known as 'dinner', and often comprised beef, vegetables, and as a reminder that they would soon be sailors, beer. Late in the afternoons a hint of boyhood returned via a glass of milk and a slice of cake. On one Sunday in the month their supper would include a special treat – roast chicken – but supper on most other days would be cold meat and bread.

The curriculum was a packed one. Spherical trigonometry, the study of charts, nautical astronomy and algebra filled the hours between drills and musters. There was theoretical and practical seamanship and navigation, but equal measure was given to fitness and exercise. At 3.30 each afternoon the boys would change into flannels or sports gear and row ashore to indulge in all kinds of recreation, such as lacrosse, hockey and cross-country running – and in keeping with the status of some of their rural backgrounds, there were even the *Britannia* Beagles. Tennis courts, a gymnasium, regular cricket and rugby all combined to ensure that wherever a life at sea might take these future officers, the social armoury of the English gentleman went with them. Often, on their cross-country runs, a Royal Marine sergeant would be hidden somewhere along the route to spot any slackers. On the water there was ample opportunity to get to grips with boating. There were four-oared and six-oared gigs, and pair-oar skiffs, which, long after the *Britannia* has gone, are still referred to in Dartmouth as 'blue boats'. Sail was important, too. Several small sailing boats were available, half-decked and rigged with a mainsail and jib.

The cadet's study workload was divided under three headings: seamanship, which included signalling and the lore of sailing; 'study', which encompassed navigation and mathematics; and 'out of study', in which Francis Cromie was to show a particular talent. It had been decided by the Lords of the Admiralty that part of any officer's training should include art, in the form of basic sketching and drawing. This was seen as important for officers keeping watch at sea. With this skill they could make quick sketches of significant geographical and navigational features: coastlines, headlands, etc. Francis was already adept with his pencils and would go on to develop this talent with watercolours. This 'out of study' element also included French. No doubt the Royal Navy's long history of facing our continental neighbours across opposing gun decks demanded that we could at least attempt to communicate in what was generally regarded as the language of diplomacy.

Punishments on board the *Britannia* were enough to bring tears to any sailor's eyes. A miscreant had a choice: birched on the buttocks with his trousers down or caned with them up. If a cadet was particularly badly behaved (and thus regarded as a 'third-class' offender), he suffered the indignity of eating in a specially set-aside mess or in the cockpit, with a white strip on his arm to signify his advanced criminality. Other offences could land him in the cells, on a grim prison diet of bread and water. 'Bad boys' often had their intransigence diluted by being made to exercise for long periods with bar bells, or go through repeated drilling with cumbersome, heavy 'Brown Bess' muskets. The old custom of flogging with the cat-o-nine-tails, strapped to a grating, might have been abolished in 1881, but these boys were under no misapprehensions – they stepped out of line at their peril.

This culture of punishment had continued down the centuries as a mainstay for maintaining discipline in the Royal Navy. Thankfully, young Francis Cromie was a diligent enough student not to have to experience some of the *Britannia*'s other treats for rule-breakers, such as being made to stand to attention long after their mates had tucked themselves into their hammocks, or being shaken from theirs much earlier in the morning than everyone else.

On the face of it, this public school of the sea seemed to offer everything expected to build up the character and ability of prospective officers. But whilst in many ways this was true, *Britannia* had her negative aspects. To begin with, decades of tradition and routine, moored away from any real naval contact along a quiet stretch of river, had created a false idea of what life in the Navy was really like. Although the masters and officers on board had their own broad experience of seafaring, what they were actually in control of was a self-contained world which bore little reality to life on board a real warship. Dartmouth, and especially the isolated stretch of water occupied by *Britannia*, saw little naval traffic. Every now and then a sail-training vessel might enter the harbour on an exercise from Portsmouth or nearby Plymouth, and even these minor representatives of seafaring must only have stirred the cadets' curiosity. The *Hindostan* and the *Britannia* may once have been fine ships of the line, but the fact was that de-masted, retired and relaxing now at their moorings, these old ladies were going nowhere. Thus those boys who could stick out their two years and not fall by the wayside must have longed for the experience of a real, moving deck beneath their feet. When they finally got it, however, it came as quite an unpleasant shock.

Francis Cromie, only sixteen years old in June 1898, had proved himself to be an able enough student on board *Britannia*. He had passed his seamanship and navigation examinations with flying colours. With only a few days' leave as respite from life in Dartmouth, his naval career proper would soon get under way.

As a schoolboy, Francis would have found Pembroke Dock a fascinating place. Shipbuilding, and especially warship-building, had been a major industry in the town since before the eighteenth century. When a ship was launched there it was always a special occasion. When Cromie was ten years old, in 1892, he may well have witnessed the launch of a new type of warship, the 14,150 ton *Repulse*. He could hardly have dreamed that, eight years on, he would be carrying his sea chest up her gangway. Commissioned on 25 April 1894, HMS *Repulse* was the first British battleship to carry her main armament of 13.5 inch (34 cm) guns on her weather deck. With her twin funnels, ten 6 inch (15 cm) guns, sixteen 6 pounders and twelve 3 pounders, this pride of Victoria's Navy would have been a source of fascination for any adventurous boy. As one of the Royal Sovereign class of warships, 410 feet (125 metres) long and 75 feet (23 metres) wide, she squatted aggressively in the water with a draft of 27 feet. She even had seven torpedo tubes.

On 1 June 1898 Francis Cromie boarded the *Repulse*,[3] ready to join her complement of 700 men. Fresh from his time on the old *Britannia*, and a tougher young man than he had been eighteen months previously, he must have felt a surge of excitement as he stepped onto her deck.

The appellation 'midshipman' may have some romantic resonance when we think of C.S. Forrester, but it was the lowest rung on the navy's sea-going ladder of command. It seemed to many young midshipmen that all they had crammed in during their terms of discipline and rigid routine on *Britannia* served for little once they joined a real working warship. For Francis, the immediate years ahead would be tough ones, but he was tenacious and dedicated enough to get through. Now he would live in the *Repulse*'s gunroom, without even the afternoon flannels and cross-country runs to break up the long watch. Both in port and at sea, midshipmen were expected to keep watches. Francis learned how to command parties of men, and arrange and manage various events on board. On the bridge, under the watchful eye of the naval instructor, he would spend long hours receiving instruction on taking sights and navigation – not now the static version, learned in *Britannia*, but vital navigation, crucial to the vessel's progress at sea. Midshipmen were also required to run the ship's boats, much preferring the vigorous activity of boat-running and keeping watches over the long periods of theoretical instruction. After two years at Dartmouth, they felt they had had enough of the latter. And a midshipman was often tired. His auxiliary duties added many extra hours to the basic watches, and sleep was at a premium. Only the stamina of their youth gave them the endurance to concentrate. It was not unusual for a naval instructor to have to dress down an exhausted midshipman for yawning.

But Midshipman Cromie was about to experience something the Royal Navy had not had too much of since Nelson's day – a taste of war. After little over a year on board *Repulse*, he was transferred to HMS *Barfleur*, under Captain J.S. Warrender. He was about to have his mettle tested.

He had a long voyage ahead. In this year of 1900, the British Empire had trouble on its hands: the Ashanti in the Gold Coast colony in West Africa, followed by the Boers in South Africa – and China, to where the *Barfleur* now headed at full steam.

Following Britain's lead, the armies and navies of the world had been modernising and expanding in the last decade of the nineteenth century. This included the Chinese, who, by the early 1890s, had built up their armed forces, and commissioned new warships which were thought to be a match for any potential aggressor. But the Chinese imperial court was on the horns of a dilemma. Whereas the rulers knew that, to face the challenge of the West, they must adopt Western ways and learn how to manufacture Western military technology, they also had to appease the greater population by attempting to stick to China's traditional values. This attempt to Westernise had only sporadic success. Chinese officials, their hearts split between respect for a Confucian heritage and a mistrust of all things foreign, did not make the best managers for the large enterprises needed to maintain Western-style industry.

In the ravaged countryside the huge, struggling peasantry looked on in confused disgust as their leaders seemingly embraced the ways of the West. Skirmishes broke out, and the brunt of this anger fell upon the foreign missionaries. Although they gathered many converts, in general Catholicism and Protestantism were both anathema to the Chinese. If this Christian philosophy was the spiritual engine which drove the industries of Europe and America, they were having none of it. Hatred and xenophobia grew and ignited into an expression of violent rage. But the pinnacle of anger and despair came when, in 1894, the detested Japanese inflicted the most humiliating defeat on Imperial China's supposedly invincible new navy and army. The Chinese population seemed to have all the confirmation it needed – so much for Westernisation. This would be a fight to the death between opposing cultures: Chinese tradition against the encroaching evil alien from across the sea.

Throughout the nineteenth century China had suffered at the hands of well-equipped foreign regiments, which often defeated entire imperial armies. Each defeat had resulted in the Emperors giving ever larger concessions to the Westerners. France, Austria, Great Britain, Germany, Japan, Italy and Russia all claimed exclusive trading rights in various parts of China. This greed-driven scramble continued until the Dowager Empress Tsu Hsi of the Ch'ing Dynasty realised that the foreigners were carving up her country into their own spheres of influence. When the USA acquired the Philippines, the Chinese became acutely aware that, with their well-armed base of operations a mere 400 miles away, the Americans would be the next nation to get their foot in the door. This added an extra tension: the Europeans were just as reluctant to admit the Americans into their profitable playground as the Empress was. John Hay, US Secretary of State, was opposed to the use of force – the warlike taking of the Philippines had strained US public opinion too much. Thus he approached the foreign powers in China with a request for an 'open door' policy, offering all trading nations the equal chance to line their pockets from China's resources.

Whilst this diplomatic ping-pong match continued, to the understandable anger of the sidelined Chinese, Tsu Hsi issued a message from the court in Peking to all her provinces:

> The various powers cast upon us looks of tiger-like voracity, hustling each other to be the first to seize our innermost territories; should the strong enemies become aggressive and press us to consent to things we can never accept, we have no alternative but to rely on the justice of our cause . . . If our hundreds of millions of inhabitants would prove their loyalty to their Emperor and love of their country, what is there to fear from the invader? Let us not think about making peace.[4]

The people of Shandong province were on the verge of starvation after a merciless drought had laid waste the land. The Empress's message matched their mood. For some time, a secret society centred on the study and practice of martial arts, the I Ho Ch'üan, (the 'Righteous Harmonious Fists'), had been attracting hundreds of new recruits. As they watched the Europeans and

28

Americans squabble over a land which was not theirs, the Harmonious Fists, who became known as the 'Boxers', now saw their membership increase by thousands. They were experts in the art of what we now know as Kung Fu, and were fearless swordsmen and archers, believing firmly in their magical powers. One aspect of this ritual belief convinced them that they would be immune to the foreigners' bullets.

The opposing factions in the imperial palace watched the rise of the Boxers in fear, because the secret society's original aim had been to bring down the Ch'ing government, many of whose members the Boxers saw as being in league with the foreign money-makers. But the wily dowager knew what she was doing. Her message removed the fear that the Boxers might storm the palace – and now, the slogan on their banners read: 'Support the Ch'ing – Destroy the foreigners!'

As the new century opened up, China became a bloodbath. The Boxers rampaged through the countryside in their thousands in the early months of 1900, killing Chinese converts to Christianity, murdering every missionary they could lay their hands on. As they began to move towards the cities, their steady advance attracted thousands more followers.

Inside the walled foreign enclave in Peking the uncomfortable diplomats issued a stream of demands to the Empress, who watched the advance from the security of the Forbidden City. She played a duplicitous hand; whilst issuing responses to the foreigners that her imperial troops 'will soon crush the rebellion', she waited, biding her time in the hope that this new, fearsome force from the provinces might just be the final answer to decades of alien intervention.

The foreign diplomats assembled and united their small military attachments to form a defence force of a mere 340 men. Russians, Italians, Japanese and American marines counted their ammunition, cleaned their weapons and began to construct defences. But it was painfully obvious that once the Boxers arrived, the 'foreign devils'' days would be numbered. It was time to call for help.

With mission stations and railways being devastated daily as the Harmonious Fists smashed their way to the outskirts of Peking, and with foreign concessions in around the port of Tientsin increasingly threatened, the British Consul in Peking sent an urgent message to the Royal Navy's China Squadron, moored off the Peiho River. The squadron commander, Vice-Admiral Sir Edward Seymour, was familiar with the ways of the Chinese. He already had two missions to China under his belt and, according to his memoirs, displayed a surprisingly liberal view for a representative of an imperial power: 'The general history of our dealings with China has been that we have forced ourselves upon them and into their country. I believe we are too apt to forget this.'[5]

The Tientsin Consul backed up Peking's plea for Seymour's men to go into action, but Seymour was reluctant. His response that the Navy's presence at Tientsin was 'only for the protection of European lives' must have proved frustrating for the beleaguered foreign community – Europeans to a man, with the exception of a small number of Americans. However, the situation was dangerous enough to call for some show of support, so Seymour sent a detachment of 130 sailors and marines, along with a 9 pounder gun, to bolster up defences at the Tientsin Consulate, and a further 76 marines with a .75 calibre gun, a naval armourer, a signalman and one sick berth attendant to the diplomatic compound at Peking.

By 9 June there were around 140,000 Boxers pouring into Peking. They made a fearsome sight and an even more frightening noise. With their swords, spears, rifles, red sashes and headbands they advanced, carrying aloft banners of white and red proclaiming death to all foreigners. They beat upon drums, pounded gongs and blew horns. Periodically they would stamp their feet on the ground in unison. For the occupants of the walled legation enclave, this rolling thunder of sheer hatred must have given them their darkest hour. Yet, as loyal subjects of their individual home countries, they felt instinctively that help would soon arrive. It was to be a much longer wait than they hoped.

By this time, after a long voyage, Captain Warrender was pushing HMS *Barfleur* at full steam ahead into the Yellow Sea. As Tientsin and the prospect of conflict drew closer, the officers, among them the young Midshipman Cromie, were briefed by the captain and the thirty-year-old Commander David Beatty, who with his recent experience of commanding gunboats on the Nile was a good man to have on board. The news was that Admiral Seymour had responded to a final desperate telegram from Peking, where the Consul had pleaded that, if there was no relief at the city soon, then it would be too late. Without awaiting any approval from the Admiralty, Seymour drew together every naval force he could in the area to assemble a relief expedition. His plan was simple, bold and fraught with danger. They would strike out to Peking along the 80 miles (130 km) of railway line from Tientsin. For this brave endeavour, which was entirely naval, Seymour drew together what one might call today the ultimate international reaction force. Its composition is worth listing, as it was a unique example of mixed nationalities, for now united with one aim, but many of whom were to be fierce enemies in the years to come:

> Austria-Hungary 25 men
> France 158 men
> Germany 450 men
> Great Britain 921 men
> Italy 40 men
> Japan 54 men
> Russia 312 men
> United States 112 men
> Total 2,072 men.[6]

With the impending arrival of Seymour's marines, this must have provided a ray of hope for the legation guards, as their combined number at Tientsin and Peking was a mere 507 men. Of these legation forces, Britain had the highest number, 82, followed by Russia with 81 and the United States with 56.

When Cromie arrived off the Peiho River in late June Seymour's force was already on its way to Peking. He had left Captain Edward Bayly of HMS *Aurora* in charge of the British naval forces at Tientsin, and there were joyful cheers of relief as help steamed into view with the welcome reinforcements on board the *Barfleur*. As the captain and Commander Beatty hastily put together their own force of 150 men, which included Midshipman Francis Cromie, ashore the Boxers busied themselves by cutting off all links between Tientsin and the Allied squadron, tearing up the railway lines from the town to the shore, cutting telegraph wires and setting fire to any building they thought had some foreign connection. For Beatty and Bayly, anchored 12 miles off the shallow estuary of the Peiho, the news from the shore had become much worse after 19 June. The Empress's imperial troops, well armed and equipped, sensing that the Boxers might well be successful in their attempted rout of the Allies, had now joined forces with them. And nothing had been heard from Seymour's expedition. The privations and difficulties they were experiencing were to be a test of tenacity and courage few of the battling sailors could have expected.

Seymour's advance along the railway to Peking was tortuous and slow. With each attempt to move forward, the Boxers ripped up long stretches of rail. Halfway to Peking, after frequent stops to replace the tracks, Seymour decided to abandon the train. But carrying on on foot also meant abandoning much of their gear. This was particularly annoying for the officers who, confident of a straightforward march to Peking, had been hoping to wear their dress uniforms upon arrival in the capital; they were forced to leave them behind.

For four days the force moved along the left bank of the Peiho. With over forty wounded men they had to commandeer four Chinese junks, which followed the slow-moving column along the river. By now, with so much material left behind on the abandoned train, the sailors were on half-rations, yet marching for sixteen hours a day, much of the time under fire from snipers. The casualties began to mount up. At one point a bayonet charge was led by Seymour's forty-one-year-old flag captain, whom many of the 450 Germans in the force would come to respect in a different way almost sixteen years later. John Jellicoe, although badly wounded in the charge, was destined for bigger things at Jutland in 1916, courtesy of the poor aim of the Harmonious Fists. Someone else fighting his way to Peking, and in many ways sharing a similar early career with Francis Cromie, who was to make his name in later years, was the young Austrian Midshipman Georg von Trapp. The bullets whizzing around his head along the Peiho were hardly comparable to the sound of music which would celebrate his long life in later years, thanks to Julie Andrews. Yet after surviving Seymour's march the eighteen-year-old von Trapp was destined, like Cromie, to play a major role in his country's submarine force in a career which even encompassed marriage to the granddaughter of the father of the torpedo, Richard Whitehead.[7]

As 22 June dawned, Seymour faced the distinct possibility of defeat. There was no more room on the overladen junks for the growing number of casualties, which had grown from forty to 230. With little ammunition left, guns lost and rations almost gone, only a huge stroke of luck could see them through. It came at Hsiku, where the Boxers had somehow overlooked an arsenal there which was packed with everything the sailors needed: food, arms and ammunition.

Bayly and Beatty meanwhile had heard nothing from Seymour (which eventually earned him the nick-name 'See No More'), and for nine days Seymour had heard nothing from Tientsin. Yet now, with arms and ammunition replenished, and the strongly fortified Hsiku arsenal as a base, the Allied force could replenish itself and hopefully strike out anew. But impressive though their progress had been, they were now halted. Seymour could not continue on his way to Peking; the Boxers were now outside the arsenal, with the result that the Allies had no choice but to dig in and hope that they could now be relieved themselves – providing their comrades had had more success back in Tientsin.

In Peking, the foreigners were, in the words of the Empress, 'like fish in the stew pan'. They knew that help had been sent, yet to their dismay there was no sign of it.

By 23 June 1900 Midshipman Cromie was armed and ashore in China. His force from HMS *Barfleur* had joined up with a squad from HMS *Alacrity*, under the command of Commander Cradock, and the relief of Tientsin was under way. During the lifting of the siege of Pei Yang arsenal, Cromie displayed exemplary courage. Captain Warrender wrote on his service record: 'Showed much zeal and ability with Naval Brigade at Tientsin.'[8] His mettle had been tested and not found wanting, and his strength of character was about to receive its first real recognition; he was to be Mentioned in Despatches.

On 26 June Pei Yang arsenal was liberated, and on the same day, a further relief force sent to Hsiku to assist the beleaguered Seymour succeeded in their mission, and the Admiral's brave but bedraggled sailors made a happy return to Tientsin. But although there was relief in Tientsin, the siege of the international legations in Peking was far from over.

A second, larger international relief force was assembled, this time numbering 17,000 men, under the command of the British General Alfred Gaselee. Its progress had little of the close-knit camaraderie of its predecessors, the naval brigades. It was dogged by international rivalry, which slowed things down to a frustrating degree. There seemed to be a race to see which nations could reach Peking first, so much so that the Austrian, German, French and Italian contingents were left behind as the four main nations surged ahead. Nevertheless, after fifty-five fearful days listening to the repeated yells of '*Sha! Sha!*' ('Kill! Kill!') from the Boxers outside the walls, on 12 August, the foreign diplomats and their small, hard-pressed bands of soldiers, marines and sailors welcomed their liberators. Within two days the siege was over. But 250,000 Chinese Christians and 100 'foreign devils' had lost their lives. The Empress Tsu Hsi had fled.

Among the foreigners murdered was the German minister. When the German troops arrived in the city, they executed a bloody vengeance, remembering the words of the Kaiser: 'Anybody who falls into your hands must be destroyed!' China was to pay a heavy price for the rebellion. In the treaty signed the following year, the imperial government had to pay an indemnity of $330 million, agree to wide-ranging foreign trading concessions and allow for large contingents of foreign troops to be stationed in Peking. It would be over four decades before the Chinese finally got their country back, with the arrival on the scene of Mao Tse Tung.

For Francis Cromie, this was only the beginning of his China experience. He would be back, and not as a brave but lowly midshipman, but in command of his own force. As the smoke and fire of the Boxer Rebellion subsided, thousands of miles away in England, the Royal Navy had made a bold move. Their Lordships had ordered their very first submarine.

CHAPTER 3

TIN FISH AND INVISIBLE MEN

The world will never have lasting peace so long as men
reserve for war the finest human qualities.

John Foster Dulles

Dulles had a point. In an age which gave us the motor car, the refrigerator, the tram, railways, electricity and a thousand other life-enhancing inventions, one could ask the question, what earthly use to humanity is a submarine? That some of the world's most inventive minds should conspire to make a metal boat capable of sinking itself, to prowl beneath the waves with only one ultimate purpose – death and destruction – seems an obscenity. A submarine is a dirty, low-down and underhand machine. At the end of the nineteenth century, even a master of war as lofty as Rear-Admiral Arthur Knyvet Wilson, VC,[1] Third Sea Lord and Controller of the Navy, was willing to slug this one out with his superior, the First Lord of the Admiralty, George Goschen. Although Goschen could see the fledgling submarine's practical problems, he none the less recognised its potential as early as 1900, even if only in a defensive role. His enthusiasm was taken on board by the Admiralty when, in October 1900, an order was duly placed with the American Electric Boat Company for five Holland-type submarines. Admiral Wilson could barely contain his disgust, and his subsequent condemnation of this machine of war immediately went into submarine folklore when he dubbed it 'a damned un-English weapon'.

Three years later, when Lieutenant Francis Cromie volunteered for the Submarine Service in September 1903, he was literally entering the unknown. Even today, submariners, as any 'Big Navy' sailor will tell you, are a breed apart. To volunteer a century ago to leave the big sky above and the relative liberty and fresh air of the surface of the high seas, opting to spend your service below the waves, would have seemed a reckless folly to most Jack Tars. The life was already looked down upon by Nelson's heirs. The submarine, regarded by many as a mad experiment, had taken men to hell and back too many times during its chequered history to date. Upon the waves, the dog could see the rabbit. Man-to-man, dreadnought-to-dreadnought, this still felt like the proper role of the Navy. Even if you lost the battle, there was always a remote chance of some kind of survival. Defeat on a submarine was an unthinkable way to go.

What it was that possessed Cromie to submerge himself is hard to say, but he was certainly not alone. In war or peace, this uncomfortable, claustrophobic and extremely dangerous life had already begun to attract a cross-section of officers and ratings. Although the physical atmosphere on early submarines could be oppressive and stifling, one might guess that one of the plus points of living in a 'can' with fourteen or more ratings and two officers was the break-down of some of the rigidly held social tradition and class etiquette of the surface fleet. In submarine flotillas new attitudes were formed. Here was a world where more than ever 'getting along with your mates' was a genuine condition of service. There was no room for too much distance between the officer class and the lower ranks. The brass may have had the bunks, but there was only a hanging blanket between them and their hard-pressed sailors. Compared to the living conditions of a pre-1914 submarine officer, a lowly midshipman in Nelson's Navy lived in luxury.

It is impossible to consider Cromie's prowess as a submariner without looking at the history of these bizarre vessels – and their main weapon, the torpedo. Like the aeroplane, which was also slowly coming into its own as a weapon, the submarine was an on-going area of research and development in warfare. Whereas, in the early part of the twentieth century, some pale vestiges of chivalry, pomp and ceremony still clung to traditional surface warfare, behind the scenes a new breed of boffin, bereft of flying colours, trumpets and gun salutes, was busily designing a dark and dreadful new weapon which would, within four decades, result in the tragic carnage of the Battle of the Atlantic. It is little wonder that many 'salt water' admirals found this new-fangled vessel so offensive to their notion of war at sea.

Our modern conception of submarines will be forever coloured by the Second World War, and then by the German U-boat. There is something inescapably dramatic and sinister about underwater warfare. It can be summed up in one word: invisibility. Invisibility provides the greatest of all tactical benefits for the fighting man: the element of surprise. The early nuts-and-bolts science of underwater navigation often seems crude and unsophisticated, but measured alongside what was going on at any given time above the waves, the submarine often looks ahead of its time. Much has been made of Leonardo da Vinci's sketches of proposed aircraft. Yet Leonardo also toyed with the idea of the submarine. His references may have been oblique and sketchy, but his basic ideas were sound. Hidden men and hidden weapons always obsessed an armourer. The Trojan horse was a fine example of dirty trickery.

As early as 1578 William Bourne, a versatile inventor in Elizabethan London, in his book *Inventions or Devises*, gave an account of the ingenious construction of a submersible boat and its method of operation.[2] Bourne's methods were, of course, extremely primitive, but the fundamental principle of buoyancy and ballast tanks is still basic to submarines over four centuries later. His vessel was a small boat, made watertight with a covering deck at gunwhale level. Jutting up through this deck was a tube, basically a hollow mast, to provide air to the sealed area. The sides of the boat were perforated, and inboard two inner walls were built. These inner walls were loose, made to move inwards and outwards by being attached to sealed watertight flaps of leather – the same principle as a bellows. There was already enough ballast in the boat to lose almost all its buoyancy, so that she had a very low profile in the water. By moving the leather-hinged walls inwards, the sailor created a chamber into which he drew the water through the holes in the side of the boat. With this ballast the boat submerged. To surface, the inner walls had to be pushed outwards, expelling the water, and thus enough buoyancy was restored to surface. It was clever, but this novel little craft only had two directions – up and down.

Several decades later Bourne's ideas were taken up by the Dutchman Cornelius Drebbel, who gave his submariners a little more headroom by splicing two boats together – one upside-down on top of the other, the whole contrivance clad in waterproof leather. In 1620 he demonstrated his device on the Thames, to the mystified delight of King James I. Claims that the monarch took a trip in Drebbel's boat between Westminster and Greenwich are best discounted – James was not known for his courage. Drebbel's contemporary spin-doctoring also had it that his boat had stayed submerged and travelled thus at a depth of 15 feet (4.5 metres) for several hours. This bit of positive PR makes no allowance for the fact that, without Bourne's hollow mast, Drebbel's crew would have suffocated to death. It is wise to remember that the ingenious Dutchman was also an alchemist – not a trade which figured much in the crew lists of the later Royal Navy.

When men of the cloth dedicate their off-duty hours to the science of war, the text from Book of Ecclesiastes, 6:29, 'God hath made men upright; but they have sought out many inventions', consigns 'love thy neighbour' to the waste-basket. Priests figure prominently in the development of war beneath the waves. In 1634 two French clerics, Fournier and Mersenne, took time off from ministering to their flocks to draw up plans for a submarine, the design of which had an uncanny resemblance in shape and style to the vessels which finally succeeded in their trials two centuries later. Unlike Noah's Ark, the priestly duo's dream boat never got further than the vestry drawing board. Fourteen years later, another great man of God, Oliver Cromwell, was impressed by his brother-in-law's undersea design prowess. As the Bishop of Chester, Dr John Wilkins obviously had time on his hands while dealing out the judgement of the Lord. In 1648 he published his book *Mathematical Magick*, in which he outlined intricate plans for a 'submarine ark', which, although in the main it would have scientific purposes, could attack other vessels and engage in surprise assaults.

Before the next Catholic priest sailed onto the scene, an irrepressible Frenchman, M. de Son, tried to bamboozle the hapless Dutch admirals with his own version of a submarine warship. This time the craft was actually built, but when it slipped into the water off Rotterdam in 1653, it hardly lived up to its designer's claims. It was robust, big – over 70 feet (21 metres) in length – and good-looking, with iron cladding fore and aft for ramming, looking every bit the submarine we recognise today. However, despite having comfortable cabins and a novel, albeit dubious, means of clockwork propulsion, it refused stubbornly to go anywhere, and simply ended up as a novelty visitor attraction.

But the resourceful sons of Rome were soon back at their inventive peak when Father Giovanni Borelli got to work on his design for a diving bell. Unfortunately, he was unable to canvass for support of his plan as he had been dead for a year when it reached the printed page in 1680.

Many more variations on Bourne's ideas came and went; the Germans had a go, as did a Devon joiner, and in 1774 a bold experiment by another carpenter, resulted in his losing his life and his crew in 20 fathoms (36 metres) of water in Plymouth Sound. The problem of water pressure crushing an undersea boat had yet to be fully realised.

But on 6 September 1776, the submarine finally began to make history. The *Turtle* was the brainchild of an ingenious American inventor, David Bushnell.[3] This one-man submarine broke with the cigar-shaped tradition by being built in the shape of an upright egg. Sturdily constructed from oak and strengthened by iron bands, it was propelled forward by a propeller connected to a crank driven by hand or foot. The pilot sat on a wooden seat, his head enclosed by a tiny conning tower which formed part of the hatch. In this were two glass eye-holes. Vertical movement was gained by a hand-drive second screw. To descend the bilges were flooded, and to regain buoyancy they were emptied with force pumps. Bushnell had really done his homework, and his efforts were just the shot in the arm the rebellious American colonists were looking for. His 'torpedo' consisted of 150 pounds (68 kg) of gunpowder encased in an oak 'bomb'. By means of an external apparatus controlled from inside the conning tower, the pilot was to drive a screw to which the torpedo was attached by a short line, into the bottom of an enemy vessel. Once the screw had been attached and the bomb released, it rested against the enemy hull, tethered by its rope, and a simple clockwork detonator would give the *Turtle* ample time to move to a safe distance.

The intended victim of Bushnell's fiendish ingenuity was the sixty-four gun HMS *Eagle*, which was taking part in the blockade of New York and was commanded by no less than Admiral Lord Howe. In theory everything should have gone to plan, but prior to the attempt Bushnell became ill. It was then decided that his brother would pilot the craft, but a further twist of fate saw him fall down with sickness at the eleventh hour. But with the American War of Independence gathering speed, there was to be no shortage of brave volunteers. One was a sergeant in the Patriot Army, Ezra Lee. Unfortunately Ezra did not benefit much from his last-minute crash course in submarine warfare. Although he made a brave and resourceful attempt, the tide carried him past his target. Using his forward screw, he was forced to surface and manfully manoeuvred the *Turtle* back towards the *Eagle*. He was spotted, however, and boats were sent after him. His only recourse now, as he frantically cranked himself along, was to release his torpedo in the path of his pursuers. To his relief this worked. The bomb exploded in front of the startled Jack Tars, and although it did no damage, it provided enough confusion to allow him to escape. The plucky patriots tried and failed on two further occasions, and the British captured the *Turtle* later that month in New York and destroyed it.

From then on, with their independence gained, it was to be the American 'can-do' philosophy which would dominate submarine development for the coming century. One of naval history's great geniuses was the American Robert Fulton, who took his own submarine, the *Nautilus*, to Napoleon in 1801. Yet despite a brilliant demonstration, during which he remained submerged for four hours and successfully 'torpedoed' a ship, Bonaparte remained unconvinced. To the French navy, this 'fish boat' had a grim lack of chivalry and was an ungentlemanly way to wage war, an attitude which stubbornly persisted for a century.

Fulton, however, was no quitter, and if the French refused to help him keep a roof over his head, then he must go to their common enemy, the British. Masquerading as 'Mr Francis', Fulton won the patronage of William Pitt the Younger's brother-in-law, Lord Stanhope. In an impressive demonstration, Fulton took his *Nautilus* below the waters off Walmer Castle and managed to attach his 'torpedo' to the hull of the brig *Dorothy*, blowing her in two. Pitt was keen on the submarine, but Admiral of the Fleet Earl Vincent displayed the same disgust for underhand warfare as his enemies, the French. However, Fulton did receive a staggering £50,000 to develop torpedoes and a clockwork boat, but when Britannia proved that she really did rule the waves with Nelson's destruction of the French at Trafalgar in 1805, no one would argue with Earl Vincent – the British Navy was quite powerful enough without recourse to Fulton's mechanical genius. Thus humbled, he dropped the 'Mr Francis' tag and headed home. Despite his failure to promote the submarine, he did manage to crown his career just before his death in 1815 with a steam-powered surface warship, the world's first – the USS *Fulton*.

A similar craft to Fulton's and Bushnell's design again sneaked up on the British in their second confrontation with their ex-colonies between 1812 and 1815. This time the Americans almost succeeded in sinking Commodore Hardy's HMS *Ramilles* and were only thwarted in sending Nelson's noble comrade to a watery grave when the screw being driven into her bottom snapped off.

The ensuing eight decades only served to prove how stubborn the idea of the submarine was – except for the British. In December 1850 the Germans displayed their inherent mastery of the concept when Wilhelm Bauer launched the mother of all U-boats, the *Brandtaucher*, in Kiel. In 1861 came the French *Plongeur*, which was driven by compressed air. In the American Civil War an underwater craft finally succeeded in sinking an enemy vessel when a Confederate submarine, the CSS *Hunley*, sank the 1,400 ton USS *Housatonic* in 1864. Sadly, the *Hunley* was the victim of her own success, also sinking with the loss of her nine-man crew.

This is, of necessity, a condensed overview of the intricate history of the submarine, but the theme of clerical inventiveness warrants one last mention before moving on. In 1879, one of the Church of England's finest, the Lancashire-based Reverend George W. Garrett, went beyond doodling on the parish notepaper and actually built a submarine. With the usual propensity of warlike priests to adapt and divert their education, he made full use of his Latin and called his submersible the *Resurgam* ('I shall rise again'). But in tests in the Mersey the Good Lord struck back, making the name less than appropriate. Undaunted, and obviously attracted by the smell of cordite, Garrett steamed off to Sweden with further plans which he placed before the top Swedish gun maker, Thorsten Nordenfelt.[4] Seven years after the words 'I shall rise again' had splashed egg on the Reverend's face, a new submarine, *Nordenfelt 1*, which incorporated his ideas, was demonstrated to an eager gathering of international military leaders. With its propensity for filling up with noxious fumes, it was not as big a success as Garrett had hoped. Back in England, he took her for further trials in the Solent and almost gassed himself in the process; he spent nearly a month convalescing. The following year the Greek navy bought the vessel for £9,000. By this time it appears that Garrett had put the church far behind him, as he and Nordenfelt continued their submarine experiments for some years.

For the submarine innovators, there was to be no turning back. But if a submarine was a warship, it had better be effectively armed. Enter the torpedo. The development of this weapon, affectionately known to all submariners as the 'tinfish', has its roots in a land-locked country, Austria. Bereft of significant coastline though she was – a mere 300-plus miles (500 km) from Trieste down to Cattaro – Austria's navy, and especially her submarine arm under the musical command of Lieutenant Georg von Trapp, was eventually to become a force to be reckoned with.

In 1867, Captain Giovanni Luppis of the Imperial Austrian Navy made a tiny unmanned boat fitted with an explosive bow. This precursor of the torpedo as we know it today was none too convincing for Austria's admirals. It was almost impossible to guide it correctly to its target, but like most inventors in this field, Luppis had no intention of being defeated. If there was some way his boat could be self-guided towards enemy ships, then he would find it. He was in luck, because working in Rijeka (then known as Fiume), tucked away on the northern shore of the Adriatic in what was then Austrian territory, was the forty-four-year-old manager of an engineering company, far from his native Lancashire, Robert Whitehead. The son of a cotton bleacher, he had left grammar school at the age of fourteen to become an apprentice engineer. After attending the Manchester Mechanics Institute, unlike many of his industrial contemporaries he opted for taking his chosen trade (he was a specialist in silk-weaving machinery) to warmer climes, first to France and then to Austria's Adriatic coast. By the time of his death aged eighty-two in 1905, Whitehead's brilliant development of Luppis's idea had become the standard torpedo technology for the world's navies. His early experiments with Luppis produced a pointed torpedo which eventually evolved into the characteristic bull-nosed missile still in use today. Using compressed air as propulsion, and eventually tackling the variable depth problem by adding his own 'secret balance chamber mechanism', Whitehead soon had the world's admirals knocking on his factory door.

He rapidly followed his breakthrough with the invention of the first torpedo firing tube, and after an impressive display of over a hundred test firings off Sheerness in Kent, the British Government gave Whitehead £15,000 for the right to manufacture this new weaponry. Within a decade torpedo boats were being built, and as early as 1878 the first successful torpedo attack was carried out against the Turks by the Imperial Russian Navy. Soon torpedoes were being built in their thousands, in Fiume, in Woolwich, and under licence to Whitehead by the US Navy at Newport, Rhode Island.

In 1898 he had bought a new invention from an inventor in nearby Trieste. Mr M. Obry's[5] gyroscope was a development of work carried some years earlier by Focault, and for Whitehead it was the answer to the perfection of an automatic steering system for his torpedoes. The weapon became even more deadly and sophisticated, increasing in speed and range from 6 knots and 200 yards (11 kph and 180 metres) in 1868 to 36 knots and 4,000 yards (66 kph and 3,650 metres) by 1907. If all this sophistication could be crammed into a 15 foot (4.5 metre) self-guided underwater bomb, why should some of these fine innovations not be incorporated into its mother, the submarine?

This brings us, inevitably, to John Phillip Holland. Holland was thirty-three when he left County Clare, Ireland, in 1873 to settle in New Jersey. As a Fenian, he had no time for the British, yet like Fulton before him he would soon end up taking their shilling. His first submarine, built in 1877, incorporated the precursor of the hydroplane. It had horizontal rudders, thus enabling its crew to exercise control when going up or down, rather than simply sinking like a stone. His sales pitch, considering the success stories coming out of Austria, was impressive: 'The submarine boat is a small ship modelled on the Whitehead torpedo, subject to none of its limitations, improving on all its qualities except speed, for which it substitutes incomparably greater endurance.'[6]

Holland's greatest achievement was his use of two complementary forms of propulsion: on the surface, the internal combustion engine; submerged, electric storage batteries. His predecessors had used steam power and electric batteries, or simply batteries on their own. Although he had his worthy competitors in his industry, Lake in America and Laubauf in France, after twenty-three years of development, John Philip Holland was to be the focal point for the Royal Navy as they made their first tentative steps towards including this 'damned un-English weapon' in their fleets.

In July 1900, whilst Midshipman Cromie continued to build his career in the stifling heat of a bloody Chinese summer on board HMS *Barfleur*, the ship-building firm of Vickers and Maxim were already planning the rest of his life. On 27 October 1900, Vickers were granted a licence to manufacture Holland boats. Britain's submarine service was about to be born.

CHAPTER 4

THE TRADESMAN'S ENTRANCE

Kipling's poem 'The Trade' is one of the few artistic accolades to the submariner. Everyone knows 'Rule Britannia'. We all had to learn 'Hearts of Oak' at school. But Kipling's imperial thunder, penned at a time when sailing submerged was in its infancy, perfectly encapsulates the Edwardian feeling of all warriors with an eye on the future. If Kipling had lived another sixty years, no doubt he would have done the same for British astronauts – had we ever had more than two.

After Francis Cromie's displays of undoubted seamanship and bravery in China, on 15 December 1901 he made the rank of sub-lieutenant. By June 1903, after a spell in HMS *Hermes*, his promotion continued, owing to an impressive success in his passing-out exams for lieutenant – four firsts and a second. Few officers could boast results as gilt-edged as these: 923 marks out of 1,000 for seamanship, 1,442 out of 2,000 for navigation (his only second), 915 out of 1,000 for pilotage, 894 out of 1,000 for gunnery, and 186 out of 200 for torpedo studies.[1]

There were many reasons why a young officer like Cromie should find sub-marine warfare fascinating. At the beginning of the century the Royal Navy had certain factions, each with its own followers and detractors. Cromie had an adventurous and creative mind – indeed, one of the few unfair references to his outlook, written years after his death by Admiral Sir Victor Stanley, KCB, his naval liaison officer in Russia, accused Cromie of having 'no view beyond his own immediate horizon'. But included on that young lieutenant's horizon was the lively, progressive 1st Baron Fisher of Kilverstone, who, in 1902, had been appointed Second Sea Lord at the Admiralty.

'Jacky' Fisher, as he was affectionately known to his sailors, had all the neces-sary respect for the Navy's long, proud Nelsonian tradition – and at the same time a keen, prophetic eye on its technical future. When Cromie volunteered for submarines in 1903, Fisher, at the age of sixty-two, had a vision of the future which outstripped that of many of his peers, who were half his age. As Second Sea Lord his immediate responsibility was for naval personnel.

Fisher had entered the Navy as a boy during the Crimean War, fought in China in 1860, and in 1863 had a taste of things to come by serving in Britain's first ironclad steam-powered warship, HMS *Warrior*. As the man in charge of personnel, however, it came as no surprise to his Admiralty colleagues that he would be one of the first men to support Lord Selborne's then radical plans for the reform of naval education. These reforms were set to ensure that in the future, all officers would possess an element of technical competence. The world of spars, sails and halyards, although important, was fast receding. With newer forms of propulsion and armoury leaving the drawing board every day,

'The Trade'

1914–18

They bear, in place of classic names,
Letters and numbers on their skin.
They play their grisly blindfold games
In little boxes made of tin.
Sometimes they stalk the Zeppelin,
Sometimes they learn where mines are laid,
Or where the Baltic ice is thin.
That is the custom of 'The Trade'.

Few prize-courts sit upon their claims.
They seldom tow their targets in.
They follow certain secret aims
Down under, far from strife or din.
When they are ready to begin
No flag is flown, no fuss is made
More than the shearing of a pin.
That is the custom of 'The Trade'.

The Scout's quadruple funnel flames
A mark from Sweden to the Swin,
The Cruiser's thundrous screw proclaims
Her comings out and goings in:
But only whiffs of paraffin
Or creamy rings that fizz and fade
Show where the one-eyed Death has been.
That is the custom of 'The Trade'.

Their feats, their fortunes and their fames
Are hidden from their nearest kin;
No eager public backs or blames,
No journal prints the yarns they spin
(The Censor would not let it in!)
When they return from run or raid.
Unheard they work, unseen they win.
That is the custom of 'The Trade'.

Rudyard Kipling 1865–1936

an understanding of engineering was becoming an absolute necessity. In the class-bound armed forces at the turn of the century, the very idea that an officer should have to do anything 'mechanical' and get his hands dirty was an anathema. With Britain and Germany as the manufacturing powerhouses of Europe, there was no shortage of skilled tradesmen from the other end of the social scale to fill the ranks of the services. Those boiler-suited chappies could deal with the engines, the guns and all that other oily stuff below decks. The officer's job was to command, organise, manoeuvre, plan – and socialise.

But Jacky Fisher knew that although this had been true, the new warships would demand a new breed of officer. In the claustrophobic, slowly growing 100 per cent technical world of submarines, the commanding combination of Horatio Nelson and Isambard Kingdom Brunel would come into its own. This was a dark, suspicious branch of seafaring. Here the mast, the funnel and the big gun meant little. This was the domain of a new kind of navigation, an unknown plunge into danger beneath the waves. Amongst the Navy's officer class, and below decks, the attitude to this modern war by stealth was split. Either it was a dastardly, unfair and 'non-cricket' form of combat or, at best, submarines were simply a defensive machine, to be hidden away in the right spot to protect grand fleets. The notion that these underwater coffins could be used principally for attack purposes was slow to be accepted, and at least in these early stages, even Fisher saw them primarily as defensive weapons.

But anyone with a keen and creative eye, like Francis Cromie, could see from the submarine's history that it was bound to carry on developing. Despite the fact that the young lieutenant was inevitably leaving the comparatively sparkling social life behind in the 'Big Navy', he was none the less joining the ranks of what would soon become an elite club of progressive sailors, all prepared to take this technological promise on board and incorporate it into their careers. In many respects, to use an airborne analogy, they were the test pilots of their day. Although it had taken some years for Jacky Fisher to take up the cause of the submarine, he had none the less devoted a lot of his time in the 1870s to the development of the torpedo, and by the time he was elevated to the rank of First Sea Lord in 1904, he was a leading proponent of new technology, helping to oversee the design of the first turbine-powered warship, the huge HMS *Dreadnought*.

With the launch of this vessel in 1906, the military leaders of the world stood back in envy. Britannia still ruled the waves – and how. *Dreadnought* left every battleship in the world in the shade, and her new form of propulsion, the steam turbine engine, was to change both commercial and naval fleets around the globe for decades to come. At 18,000 tons and with a speed of 21 knots (39 kph) *Dreadnought* became both a benchmark and a beacon for the world's admirals. Germany took up the challenge and a building race was on to increase her own fleet to a standard to match Britain's.

Dreadnought was a reminder of Britain's recent 'bulldog' past, and although the spirit of Victoria, General Gordon and the old Empire still remained strong, there were cracks appearing in the social fabric which would eventually change the old order for ever. On 7 February, only three days before *Dreadnought* slid down the slipway, the general election had swept the Liberals to power with 399 seats. The Conservatives trailed behind with a mere 156 seats, but it was the impressive gains by the working class via the Labour Party, with 29 seats, which set the proverbial cat among the pigeons. The realm was changing – very slowly, but within two decades there would be a political upheaval throughout the world. On 8 March a large demonstration of the unemployed marched from the Midlands to central London, but were met with little if any sympathy. So for now the establishment and the Admiralty could enjoy their unchallenged European supremacy.

It is little wonder that the more progressive, free-thinking younger men of the officer class, and especially those, like Cromie, who were not from the landed gentry, should watch and listen for every piece of news coming from the progressive Admiral Fisher. If you had your eye on future promotion, Fisher was the man to follow.[2] His attitude to submarines had become the total opposite of many of his fellow admirals, who still regarded this new-fangled machine as nothing more than an experiment in defence. But if the French and the Americans were building submarines, then it was high time that the British followed suit. Thus in 1901 Lord Selborne, revealing the Naval Estimates in March that year, finally went public with the news that the Royal Navy was about to incorporate the submarine into its fleet. Of course, the old stalwart, Admiral Wilson, was still of the opinion that the use of the submarine as an attacking vessel ought to be prohibited, adding that if captured, we should 'treat all submarines as pirates – and hang all the crew . . .'

In Barrow-in-Furness, Vickers shipyard was now busy building the first five submarines for the Navy, under licence from the Electric Boat Company. On 2 October 1901, *Holland 1* was launched, quickly followed by *Holland 2*. To oversee the opening up of this new branch of seafaring the Navy put in charge one of its most competent torpedo experts, Captain Reginald Bacon. As Inspecting Captain of Submarines, based in the Controller's Department at the Admiralty, Bacon must have been a lonely man at first. Even his own technical adviser, the Director of Naval Construction, Sir William White, was a supporter of the anti-sub Wilson faction – and not without sound reason. As a clever engineer, Sir William agreed with Chief Engineer Sir John Durston that working in a tight, enclosed space with petrol engines on board a submarine was simply asking for trouble.[3] As the rumours got around the 'Big Navy' about what life was going to be like in the newly formed submarine service, the conditions seemed to smack more of a punishment duty than a leap into some glorious future.

Consider the little Holland boats: just under 64 feet (19 metres) long and less than 12 feet (3.5 metres) wide at maximum beam. Even at full throttle, on the surface, the puny four-cylinder petrol engine could only just manage 9 knots (17 kph). Submerged, and propelled by a sixty-cell battery, it would be lucky to make 5 knots (9 kph). The interior was so cramped that the seven-man crew hardly had room to operate the machinery, and certainly no room for anything else, such as sleeping. The atmosphere was dank, cold, reeked of oil and the filth of bilge water, and – most deadly – it was thick with dangerous petrol vapour.

This, combined with frequent electrical sparking, was a recipe for disaster.

These early boats had only a standard compass, not fitted inside the boat but mounted on the exterior, to avoid magnetic interference. There was no conning tower, and to look at his compass, the commander had to use an odd periscope-type of fitting encased in a tube with angled mirrors. As to the periscope proper, on these pioneer subs this was a primitive device. Lenses became dirty, and the horizon appeared differently as the periscope was moved around. Looking astern, the horizon was upside down. With only one bow torpedo tube, and all these negative features working against the crew, it is a wonder, looking back, that the Navy even bothered to move ahead with the service at all.

Just one day working in this horrendous environment might be expected to be enough to make strong men baulk, and yet, as those early Holland trials progressed throughout the winter and summer of 1903, there were men ready and willing to sign up. In September 1903, Lieutenant Francis Cromie was making his way towards Portsmouth to join HMS *Thames*, the little flotilla's base vessel.

This fledgling submariner was a world away from the eager, inexperienced midshipman of five years before. With his time at sea on *Repulse* and *Barfleur*, two of the Navy's finer vessels, plus his hair-raising adventures in China, he was now the energetic epitome of the Edwardian naval officer: confident, cool and in command.

Beyond existing photographs, it might be hard to form an accurate picture of this bold young man, but forty-five years after Cromie's death, in 1963, Rear-Admiral C. G. Brodie recalled in the *Naval Review* his own early days as a young lieutenant in Portsmouth:

> The most picturesque of the pioneers was Cromie, captain of one of the Holland boats in 1904. Tall, good looking, with curly black hair and dark Irish eyes, he wore short side-whiskers and whether in sea-going or any other rig, was always carefully dressed. Also, in contrast with some contemporaries, he was polite to the training class in his slightly aloof manner. Living ashore on 'lodging and compensation' he was cut off from ward-room life, but we recognised him as out of the common run. In February 1905 he recommended diggings to me and for a few days we shared a living room. Cromie had hired a piano, which I enjoyed for a month while Ma B. (the landlady) was holding his rooms in hopes of his return. She thought highly of Cromie and when on later returns to Portsmouth I looked in upon her, she always asked after him and murmured, 'A lovely man . . .' He was certainly, at twenty-two, a romantic figure, and it is not wholly hindsight after his heroic end in Russia that kept him for me on a pedestal, when others had fallen off. His whiskers were long, and in place of the spotless white silk scarf that picked him out from the other grubby sweater-clad Holland boat officers, in 1904, he wore an astrakhan collar to his great-coat, and his medals wherever possible. He neither smoke nor drank, yet was undoubtedly the type of leader for whom Englishmen will perform prodigies that surprise themselves, and whom foreigners will admire and trust.

Francis would have been attractive to any available young lady in the Empire. The fact that he was a sailor was enough, but with his good looks, his youth and his rank, the world really was his oyster.

By 1903 the five small Holland boats had finally made it from Vickers' yard in Barrow all the way to Portsmouth. Here they became the centre of attention as officers and sailors alike scrutinised these bizarre little vessels. There was not much to see; with most of their bulk below water, all that remained in view was a tiny deck area, the diminutive hatch and the periscope. Compared to the lofty might of a dreadnought, this new investment by the Navy, officially dubbed the Submarine Branch, looked about as threatening as a pea-shooter.

Their early trials did little to build a reputation, either. Not long after assembling at Portsmouth, it was decided that the Hollands' first exercise would be a simple trip, on the surface, around the Isle of Wight and back again.

Only one of them made it to Cowes. Three threw in the towel after less than five miles (8 km), citing engine trouble; another managed a further couple of miles before also succumbing to mechanical failure. However, Captain Bacon and his young officers were far from despondent. There was work to do. On board HMS *Thames* the problems of each subsequent exercise became the subject of long discussions between him and his young pioneer submarine commanders, among them the keen and attentive Cromie.

Little by little these hardy young trailblazers got to grips with the challenging new art of diving below the waves. During 1902–3, the five Holland boats threw up more questions than answers, but the ingenuity of the volunteers continued to offer up new refinements, suggestions and ideas for improved design. A new boat, the *A1*, which was launched in July 1902, incorporated Captain Bacon's suggestions, and was the first British-designed submarine. To begin with, she had a conning tower, and at 100 feet (30 metres) was much longer than her five predecessors. The conclusion was that the first five boats could not be used for anything other than coastal defence. They were too small for the deeper waters beyond the coast, but even so they were about to prove once and for all that the Submarine Branch was here to stay. In March 1904 the Navy carried out manoeuvres in the Channel. Although the Hollands had been given the assignment of defending Portsmouth, they gave an impressive display of stealth when they managed a mock torpedo attack which theoretically 'sank' four of the Channel Fleet's battleships.

The aloof, haughty officers of the 'Big Navy', who had already designated the new submariners as some kind of lesser breed of 'below stairs' operative – and with all the acute class vitriol Edwardian society could offer had dubbed them 'The Trade' – now had to sit up and take notice. Perhaps the most egg was on the faces on the bridge of the 'torpedoed' fleet flagship, where none other than the submarine's arch opponent, Admiral Wilson, strutted up and down as these oily, hidden 'pirates' enraged him by scoring a hit on his ship.

But although there was a slight air of triumph among the mariners, it was all but obliterated by a terrible tragedy. On 8 March 1904, the final day of the manoeuvres, the new *A1* collided with the passenger liner SS *Berwick Castle*, which was *en route* to Hamburg. Her skipper had been under the impression that he had been hit, like Admiral Wilson, by a practice torpedo. What he did not realise was that the *Berwick Castle* had ripped a hole in the *A1*, and as he sailed innocently on towards the German coast, the stricken submarine lay on the seabed. All hands, including her commander, Lieutenant Mansergh, perished.

Yet within a few weeks the *A1* was salvaged, brought to the surface and repaired, to become the sea-going classroom for one of Francis Cromie's legendary contemporaries, Max Kennedy Horton.

There would be other accidents with the new Hollands; *A4*, *A5* and *A7* all bore the scars of their research into the unknown. *A7* eventually sank with all hands. *A5* lost six of her crew with twelve injured, following an explosion. *A4*, under Lieutenant Martin Nasmith (who was later to win the VC for sinking twelve ships in nineteen days in the Dardanelles in 1915) almost suffered the ultimate fate by plunging to the bottom, but was saved by First Lieutenant Herbert, who managed to blow the tanks.

However, it was Lieutenant Francis Cromie who, despite a tragedy on his own boat, *A3*, became the hero of the hour on the cold afternoon of 5 February 1906.

Both the national press and the papers in his home town eagerly took up the story.[4]

LIEUT. CROMIE'S BRAVE EFFORT

CHIEF CONSTABLE'S GRANDSON

Some of the London papers on Tuesday gave great prominence to a splendid deed of heroism by a naval officer off Spithead, and Haverfordwest people experienced a thrill of pride when they discovered that the officer was none other than Lieut F.N. Cromie, grandson of the Chief Constable of Pembrokeshire, Mr T. Ince Webb-Bowen.

The following is the description of the affair given in the *Morning Leader*:

Our Portsmouth correspondent telegraphs: Another fatality in connection with the exercise of a submarine vessel at Portsmouth occurred under thrilling circumstances. A seaman, named Thompson was swept off the deck of one of the A Class of submarines while at Spithead, and, notwithstanding the gallant attempt of Lieut F.N.A. Cromie, the commander of the vessel, to rescue the man, he was drowned.

It appears that shortly after noon two submarines, accompanied by torpedo boat No. 26, were carrying out exercises at Spithead when one of the vessels came to the surface, and the commander, Lieutenant Cromie, and Able Seaman Thompson, went on deck, presumably to have a look round.

VESSEL SWEPT BY A BIG WAVE

A heavy sea was running at the time, and a big wave swept over the little vessel with such force that Thompson was washed off the deck into the sea. He was wearing very heavy sea boots and waterproof overalls, and at once shouted for help.

Lieutenant Cromie, with splendid bravery, unhesitatingly leaped into the rough sea, although he, too, was wearing heavy boots, and succeeded in getting hold of the blue-jacket. The absence of the lieutenant and Thompson was not noticed for a minute or two, and by this time the submarine had gone on two or three hundred yards, leaving the two men struggling in the sea.

When the accident was discovered the vessel was put about at full speed, but before the officer and the sailor could be reached, they had both become exhausted, and Thompson sank and was not seen again.

PICKED UP UNCONSCIOUS

The lieutenant was picked up in an unconscious condition and placed on board the torpedo boat, and there he was revived by artificial respiration, after 90 minutes' unceasing work. He was then conveyed on board the torpedo boat to Portsmouth Harbour, where he was taken to the sick bay of HMS *Thames*, the parent boat of the submarine flotilla, for treatment.

The gallant act of Lieutenant Cromie is one of the most self-sacrificing and heroic recorded at Portsmouth for many years.

Not only Haverfordwest and Pembrokeshire, but the whole of the country may well be proud of the knowledge that our Navy contains such men as Lieut Cromie, who unhesitatingly incurred the gravest risks to his own life in attempting to rescue that of his comrade. All our readers will join with us in congratulating the Chief Constable on possessing a grandson of such mettle, and at the same time wishing him a speedy recovery from the effects of his terrible ordeal.

This brave attempt to save Able Seaman Thompson's life did not go unnoticed by the Admiralty, who thought highly enough of Cromie's gallantry to forward details of the event to the Royal Humane Society. When the Humane Society's committee met in London on Thursday, 15 March 1906, they discussed many similar cases of selfless sacrifice upon the water, such as that of James Gorvin, a Dock Boatman in Cardiff, who had rescued his colleagues from a capsized boat, and Gunner Thomas Connolly of HMS *Theseus*, who had saved a fellow sailor from drowning in Devonport. But they were all overshadowed by case number 34480. The entry in the Royal Humane Society ledger reads:

12.15 p.m. 5th of February 1906, the Sea, Spithead;
The man was washed overboard from submarine, speed 10 knots;
a nasty sea, very cold. Lt Cromie jumped in and held him up for some time, but had to release his hold and was got on board by a line.

This was enough for him to receive the society's coveted Bronze Medal. With his

China Medal with Peking Bar and this, Cromie had a good start to a collection which was to grow over the next twelve years.

In fact, the year 1905–6 had been one of his most fulfilling and exciting yet. At the age of only twenty-four, he was in command of one of the new A Class submarines. By 1907 he was married to Gwladys Cromie. The coincidence of her surname is not surprising. Many of the County Armagh Cromies, distant from the American branch, came and went between Ireland and Pembrokeshire at the end of the nineteenth century. If life was not rounded enough, on 11 April 1907, Gwladys gave birth to their daughter, Dolores Anthea.

Now that the Navy was irrevocably committed to submarines, Francis could feel that he had made the right decision in volunteering for the service. Across the water, the German Navy was also taking the subject seriously; they had ordered the building of their first *Unterseeboot*, propelled by paraffin and electric motors, the *U-1*.

Against all the odds, the Admiralty was now behind 'The Trade'; already, by 1906, a new class of submarine, the Bs, were leaving the slipway, to be followed shortly by Cs and Ds. At last the Submarine Branch, branded by the snobs in the surface fleet as '*unwashed chauffeurs*' was a force to be reckoned with, and it would dominate Cromie's life, and that of his family, from now on.

CHAPTER 5

LENGTHENING SHADOWS

*For us a great fleet is a necessity, for Germany a luxury. It is
existence for us; it is expansion for them.*

Winston Churchill

The years between 1905 and 1912 were good for the young Lieutenant Cromie.
With his wife and child living at 3 Russell Road, Lee-on-the-Solent, he could
enjoy what shore leave there was with Gwladys as they watched Anthea grow.

By 1908 he was in command of one of the new C Class submarines, *C5*. His
daily training work with the growing membership of the Service involved the
study of every aspect of the new science of submarine warfare, from the principles of buoyancy through to the firing of torpedoes. Cromie and his officer
colleagues who had volunteered in the first wave now had an indisputable lead
in both knowledge and experience over all who came after them. Alongside
Cromie and above him were men who would become legends in the coming
conflicts of the twentieth century: Captain Roger Keyes, and Lieutenants Noel
Laurence, Martin Nasmith, Courtney Boyle and of course, Max Horton. Like
the early aviators, these men were a breed apart from their contemporaries. What
attracted sailors to the 'Big Navy' may have been the high-profile glamour of
traditional naval life, but what drew young men into 'The Trade' was a quest for
something different, an adventurous leap in the dark. And now their machines
were getting bigger, better and more sophisticated. The original, tiny Holland
boats appeared like toys[1] alongside the new classes which were being built, not
only at Vickers but also at the royal dockyards.

In many ways this was a good time to be in naval uniform, for despite what
was happening in the civilian world, naval ship-building was going ahead at a
rate of knots and was constantly in the news. There had been wars and international flash points, from the Boxer Rebellion to the Boer War, yet, in general,
for the Royal Navy there had been no major battle at sea since the time of Nelson.
With its huge building programme and massive injections of public money, this
muscular peacetime force stood as the potentially aggressive guard dog on the
boundary fences of the Empire, ready to savage any intruder. Between the relief
of Mafeking and Ladysmith in 1900 to the outbreak of the Great War in 1914,
Britain appeared to have a firm enough grip on her possessions not to have to
fight for them on any grand scale. Although what was happening in the Balkans
and throughout Europe, including the Anglo-French Entente of 1904 and the

Austrian annexation of Bosnia and Herzegovina in 1909, was worrying enough for politicians with a less blinkered and more prophetic world view, for the average Briton, flushed with jingoism after six decades under Victoria, the prospect of anyone across the Channel daring to push Britain into war appeared unlikely. In any case, with our own royal family's German connections, perhaps the arms race with our Teutonic cousins was simply a kind of sibling rivalry. But Winston Churchill, with his eye as ever on historical possibility, could see the potential for disaster between Europeans.

Early in 1911, at the request of the Sultan, the French sent troops to Morocco, where the Germans had already established commercial interests. Although the French troops had been sent to quell a Moroccan uprising, the Germans, concerned that their Gallic neighbours were seeking to establish a protectorate, despatched a gunboat, the *Panther*, to the port of Agadir. Known later as the Agadir Incident, this brought Germany, France and Britain close to war. Britain had no choice but to support her Entente partner, and conflict was only avoided when a treaty was signed on 4 November 1911 which resulted in Germany retreating from Morocco, whilst at the same time receiving extra territory on the Cameroon border. It was a close-run thing and an early spark of enmity which would ignite a broader hostility before long, but Churchill and other leaders sighed with relief that it had not led to a greater tragedy at the time.

Yet there was continuing consternation about the obvious arms race the British had entered into with the German navy, which had announced that its new warships would be the most heavily armed vessels in the world. In August 1907 Edward VII visited the Kaiser to discuss the naval situation, yet no conclusion was reached. So perhaps Germany was just a powerful, if unpredictable, neighbour (described by the writer Rebecca West as 'like a wasp at a picnic'). Otherwise the Kaiser would surely not have travelled to Oxford on 22 November 1907, to receive an honorary degree.

After the launch of the first *Dreadnought*, the government announced that it would be spending less on the Navy – yet still ordered three more dreadnoughts. On 16 March 1907, a new class of battleship, designated a battlecruiser, HMS *Indomitable*, was launched on the Clyde. In July 1907, the mighty HMS *Bellerophon* made her debut at Portsmouth. In September Britain's first military airship flew at Farnborough.

As the Royal Navy's Submarine Service continued to expand, it might have been reasonable to expect the higher echelons of the Grand Fleet to begin to afford 'The Trade' a little well-earned respect. But it was not to be. In the main, almost all the men in command of submarines were young and of low rank. As history would eventually show, being members of this select breed would not be a bar to future advancement, but during those first two decades it must have almost seemed as if there were two Royal Navies: the traditional one, with its mighty capital ships, scrubbed decks, brass, spit and polish, and this smelly, hidden oily one, occupied by men who were often a complete enigma to their surfaced comrades.

In 1910, Admiral John 'Jacky' Fisher was sixty-nine years old and had been in the Royal Navy for an incredible fifty-six years. Although the decision disappointed many, it came as no surprise when he resigned.[2] In this same year the dynamic Captain Roger Keyes took command of the Submarine Service. On 8 August 1910 Francis Cromie was moved to Devonport to begin service with the submarine flotilla, attached to HMS *Onyx*, which was assigned to the depot ship for the A and B Class boats, HMS *Forth*. Another memoir briefly describes him in action at this time:

> Cromie, aged 28, took an absorbed interest in training his four juvenile captains – his juniors by about four years – in the handling of their obsolete and unhandy boats, and rarely a day passed but he was out in Whitsand Bay on board the lumbering old tender, which was the only target available upon which the out-of-date 'A' boats could practise . . .[3]

On 15 June 1911, he was promoted to Lieutenant-Commander. Over the following two years under Captain Keyes's watchful eye he honed his skill and ability as a commander and a leader of men. By the age of thirty, in August 1912, he had gained both the maturity and the confidence in his chosen occupation to be offered the command of a brand-new boat, one of the larger E Class, HMS *E4*. Now he was once more working out of Portsmouth from his base aboard HMS *Maidstone*.

By this time British submarines had entered the international arena. In 1910 six B Class boats had been sent out to Malta and Gibraltar, and that same year one of Jacky Fisher's last bold moves prior to his resignation was to send three C Class submarines, *C36* commanded by Lieutenant Godfrey Herbert, *C37* (Lieutenant Athelstan Fenner) and *C38* (Lieutenant John Codrington),[4] on an expedition many considered to be almost impossible. Together, accompanied on various stages by HMS *Diana*, HMS *Pelora* and HMS *Bonaventure*, they were to complete a staggering journey all the way to Hong Kong. After a voyage the sailors would remember for the rest of their lives, the submarines finally arrived and the Hong Kong Submarine Flotilla was established.[5]

Back in Portsmouth, Cromie was to spend just over a year mastering his new E-boat. However, Captain Keyes's plans for his brightest commander meant that his days of training and manoeuvring off the British coast were numbered. He had been chosen for something special, and was about to refamiliarise himself with the country which had done so much to form his character – China. After saying goodbye to Gwladys and Anthea, Francis Cromie stood on the threshold of the toughest, fullest – and sadly the final – phase of his career. During the coming six years, he would only see his young family again for a few short weeks.

As he left Portsmouth on 5 November 1913, the Britain he was leaving behind was already vastly different from the country he had known as a boy in Pembrokeshire. People had already begun to question their place in society. The suffragette movement had outraged the establishment by planting a bomb in St Paul's Cathedral and another which destroyed Lloyd George's house. Both Sylvia and Emmeline Pankhurst had been imprisoned. At the same time, the first sickness, unemployment and maternity benefits were introduced.

And in the face of Germany's quickening pace in the arms race, Britain's Navy was still turning out new ships; in October 1913 came the first oil-powered battle-ship, HMS *Queen Elizabeth*, followed eight weeks later on the Clyde by the mighty battlecruiser HMS *Tiger*.

Despite the uncomfortable feeling that something was about to happen in Europe, Francis Cromie, like everyone else in 1913, could have no idea how or when that 'something' might be triggered. But within seven months of his leaving Britain, his life and everyone else's in Europe would be irrevocably altered and placed under threat by the actions of a young Bosnian Serb, Gavrilo Princip, a fanatical linotype operator on a Serbian newspaper. When Princip squeezed the trigger of the gun which killed Ferdinand, the heir to the throne of Austro-Hungary, and his wife Sophie on that fateful sunny day in Sarajevo, 28 June 1914, he unleashed the most vicious dogs of war the world had ever seen.

Cromie was now in command of the complete Hong Kong Submarine Flotilla. Based on board HMS *Rosario*, this must have been a pleasant posting after the years of ploughing up and down the English Channel with its attendant bad weather. He now had time to devote to his watercolour painting, and lost no opportunity when off duty to set up his easel on deck and complete colourful representations of passing vessels. Yet as the months progressed and tension grew in Europe, frustration began to set in among the men of this far-flung flotilla. After many decades of building and training the mightiest navy in history, it was time to put it to the test. But it would not be here, in the balmy waters of the South China Sea. The real battle for sea power between Britain and Germany would be played out in the North Sea and the Baltic.

On Tuesday 4 August, Britain issued an ultimatum to Germany, to cease military operations against Belgium.

When Britain's ultimatum to Germany expired at midnight, British time, the Royal Navy had already been officially at war with Germany for an hour, as Churchill, with characteristic belt and braces style, had insisted that they should receive a telegram at 11 p.m.

As the news of war in Europe was received in Hong Kong, the men of the flotilla were primed and ready for a return to Britain. After the call from the Admiralty, winding up the flotilla's operations in Hong Kong was no overnight job. The trip alone from China back to Europe was a long one. Cromie arrived home in March 1915 to enjoy a well-earned leave with Gwladys. On 21 April he was once again serving in HMS *Maidstone*, and received news that his new command, submarine HMS *E19*, was ready for inspection at Vickers shipyard in Barrow-in-Furness. He would take command of his new boat on 1 July.

On 22 April 1915, across the Channel in the verdant rolling fields of Belgium, the second battle of Ypres began, a month-long catalogue of death and horror which saw the Germans use gas for the first time. After all that, however, neither side gained any ground. Compared to the slaughter in mainland Europe and in far away Gallipoli, where conflicts would soon claim both of Francis's half-brothers, with the mud, the constant shelling and the fear of gas, the life of a submariner, despite its threat of fearful death and danger, must have seemed like liberation.

Now the years of study and training for Lieutenant-Commander Francis

Cromie were to prove their worth. No longer were the men of the service on pretend manoeuvres or exercises. This was war – the real thing – and, although somewhat behind in the building department, the German navy had taken the submarine every bit as seriously as the British.

Entering The Baltic 1914–15

CHAPTER 6

DANGEROUS MISSION

> The submarine cannot capture the merchant ship; she has no
> spare hands to put a prize crew on board; little or nothing would
> be gained by disabling her engines or propeller; she cannot
> convey her into harbour; and, in fact, it is impossible for the
> submarine to deal with commerce in the light and provisions of
> international law. There is nothing else the submarine can do
> except sink her capture . . .

> Admiral Lord Fisher, January 1914

At the outbreak of war the 8th Submarine Flotilla with HMS *Maidstone* at
Harwich boasted no fewer than eleven of the latest vessels out of the Royal
Navy's seventy-three undersea boats, and there were new ones waiting on the
slipways. The Germans, on the other hand, had twenty boats available, but only
sixteen of those were fit for war. There were U-boats being built – eighteen diesel-
powered versions, larger and more efficient, had been ordered in the previous
year, but only three were nearing completion. Of the U-boats that were fit for
service, *U-5* to *U-18*,[1] the best that could be said was that they were a liability
when running on the surface. Their engines burned heavy oil and the ensuing
smoke and sparks did little to enhance their capacity for stealth.

The Harwich flotilla, commanded by Captain Arthur K. Waistell, had E Class
boats *E1* to *E9*, plus HMS *D2*, *D3*, *D7*, *D5* and *D8*.[2] This flotilla represented the
cream of the service, and included a quartet of commanders destined to go down
in 'The Trade's' history: Martin Nasmith, Noel F. Laurence, Francis H.H.
Goodhart and Max K. Horton. It was into the ranks of this exclusive club that
Francis Cromie would eventually be welcomed. But for now, still thousands of
miles away from the action in the steamy heat of Hong Kong, all he and his crews
could do was wait impatiently for instructions.

The problem was the submarine itself. Over the decade prior to the war, both
Germany and Britain had been obsessed with bolstering their surface fleets by
building ever bigger, tougher and more heavily armed warships. The only reason
everyone, from the Germans, the French and the Italians to the USA, kept
building submarines was that everyone had them, and no one wished to be left
behind. Yet still the general feeling among the deep-water admirals was that the
vessel could never play a significant role in a sea battle. It was still regarded as
too underhand, and the idea that submarines could one day attack merchant
tonnage was simply beyond the moral pale. Although everyone had these boats,

it was still largely unknown what they might be capable of in an all-out war.

The Hague Peace Conferences of 1899 and 1907 had also set some rules of engagement for submarines. In comparison with what these vessels were to do within three decades, the laws seem chivalrous to a fault:

> Any boat intending to sink an enemy vessel must first stop that vessel, then give her captain a clear warning of the proposed sinking; the submarine captain must then make provision for the crew of his victim, and ensure their safety. It is permissible to stop neutral vessels to discover if they are carrying war materials for an enemy, and if this is so, they should be escorted to a port for internment.

Needless to say, these laws were seen by all participants in the war as a bit of a straitjacket. It seemed to turn the whole purpose of the submarine – its invisibility, its stealth – on its head.

Cromie was still in Hong Kong when the keel of his new boat was being laid down at Vickers' Yard, Barrow-in-Furness, on 27 November 1914. She would certainly be an improvement on the three C Class submarines he was working with in China. HMS *E19* displaced 664 tons surfaced and 780 tons submerged. She was 181 feet (55.2 metres) in length with a beam overall of 22 feet 9 inches (6.9 metres). Her mean draft was 12 feet 6 inches (3.8 metres). With twin screws, two 800 bhp diesel engines and two 420 bhp electric motors, she had a maximum surface speed of 14.5 knots (26.9 kph), and 9.5 knots (17. kph) submerged. With just under 42 tons of fuel she had a range of 3,000 miles (4,800 km). Compared to what had gone before, the E Class were, to the British sailor at the time, the de luxe branch of 'The Trade', but this was not saying much. They were still very uncomfortable vessels to live in. In terms of foul-weather clothing, the British submariner was ill equipped when compared to the Germans. On the surface, the tiny platform atop the conning tower, encircled by slender handrails, was totally exposed to the elements, barring a flimsy canvas bridge screen, so that anyone on lookout in bad weather was guaranteed to be soaked to the skin and, if not lashed to the periscope standards, stood a fair chance of going overboard. The early Es lacked many of the navigational refinements of later boats. For instance, *E9* had no wireless telegraph. The gyrocompass was one navigational refinement which had made life less hazardous, but it was still a fickle instrument.

The gyrocompass is not dependent on the earth's magnetism. To indicate direction it relies on the force produced by the earth's rotation about its axis, on the force of gravity and on the principle of the spinning wheel. Part of the gyrocompass involves an electrically driven high-speed wheel, the spindle of which, if free to do so, will take up a position parallel to the earth's axis. This wheel is known as the master compass and is kept in a sheltered position below decks. From this master compass can be run repeater compasses, to any chosen area of the vessel, each simultaneously reading the same course. Without a repeater, it was not unusual for the sailor at the wheel to discover he was steering the wrong course.

The boat's periscope, although an improvement on earlier models, was still small and basic. These were the days before radar and asdic, and such devices as the simple ship-detection apparatus – the hydrophones – which enabled submarines to listen out for other vessels approaching, were, at the start of the Great War, primitive and barely efficient. Much British optical equipment, such as binoculars, was inferior to the enemy's. Depth gauges only registered up to maximum of 100 feet (30 metres). Although the E Class was referred to as an 'overseas' boat, it seemed on the face of things to lack any basic comfort for the men who would sail it to foreign climes. The toilet facilities were a slight improvement on the regulation bucket on board the C boats, but this description by *E19*'s telegraphist, Ben Benson,[3] gives some idea of what spending a submerged penny was like:

> We did have a toilet, it was as near aft as you could get, where the stokers' mess was in fact. It was only about two feet by two feet square, just high enough to get in to. It was fitted into a convenient corner and held all the necessary paraphernalia for getting rid of it over the side. The door opened outwards and you got in and closed it and on the back of the door were all the instructions . . . When working this most amazing thing, you had to open and close valves and also a pump arrangement. If you weren't very careful you blew the whole lot back in your face. It was a terrible business. I remember Captain Cromie, on occasions when he had to use the place, would generally give one of the stokers a couple of bob to clear it out for him because I believe he had blown it back in his face on one occasion!

These privations aside, however, Cromie's early days, with their endless discussions and recommendations, aboard the old As and Bs in the Channel were now coming to some fruition with the innovations and features of the E Class subs. *E19* had a 6 pounder gun on deck, and boasted five 18 inch (46 cm) torpedo tubes; two in the bow, two in the beam and one in the stern. With ten 'tinfish' to play with, with any luck the 'tradesmen' could get down to causing some real damage to the enemy.

By the time Francis Cromie finally arrived home from China in 1915, the war had really got under way. Sadly, he had missed the opening action. The 8th Flotilla had been one of the earliest entrants in the conflict when, less than four hours after war had been declared, the destroyers *Ariel* and *Amethyst* towed HMS *E8* (Lieutenant-Commander Goodhart) and HMS *E6* (Lieutenant-Commander Talbot) out into the North Sea. There they joined a force which was making all speed for the Heligoland Bight, to be followed later that morning from Harwich by four more of the 8th Flotilla, all cheered on from the seafront and pier at Shotley as the early August sun came up. But although the surface fleet saw early action, sinking the German minelayer *Königin Louise*, for the submarines life on this first sortie was to be a little more routine and humdrum, submerged by day and surfaced by night on what must have seemed interminably uneventful combat patrols. Their big adventure was still to come.

For the Germans September 1914 had offered mixed blessings in submarine warfare. The U-boat arm was still smarting from the previous month's loss of

U-15, sliced in two by the light cruiser HMS *Birmingham*, and the embarrassing sinking of *U-13*, which had inadvertently sailed into a German minefield.

But on 5 September naval history of a grim kind was made off St Abb's Head near the Firth of Forth when *Kapitänleutnant* Otto Hersing in *U-21* sent the light cruiser HMS *Pathfinder* to the bottom with a single torpedo. Only 37 of her 296 man crew survived. Seventeen days later, on 22 September *U-9*'s *Kapitänleutnant* Otto Wedigen became Germany's first U-boat 'ace'[4] when, all within a single hour, he sank no fewer than three British cruisers, *Aboukir*, *Cressy* and *Hogue*. A total of 1,459 men lost their lives – a shocking figure – and Lord Fisher angrily pointed out that this represented more men in a single engagement than the whole figure for men lost in all of Nelson's battles.

It was the dashing Max Horton on HMS *E9* who provided the first impressive honours for the 8th Flotilla. Not long after dawn broke over Heligoland on 13 September 1914, *E9* launched a torpedo which soon sank the German cruiser *Hela*. Other members of the flotilla had also been making the Germans jumpy; both Lieutenant-Commander Talbot in HMS *E6* and Lieutenant-Commander Leir in *E4* had been causing the Germans some concern, and in the first week of October Horton struck again by sinking the enemy destroyer *S116*.

Four days after Horton sank the *Hela*, on 17 September 1914, an extremely important meeting was held to discuss the war at sea on board Admiral Jellicoe's

Cdr Max Horton in 1915. *(RN Submarine Museum, Gosport)*

flagship, HMS *Iron Duke*, moored in Loch Ewe on Scotland's west coast. In attendance were Roger Keyes, in charge of submarines, and Reginald Tyrwhitt, in
charge of destroyers and light cruisers at Harwich. As a measure of the gravity of
the gathering, the Chief of the War Staff, Vice-Admiral Sir Doveton Sturdee was
present. Sturdee, Chief of the Naval War Staff, and in charge of the Harwich force
of light cruisers, was accompanied by the First Lord of the Admiralty himself,
Winston Churchill. The fact that Jellicoe had moved his fleet from Scapa Flow
around to the relative safety of Loch Ewe spoke loudly of the threat, even that far
north, of German submarines. There was not, as yet, a comprehensive grasp of
the notion of anti-submarine tactics. The depth-charge had not been invented at
this stage, but there was one basic display of anti-U-boat vigilance which, almost
a century later, presents such a madcap image that one can only smile. Their lordships had decreed that, in order to deal with any enemy submarine which might
make its way into the vicinity of the anchored Grand Fleet, a small flotilla of two-
man anti-submarine picket boats should patrol the waters. Their anti-U-boat
equipment included large brown paper bags and a hammer. Should a periscope
appear, the idea was to row up to it, place the bag over the enemy lens and begin
to thrash it with the hammer.[5] That would teach those Huns a thing or two!

At this conference, the subject of the Baltic figured prominently. Although all
kinds of plans had been mooted before the war concerning possible operations
against Germany either in the Baltic or in Kiel Bay, using ships from the Grand
Fleet, the threat of the chosen areas now being heavily mined had somewhat
neutralised these lofty proposals. But now the Navy's new technology –
submarines – could come into play. Commodore Keyes put forward the idea that
two submarines in the Baltic could cause a lot of damage and consternation for
the enemy. But first he had to face up to the thorny problem of actually navigating a passage into the Baltic via the Kattegat and the Skagerrak, and through
the treacherously shallow Sound between Denmark and Sweden. Could it be
done? Before this could be decided, reconnaissance was required.

Keyes sprang into action as soon as he arrived back in Harwich. On
22 September *E5* (Lieutenant-Commander Charles Benning) and Lieutenant-
Commander Noel F. Laurence in *E1* sailed out of Gorleston, just south of
Great Yarmouth, to rendezvous with two destroyers which would give them
a lengthy fuel- and battery-saving tow across the North Sea. The plan was for
E1 and *E5* to scout around the approach areas for the intended Baltic mission for
two to three days, check on the traffic in the Kattegat and Skagerrak and examine
possible anchorages. Following this the two submarines would join a force of
destroyers back in the North Sea, which would escort them back home. With
hindsight, it seems hard to imagine what great benefit this reconnaissance trip
was to provide as neither submarine went near the main area of contention – the
Sound – where some accurate feedback would have been most welcome. This part
of the passage would be the most dangerous element of an entry into the Baltic.
Nevertheless, Laurence and Benning collected enough information to take the
pioneers through from Hantsholm, past Gothenburg and all the way south to the
mouth of the Sound between Helsingborg in Sweden and Helsingør in Denmark.
Their voyage did therefore enable Keyes to feel that the required research had

been carried out. And apart from a two-day delay for Laurence owing to *E1*'s repeatedly poor mechanical condition, both boats got safely back to Harwich.

By October 1914 the war was two months old and the citizens of Harwich had grown used to submarines, busy bluejackets and all things naval coming and going from the port. Thus the crowd which lined the quay on the 13th was a thinner one than that which had cheered off Goodhart and Talbot on that first sunny August morning of the war. But the men who sailed out on this October afternoon could hardly have imagined what lay ahead. For most of them it would be over two years before they saw old Blighty or their loved ones again. They were not only sailing into war, but into a massive change in history – revolution. Most of the ratings on board had little idea what their mission might entail – least of all that, within a few days, they would be living in Russia.

Keyes had selected what was probably the finest trio of submariners available in the Royal Navy at that time. Lieutenant-Commander Noel Laurence, the Senior Officer, would take *E1* and, this time, complete the mission; Max Horton would follow in *E9* and Martin Nasmith in *E11*. The idea was to attack the German fleet which would be exercising in Kiel Bay, and once the submarines began to run low on fuel, they would sail to the port of Libau (which later became Liepaja, Latvia), where the Russians would look after them. Yet the proposed length of their mission was vague and, surprisingly, there was no 'military precision' in the planning; the Russians had no idea that the submarines were coming.

As early as 1908 Admiral Fisher had put forward plans for the large-scale use of ships from the British Fleet in the Baltic. By 1914, Winston Churchill had even been given a green light to build three enormous, fast battle cruisers, each with a shallow draft suitable for the Baltic. But despite Churchill's unbridled enthusiasm, the vessels never entered the Baltic and ended up between the wars as aircraft carriers.[6] Although Churchill had written to the Grand Duke Nicholas, the Russian Commander-in-Chief, in August, his letter had only outlined a rough plan possibly to send ships from the Royal Navy's Grand Fleet into the Baltic. The unexpected arrival of submarines, although highly appreciated, would raise a few Russian eyebrows.

It had been decided just prior to the three boats departing, after a careful study of the charts, that they would not have enough depth of water in the Sound to submerge. Horton came up with the idea that they should make a dash on the surface during maximum darkness. It was known that the Germans had regular patrols of destroyers at the southern end of the Sound. The journey was therefore going to be fraught with danger and also required, when running on the surface, that the boat should be trimmed as low in the water as possible to present the minimum profile.

At 0500 hours on 15 October 1914 Laurence in *E1* and Horton in *E9* left Gorleston, having left Martin Nasmith's *E11* behind for repairs. But their plans to commence their Baltic mission as a trio – and now a duo – were further confounded when *E1* developed engine problems, the repairs putting her behind Horton in *E9*. Laurence did, however, manage to eventually overtake Horton. Poor Nasmith was delayed even longer with mechanical problems at Gorleston, not making it into the North Sea until 15.00 hours on the 15th, with only one engine running.

Laurence ploughed on, through the Skagerrak and into the Kattegat as the light began to fade on Friday, 16 October 1914. He immediately took *E1* down to wait for darkness. Ahead of them was Oresund, the Sound, flanked on both sides by neutral countries, Denmark to the west and Sweden to the east. Straying into their territorial waters was almost as tricky as meeting the Germans. Then there were the many obstacles; in the 75 miles (120 km) between Helsingborg in the north and the island of Saltholm at the Baltic end lay a series of treacherously shallow stretches of sea punctuated by the island of Hven. Once south of Hven the nocturnal naval raiders had to face the possibility of being spotted not only by the Germans but by one of the hundreds of vessels plying the busy route across Oresund between Landskrona in Sweden and Copenhagen in Denmark.

As darkness fell, the low, glistening black silhouette of HMS *E1* broke the surface of the Scandinavian waters and trundled forward into the Sound. Four hours later, Laurence was relieved; the trip, though nerve-racking, had gone smoothly, and they had not been spotted. Just before 1 a.m. on 17 October the first British submarine had entered the Baltic.

Meanwhile, Max Horton in *E9* was several hours behind, but had managed to repair his damaged engines which had delayed him. It had been a difficult trip, as he had been forced to dive repeatedly as their path crossed that of the many vessels in the area. And now, as darkness fell on the 17th, HMS *E9* was sitting on the bottom at one end of the Sound with Commander Laurence also submerged at the other end, with no means of knowing whether Horton was ahead of him or behind. As dawn broke on the 18th, Laurence and his crew finished their submerged breakfast and *E1* came up to periscope depth for what was to be the first day of action for 'The Trade' in the Baltic. It was to be a busy one. The enemy was soon in evidence and by mid-morning Laurence had the German cruiser *Victoria Louise* in his sights for a torpedo attack.

Although he fired two torpedoes, both ran too low and missed. It was one of those frustrating anomalies of the early part of the war which denied Laurence an early hit. The real warheads on the tinfish had turned out to be heavier than the practice heads used during peacetime manoeuvres, thus causing the torpedoes to run downwards rather than straight. There was also an inherent design fault in the depth-keeping mechanism which was the cause of much frustration in future attacks. It would have made things much better for both British submarines if the *Victoria Louise* had been hit, because the German lookouts had not failed to see the trails of bubbles and without any hesitation made the correct assumption, shocking though it seemed, that British submarines had somehow entered the Baltic. Immediately the German High Command threw everything it could into preventing any further entry through the Sound – just as Max Horton was about to make his attempt.

As with Laurence, after surfacing in the dark, Horton's passage through Oresund on the night of 18 October went better than expected – at first. But once past Malmö towards the Baltic end he was dismayed to find the channel criss-crossed with searchlights and bustling with German patrols. Horton, as always, pushed his prodigious luck and crept slowly forward on the surface until, at one point in the jet black darkness, the lookout shouted that the shape looming closely ahead off the starboard bow was a destroyer. Horton hastily ordered 'Dive!' but within seconds realised the folly of this as *E9* thudded to a sudden, booming halt – the sea was a mere 14 feet (4.03 metres) deep. This might have been the end of the *E9* and her crew, but miraculously, the German patrol had missed the boat, which had been less than 200 yards distant.

Now the skills and bravado of the master submariner came into full play. After less than an hour with perilously little water hiding the top of her conning tower, Horton gently brought *E9* to the surface, careful not to let her get too high out of the water. He delicately raised the hatch and peered out; he was shocked to discover that the destroyer was still there, although this time much closer than before – yet still the Germans hadn't spotted the submarine.

Horton had little choice but to submerge yet again, but this time only deep enough to leave some clearance beneath *E9*'s hull and the seabed. Considering the dangerously shallow water and the dark bulk of the submarine, what Horton got away with was not only down to luck, but a nail-biting display of good old stiff-upper-lip courage. With one electric motor running at dead slow, and with just inches of water above her and just over a half-fathom (1 metre) below, he took *E9* close by the German destroyer, and slowly past her and silently stole away, until at last deeper water was reached. It was to be several hours before this snail's-pace escape put enough distance between *E9* and the destroyer. Whilst submerged, they were reasonably safe, but the Germans were up there on the surface, waiting, watching. By now the air on board the submarine had become almost unbreathable, causing the crew to retch and vomit. And after such a long, slow progress on the electric motors, the batteries, which could only be charged up by running on the surface with the diesels, were running dangerously low. Horton decided to surface. The opening of the hatch and the sudden intake of fresh Baltic air was, for the crew, as welcome as an iced lager in the middle of the Sahara. But the relief was short-lived; just minutes later, without even time to begin charging the batteries, Horton ordered 'Dive!' again as a destroyer, which had obviously spotted them, was sighted, making full speed in *E9*'s direction. There was nothing for it now but to push on and use whatever battery power was left to get out of the Sound and into the Baltic proper. After a long and difficult passage, they finally made it into deeper, comparatively safer water, and as darkness fell after what had been a long, nervous day, they surfaced, took in precious fresh air once again and at last were able to take the opportunity to charge their batteries. Then it was down to the bottom for a quiet night's rest, before setting off at dawn for their meeting point with *E1* and, hopefully, *E11* at Libau.

Laurence, in the meantime, hoped on the morning of the 20th to make up for the disappointment of missing the *Victoria Louise* by taking the risky and brave decision to submerge and enter the lion's den – Danzig Harbour. Although there were some choice German warships berthed there, their positions in the basin were too awkward to make them good targets. Realising that discretion was the better part of valour, Laurence cut his losses and, like Horton, set course for their rendezvous at Libau.

If Horton and Laurence had been blessed with good luck, poor Martin Nasmith was certainly being denied his share. Later on that first day, 15 October, after lengthy repairs to *E11*, he had set out across the North Sea, only to break down yet again – not once, but twice. He did not arrive off the Sound until late on the 17th, and over the next six strenuous days the crew of the ill-fated boat faced a number of trials. To begin with, Nasmith was perplexed at the sheer volume of merchant traffic each time he surfaced. Neutral or not, to be spotted by any of these vessels inevitably meant being reported. At one point, whilst sailing in darkness, he attempted to fool the merchant steamers by ploughing on merrily with his navigation lights on full display, in the hope that *E11* would appear to be a small trading vessel. But still he had to keep diving and ducking to avoid the thoroughly alerted enemy, and even then, as the days passed and the fatigue of the crew grew greater, he seemed no nearer to entering the Sound.

The waiting reached a high point, when Nasmith took *E11* out of neutral waters for a surface run to charge up her batteries. Suddenly, ahead on the horizon, he spotted a submarine, which he believed to be the German *U-3*. Wasting no time, he lined her up in his sights and sent off two torpedoes. Both missed their mark, a fact which, looking back, Nasmith must have blessed, because although this was indeed a submarine bearing a large figure 3 on her tower, she was not a German, but the neutral Danish boat the *Havmanden*. It was an easy mistake to make (he was unaware the boat was Danish until he got back home), especially in such busy and confusing waters with so many vessels, both warships and merchants, neutral and belligerent, crossing one another's paths.

He had another surprise when *E11* was buzzed by a German plane. The use of aircraft at this stage of the war was still relatively uncommon, and on top of everything else it must have been galling for him to have to face up to this irritating rarity. By the 22nd, his crew exhausted, his mission no nearer to completion, Nasmith made the very hard decision – he must abandon the attempt to enter the Sound and go home. Tired, dissatisfied and frustrated, the men of HMS *E11* arrived back in Gorleston on the 24th.

By this time both Laurence and Horton had arrived in Libau. Their appearance in this port – indeed, the very fact that they had successfully entered the Baltic – must have come as quite a shock to the Russians. As Churchill wrote later, 'The Russians . . . were imperfectly acquainted with their project and possible arrival.' The devastated state of Libau also came as a shock to Laurence and Horton. Had advance planning and communication around this mission been given more careful attention back in Britain, then someone at the Foreign Office (FO) two months earlier might well have seen the advantage in letting the Admiralty know that their reports indicated that Libau, which was in danger of falling to the enemy, had already been hit by the Germans and had been subjected to some Russian 'scorched earth' tactics. Forts had been destroyed, the dockyard seriously damaged, and coal, ammunition and other stores had been put to the torch. But on top of this, when Laurence and Horton were met by a surprised

Russian patrol boat, they had to listen in horror as the Russian officers offered their congratulations for just making it into Libau through a large German mine-field – another fact which, courtesy of the British Embassy reports, was known to the Foreign Office but not communicated to the Admiralty.

This must all have added to the Russians' perception of the Royal Navy submariners as devil-may-care pioneers with nerves of steel. Whereas this is probably an accurate description when looking at Horton and Laurence's successes, no doubt both they and the Russians would have made quite a few different moves had the E-boats been given accurate information about Libau.

Once Horton had caught up with Laurence, the Russians were keen for them to move into safer moorings in the Gulf of Finland. However, this was impossible, as they still had no idea what had happened to Nasmith. Against their hosts' advice and wishes, both *E1* and *E9* waited for a further seven days in the wreckage of Libau, going on patrol in a vain attempt to find *E11*, not realising that, far from their grim assumption that she had fallen prey to the Germans, Nasmith and his crew were safely at home gearing up for their next wartime mission. Within five years Martin Nasmith would be back in the Baltic, however, this time as a holder of the VC and in command of another flotilla, fighting the same Russians to whom the British were allies in 1914.

In the spring of 1915, once the vicious ice of the Baltic winter had loosened its grip, Horton and Laurence set about reminding the Germans that they had more to worry about now than the Russians. Horton modestly referred to this activity in a letter: 'During this period, we really have been busy, even more so than at the beginning of the war, 7,000 miles in two months . . .'

On 20 May a great blow was dealt to the Russian navy when their highly efficient and respected Commander-in-Chief, Admiral Nikolai von Essen, died of pneumonia. In von Essen the British had a man they could respect and deal with. After a temporary stewardship by his Chief of Staff, Vice-Admiral L.F. Kerber, von Essen's permanent replacement, Vice-Admiral Viktor Kanin, made an auspicious beginning by expanding the fleet's operations, taking control of the Gulf of Riga and adding to the defences of Moonsund and the Aaland Islands. But the loss of the talented and efficient von Essen only added to the Imperial Navy's growing problems.

Several thousand miles away, Francis Cromie was packing his bags for an eager return to Britain and a chance to wage war. From St Petersburg, Commander H. Grenfell, the Naval Attaché at the British Embassy, had made strong recommendations that the Royal Navy's Submarine Flotilla should be expanded. When Cromie arrived back in the UK in March 1915 the boat he was to take command of was still being built on the slipway at Vickers' yard at Barrow-in-Furness. On 21 April he took command of HMS *E19*[7] whilst she was still completing at Barrow. The success of the flotilla, now based in Reval (present day Tallin, Estonia), had become a source of some pride, but in far-away Russia there were fault lines appearing. Laurence and Horton both possessed fine qualities, but in terms of personality they were oil and water. Max Horton was a dashing, Biggles-type character, a gambler, loved by women. Not one to stand on ceremony when expressing his opinions about fellow officers or their decisions, he could be regarded unfavourably by some. Noel Laurence, on the other hand, was a much more formal, disciplined character, in stature surpassing six feet, and a classic example of the naval disciplinarian. Both men were highly regarded by their crews, but the strain of their enforced absence from home in a strange land, serving alongside a very different navy from their own, was bound eventually to raise tensions.

As the summer of 1915 rolled on, Cromie assembled his crew and put *E19* through her rigorous trials whilst the Admiralty began to formulate its plans for expanding its Russian campaign. Four more E-boats were to fill out the Baltic Flotilla. The first two would be HMS *E8* (Lieutenant-Commander F.H.H. Goodhart) and HMS *E13* (Lieutenant-Commander G. Layton). Additional British submarines could not arrive too soon for the Russians, as Admiral von Hipper's 1st Scouting Group of the German navy in the Baltic, with reinforcements transferred from the North Sea, had set its sights on the Gulf of Riga. If the port of Riga fell, this would deal a decisive blow against the Russians.

As Horton, Laurence and Nasmith had done a year before, Goodhart and Layton took their boats out of Harwich on 15 August 1915 and headed across the North Sea for the Kattegat. Fortunately, this time someone in the Baltic knew they were coming, as their instructions were to rendezvous with Max Horton's *E9* off Dagerort, just outside the Gulf of Finland. Although, after brushes with a destroyer and a torpedo boat and a repetition of Horton's shallow dive, *E8* made it to the rendezvous, the hapless *E13* lived up to the reputation of her number. Both submarines had managed to keep in contact until just before the approach to the Sound. The usual problem dogged them both – having to dive at ever shorter intervals to avoid being spotted by the ubiquitous commercial shipping in the area. But a serious fault with *E13*'s gyro-compass resulted in bitter tragedy. After steering as much as 20 degrees off course, the submarine, after almost making it through the Sound, ran aground in shallow water, shuddering to a permanent halt in the sticky mudbanks off the Danish Island of Saltholm. Try as he might, Layton could not free the stricken vessel, which by early light the following morning (the 19th), had attracted the attention of the neutral Danes. The captain of the Danish torpedo boat *Narvhalen* left Layton under no misapprehension – either he got his boat out of these neutral waters in the next twenty-four hours, or he and his crew were all bound for a Danish prison.

This seemed bad enough, but at least the British Navy was not at war with the Danes. Hearts must have sunk when the Germans, in the warlike shape of *Leutnant zur See* Graf von Montgelas, commanding torpedo boat *G132*, hove into view to take a surprised and hungry look at what was a sitting target. But the *G132*, like the *E13*, could do nothing in these neutral waters but take notes and steam away to contact superiors in Kiel for advice.

Many miles away, at the north-eastern end of the Baltic, just as Layton and his exhausted crew were locked in a struggle to lighten their boat and float her off the Danish mud, HMS *E1* fired off a torpedo at the German flagship *Seydlitz*. The tinfish missed, but cruised on and found a target in the nearby 25,000 ton battlecruiser *Moltke*. Although its torpedo lacked the destructive power to puncture and sink the huge, heavily armoured German, it nevertheless made a grim mess of her forward torpedo room and despatched eight German sailors in the process. It was enough for the Germans to high-tail it to Danzig to repair the damage and, eventually, withdraw its High Seas Fleet units from the Baltic. Yet, as the Russians prepared to fête Noel Laurence for ultimately preventing the port of Riga falling to the enemy, the news of the damaged *Moltke* sent the enraged Germans into a savage and illegal act of vengeance off the Island of Saltholm. One British submarine had stood between the German navy and Riga, and now the reckless British had the temerity to send yet another boat into the Baltic. This would not be allowed.

As Layton and his men continued their fruitless struggle, three Danish torpedo boats, the *Tumleren*, *Søulven* and *Støren*, had all now reluctantly gathered to witness the embarrassment of the Royal Navy. That would have been bearable, but on the horizon *Leutnant* von Montgelas, on board *G132*, was returning full ahead – and this time he had come mob-handed with a further torpedo boat bringing up the rear. One of Britain's greatest naval strategists and historians described what followed as 'an outrage, perpetrated in cold blood, by men under control of their officers, upon a helpless wreck on a neutral shore. For a cumulation of illegality it would surely be hard to match in the annals of modern naval warfare . . .'[8]

Even allowing for the effect of the news of the damaged *Moltke* on the Kiel-based German Rear-Admiral Mishke, *Leutnant* von Montgelas's retribution certainly did fall well outside the law. But Mishke's instructions were that neutral waters or no neutral waters, yet another British submarine must not be allowed into the Baltic under any circumstances. Perhaps the argument was that, even if Layton did break free, with the Germans waiting just outside Danish waters, *E13*'s fate was sealed in any event; much easier to cripple her for good whilst she lay aground.

The Germans' first act was to fire a torpedo at *E13*, which surprisingly missed, but exploded upon hitting the mudbank. Then, from a range of only 300 yards, the Germans began shelling the submarine; within minutes she was ablaze. Because of the awkward angle at which the boat was lying, it was impossible for Layton to retaliate in any way, and within seconds nearly half the *E13*'s crew were dead or dying. Layton gave the order to abandon ship and the rest of the men took to the water, where the enemy showed no mercy, continuing to fire on the survivors. Thankfully, the intervention of the Danish boat *Søulven*, which moved between the *E13* and the German patrol *G132*, prevented even further bloodshed. Fourteen men had died, and a fifteenth body was recovered later. Their bodies were eventually shipped back to Britain on board the merchantman SS *Vidar*.[9] Fourteen German shells had wrecked the *E13*. Layton and the survivors were taken as internees to the naval barracks in Copenhagen. Although Layton and his first lieutenant, Paul Eddis, managed to escape from Denmark to continue their fight against Germany,[10] the remaining crew members were to spend the duration of the war as prisoners of the Danes – not, according to some records, as bad a prospect as might be imagined.

Goodhart and Layton had no knowledge of each other's fate. Goodhart's *E8* was now well into the Baltic and heading for her rendezvous with the Russians and Horton's *E9*. But it had not been an easy run. There had been some nerve-racking cat-and-mouse games with the Germans and some hair-raising dives in water so shallow it hardly covered the boat. At one point *E8* had lost the blades on her starboard propeller. German patrol activity was at a fever pitch – following the *Moltke* incident and the crippling of the *E13* the German lookouts were on a nervous alert. Had another submarine got into the Baltic? At the moment, they did not know.

On the morning of 22 August Goodhart and his crew, tired and nervous, ate a quick cold breakfast as Goodhart scanned the horizon through the periscope. To his delight, a Russian destroyer was approaching, accompanied by a submarine – HMS *E9*. This time surfacing was a joy as Goodhart and Horton met, and the Russians congratulated this new addition to the Allied flotilla. But as the three vessels cruised towards their Russian base at Reval, the news broke about the fate of *E13* and her crew. The sadness of losing so many of their comrades,

Cdr Cromie on *E19*.
(*Imperial War Museum*)

and so early in the mission, cast a cloud over what should have otherwise been a joyous occasion.

Back in Harwich Francis Cromie was drumming his fingers on the new, polished chartroom table of the *E19*. He was anxious for orders. There were men in the Baltic, the Dardanelles, men in the North Sea, patrols in the Channel. When was his adventure to begin? Despite his new command, his new submarine, all the trials and activity, the four months since returning to England seemed to have dragged on interminably. But he did not have long to wait.

Not knowing what his orders might be, Cromie had outlined the possibility of a long absence to Gwladys, Dolores Anthea and his mother, all now living in central London. From there Harwich was an easy train ride when leave came up, and certainly a less fraught journey than to either Hampshire or Pembrokeshire. But the advantage was short-lived; HMS *E19* and HMS *E18* were transferred from Harwich to the Tyne Flotilla, with their depot ship the HMS *Bonaventure*. Francis Cromie was about to say goodbye to Britain, and to his wife, mother and daughter, for good. Ahead of him lay the most adventurous – and tragic – assignment of his career.

CHAPTER 7

EMBRACING THE BEAR

24 August 1915 St Petersburg

To His Majesty The King,
I have heard with much pleasure that the British submarine *E8*
has joined My Naval Forces and wish to express to You My
cordial thanks. The Baltic Sea represents a most favourable field
of operations for submarine activity and the presence of British
boats of that type will render a most important service to our
general cause. I am sure that *E8* will perform deeds as brilliant
and successful as *E1* quite lately again. I beg you to accept my
deepest sympathy for the sad and heroic loss of submarine *E13*.

Nicholas[1]

Francis Cromie's experiences in China had given him a broad enough education
in the perceived inscrutability of cultures far removed from that of his native
Britain. The combination of his time during the Boxer Rebellion and his return
with the Hong Kong Flotilla thirteen years later would have removed any false
notions this young officer might have had that there was only one way of doing
things – the British way. Russia, like China, was a very big country, and quite
soon Cromie and his men were to discover that although in many ways her cities,
industry and terrain looked familiar, her social fabric would seem every bit as
alien and archaic as Imperial China's. As for her navy – it may well have looked
the part, smart, imperial and disciplined, but beneath the lofty ladder of rank and
privilege and the ostentatious gold braid of its martinet titled officers, below
decks, even in 1915, this was a force seething with anger and resentment, a social
powder keg just waiting for a spark.

Russia's pride and prowess as a sea-going nation had always been fuelled by
the image of Peter the Great, who had forced his way into the Baltic in 1703 after
successfully attacking the Swedes in their fortress at the mouth of the River Neva.
Peter, certainly no palace-bound monarch, was in love with the sea – in fact he
relished every scrap of knowledge and experience he could collect on all things
maritime. After spending hours in the Dutch quarter of Moscow, listening to the
tales of the navigator and sailor Franz Timmermann, he wasted no time in travelling to Holland to see her shipyards, and then even worked for a spell in
Britain's naval dockyards, such as those at Deptford, where the King's growing
fleet of warships was being built. When at home in Russia he took up sailing on
Lake Izmailovo.

All this inspired the young Tsar to recruit his own men and set up the Imperial

Russian Navy. After twenty-one years, during which he had rid the eastern Baltic of the Swedes, and, after battling with the Turks, at one time had a clear access to the Black Sea via Azov, he had become the proud master of a great navy, with no fewer than 800 ships under his command. He also built Russia's most beautiful city, which was proclaimed to be a 'window on the west' and modestly named after him – St Petersburg. Here Peter's Admiralty would look out with pride from its superb palace buildings on the banks of the broad, flowing Neva to the sea beyond.

When Catherine the Great took the helm, she gave the Imperial Navy just as much attention, and by 1774 the force was strong enough to secure an impressive defeat over the Turks and give Russia permanent access to the Black Sea. This meant the building of yet another great war fleet which would further enhance Russia's power in the south. Yet although the will to be great sailors has always existed amongst the Russians, the geography of her empire has fractured and diluted her navy. The Baltic is virtually enclosed, as is the Black Sea. In the north, only remote Murmansk offers an ocean outlet to the rest of the world. For a great part of the year, ice is the Russian sailor's greatest enemy. Great stretches of the Baltic, from St Petersburg to Helsinki and down the coast of Estonia, become the prisons of ships from November until the spring.

By the time the later Romanovs of the nineteenth century came to power, the great days of Peter and Catherine were nothing but a golden memory in naval terms. Russia's royal and military establishment at the end of the nineteenth century was flushed with its own insular self-importance. Whereas the social fabric in the rest of Europe and in the USA was constantly being improved (albeit excruciatingly slowly), in Romanov Russia the peasantry and the urban working class suffered a life so feudal and medieval that it is no surprise that one of the most popular pastimes amongst the intelligentsia was plotting some form of revolution. Ordinary Russians had suffered throughout the centuries at the hands of autocratic despots, but sadly, as history has shown, this situation was to be self-perpetuating.

To the Tsar and his military hierarchy the navy and army were simply reliable showcases of Russian might, to be polished and displayed every so often in the face of any potential aggressor. But because of the almost God-like nature of the Romanov dynasty, progressive wisdom and good advice rarely filtered through to the big guns. Treatment of the lower ranks in both services was appalling. Conditions of service bordered on slavery, the food was fit only for pigs and the discipline and regime of punishment made that of Nelson's navy seem humane by comparison.

The humiliating defeat of the Russian navy by the Japanese fleet at Tsushima on 27 May 1905 was not only a major military turning point, but a social one. After sailing from the Baltic in October 1904, via the North Sea (where they had mistaken Hull trawlers for Japanese torpedo boats, sinking one vessel and killing two fishermen), the hapless Russian fleet of forty-five assorted warships, many of them well past their prime, continued their 18,000 mile (29,000 km) voyage to their doom. The aim was a heavy-handed show of force to relieve the Russian First Pacific Squadron, which was trapped in Vladivostok and Port Arthur, under siege by the Japanese navy under Admiral Togo. Unlike those of other navies, such as Britain's, the Russian vessels were not a regular feature beyond their own theatre of operations. Whereas, historically, the Royal Navy had established a chain of command, bases and supply points stretching around the globe, the Russians, once outside the Baltic, faced a long and isolated journey to Japan.

Their general overall speed did not exceed 8 knots (15 kph), and to refuel during the six month voyage, the expedition leader, Admiral Zinovi Rozhdestvenski, had to depend on unreliable, prearranged meetings at sea with German colliers. To ensure that the fleet kept moving, so much coal was sometimes taken on board that it was piled on decks, in cabins and even in messdecks or officers' bathrooms. The Baltic Fleet's eventual arrival in the Straits of Tsushima, between Korea and Japan, was a disastrous climax to the previous six months of sacrifice. Admiral Togo proved to be no Oriental pushover. Despite Japan's remoteness from Europe, her navy had much more in common with the British Royal Navy than Admiral Rozhdestvenski could have imagined. In fact, the son of a Samurai, he had studied naval warfare in England during the 1870s, and as he rose through the ranks he had been determined to base Japan's navy, from the status of its vessels, right through to the sailor's uniforms, on the British model. Togo's study of naval tactics and his unbounded admiration for Horatio Nelson was to stand him in good stead.

With their tight discipline, superior training and state-of-the-art warships, the Japanese saw off the tired, motley Russian fleet in less than twenty-four hours, sending nearly fifty warships to the bottom and 4,830 Russian sailors to their deaths, and wounding a further 5,917. Only three vessels got through to Vladivostok – the Russians under siege at Port Arthur having surrendered five months before the Baltic Fleet arrived. The Japanese lost 117 men with 590 wounded, and just three torpedo boats. The shock waves of shame went through the ranks of Russia's armed forces right up to the Tsar's Winter Palace in St Petersburg. Tsushima was a disaster.

All this was a crushing blow to public morale throughout Russia, highlighting the claims of the revolutionary groups that the old order was bankrupt and ripe for replacement. As for the navy and the army, a mutinous mood of dissatisfaction festered, matching in many ways that of the growing civilian political reform movements. Although the first attempted revolution in Russia during that same disastrous year, 1905, was eventually quashed, for the administration which had produced the Tsushima débâcle the writing was firmly on the wall. In some ways, the arrival of the Great War in 1914 must have been viewed by Nicholas and his entourage as a much-needed diversion, another point in history around which the embattled citizens of Mother Russia could unite. But for Vladimir Ilyich Lenin and Leon Trotsky this huge but futile conflict would be the seedbed of revolution.

Although he could not have realised it at the time, the Russia Francis Cromie was about to arrive in was teetering on the cusp of perhaps the biggest political explosion in history. Had the *E19* been bound for any other destination, then no doubt the Royal Navy's task would have been just as dangerous, but at least it would have been carried out in a more orthodox atmosphere of wartime conflict, namely, one side against the other, with no added complications to interrupt the line of fire.

Such was the mixture of bumbling bureaucratic inefficiency and continuing mindless subservience to the Tsar that the Romanovs had only themselves and their advisers to blame for the peril into which their country was about to plunge. Alexander Kerensky, at one time Premier in the post-Romanov Provisional Government, gives a perfect example of the constraints under which some of the country's more talented military leaders operated.[2]

> Wishing to avoid aggravating the Germans, the Tsar forbade the navy to lay minefields in Baltic waters without first asking his consent. On July 17, the Admiralty received a report that the German fleet had left Kiel and set sail for Danzig. Aware of the Tsar's orders, Admiral Essen, commander of the Baltic Fleet, telegraphed the chief of naval staff, Admiral Rusin, urging him to ask the Tsar for permission to lay mines at once. The telegram was received at about midnight on July 17. The chief of staff, accompanied by his closest aides, went to the minister of the marine, despite the lateness of the hour, and asked him to wake up the Tsar and request his permission to lay the minefields. The minister of the marine flatly refused to do so. Attempts to secure the assistance of the Grand Duke Nicholas were also a failure. It was at about 4.00 a.m., when the officers sent by Rusin to see General Yanushkevich, a regimental comrade of the Tsar, had not returned, that the Admiral decided to go against the Imperial command and to order the mines to be laid. Several minutes later permission was received from General Yanushkevich . . .

Less than twenty hours later, they had no other choice than to wake His Majesty, for at midnight on 18 July, Russia was at war with Germany.[3]

At the outbreak of war, the Russian Baltic Fleet, alongside which the British submariners were now fighting, possessed some grand battleships but was greatly outmatched by the German fleet, which boasted no fewer than thirteen new dreadnoughts as well as an impressive array of other vessels. But with Admiral von Essen the Russians did at least possess someone with decisive, bold leadership. In fact, once von Essen had made the decision to lay mines as he waited for the Tsar to wake up, within four hours the Baltic Fleet had laid no fewer than 2,124, which effectively blocked any German entrance to the Gulf of Finland.

On 13 August 1914, the Russians had a stroke of luck which would last for the rest of the war. There was heavy fog that night in the vicinity of the island of Odensholm in the Gulf of Finland when one of Germany's finest warships, the cruiser *Magdeburg*, ran aground on the island's reefs. The Russian Baltic Fleet vessels *Bogatyr* and *Pallada*[4] soon captured the *Magdeburg*'s captain and over fifty of her crew. But more important, they seized code tables and signal logs which gave them the unprecedented advantage of being able to decode German radio transmissions.

The Russian Baltic Fleet which awaited the arrival of Francis Cromie was, in appearance, a fine, traditional organisation with its fair share of battle honours, but the painful disgrace of Tsushima always hung in the air. Unknown to Cromie and his crews there was also a moral bankruptcy running from the Admiralty right down to the officer classes, and a hateful range of outmoded attitudes towards ratings which had only been made worse since the rebellions and mutinies of 1905. But all this complicated background was yet to be faced.

Back in Newcastle, the crew of HMS *E19* were still curious as to what exotic posting Cromie might reveal once he'd opened his sealed orders. As the war got into its grisly stride Cromie worked around the clock to make sure that the submarine was ready for her first big adventure. Together with HMS *E18*, under the command of Lieutenant-Commander R.C. Halahan, he was to follow the dangerous routine as established by *E1*, *E9*, *E8* and the brave but doomed *E13*. However, after almost a year of operations in the Baltic, at least Cromie had some intelligence from the flotilla on the nature of the mission. He knew what dangers to expect, as did Halahan.

Leading telegraphist Ben Benson had received his orders. He knew by the amount of kit he had been told to pack that they were going somewhere, and that it probably was not the Mediterranean. At the moment it was all hush-hush, but the idea of the Baltic had been bandied around. After a short leave, towards the end of August Benson made his way to Newcastle and arrived back on board *E19*. One of the early tasks in making ready for the voyage was to sail out to the Tyne estuary to 'swing compasses'.[5] During one of these exercises *E19* burned out one of her main armatures. Able Seaman Wingrove recorded the event in his diary.[6]

> Monday: went to swing compasses and with the luck of Old Nick managed to burn out our starboard motor. Josie[7] nearly jumped over the side with anxiety. By dint of slaving all day and half the night then a further two days and nights, we got the damaged motor out and replaced by a new one from Vickers, all this being done to accompaniment of much growling because we got no leave and *E18* were ashore every night.

And Benson recorded in his diary: 'Cromie our Skipper was almost demented over this.'

The skipper's dementia was to get worse. After limping back into dock Cromie sent urgently to Vickers at Barrow for a new armature. By now he knew that before long he would be making his way into the Baltic, where he would be rubbing shoulders with the already legendary Max Horton. Anything which delayed *E19*'s departure was a curse. Wartime or not, the obstinacy of the British dock worker, even in 1915, could easily stand in the way of a demented submarine captain. Taking their own steady pace, the shoreside engineers infuriated Cromie with their laid-back performance installing the repaired armature, driving him to issue a constant stream of threatening orders to speed things up. This got to such a pitch that the foreman simply joined his men and downed tools. In the face of such civilian belligerence, the Baltic now seemed further away than ever.

However, as his character would always demonstrate, Cromie was not about to be delayed by a little industrial action. If the shore crew would not do the job, then the sailors would have to take over. All shore leave was suspended and the men were set to work on twelve-hour shifts, around the clock, fitting the repaired armature. According to Benson, this task lasted seven painful days, with Cromie overseeing the job almost without a break. As he recalled:

> All leave being stopped and Cromie acting as slave driver and becoming very unpopular. I remember our chief stoker, who had a very high-pitched voice, was working up a small wooden ladder, slackening overhead nuts with a hammer and spanner, and calling the skipper all the blankety-blank so-and-so's he could think of, with Cromie standing at the foot of the ladder and saying, 'Yes, Eyres – I *know* I'm all that but *hit it*!!'

To the skipper's relief, the job was finally done and the motor appeared to be working correctly. Cromie, although a teetotaller and a non-smoker, knew how to show his gratitude to his crew who had worked so long and so hard. As the repaired *E19* tied up for her final day, 4 September 1915, alongside HMS *Bonaventure*, he made a deal with his men that they could go to the depot ship's canteen for two pints of beer per man, which he would pay for, on condition that they were all back on board in good time for their possible departure that evening. Their sailing orders arrived that afternoon.

Later that evening, the aroma of good Tyneside ale filled the interior of the *E19* as she at last slipped her moorings. As they cruised along the Tyne, heading for the open sea, there was still an air of mystery about their ultimate destination. Could it perhaps be, after all, the milder climes of the Dardanelles and into the Sea of Marmara, where the E boats had already won substantial honours? There, the battle had been taken to the surprised Turks, first by the Australian submarine *AE2* (Lieutenant-Commander H.D. Stoker), and then by Lieutenant-Commander E.C. Boyle in HMS *E14*. And although Lieutenant-Commander Nasmith may have suffered disappointment when HMS *E11* failed to make it into the Baltic with Horton, he had certainly made up for it with the very same boat in the Dardanelles. Both he and Boyle won the VC.

With *E19* trimmed and making a stable headway, Cromie gave out the order; 'Take her down to sixty feet.' In the velvet silence beneath the North Sea, he gathered the crew together in the control room. He had opened his sealed orders. The semi-circle of attentive faces waited patiently for his words. 'Gentlemen – we are bound for the Baltic.'

HMS *E19* leaves Barrow on being commissioned, July 1915

Walter Leonhardt, 1,261 tons. Sunk by HMS *E19* on 11 October 1915

Svionia on fire after *E19*'s attack on 3 October 1915

The German cruiser *Undine*, 2,450 tons. Sunk by *E19* on 7 November 1915

Svionia, 2,500 tons. She was shelled and torpedoed by *E19* on 3 October 1915

Direktor Rippenhagen, 1,683 tons. Sunk by *E19* on 11 October 1915

☠ **Cromie's Victims** ☠

Vessels Attacked by HMS E19
1915
Svionia 2330 tons October 3rd
Lulea 2,250 tons October 10th
October 11th.;
Walter Leonhardt 1262 tons
Gutrune 3000 tons
Direktor Rippenhagen 1683 tons
Nicomedia 1933 tons
Germania 1933 tons

Nike 1800 tons October 12th
Suomi 1000 tons November 2nd
Undine November 7th
Friesenberg 1300 tons December 4th

Stockholm

Gotland

☠ *Nike*

SWEDEN

Oland

KALMAR

☠ *Direktor Rippenhagen*
☠ *Gutrune*
☠ *Nicomedia*
☠ *Walter Leonhardt*

Baltic
Sea

Copen-
hagen

Germania ☠

☠ *Suomi*

Bornholm

☠ *Undine*
☠ *Friesenberg*
☠ *Lulea*

☠ *Svionia*
SASSNITZ

Danzig

STETTIN

GERMANY

Suomi, 1,000 tons. Sunk by *E19* on 2 November 1915

CHAPTER 8

VOYAGE OF DESTRUCTION

Strange, is it not? That of the myriads who
Before us pass'd the door of Darkness through,
Not one returns to tell us of the Road,
Which to discover we must travel too.

Rubáiyát of Omar Khayyám

How much easier entering the Baltic would have been if the Germans had not mined the Belts. But this was war. The passage through the Sound was not a prospect Cromie relished. Fortunately, any element of uncertainty had been diminished by Laurence and Horton's successful attempt the preceding year. But the fact remained that entering the Baltic Sea in a submarine, challenged not only by the astute and trigger-happy enemy, but also by the fact that much of the journey was through neutral waters, was no easy feat of navigation. In addition to this, Horton in *E9* and Laurence in *E1* had possessed the element of surprise. For Halahan in *E18* and Cromie in *E19* things promised to be a little more hazardous. After almost a year of this new British threat, the seas south of the Flint Channel were now infested with German warships, nervously reacting to any suspicious ripple on the water.

Halahan and Cromie sighted the Hanstholm Light in the Skagerrak at 3 a.m. on 6 September. During the day Cromie was forced to dive several times. Every puff of smoke on the horizon, every sail, neutral or otherwise, could prove to be a threat. At 8.30 a.m. the *E19* rounded the Skaw and shaped for the Swedish coast. Along this dark and choppy sea it was hard to know what to expect. With the Swedes and the Danes neutral, the traffic – cargo vessels, fishing boats and two vigilant Scandinavian navies desperate to keep the European war out of their territories – was busy and confusing. Nothing could be taken for granted. There was nothing to stop any skipper reporting the sighting of a submarine – and any such report would soon be in the hands of the German fleet.

At 10.30 p.m., just as *E19* was making steady headway on the surface, the lookout spotted two white lights ahead. Cromie bellowed the order – 'Dive!' It was a narrow escape. What appeared to be a German destroyer steamed towards them, intent on ramming. Sitting in the malodorous, menacing blackness on the seabed, the exhausted crew of the *E19* listened as the destroyer prowled overhead. An hour passed, and as silence returned, Cromie surfaced. The destroyer had vanished. With only a few small motorboats about, the dark, unlit silhouette of the *E19* slid on through the waves. At 12.50 a.m. on 7 September she passed the Vinga Light.

Cromie had no idea in these dark small hours where Halahan's *E18* might be. Just after 1.30 a.m., however, he was to find out. As the lookout peered ahead into the night, a familiar outline presented itself only yards ahead. Cromie barked, 'Hard a-port!', and the *E19* swung around, narrowly missing her sister. Panic was replaced with relief as the crews all realised they were not alone. Within minutes, however, fear regained its grip as what appeared to be a German patrol loomed into view. Within minutes *E19* was back on the bottom. Fortunately, she had not been spotted. But the tension was taking its toll; it was decided it was time for a well-earned rest.

After a fitful sleep followed by a breakfast of ham and eggs Cromie surfaced. A steely light had broken over the sea, which now appeared empty of shipping. At 10.30 a.m. they passed west of the island of Anholt. Between *E19* and the rigours of the Sound there was now only 50 miles (80 km). To the south they spotted a fast steamer which soon disappeared over the horizon. With her engines at full speed, the submarine raced on until 2.10 p.m. when yet another German patrol was spotted. Once more *E19* dropped from view beneath the waves and, changing over to electric motors, edged quietly onward. Cromie, keeping a diligent watch through the periscope, was now alarmed at the number of merchant ships criss-crossing the sea above. He decided to carry on submerged until night fell. At 7 p.m., once more on the surface, the sea had cleared and as the darkness thickened *E19* cruised on for an unhindered five-hour stretch.

As 8 September dawned, the *E19* reached the busy waters off the Sound and was now faced with the prospect of being spotted, if not by the Germans then by the Swedes and Danes. Shortly after midnight they dived rapidly to avoid a ship, but had no sooner broken the surface less than half an hour later, than they were picked out in the bright acetylene light of a fast motor boat which was heading out from the Danish shore. The submarine once more plunged down, coming to rest on the bottom at a depth of 70 feet (21 metres) at 1.30 a.m.

Ben Benson recalled the sheer, nerve-wracking tedium of their passage through the Flint Channel, in his memoir:[1] 'All I remember is the hours it took and the mucking about between the Skagerrak and the Kattegat. All I heard was the Skipper saying "Keep her tail up! Keep her tail up!" so that we wouldn't strip our propellers.'

The perils of the German navy were one thing. Less predictable was the mechanical behaviour of Cromie's boat. After twelve claustrophobic hours of silence on the seabed, he was suddenly faced with a new problem. The steering gear had jammed solid and *E19* refused to surface. The hardy crew, with Chief Stoker Eyres's high-pitched swearing in full flight, spent the next four hours in a desperate repair job which eventually proved successful.

Cromie's terse log for 8–11 September illustrates the drama and chronicles the knife-edge tension which was growing by the hour.[2]

5.00 p.m.
  Finished repairs and got under way. Everyone sick and suffering from bad atmosphere.[3] Trim entirely lost and very difficult to regain (20 tons different) Ran ashore on Hven and took a big list. Blew everything until boat shifted astern and then did stern dive to 50 ft.

Boat picked up alarming angle about 30 degrees down by the stern but recovered well after breaking up most of the moveable gear. The crew behaved very well indeed.

7.35 p.m.

Surfaced 1.5 miles west of Hven found one arm of the conning tower hatch compensating weight broken, and jambing [sic][4] the lid. Managed to crawl out to look around but could not get in again. After a severe struggle I managed to break off the other arm and so free the lid of the fouled weight. Dived until dark.

7.58 p.m.

Started up engines and both main motor bearings ran hot due to having spilt the oil out of the bearings during the stern dive. Proceeded towards Malmo on one engine fixed and started to go through at 11.45.

Sept. 9

0.30 a.m.

Touched bottom whilst trying to avoid the many ships lying in the Channel; at the same time a large number of star shell and search-lights shewed up to the SW so I decided to await until both motors were available and I returned to deep water off Landskrona. My return was reported so the ships in the Channel are evidently spies.

Charged until daylight then retired to bottom for repairs. Found considerable acid had been spilt. Spent the day wiping over the battery and rebedding port main motor bearings.

7.20 p.m.

Came to surface and found boat had drifted once more close under Hven. Proceeded towards Malmo. The only lights of any use being the Middlegrund Nodre Rose on Danish side and Malmo high light and Roderprick buoy on the Swedish. Decided to start from buoy and so avoid ships in the Channel. Night was dark, clear and slight ripple but very strong searchlights on the Danish coast. Trimmed right down and went slow on one engine.

Sept 10

12.30

Sighted destroyer without lights 500 yards on port bow. Dived in 30 seconds and hit bottom at 16 feet. Had to alter towards the destroyer to get into deeper water. Proceeded at full fields grouper up bumping heavily on a stony bottom got into 20 ft. on gauge and altered to proper course. Continued bumping at 15 to 20 feet on the gauge until 1.36 p.m. when I considered Drogden Light would be abeam then altered to 220° and gradually got into deeper water. Boat made good 4½ to 5 knots bumping on the bottom.

2.50 a.m.

Came to surface and proceeded on engines.

3.50 a.m.

Sighted ship in the twilight 2 miles on port beam steering the same course. Found her to be a small cruiser of the 'Nymphe' class: too dark to attack so kept her in sight.

4.10 a.m.

Dived to attack but she altered north at 1,500 yards range. Watched her out of sight and saw another ship coming end on. She proved to be a large destroyer probably of G 127 Class. Fired a double shot (Gyro 3½ spread). Unfortunately through a misunderstanding the 2nd Coxswain dipped the boat to 50 feet and got her out of hand. Shortly after there was a loud explosion and at the same time distinct noise of propellers overhead. Thirty seconds later an even louder explosion but propellers were still overhead. For some ¼ hour I was unable to get away from the propellers. Afterwards I had a look round and found a destroyer 1 mile astern steaming fast. It is impossible to say if the explosions were those of a sweep or a torpedo.[5] The destroyer I fired at would not have had time to explode a sweep so quickly. The destroyer continued to dog me all day and I eventually found a Zeppelin was directing her and so retired to the bottom with battery at 11.46. Rose at dusk and proceeded for Bornholm. Passed two destroyers in the dark north of Bornholm. Night clear and very dark.

Sept 11

8.00 a.m.

Bright clear sea like glass visibility only limited by height of eye.

Off Oland sighted two grey destroyers steaming at high speed. Dived for two hours to avoid them. Water extraordinarily clear. Proceeded without further incident to Dagerort where I was met by E9.[6]

The glorious vision of E9 on a crisp autumn morning in the Baltic, accompanied by a Russian destroyer, was a sight of sheer joy for the crew of E19. And there he was, the splendid Lieutenant-Commander Max Horton, now in proud possession of his DSO with the added glory of a Russian decoration – the Order of St George – for not only entering the Baltic but, amongst other daring feats, putting the German cruiser Prinz Adalbert out of action for several weeks. And now Francis Cromie was here, too; here was a big war with the open opportunity to prove one's worth. This fine first morning of a new campaign was made even happier as the relieved sailors aboard E19 learned quickly that their comrades under Lieutenant-Commander Halahan in E18 were waiting for them.

Their welcome in Reval must have taken some of the sailors' breath away. Arriving early in the morning, 6 a.m., on 13 September, they passed a Russian cruiser squadron, at anchor close to the harbour. Soon the Russian decks were lined with sailors, who loudly cheered the passing British boats. Once in the harbour, another delight was in store – a brass band, blowing for all they were worth in honour of their new guests.

Reval's naval harbour was separated from the commercial port which was now, owing to the war, bereft of much of its traffic. Only a sparse shipping trade with neutral Sweden gave any inkling of the port's former prominence as a prosperous maritime centre. But where commerce had withdrawn, the navy had moved in. The five British submarines which now made up the Baltic Flotilla, although still nominally under the tutelage of the 8th Submarine Flotilla in Harwich, were intended to become an effective force for the Russian navy. Already Commander Max Horton's exploits in the Baltic had earned the new force a respect among the locals which bordered on adulation.

In 1915 Reval was a bustling town with a population of over 75,000. Timber, textiles and a growing shipbuilding sector provided employment, but the year-old war with Germany was taking its toll. Britain, long acknowledged for her prowess in the textile industry, had provided a wealth of expertise in Russia. The British sailors with the new submarine force were eventually to find many comforting reminders of home at parties held in their honour by a substantial expatriate population of British textile workers. In command of this far-flung outpost of His Majesty's Royal Navy was Commander Noel F. Laurence. Above him, in charge of Russia's Baltic submarines, was Commodore Podgursky of the Russian navy. He, in turn, reported to the Commander-in-Chief, Vice-Admiral Kanin.

Laurence's and Horton's men had already settled in to a somewhat rudimentary existence aboard an old Russian warship which was used for accommodation, the *Ruinda*, a 3,540 ton cruiser of 1885 vintage.[7] On board this museum piece they shared mess decks with their Russian counterparts. With the arrival of Cromie and Halahan, new berths had to be found for another sixty souls, with more spare crew already being sent out from England. This accommodation took the form of an old sloop, the *Voyne*, which was moored alongside the *Ruinda*. Ben Benson recalls the *Voyne* as 'a little yacht' although she was a 1,280 ton sail and steam training ship, built in 1893. Characteristically, Ben set about making himself at home.[8]

I remember one volunteer from each boat was required to act as 'Cook of the Mess' for the two boat crews. I volunteered for my boat and an Able Seaman volunteered from the other. We took over the job and the first thing we enquired about was getting a man from the shore who would supply the food, in fact he was already around and we had to learn the names of things. He spoke fairly good English, this chap, and we asked him for the various things we would like to have, for example, mutton and beef or pork, or whatever we could get. Ham and eggs, of course. In fact the first meal we had was ham and eggs, but the ham turned out to be not pork ham – but bear ham. But it was very nice. Slices of bear ham, young bears or not – it was quite tasty. We soon learned the names. The first thing I asked for – to get the Russian name for it – was vinegar. It turned out to be *Ooksus*. And you remember those great big cheeses you used to see in grocery shops – about eighteen inches across and a foot thick? We had about four of these to last at least thirty of us for three weeks ... The fore end of the boat was pretty well full up of bread and everything you could think of. Tinned stuff – there was so much, we had to put it all in the bilges and some of it was there almost to the day we packed up years afterwards. All the labels had come off after a time – you would just open a tin and hope for the best. Soup, tinned fruit, cakes and I discovered a tin of asparagus. I kept that in a cupboard and it came out on the day that we sank the cruiser, *Undine.*

This local opulence was not to last, but in the coming years the British sailors' stores, delivered by transport ships from home via a tortuous route from Archangel and thence by train, were always infinitely better than the slops fed to the poor Russian ranks. In the first year of the war, 1914, when Horton's and Laurence's crews had been in Reval for several months, their supplies of traditional navy rum had expired. To the Russian sailor, aware of the amount of champagne quaffed daily in their officers' ward rooms, the idea of a fighting force's lower ranks being allowed an official daily measure of alcohol was redolent of a society where freedom had run riot. Envy of their British counterparts was hard to conceal. But the notion of Jack Tar fighting the Hun without his daily ration was as abhorrent to Laurence as it was to his ratings. As Senior Officer, he approached the official channels to correct the situation. His request at first baffled the Russian bureaucracy, passing upwards through the higher echelons until it finally landed on the desk of the Tsar himself. Already impressed by the Royal Navy's disciplined fighting prowess, the monarch granted the request, but as rum was unavailable, vodka had to be substituted. In agreeing, however, Nicholas displayed the lofty naivety of the upper classes which was eventually to cost him his life. Why did the British sailors have rum? Part of the British reply was to mention the extreme winter climate in the Baltic. 'But,' queried the Tsar of All the Russias, 'If they are so cold, why can't they wear two shirts?'[9] Francis Cromie had no need of alcohol or tobacco. It was in his character to maintain a clear grip on reality at all times. But for everyone else, vodka was to be one of the few comforts on hand in Reval.

Contact with Flotilla HQ at Harwich was usually by telegraph, but the problems of sending and receiving mail were a major bone of contention. One of the main themes running through many of Cromie's letters to the Admiralty is that of poor or non-existent postal communications. For men trapped in an ice-bound harbour in sub-zero temperatures, letters from home were a great comfort. And yet, somewhere between Archangel and Reval they would often vanish, then turn up in a batch months later – and on one occasion, as we shall see, via Germany!

Once the crews had adjusted to their strange new surroundings, Cromie proceeded with the pressing business of war with Germany. Having the legend of Max Horton in the wardroom was a big challenge. Cromie must have wondered if the success Horton had so far enjoyed against the Germans could ever be matched. He was not to be disappointed, however.

His initial quarry was to be German shipping *en route* between the southern Baltic coast and Sweden. His mission began somewhat ignominiously on

2 October with an event which almost cost him and his crew their lives. As the pale light of dawn broke over the grey sea *E19* spotted what Cromie thought was a transport or merchant vessel. As the light was too poor, he decided not to attempt an attack but to follow the indistinct silhouette until his chances improved. Suddenly *E19* shuddered to a halt; they had become entangled in a submarine net. All efforts to break free only resulted in a worsening of the situation. Tiny charges attached to the steel mesh of the net were exploding against the submarine's tortured hull as the heavy wires fouled and snagged both her rudder and her hydroplanes. Ballast was blown, but to no avail. Cromie then attempted to go full astern yet still they were trapped. The crew stayed calm, but one can easily imagine the growing dismay.

Meanwhile, above the waves, the vessel Cromie had selected as prey became the hunter. She was the German patrol ship, the *Sylvania*. On board *E19* the situation was becoming increasingly hopeless. Cromie addressed his crew. If all else failed, he told them, he would have to surface so that they could abandon ship and take their chances. His role would be to remain on board and set the demolition charges. This, of course, would mean death for Cromie, but it was a plan he offered unflinchingly, totally in keeping with his character. His men, as always, were his prime concern. It was this kind of selflessness which remained in their memory for the rest of their lives. But fate still held a few cards for the gallant lieutenant-commander. Over two hours had now passed, and the menacing propellers of the *Sylvania* above only increased the sense of doom. Twice the stricken submarine, still entangled in the grim steel web, rose like an agonised leviathan above the waves and the Germans, in a frenzy of anticipation, pumped shells in her direction, but they scored no hits. Two death-defying hours had passed. Once more Cromie ordered full astern. With a grinding, crunching wrench, the entrapped submarine suddenly broke free. Silently, stealthily, she edged away beneath the eager *Sylvania* until the sound of the German propellers finally receded.

The sense of relief and liberation following this incident was tangible. The following day, 3 October, seemed like a quiet cruise of redemption until, at 5.30 p.m., Cromie peered into the periscope and spotted the 2,500 ton *Svionia*. Unaware of her impending fate, the German vessel sailed on. Minutes later, the waves ahead became a slash of white foam from which the intimidating shape of *E19* emerged. Cromie's men jumped onto the glistening deck and manned the 6 pounder gun. The order was given for the German to stop, but it was as if the merchantman pretended there was no threat; Cromie therefore, ordered shots fired.

The Germans got the message and began to abandon ship. Once her captain and crew were at a safe distance, *E19*'s gun went into action again, putting several shells into the *Svionia*'s hull. The result was hardly impressive. There seemed to be no chance of sinking the vessel this way. Cromie then ordered a torpedo to be fired. Torpedo technology in 1915 left a lot to be desired, and the first left the tube only to fizzle out like a damp squib and fail to run. The second ran deep and missed. Eventually the stricken ship ran aground. It was a success of sorts, but not a victory.[10] But Cromie had had a taste. The *Svionia* was only an entrée – the main course was yet to come, but the service was poor. The weather, already bad at the time of the attack, had become atrocious and remained so for several days.

In the afternoon of 10 October Cromie surfaced after spying the 2,250 ton *Lulea*. Now he was in a tricky position. Neutral Denmark's territorial waters to the north-east were perilously close. The lofty white façade of the Moen Island cliffs were clearly visible. Yet here before the *E19* was a German target less than 60 miles (95 km) from her destination, Lubeck. It was irresistible. Within minutes of Cromie's warning, the crew of the *Lulea* knew what they had to do; they abandoned ship. But again the curses rang out through the *E19* as the first torpedo malevolently turned back on the submarine in a wide circle, narrowly missing her stern. Another faulty gyro. The second made contact with the *Lulea*'s stern, yet nothing happened. No explosion. Angrily Cromie ordered a third to be fired. It ran deep. Surely they would be fourth time lucky. Not so – the fourth torpedo passed harmlessly ahead of the abandoned vessel. Leading Stoker Holmes describes the occasion in his diary:[11]

> Sunday 10 October; A better day. We saw several large merchant vessels during the day and towards 1600 the skipper decided to have one so we went up to the surface and hoisted the signal. She hoisted the ensign which we took to be Dutch. But on our making a signal to her to send her papers on board, reversed it and admitted she was a Hun. We then made the signal 'Abandon Ship' which the crew did in a terrified panic, which was quite unnecessary. After they had left we fired four torpedoes in succession and every one missed. The skipper raved and after that we went for a homeward course . . .

With seas running high in the whiplash gale, gunnery was out of the question. Cromie reluctantly clambered back below and set sail for Bornholm. The unharmed, drifting target was eventually salvaged from a reef by the Germans, her cargo intact.

So much effort without result did not dishearten Cromie. He pressed on. The dawn which broke the following day, 11 October, heralded the making of a legend. As Cromie finished breakfast the iron ore carrier *Walter Leonhardt* was sighted. All the etiquette of submarine warfare then took place. Her crew, duly warned, were spared the damp prospect of an open lifeboat when Cromie stopped a passing Swedish steamer, the *Fernebo*, which took the Germans on board.[12] This time there would be no untrustworthy torpedoes. Despite the initial setback of a damp fuse, a charge was eventually set in the bowels of the ore carrier, and once safely back aboard *E19*, Cromie and his men enjoyed their first triumph as the subsequent explosion ripped through the *Walter Leonhardt*. Within minutes her stern disappeared beneath the waves, and then, complete with her valuable cargo of ore, she was gone.

As if the gods had decided to shine on *E19*, the awful weather began to clear as yet another German target came into view. She was the 9,000 ton *Germania*, bound for the German port of Stettin with a full cargo of iron ore. Cromie could not believe his luck, but the Germans thought that if they disregarded his signal to heave to they might steam ahead fast enough to make neutral Swedish waters. They pressed desperately on, and a shot from Cromie across the bows had no effect. In his panic to escape, however, the German captain miscalculated his position. His ship shuddered to a halt as she ran aground. As the *E19* raced towards her, Cromie was relieved to see her crew abandoning ship. Once along-side he boarded her. After searching the captain's cabin, he removed the ship's papers and instructed a sailor to take a supply of fresh meat from her galley for use aboard *E19*. He then issued instructions to the crew that an attempt would be made to tow the *Germania* free so that she could be scuttled. After several attempts, however, with the *E19*'s engines working flat out, the towing attempt was abandoned.

Cromie was unaware of the diplomatic can of worms he had just opened. In his zeal to kill his prey he had not noticed that the *Germania* had actually made it into neutral Swedish waters. She was within 2 miles (3 km) of the Swedish shore. Moreover, an explosion had occurred in her engine room, which the Germans insisted was a charge set by Cromie. If this had been the case, and the *Germania* was indeed in neutral waters, then Cromie would have been guilty of a major infringement of international law. The enraged Germans also insisted that Cromie had continued firing almost up to the point they abandoned ship.

One thing is certain, he had offended the Swedes in a big way. For weeks after-wards they and the Germans bombarded the diplomatic community with notes about the *E19*'s flagrant breach of Swedish neutrality. But like one of the sub-marine's enigmatic torpedoes, the controversy eventually failed to find a target and fizzled out – especially after the *Germania* was towed away, repaired in Germany and put back into service.

Disappointed though Cromie was as he left the beached *Germania*, unaware of the diplomatic hurricane which was to ensue, his luck was still in. Shortly after 2 p.m. he had another victim in his periscope sights, another German, the 3,000 ton *Gutrune, en route* from Lulea to Hamburg. This time her master erred on the side of caution and heeded Cromie's signal to stop. He even sent a boat across to the *E19* with his papers. Cromie sent a boarding party back. Once her crew had taken to the boats, he ordered the vessel's main inlet valve to be removed. Back aboard the *E19* the gun spoke again, putting three shells into the *Gutrune*'s hull below the waterline. Within minutes, the ore carrier with her full cargo was on the bottom of the Baltic Sea. Cromie still found time to tow the German's lifeboats to a passing Swedish vessel, which took the stunned seamen on board.

By now the *E19*'s crew must have been dazed by the busy activity of the day. But Cromie was far from finished. Later in the afternoon he stopped the Swedish freighter the *Nyland*. Satisfied that her papers proved she was *en route* to Rotterdam, he wished her captain 'God speed' and let her continue on her voyage. But whilst he had been dealing with her, another vessel had inadvertently strayed in *E19*'s malevolent path. The 1,700 ton German *Direktor Rippenhagen*, also carrying ore, had sailed her last voyage; Cromie's men scuttled her. It was time for tea but Cromie had the *Direktor Rippenhagen*'s shipless crew on his mind. His problem was solved when he stopped the Swedish *Martha*, carrying a

A view from the bridge of *E19* looking down to her 6-pounder gun. *(Ashmore Collection)*

E19 diving. *(Ashmore Collection)*

cargo bound for Newcastle. With the stricken Germans safely aboard the Swede, and night falling fast, Cromie could well feel satisfied with his day's work.

As the darkness gathered, however, one more target appeared. Cromie was about to bring about another diplomatic row, but this time he was in the clear.[13] The German vessel *Nicomedia*, of 4,000 tons, was brought to a stop by a shot across her bows. Soon after, her hapless crew rowed away whilst the *Nicomedia* slipped slowly beneath the waves. It was cocoa all round in the tiny wardroom that night. There was a sense of purpose and achievement, plus a satisfying bonus, especially for Cromie. Throughout this momentous day, not one seaman's life had been lost.

Cromie arose from his bunk the next morning, 12 October, in anticipation of another turkey shoot. But he was puzzled. The day before the sea had bristled with German targets. This morning he could only find Swedes. As the day wore on he decided to stop a Swedish ore carrier, the *Nike*. He was indignant when he discovered from her papers that she was on her way to the German port of Stettin with a load of iron ore. Despite her captain's insistence on his vessel's neutrality, Cromie had a good case to argue; the vessel might well be a neutral Swede, but her cargo was bound for the enemy. He immediately put *E19*'s Navigating Officer, Lieutenant Cecil Mee, on board with two armed sailors as a prize crew.[14] With the submarine leading the way, Cromie was determined to take the *Nike* into Reval as a prize. *En route* he found time to stop yet another Swede, the *August*, which, to his delight, was bound for England with a load of timber. Stopping her held more delight for *E19*'s hungry crew, as the Swede's generous cook sent over a batch of newly baked bread.

At sunrise on the 13th the *E19* was met off Reval by the Russian navy's torpedo boat, the *Dostoini*. Mee boarded her and the Russians took charge of the *Nike*, whilst Cromie waited impatiently nearby aboard the *E19*. If anyone thought that a short stay in Reval for a breather was on the cards, they were soon to be disappointed. Cromie was keen to get Mee and his two armed sailors back on board: the *Nike* was simply a diversion; the skipper was keen to get back into the fray.

Mee must initially have been puzzled by the awe displayed by the Russians as he handed over his charge. Locked away for two weeks in the claustrophobic world of the submarine, and especially following the hectic activity of the previous three days, the Royal Navy – which was simply performing the task it had been sent to do – had not had time to assess the effect they might have. The Russians soon put Mee in the picture. Apparently the telegraphs around the Baltic coast had been buzzing. Mee was told of the German commercial trade's panic following *E19*'s swath across the waves. In ports around the coast, all German merchant shipping was refusing to move. The German High Seas Fleet was now faced with the unwelcome prospect of allocating two flotillas of destroyers and two cruisers to act as escorts, as nervous, immobile merchantmen awaited protection from the voracious British submarines.

Cromie and his crew had not been in Russia long enough to appreciate how much more disciplined and effective the Royal Navy was, compared to its Russian counterpart. There was no doubting the Russians' bravery, but compared to society back home in Britain, Russia must have seemed positively feudal to Jack Tar. The Russian sailor was ill-treated, ill-fed, and the brunt of an arrogant, insensitive leadership which regarded their ratings as animals. When addressing an officer, a Russian sailor was duty bound to stand at permanent salute, and use the archaic appellation 'High-born Excellency'. Russian officers were often very young, upper class, well-heeled martinets with little or no experience of the real art of leadership. Their men were, in the main, illiterate and poorly paid. Where the British sailor had his rum ration, three square meals and, by the standards of the time, a reasonable wage,[15] the Russian sailor lived in a 'dry' world where he was lucky to earn that much in a month. His food was a miserable gruel laced with vegetables.

For even minor infringements of navy rules, misdemeanours which might have earned the British sailor a few days' stoppage of pay or leave, or incurred extra duties, the poor sons of the Steppes could be guaranteed a ten-year exile to Siberia or worse – a spell of several years in the prison of the Peter and Paul Fortress.[16]

Following the first failed attempt at revolution in 1905, the imperial orgy of punishment against the people and the armed forces had done nothing to ease the grim life of the Russian proletariat; it had simply bought a creaking feudal system a little more time. Russia was beginning to fall apart, whilst the Bolsheviks plotted and waited. The Great War may have seemed to many in Russian royal circles and the Duma to be a welcome diversion, a way of replenishing the great Russian soul. But the children of poverty – disharmony and mass dissent – were growing fast. With this as a backdrop, it was hardly surprising that the repressed lower ranks of Russia's archaic navy were a hotbed of resentment. One of Francis Cromie's heartfelt pleas to the Bolshevik officers who ruled after March 1917 was 'Discipline! You must have it – you will never fight and win without it!'[17]

Presenting the *Nike* to the Russians as a prize turned out to be more trouble than it was worth. Although it had not been ratified by Britain, the Germans wheeled out the 1909 Declaration of London which stipulated that iron ore was not contraband. The Russians, with only neutral Sweden left in the Baltic as a source of trade, were loath to upset the neutrals. To Cromie's and Mee's bitter disappointment the *Nike* was handed back to the Swedes.

As October wore on, *E19* enjoyed a welcome break in Reval where Cromie and his hardy crew were beginning to enjoy some of the star status Horton was used to. The Russians, with their comparatively ineffectual submarine force and increasingly truculent ratings, could only look on in grudging admiration. At the end of October, Cromie, hardly able to stand as he was suffering from a severe bout of influenza, once more took *E19* out into the Baltic. Still smarting from the *Nike* débâcle, he was hell-bent on retribution against the Hun. He did not have long to wait.

For the first few days of his patrol, he gave his orders from his bunk, attended to as ever by the faithful Benson. On 2 November he was back in business, stopping the trader *Suomi*, which was taking the risk of transporting a large load of

A group shot of officers of *E1* with three Russian officers taken at Reval in 1915.
L to R: Messing, Cookhill (Russian engineering Officer), R.W. Blacklock,
N.F. Laurence, Ivanoff and R.A. Thorburn. *(RN Submarine Museum, Gosport)*

timber to the enemy. With the captain and crew of the ill-fated vessel safely
disembarked, Cromie's men set fire to her, and as the *E19* moved away into the
night the huge flames from her cargo of wood lit up the ocean until they were
dowsed as she slowly sank, stern first.

But Cromie was growing impatient. Merchantmen seemed easy prey; he
needed to cut his teeth on something more susbstantial – the German navy. On
7 November to the west of the island of Bornholm, Cromie's officer of the watch,
Lieutenant Sharp, acted calmly as a challenging vision appeared in his periscope
sights: the German light cruiser *Undine*. *E19* dived and crept close to the un-
suspecting warship. Twenty-five minutes later Cromie had her in his sights, now
only 1,100 yards (1,000 metres) away. The crew in the control room looked
around at each other, anxious. Would the torpedoes let them down? And what
if they failed? This was no turkey on the waves above – this was a wolf. Cromie
took a deep breath then uttered the word 'Fire'. With gritted teeth and crossed
fingers they waited.

On board the *Undine* the anguished lookout spotted the foaming track coming
towards them. Responding to the bellowed warning, the German captain
shouted a manoeuvring order, but it was too late. The tinfish struck the *Undine*
amidships and the violent explosion caused a cheer to run through the *E19*. As
panic developed on the blazing ship, Cromie spotted a destroyer, the *V154*,

coming alongside the cruiser. To Cromie, it appeared that the *Undine*'s wound might not be as mortal as he had hoped. As the survivors from the cruiser clambered onto the *V154*, he took the *E19* down, daringly manoeuvring her under the destroyer and placing himself in a position by the stern of the *Undine*. Torpedo number two, like its predecessor, behaved well. She struck aft, obviously in the vessel's magazine, as a mighty detonation reverberated through the water, rattling all on board the *E19*. Twenty-four Germans were killed, the remainder being picked up by a passing ferry. *E19* crept away; her first blood had been spilled.

As Ben Benson pondered over the menu for dinner that night, he reached for the store cupboard. Tinned asparagus had never tasted so good.

Later that month the admiration in which the British submariners were held evolved into a lofty official recognition. For sinking the *Undine*, Cromie was presented by the Tsar himself with Russia's highest award for bravery – the Order of St George. This was in addition to the Order of St Vladimir, received for *E19*'s entry into the Baltic, and the Order of St Anne for the destruction of merchant

British and Russian officers aboard the depot ship *Ruinda* at Reval during October, 1915. Back row L to R: Lt Thorburn RNR, Russian Officer, Lt Simpson, Russian Officer, Lt Blacklock, Lt Miller, Lt-Cdr Francis Cromie and Lt Urich Dvoyitski. Middle row L to R: Lt-Cdr Goodhart, Cdr Horton, Russian Officer, Cdr Laurence, Russian Officer, Russian Officer, Russian Officer. Front row L to R: Lt Peirson, Lt Chapman, Lt Greig, Lt Smith RNR and Lt Otto von Essen.
(RN Submarine Museum, Gosport)

shipping. Within a year, the slow-moving Admiralty would also acknowledge his work, adding the DSO to these medals of war.

That night the handsome lieutenant-commander was invited aboard the Tsar's royal train for dinner, as outside, the heavy snows of the advancing winter began to fall. The medals were beginning to line up on Cromie's unorthodox, astrakhan-collared greatcoat. As reminders of momentous deeds, they were to become a shield against the troubled times ahead.

CHAPTER 9

FROZEN ASSETS

From Lt. J.J.R. Peirson, HMS *E9*
12 May 1915

My Dears,

How different must our surroundings be. There you are at home, out on the lawn perhaps, looking down and watching something on the beach, whilst here am I within three miles of a certain bit of Germany able to see plainly the fields, buildings etc., on the shore. A contrast isn't it . . .

You see up here now it is only dark at the most between 11 p.m. and 2.45 a.m. to 3.00 a.m. so it means that when we are doing our job properly we are 20 hours out of the 24 below the surface.

This means no air, worth the name, it is not more than ten hours before a match refuses to burn, no exercise, and sometimes very little cooking; the whole contributing frequently to the slight upsetting of livers. This is alternated with at times the eye strain of, by day, searching the sea through the periscope, and by night through glasses . . .[1]

There would be many such letters to families, written in pencil on poor notepaper in the long, damp silences whilst sitting out the hours on the seabed. Nowhere in the Navy could one expect such lengthy enforced periods of silence and inactivity as those experienced in submarines. For this we can be thankful, as any sailor who realised the history he was helping to make would soon find himself, like Lieutenant Peirson, sharpening his pencil and jotting down his thoughts. And the Baltic campaign had an extra dimension of inertia – a deeply frozen winter.

Thus far 1915 had been an impressive year for the flotilla. Before Cromie's arrival both Laurence and Horton had been extremely busy, the thirty-one-year-old Horton in particular causing such havoc for the Germans that already the Baltic was being referred to as 'Horton's Sea'. In fact, such an impact had the Royal Navy made that the German Commander-in-Chief, Prince Henry of Prussia, was under the impression that there were more submarines than the dynamic duo of *E9* and *E1* assailing his fleet. Although the Russians, who had also added to the submarine force when their boats the *Bars* and *Gepard* joined as reinforcements, were not without their successes, it was the staunch discipline and technical superiority of a belligerent force on a more equal footing to the Germans which prompted Henry to announce:[2] 'I consider the destruction of a Russian submarine will be a great success, but I regard the destruction of a British submarine as being at least as valuable as that of a Russian armoured cruiser.'

It was common, from the end of November through to March, for the port of Reval, like most coastal locations at the northern end of the Baltic, to be trapped in ice. This would also mean that there were noticeably fewer targets around, but the flotilla still took any opportunity it could to carry on fighting. Goodhart took *E8* out on a hunt off Brusterort which almost paid dividends, but his well-aimed torpedo in the direction of the German collier *John Sauber* failed to detonate.

However, returning to Reval from this mission in the dark, *E8* was involved in a collision with the Russian submarine *Gepard*, and, although this incident failed to knock the shine off the flotilla's glorious entrance, it did result in *E8* being out of commission for several weeks whilst repairs were completed. Repairs in Reval presented much more of a challenge than they would have back in Britain.

Cromie made up for all this and topped off the year by pulling off yet another impressive stunt east of Moen. There he stopped the 1,300 ton ore carrier *Friesenburg*. In charge of the boarding party was Lieutenant George Sharp, who soon had the vessel, with her 3,861 tons of iron ore, scuttled. Even as Christmas ticked over into 1916, Halahan braved the ice and took *E18* to sea, but winter could no longer be denied its grip.

This was the time when the crews took the opportunity to overhaul their boats, and during the long periods off watch, to get to know their hosts. After their initial settling in, the British contingent were given a new accommodation berth on board the ageing cruiser *Dvina*. After the cramped conditions on the old sloop *Voyne* and the warship *Ruinda*, this offered much-needed extra leg room and a little more dignity for Jack Tar, but sharing this larger space with his Russian counterpart only helped to highlight the acute social differences between the two navies. The *Dvina* had a chequered history, having been one of the miscreants in the mutinies during the abortive 1905 revolution, and would eventually have an extra colourful chapter added to her life. The conditions of service for the British sailor made those of the poor Russians stand out as a poorly rewarded life of total subservience. The British were paid better, received fairer treatment and between the ratings and their officers there was a high degree of mutual respect. With the difficulty the Admiralty had of transporting supplies to the British flotilla via a circuitous route through Murmansk, Archangel and then by an over-strained, unreliable rail link to St Petersburg (now renamed Petrograd to make it sound less Germanic), it was down to the Russian authorities to bridge this gap by provisioning the flotilla in the manner to which they were accustomed.

On board the *Dvina* the Russian crew were responsible for working and manning the ship, but while the British and Russian officers shared the same wardroom, ratings lived apart in their own separate Russian and British messes. The British were only responsible for keeping their own accommodation clean and ship-shape. When the Russians saw the quality of victuals the British enjoyed, the first rumblings of jealousy set in. Even from the start, the Russian Admiralty, oblivious to the sensitivities of their own hard-pressed crews, made sure that His Britannic Majesty's Navy had the best. Ben Benson, apart from his many other duties as telegraphist, Cromie's servant, secretary, musician and concert party supremo, was increasingly proud of his role as *E19*'s 'cook of the mess'. There was already an established chain of supply from the shore for Laurence and Horton's crews, and Ben had wasted no time in establishing a connection and reaping the benefits for *E19*'s shopping list. The Russian chandler was able to offer his British customers something his own navy's cooks would have found a luxury – a choice.

He was further elevated to 'officer's chef' and became adept at making use of the stock brewed from his vegetables by adding tomato sauce, cornflour and anything else he had to hand to create what Cromie came to know as 'Benson's Special'. There were huge quantities of eggs for the British – something which must have rankled with the poor Russians in Reval. At one point, on board HMS *E19*, Ben had stored some baskets of eggs at the foot of the ladder leading down from the bridge. George Sharp, Cromie's First Lieutenant, over six feet tall and size 12 in seaboots, had the misfortune one day to descend from the conning tower and arrive at the bottom of the ladder to the sound of crushing eggshells. Cleaning his boots must have been a sticky business.

There was also an example in each boat of the lofty insensitivity of the Russian naval hierarchy, in the person of the Russian liaison officer. One of the greatest luxuries a submariner had in those days, both rating and officer alike, was the facility to keep clean. Even the most basic ablution such as washing one's hands took up valuable water. One of *E19*'s Russians, Lieutenant Vorgiski, was, to quote Ben Benson, 'a bit foppish'.

> We had to cure him of washing his hands every five minutes in the little wash cabinet in the wardroom. There was a copper jug with water in it as a rule, so we made a change and put some oil in it. It looked like water until he put his hands in it. That cured him of using the water!

But there were some Russian officers with a better grasp of the gap in social attitudes. Vorgiski's replacement, Baron Fearson, spoke perfect English and eventually joined the Bolsheviks. He had his roots in Scotland, and, upon hearing that Benson was living there at the time, took a shine to the young telegraphist and actually presented Ben with one of his golden uniform epaulettes as a souvenir during the Revolution. The removal of these from an officer's shoulder became *de rigeur* when hostilities broke out, but there was already a quaint tradition amongst Russian naval officers who, upon achieving the rank of captain, would have all the real gold in their epaulettes melted down to be made into cigarette cases.

But what shocked Cromie and his men more than anything was the absolute arrogance endemic in the behaviour of their host officers towards their own ratings. It was common when ashore to witness a young Russian officer, either alone or out promenading with his girlfriend, homing in on some hapless passing rating, probably out with his own lady, to demonstrate his social superiority. This took the form of first accepting the rating's salute, then spitting in the young lad's face and commanding him to turn around and bend down to be kicked violently on the rump. Ashore the Russian sailors were never allowed into anything but the poorest seats in the theatre or cinema, and in cinemas the cheapest seats, rough wooden benches, were *behind* the screen. Most of the films emanating from the Western world were subtitled, so the Russian ratings had to learn to read the captions backwards. On the other hand, the British sailors, who could afford decent seats, frequently enraged the Russian officer class by appearing in the same plush pews as them. To Cromie's credit, when approached about this by his hosts in the wardroom, he made it quite clear that his sailors were free to enjoy their leisure in any way – and in any seats – that they chose. Ben Benson further illustrated this growing contribution to the tension:

> It was the custom when a senior Russian officer arrived or got up to leave that all junior officers sprang to attention. We boys, understanding that this sort of thing was part of the Russian discipline, also went through the performance until we realised that if one of our own senior officers appeared, the Russians remained seated. Thereafter we did the same – even if a Russian Admiral appeared. Complaints from the Russians to our officers brought the answer that we could please ourselves in such cases.

Even minor infringements of Russian Admiralty law, the kind of offences which would have resulted in a British sailor losing leave or being placed on fatigue duty, frequently resulted in a poor illiterate son of the Steppes being exiled to Siberia for two or more years. With this age-old and increasingly repellent behaviour, the Russian ruling classes were simply adding extra weight to an unnecessary feudal folly which, before long, would explode in their faces.

Cromie now faced an added challenge. Overhauling the more sophisticated British submarines in the crude and comparatively primitive Reval dockyards demanded a new level of inventiveness. As the rigid winter set in, requests placed by Laurence and Cromie with the Admiralty for valuable spares, especially for the boats' batteries, seemed to take an age to fulfil. After a lengthy, vicious sea voyage, braving not only the possibility of enemy attack but the horrendous conditions to be navigated into the Barents and White Seas, transports would arrive at Murmansk or Archangel to offload valuable materials for the boys in the Baltic, only to have them virtually vanish into the slow, tortuous Russian railway system between their port of entry and Petrograd. Often, as Cromie's letters illustrate, valuable packing cases would arrive damaged, their contents beyond repair.

With temperatures frequently falling to 40 degrees below freezing, much of the crews' time would be spent simply keeping their trapped boats as free from the threatening ice as possible. Yet as least they had food, a certain amount of freedom and the possibility of some peace and quiet every so often. Far away, as the war on land tightened its bloody, stalemate grip on the wretched lives of thousands of trench-bound troops, this same winter offered nothing but death and misery. There was little for the French to celebrate other than the return of the actress Sarah Bernhardt to the stage in Paris at the age of seventy-three. Back in Britain, Churchill had resigned from the Cabinet in the wake of the failure of the Gallipoli campaign. As for the Russians, the opening weeks of the war a year previously, when crowds had thronged the streets and cheered 'Long Live the Tsar!' outside the Winter Palace seemed to be nothing but a bitter memory. This pocket of positive warlike activity, the Baltic, although supremely significant for the men on both sides who ran it, would have seemed like a fresh-air holiday to the ill-equipped and starving Russians on the Eastern Front.

Following the sinking of the *Undine* the crew of HMS *E19* had begun to match Laurence and Horton's exploits and had proved to the Russians, if proof were needed, that the success of the first wave of British submarine expertise was certainly not just a lucky fluke – these disciplined bluejackets from over the water really did know their stuff. Cromie was to express some embarrassment to Benson, who by now had become a kind of unofficial valet to his skipper, over the fact that his mother in London had passed on one of his personal letters to her to the editor of *The Times*. It was simply the act of a proud mother wanting to tell the world of her son's effort, but it is characteristic of Cromie's modesty that he should have found his words, reproduced in the national press, such an embarrassment. However, we can thank Mrs Cromie because otherwise her boy's 'breezy' note might well have been lost to posterity, like so much of his other personal correspondence. *The Times* of 14 December 1915 reported:

The Sinking of the *Undine*
A Breezy Letter from the Hero of the Feat

Lieutenant-Commander F. N. A. Cromie, who was personally decorated by the Tsar with the Cross of St. George, in a letter to his mother, says:

On Wednesday the Tsar came to inspect the fortifications and the submarine. I had a very pleasant surprise in being decorated by him with the St George's Cross – the Russian VC, and the best war order they have. Five men of my crew got the Silver Cross. So we have not done so badly in our two months out here. We did the first two days out with the 'flu, and so directed operations from my bunk. We met a German submarine and had to dive in a hurry, and found ourselves down at 140 feet before I could get out of bed to take charge. The third day we found a lot of 'wood' outside neutral waters, and after a short chase we made a lovely bonfire, being unable to sink the stuff.

The 'inhabitants' left hurriedly, leaving a small puppy dog which we rescued. Its father was a great Dane and its mother a pug, but considering it is a 'Hun' it is not half bad and is a great favourite.

Nothing travels by daylight since our last raid on the 'hen run', so my special haunt was very dull, and I gave it up after four days, and tried another spot where I knew train ferries must pass. We had an exciting chase, but it was spoilt by two destroyers and a cruiser turning up. Guessing that they would come back again I lay low, and sure enough I caught the *Undine* in the afternoon. The first shot stopped her and put her on fire, but she was not going down quickly enough, so avoiding the destroyer that was after us, I dived under the *Undine*'s stern and gave her another from the other side. It was a very fine sight and made one feel that one did not care a — for the destroyers firing at one all the time . . .

We arrived covered in ice. The Emperor was very polite and nice, and said our work had made all the difference to the country. In the evening we dined with all the Kings and Princes etc., in the train, which was a palatial affair. We sat down 28 at one table and still left room for waiting. Nearly all spoke English, and said all sorts of nice polite things, and I sneaked a menu card as a souvenir, but had not the cheek to ask for signatures.

Being a Chevalier of St George I am pretty safe, as no-one can arrest me without an armed escort and a band to take me to prison, and both of these are pretty scarce now. I think I told you that the other cross gave me the right to go into girls' schools and taste the food and express my opinion! I only hope now that we shall not be at sea on 25 November (St George's night) when all the members of the Order dine in the Palace and take the plate home with them as souvenirs!

To little Anthea, Gwladys and her mother now living in the relative safety of patriotic London, all this must have made the war look as if it were running along the lines of a penny dreadful, jingoistic novel. With the Legion of Honour from the French Government also about to grace Francis's chest, in addition to his medals of St George, St Vladimir and St Anne, the Cromie family had the makings of a solid gold hero to set against the rigours of the ongoing conflict. But Francis Cromie was no fool. Compared to the atmosphere which was building up in this distant, frozen posting, running a submarine and sinking ships was almost a walk in the park. The news from the Russian front was nothing short of disastrous. Even before *E19* and *E8* had left Newcastle, the Tsar's soldiery had suffered defeats and setbacks which only the vastness of the terrain and the broader strain placed on the German war machine had prevented turning into a major Russian defeat.

The ghost of 1905 was far from dead, and the seeds of discontent had already sprouted strong red shoots. In Moscow and Petrograd the ordinary people were starving whilst the upper classes still thronged the fully functioning luxury hotels. Bread riots had become a common occurrence, yet for those who had the money, and the class to go with it, there was a certain gaiety of life outside the duty of war which was still illuminated by chandeliers and lubricated by caviar and champagne.

The grim struggle of the masses appeared almost as a tragically interesting side-show to those members of the elite who managed to record it. 'Helping the war effort' was a noble pastime, and was in many ways, for those private-incomed relations of the diplomatic corps, similar to our modern notion of 'slumming'. Take for instance the finely written memoir of Meriel Buchanan, the daughter of Sir George Buchanan, British Ambassador in Petrograd. Her compassion was without bounds, yet, like her Russian aristocratic counterparts, she failed to see that the starvation, misery and distress of the common people she imagined her nobly intended voluntary work might assuage was the direct result of her Tsarist friends' relentless grip on Russia, and their devotion to keeping the old order alive at all costs. She gave much of her time to nursing the soldiers from the front, and here she gives one of a selection of poignantly penned descriptions of the servile, wounded recruits she attended to in her nursing role:[3]

> Pavloff, the boy with the golden curls and the dark blue eyes, who, shot through the lungs and paralysed as well, lay there for months growing every day weaker, thinner, paler, suffering more and more intensely, always with that patient, tragic smile in his eyes, the husky tired voice that whispered so pathetically, 'If only I was not in such pain how comfortable I should be, with so many people looking after me. Just as if I was a gentleman . . .'

Meriel wrote lucidly of many such cases, and about starving peasant women, babies dying in the street, mothers begging for milk, yet failed to recognise the obscene contrast between her 'day job' and the fact that, only a few nights later, she would be out dining (a favourite pastime) with General Polivanoff, the Minister of War, who presumably did not have to indulge in a bread riot to be presented with a roll for his soup.

But the complications of Russia's imminent social upheaval, exacerbated by arriving in the middle of the worst war in history, were to be faced in more fraught ways and on a much more dangerous front by those who remained, such as Francis Cromie, long after the Buchanans and the rest of the diplomatic community had returned to the comfort and safety of their English estates.

Not long after Cromie and Goodhart arrived in Russia, it was felt that some members of the first force might be better employed elsewhere in the conflict. Thus at the end of 1915 Charles Chapman, First Lieutenant on board *E9*, and Ronald Blacklock, First Lieutenant on *E1*, were lucky enough to escape another Russian winter by returning to Britain, where they subsequently became commanding officers. In many ways the loss of these two officers from the Baltic Flotilla was a sad one for Cromie. Both were dependable, experienced submariners and most importantly, they got on well with the Russians. This left behind very different personalities at the head of the force. In command was Noel Laurence, a substantial man by any measure, a strong, tall, precise character whose fair and firm grasp of discipline stood him in good stead with his men. Like so many of the early submariners, he had his own way of doing things and left those under his command in no doubt of the fact. But Max Horton was different in many ways from both Laurence and Cromie. Whereas Cromie, although a great mediator and very compassionate towards his crews, neither drank nor smoked – and this in an age where tobacco at least was one of the few pleasures in war – Horton was almost cast in the Errol Flynn mode. For instance it was Horton who began the tradition of the Submarine Service flying the Jolly Roger – a fine example of his unorthodox approach. He was dashing, humorous, loved by the ladies and possessing the ability to sink as much vodka as any Russian challenged him to, a fact which ensured his enduring popularity with his hosts.

Laurence and Horton had now spent fifteen hard-working months of solid achievement in the Baltic, and here they faced another claustrophobic winter with its enforced indolence, further complicated by the frustrations of being

RUSSIA

Gulf of Bothnia

FINLAND

KRONSTADT

HELSINGFORS

Gulf of Finland

PETROGR.

AALAND
ISLANDS

HANGO

REVAL

DAGO
Island

ROGEKUL

ESTONIA

Moon Sound

OSEL
Island

PERNAU

Irben Straits

Gulf
of
Riga

Baltic Sea

RIGA

CROMIE'S
WORLD
1915-1918

poorly supplied from home. Horton was no diplomat in the wardroom; if he had an opinion on the way the campaign was going, he was not the man to hold back, much to Laurence's chagrin. This personality clash between these two fine yet different men was not conducive to running an efficient fighting unit so remotely based.

Perversely, this incompatibility was further complicated by the flotilla's obvious success when measured alongside that of the Russians. A rash of petty jealousies emanated from the Russian officers, and this, together with his oil-and-water relationship with Horton, was the cause of some concern to Laurence. When Rear-Admiral Richard F. Phillimore, the Senior British Naval Liaison Officer at the Russian Imperial HQ was informed by Admiral Kanin, the Russian Commander-in-Chief, that Laurence had written to him regarding the atmosphere at Reval, the inevitable result of their discussion was that Laurence should be sent home. Kanin was keen for Horton, who had given the German cruiser *Prinz Adalbert* such a bloody nose, now to take command of the flotilla, but despite his bravado and success, the Admiralty in Britain had different ideas. As the Second Sea Lord commented, this purveyor of Jolly Roger drama was 'not at all fitted for the position of Senior Naval Officer in the Baltic'.[4] He was therefore also recalled.

On 2 January 1916 he was fêted at a huge luncheon in Reval and his journey to the railway station was a colourful affair, including a brass band, all the British flotilla officers and a large proportion of the Russian command. Of course, Ben Benson, wearing his musical hat, was in the entourage with his mandolin, accompanied by the members of his recently formed concert party. Seven days later, Laurence, at his own request, left quietly, without a note being struck.[5]

It is worth mentioning the popularity of these officers in those early months of the campaign. When Blacklock and Chapman departed on 10 December 1915, they were invited to a series of dinners and parties before collecting their fake passports from the British Embassy. To return home, they were, in effect, travelling as civilians, so when they were both informed that not only had they been invited to the ballet, but also to visit the the Tsar to say goodbye, the then Naval Attaché at Petrograd, Commander Grenfell, had to lend them a uniform apiece!

The decision to send both Horton and Laurence home had at least one benefit for Cromie and Goodhart – on 31 December 1915, they were both elevated from lieutenant-commander to commander. With Laurence gone, Cromie was now senior officer. *E9*'s command was taken over by Lieutenant-Commander Hubert Vaughan-Jones, and Lieutenant-Commander Athelstan Fenner replaced Laurence on *E1*.

It had been an eventful Yuletide for the sailors on board the old *Dvina*. There had been a splendid concert party, organised by Ben Benson, and dazzling displays of Russian talent, especially on the balalaika, and much vodka had been quaffed, whilst ashore, in Reval and surrounding areas, the expatriate British community had welcomed these bluejacket reminders of the Empire into their homes with warm, open arms. Despite the snow, the ice and the rigours of war, life in Russia was not turning out to be too bad after all. But no one, especially Cromie, was fooled into believing that their initially impressive debut would last.

Cromie was already having serious doubts about overall Russian morale, and had received some disturbing news. During November 1915 there had been mutinies on two Russian battleships, the *Imperator Pavel* and the *Gangut*. Strikes and industrial action ashore were becoming more regular, but the discontent displayed by mutinous sailors was, for Cromie, the most disturbing aspect of the increasingly tense atmosphere. As he looked out from the snowbound deck of the *Dvina*, in the new year of 1916, his thoughts of Gwladys and Anthea back in London must have fought for space alongside those of the difficulties he was now about to face. Moored alongside were his precious submarines, festooned and encrusted with the vicious Baltic ice, locked in a merciless frozen ocean which stretched as far as the eye could see. Only when the thaw came could the flotilla return to its real task – fighting the Germans. But that thaw promised to be a melt-down laced with menace.

Mrs Kinna's advertisement (see page 105)

CHAPTER 10

OUR FRIENDS IN THE NORTH

HMS *E19* Reval
Sept. 26th 1915

This morning I saw an advert in one of the papers, a certain Mrs
Kinna who gave lessons in English, and as I thought the name
sounded English, I made up my mind to call upon her this afternoon about three. I found her address quite easily, enquired for
Mrs Kinna, who appeared immediately and invited me in. She
was not English, but Russian, and the widow of a Scotsman, so
her English was very good. She asked me to stay for tea, her
sister-in-law came in and invited Mrs Kinna and myself to
her house next door for tea. They were a nice family. Two children, girl and a boy, quite jolly and most kind . . .[1]

So wrote Lieutenant Cecil Mee in his diary. He also revealed that both
Commander Goodhart of *E8* and Francis Cromie had discovered the very useful
services of Mrs Kinna, too. Both were regulars in her parlour, where she was
slowly revealing to them the intricacies of the Russian language and guiding them
through the difficult Cyrillic alphabet. It is to all three men's credit, and that of
many of the flotilla's sailors, that they were keen to immerse themselves so fully
into their new surroundings.

Cromie wasted no time in forming relationships ashore. He was soon into the
swing of Russian society after taking several trips to various locations in the
company of Admiral Phillimore, Britain's senior naval representative at Imperial
Headquarters. Phillimore's letters home to his wife in Shedfield, Hampshire,
often include references to dinners and lunches with various Russian VIPs with
Cromie in tow.[2] Everywhere Cromie went his innate modesty was to be sorely
challenged by the respect and admiration shown to him by the military community and their civilian relations. Of course, the trail into this social whirl had been
opened up for him during the previous year by Laurence and Horton, and
although the dashing, swashbuckling Max had now gone home, in image terms
at least he had a worthy replacement in Francis Cromie. Charming, a witty
conversationalist, always immaculate, medals on display, his dark good looks,
flashing eyes and stylish sideburns, as we shall later see, were an immediate
magnet for the ladies.

Laurence's forays into the social scenes of Reval, Narva and Petrograd during
1915 had introduced the new members of the Baltic Flotilla to one of their most
valuable homes-from-home – that of the Honorary British Vice-Consul in Reval,

William Girard. Girard had welcomed the British sailors, both officers and ratings, with open arms. Christmas 1914 had seen his house full to capacity as he wined and dined Laurence's and Horton's men, and even though the numbers had doubled with the arrival of Cromie's contingent, he repeated this unbounded generosity the following Christmas by hiring a hall in Reval to keep the homesick bluejackets fed and entertained. Football teams were formed, and the sailors tried their hands at various Russian winter pastimes such as tobogganing and skating. And there was much more to the British community, too. In both Reval and in Narva, 120 miles (190 km) north along the coast by the Russian border, there were further outposts of British expatriate hospitality. These people had come to Russia and Estonia where their expertise in the textile and timber industries were highly valued. In Reval, in addition to the Girards there was also the Sewell family, who offered their own amicable reception, and in Narva the Butlers and the Wallworks.

Almost a century later, the memories of those men who took part in the Baltic campaign still echo down the years, and many relationships from Cromie's time put down strong roots which are still evident today. It is hard to imagine that, almost nine decades since his death, there would be anyone living who recalls meeting both Francis Cromie and his men in Russia – but there is.

Lilian Nield, formerly Lilian Wallwork, lives today in a cosy bungalow in Radcliffe, Manchester, with her son Peter. Although now in her nineties, she is a spritely, charming and communicative lady, a vibrant living archive of a long-vanished past. She can look back on a wondrous, charming early childhood even Walt Disney would have been challenged to imagine. Visiting her in Manchester was a pleasure never to be forgotten. Those who read her own colourful testimony of her days in Russia[3] can be left in no doubt as to how important the arrival of the Royal Navy in their midst was in the trying years leading up to the Bolshevik Revolution.

Lilian's father, Joseph Arthur Wallwork (known as Arthur), a textiles engineer for Platt Brothers of Werneth, Oldham, was twenty-nine when he was sent to the Coates Cotton Mills in St Petersburg on 3 March 1909. There he found a flourishing community of Lancastrians, for most of the senior posts in Russia's busy textile mills were filled by British experts. Lilian's mother, Annie, remained behind in Oldham until Lilian came into the world on 15 July 1909. Six weeks later she was enjoying the comfort of an improvised cot in a laundry basket, travelling with her mother, accompanied by her sisters, Hilda, aged eight, and Amy, three, to Hull, where they boarded a Wilson liner bound for the Baltic. On 9 September 1909, at 9.30 in the morning, they docked in St Petersburg. They were soon settled in at number 54, Suvorovsky Prospekt.

Arthur Wallwork, impressively fluent in French and German, was already getting to grips with Russian. In St Petersburg there was the British Club, a favourite gathering place and watering hole for many expatriates. Arthur, also a consummate musician, was always in demand for his skills as a pianist and mandolin virtuoso. As Lilian says, 'I can never hear "Alexander's Ragtime Band" being played without seeing in my mind's eye my father playing it at the club.'

As Lilian grew up she became as much Russian as English. Life for the

106

Wallworks was very different from what it would have been back in Oldham. They had servants, and enjoyed an envied status in the community. One of her abiding memories is of the regular journeys the family made along the frozen River Neva in a horse-drawn sledge, a *troika*.

> We would put on our fur coats and caps with the ears pulled well down, climb in and pull the fur rugs around our faces and snuggle down. The *yamschcik* [driver] would sit well up on his seat in his wadded coat right down to his ankles. He wore a fur hat and his beard and eyelashes used to be frozen. The horses had bells on their yokes. When they galloped along the bells used to tinkle. We rushed along with our cheeks beginning to freeze. It was so exhilarating to hear the horses' muffled hooves and we could look at the steam coming out of their nostrils. If it was dark, we'd look up at the sky and see the stars and the Milky Way. It was lovely . . . I do like to remember it . . .

At Easter, Lilian would attend the Russian Orthodox church with one of their servants, Marsha. On Easter Sunday there would be hard-boiled eggs in all colours and little pancakes, *blinis*. At night she could hear the servants upstairs praying aloud and banging their heads on the floor in supplication to God in front of their icons. She would be taken to see the guards on their horses outside the Winter Palace, and in addition to the exotic treat of the Russian church, her Anglican education still remained intact by regular attendance at the English church and Sunday school.

Regal Russia was, for a small child, a visual wonderland. In 1913 the Romanovs celebrated 300 years on the throne.

> I remember that very well. Thousands of people crowded into the Palace Square to pay homage and cheer their Little Father of all the Russias and his Tsarina . . . The celebration was actually on 13 July, and my father had accepted a post with the Krahnholm Mills in Narva, so we had to remove to live there. We left for Narva on 22 July 1912.

At the end of the nineteenth century, Krahnholm Mills was one of the largest textile complexes in the world. It was owned by Baron Knoop, a legend in the Russian textiles industry as an importer of machinery, having already fitted out over 120 mills in his native land. The mill comprised impressive buildings on islands along the River Narva. In their lofty interiors 13,000 employees worked 700 looms which devoured 480 bales of cotton each day. Huge deliveries of cotton were unloaded daily, with ninety men running the company's transport fleet. During the winter fifty men were employed simply blasting the ice from the turbines to keep the operation running. Krahnholm Mill had another important social function, too: the company generated its own electricity and this was supplied to eager customers up to 50 miles (80 km) outside Narva. In Narva, there were no English schools and Lilian had a governess, an Estonian Russian lady, Ella.

The Butlers, Jim and Nellie, were the Wallworks' closest friends in Narva and the other great benefactors of the Royal Navy's submariners. Life in Narva for the British was every bit as wholesome as it was in St Petersburg. There was a swimming club, a large oblong tank construction which sat in the river, which was very popular with the Butlers and Wallworks. Nellie Butler was, in her bright red silky swimsuit, 'the star of the club', according to Lilian. Lilian's best friend in Narva was Nadeusha Sansonoff, the daughter of the town's police chief. However, despite the good times and the comfortable living, even at such a young age, Lilian found certain aspects of Russian life unsettling. Living with the chief of police was an old aunt, who was dumb.

> She had had her tongue cut out for bearing false witness when she was young. This absolutely horrified me. She was probably in her sixties then. Life was very cheap, cruelty and beating and brutality were accepted as a way of life.
>
> On more than one occasion I saw prisoners stripped naked in the snow and tied to a post and whipped whilst the big guard dogs snapped at them. Mr Sansonoff did not think he was cruel, only being firm, which everybody understood and accepted. Everyone was afraid of being sent to Siberia though. I remember one night hearing a scream from the servants in our kitchen. My father rushed in to discover a demented workman. He was flourishing a knife and demanding the life of my father. They fought fiercely until my father overpowered him. The man was called Baraban, and when my father explained to him that it was not he who was responsible for his son being sent to Siberia for some crime committed at the mill, Baraban flung himself on his knees in front of my father and with tears streaming down his face begged my father's forgiveness and pleaded not to be sent to the police. Of course my father did not report him. Baraban embraced my father's feet and legs and kissed his hands. We had all witnessed an awful fight and we were so thankful to give him a warm meal and send him on his homeward journey.

The Wallworks were great friends of the Sewells in Reval, and despite the 120 mile (190 km) journey, would often exchange visits. October 1914 was a very exciting month for the British community, for the Royal Navy had arrived in Reval. Like many expatriate children, Lilian was to see a lot of the bluejackets during their stay. The presence of these British families and their children must have provided a valued dimension of domesticity for the sailors, far from their own homes and loved ones. To the children these tall, confident men from home, dressed in their navy blue, appeared as immense heroes, a confirmation of their parents' patriotic views in this time of war.

> I can remember playing with Max Horton and Noel Laurence. It was always a happy time when they came to visit us. I particularly remember Joe Langford, a Chief Petty Officer on *E1*. He used to stay with us and we called him 'Captain' Langford. He was a very kind man and always made me feel safe and very secure. I remember very well, with great love really,

Claude Fry, a stoker on Captain Cromie's *E19*. He was very young and smart in his sailor's navy blue uniform. He used to play with me and call me his sweetheart and I was so pleased when he gave me a special photograph of himself wearing the medal of St George of Russia. And there was Paddy Ryan, Petty Officer on the *E9* – he spent a lot of time with us and the Butlers. He was fortunate not to lose his life when his submarine was sunk in action. Paddy's good luck was that he had the measles and was not allowed to sail. Funny how fate decrees what happens to you . . .

When one talks to Lilian Nield today about her memory of Cromie, the response borders on reverence. She recalls him coming to dinner at their house or at the Butlers. One occasion in particular offers an insight into how he was regarded by his peers:

There was one night when the submarine officers all came to dinner, and seated at the table was Captain Cromie. I had been packed off to bed but I enjoyed these sailors coming to the house so much that I couldn't resist creeping from my room and tip-toeing along the landing. From there, I could peep over the banisters and watch the dinner in full swing, with lots of laughter and jolly conversation. At one point Captain Cromie, a tall, handsome and charming man, excused himself for a few minutes and after he had left the room, there was a hush fell over the gathering. They all looked at one another, then one man said, 'Now *there* goes a man you can *rely* on.' It was obvious that they held him in such high esteem . . .

The onset of the revolution was to have as great an effect on the placid, pleasant lives of these expatriates as on any of their Russian hosts. Within two years of all this pleasant party-going, the Wallworks, together with many of their Lancastrian friends, were to find themselves back in Britain, struggling under the yoke of a wartime economy, and having to readapt themselves to a totally different way of life.

With the ice still exercising its firm grip on the flotilla in February 1916, Cromie accepted an invitation from the Russians to form a party of submarine officers who would be taken on a specially organised visit, similar to one which Horton and Laurence had experienced the year before, to witness the army in action on the Russian front line. However grim this would turn out to be, it was to be a reminder of the very real war they were still in, and in a perverse way, a welcome break from the enforced kicking of heels in Reval.

Accompanied by Admiral Nikolai von Essen's son, Otto, and Boris Miller as liaison officers, *E9*'s Lieutenant Peirson and his navigator, Charles St John RNR, joined the party with Bertram Smith RNR of *E8*, with Cromie, Vaughan-Jones, Fenner and Goodhart in the vanguard. For Goodhart whatever relief this experience away from the frozen Baltic might provide was obliterated by the fact that for most of the time he was suffering from a prolonged bout of bronchitis.[4]

They were away for a month, experiencing extremes of both discomfort and luxury. Travelling conditions were difficult and unpleasant to say the least, in a country where the infrastructure had been severely tested. Everywhere the wounded were to be found, drifting back from the front, whilst in the war zone itself the poverty of the Russian soldiers, fighting against superior odds in the merciless winter cold, made these hardy members of the Royal Navy realise that their own occupation, however fraught with danger, was infinitely preferable to this grim world of frozen mud and twisted corpses. Travelling via Petrograd and Moscow, their tortuous journey took them to Kiev, Sebastopol, Balaclava and Yalta.

Moscow was one of the less strenuous stops on the journey, and one occasion there not only illustrates the British Navy's popularity at the time, but established Cromie's reputation as an inventive, spontaneous orator, and won for him star status among Russian society. The event in question was recorded in the diary of a man who was to become important to Cromie during the coming months.

Robert Bruce Lockhart was twenty-eight when he met Cromie in 1916. He had already spent three years in Moscow attached to the British consular staff. His diaries and, in particular, his autobiographical *Memoirs of a British Agent* offer much in the way of a counterbalancing view of this stormy period in Russia's history. He was a skilled linguist, fluent in Russian, and often kept his diary in Malay. Although, eventually, he would appear as an imperialist to the core, Lockhart was also a realist in many ways. He knew early on that the only way forward was to deal with the Bolsheviks as the future power in Russia, yet his assessment of the situation and his reports to the Foreign Office often fell on stony ground. Lockhart was living at the time with his wife in a Moscow flat, but there is ample evidence of a strained relationship between them. Like many of the diplomatic corps, his position gave him a valued freedom of movement in higher society. Like them, he was an avid party-goer and, by all accounts, lived life to the hilt and on the edge. There is no doubt that from the start he found Francis Cromie to be the most impressive of the submarine officers, as he recorded in his diary:

> Thursday, 17 February 1916
> 'Rout' for the submarine men (from the British Baltic Fleet) at the Duma. Huge crowd there and half Moscow to meet them. After the 'rout' went to the Altr where the club gave a splendid show for us. Many of the best artists sang, and Novikov and Anderson danced. Cromie (Captain commanding submarines) made a very good speech:
> 'Gentlemen,' he said, 'you are creators. What you create will live long after you. I am only a simple sailor, I destroy, but can say truthfully that I destroy in order that your works may live.' This made an excellent impression.

But such glittering occasions were only a minor oasis on a grim trip which demonstrated the true horror of the war. During the time they spent on the actual front line in Galicia, the Austrians at one time had the party in their sights and had opened fire. Fortunately, none of the bullets found its mark. Between the frozen mud and piled-up corpses came brief nights of comparative comfort when the army staff entertained the party at a sumptuous level. Nevertheless, they were relieved to get back to base. Cromie would have much to tell the men of the nastier side of this war should anyone make the error of thinking the Baltic was a difficult posting.

Whilst they had been away, work on the boats had continued and the crews who remained behind had been busy. Prior to his time as a submariner, Cromie's navigator on *E19*, Lieutenant Cecil Mee, had gained some experience working with anti-submarine nets and had put this to good use by working on them along-side the Russians. Now the promise of a thaw was drawing nearer, and Cromie was becoming impatient; it was time for some action.

It was to be the end of April before the submarines could move from Reval. Both *E18* and *E1* ventured out through the melting ice floes. But it was an in-auspicious start, and changes in both Russian and German sea-going war policy were about to make a repetition of the flotilla's 1915 success more difficult. Because of the threat the flotilla posed, the Germans were now playing a clever card by using Swedish-registered vessels to carry goods whenever possible. Following the *Nike* incident the Russians had decreed that, whether or not they were carrying contraband, the vessels of neutral nations should not be attacked. It had also been decided that the Russian boats would be the ones to attack merchant shipping, whilst the British contingent would face up to German war-ships. Cromie, as eager as ever to keep the flotilla record up, faced a perplexing period. On 26 May *E18* inflicted major, although not fatal, damage to the German destroyer *V100*. It was subsequently discovered that the *V100* had sur-vived to be repaired and fight on, but Cromie, after returning from a five-day reconnaissance trip in *E19*, became increasingly concerned when Halahan's *E18* failed to return. The sad conclusion was eventually reached, after a long and fruitless wait, that *E18* and her crew had perished after hitting a mine.

It was a sad blow for all, and was taken badly. It was at this time that Cromie began his despatches to his superiors, Commodore S.S. Hall, and Admiral Phillimore. Thus, from this point, Cromie's story can often be taken from his own detailed and thorough letters. In his first existing despatch to Commodore Hall, dated 29 May, he still expected *E18* to return, and there are hints at a slight sea-change in how the Russian command was perceived by the British. In some ways, the honeymoon was beginning to fade.[5]

Dear Commodore Hall

We are in full swing once more, but oh, the begging and 'weeping' I have had to get the staff to move, and the lies they kept putting me off with, with what idea I never discovered. Now I am doing my best to persuade them to keep at least two boats always at sea in two positions, having direct offensive bearings on any naval movement against Riga, viz. Libau and Steinort. I reconnoitred these positions last trip and located swept chan-nels, patrols and courses used, and went right up to Libau, counting five cruisers inside, but they never stirred out. *E9* reconnoitred the patrols and route west of Gotland, north and south of Bornholm. At present *E8* is off

Libau and Steinort 'looking for mines' but we have a German report of a TBD damaged by a torpedo, so we have great hopes that it is (?good). Another report is *E18* on the patrolled transport route off Memel. *E1* is off Pomerania. Yershoff, Lieutenant with the Russian boats, is on the Swedish trade route, doing well, but now we have news that the Germans are arming all merchantmen with masked guns, and have a white ring to hoist around the funnel, and canvas painted in Swedish colours to put over the side – and this from a German skipper.

Cromie was only just over seven months into his mission, but with Horton and Laurence gone, he was now the Senior Officer, and the rigorous responsibilities of keeping this show on the road so far from home were beginning to bite. No one had been paid – Cromie had to rely on borrowed money from the Russians. Stores requested from home failed to appear. Mail was months in arriving, and the men, who arrived inadequately equipped for a Russian winter, after having already been generously kitted out by the Russians with suitable Arctic clothing, were still awaiting fresh uniform kit from home.

He suggested to the Admiralty that they make his flotilla of five boats a separate one, with their own book-keeping and a paymaster, independent of the 8th Flotilla under HMS *Maidstone* back in Harwich. It was a strong argument. The level of communication he was now expected to maintain outside running *E19* took up most of his off-watch time. Not only was he required to keep the Admiralty informed, but also Admiral Phillimore, the British Embassy in Petrograd, and the Foreign Office, and he had to deal daily with the Russian authorities, whose different way of doing things was already causing him some concern. In the midst of all this he was struggling to learn the Russian language. Sharing a ship partitioned down the middle with British sailors on one side, under the constant and increasingly jealous stare of the Russians on the other, required the skills of an experienced referee. Putting to sea in *E19* must have seemed almost recreational.

Cromie showed in his despatches just why his men thought so much of him – he was never afraid, like Laurence before him with the rum ration, even when writing to a Commodore, to stand their corner.

> As things are I have the whole responsibility with none of the rights of in-dependent command . . . One of these days I will fall between some of the stools if I have no real standing.
>
> If you will consider that we have more officers, men, boats and impor-tance than the *Rosario* in peacetime, and are far more distant as far as correspondence and stores are concerned, you will realise that my sugges-tion is not one of self-aggrandisement or of a distaste for serving under the *Maidstone*, but one for the interests of the service. So many things could be dealt with on the spot if we had our own books. Now that we have six crews out here there is really more for me to do than you would at first think, and if I had not a trusty 2nd Officer, and had to oversee every job in the boat myself, I don't know how I should manage. Things are somewhat different now to when there were two boats under the personal orders of Admiral

Essen. I like and admire our Commodore, Podgourski, but even he cannot always persuade the C-in-C from doing useless stunts with the boats . . .

At the present moment the men have a not unwarrantable grievance in the matter of pay and clothing. I consider it necessary that the men be at least allowed to draw the whole amount of pay due to them, and I beg of you to consider the matter (once more) of extra pay. It really is serious – the men work in rags, and I have been into the matter very carefully and I cannot in justice make them work in better clothes. I have obtained a grant (on paper) of white duck from the Russian government, but they have not yet been able to obtain it. Serge and flannel cannot be bought at any price, so in desperation the men work in thin cotton overalls which I obtained gratis to cover the nakedness of the land. Serge or flannel ordered through the Russian government last July has not yet arrived. This great pinch has only been felt since the parcel mail stopped last Xmas. The PMG informs me that parcels have been sent regularly in accordance with Admiralty instructions, but we have only had one lot via Canada since Xmas.

The officers are in much the same way, with the addition of the expense of warm clothing and entertaining. Our winter trip cost 900 roubles in entertaining, over and above personal expenses . . .

Even at this early stage in the campaign the British officers, although looked up to by Russians sharing the same ranks, were entering an embarrassing phase of penury owing to their increasing inability to match their hosts' penchant for high-octane off-duty living. Cromie had concerns about his salary (which was to become a recurring theme), complaining that he had heard through Horton that extra pay for officers in this posting would not be forthcoming from the Admiralty. Although he agreed that they could live 'comfortably', they were not able to dress properly, entertain and become too involved in social life. The off-duty life of the overseas naval officer was highlighted when he wrote, regarding social life, 'At least give us "table money". I am afraid my letter has been one long moan, but it is better that you should know the facts as they are.'

From these despatches we also learn that many of the men were somewhat annoyed with their shipmates, some of whom were already marrying Russian girls. For instance, Lilian Nield's favourite, Petty Officer 'Paddy' Ryan, soon had a Russian bride, as did Able Seaman Tom Rayner and Stoker Petty Officer Ellis Godfrey. It is worth mentioning also that, despite these marital arrangements being far from home, even starting a family was not out of the question. Mr William Dudley of Lymington in Hampshire is in his mid-eighties, and like Lilian Nield can claim a direct link back to Cromie's flotilla. Bill is also an ex-Navy man, and even at the age of ten served in the Submarine Cadet Corps. In later life he became a crew member of Admiral Jellicoe's one-time flagship, HMS *Iron Duke*, and was in Scapa Flow at the time the *Royal Oak* was torpedoed. His father, Stoker Bertie Dudley, who was an engine-room rating on Cromie's *E19*, fell in love with an Estonian girl and asked Cromie's permission to marry.[6] They did so on board the *Dvina*, with the Chaplain, Revd B.S. Lombard in attendance, in the depth of winter with relatives and friends arrived by horse-drawn sledge.

Fortunately, as part of their musical armoury, the ship's concert party possessed a gramophone record of church bells, and this was played as the wedding party approached the vessel. It was a colourful and unusual occasion for the British sailors.

A year later, Bill was born and christened on board the *Dvina* in Reval, using the up-turned ship's bell as a font. As is the way with travelling military men, some of these liaisons did not last. Bill's father, cast in the mould of a loveable rogue, hoodwinked his Estonian wife into believing that he was the proud owner of a large house back in Blighty. She must have been impressed with the photograph he showed her of his stately pile, but she discovered, when she finally arrived in England, that the building in question was her husband's local pub!

Ben Benson was thankfully happily married with a wife back in Scotland, but he recalls with relish all the amorous goings-on in his memoir:

> It was a rule that all hands should be on board when the Chaplain came to hold a service. He would usually arrive a day or two beforehand to enable him to be available for anyone having personal problems and wishing advice, etc.
>
> On at least one occasion he performed a couple of weddings between our chaps and Russian or Estonian girls. One of these girls was notoriously well known to quite a number of the chaps and it was strange how most of these lads sat in the front rows! Another of the girls – quite a good looker – who shortly after her wedding on ship took advantage of her husband being at sea and got mixed up with someone else. As a result of this Captain Cromie and the padre were able to arrange a divorce.

It is easy to imagine the tensions these courtships and marriages would have brought into the mess deck of some 200 sailors engaged in a war. It is to Cromie's credit that he allowed his men such romantic leeway, but the colour and gaiety of what were, in civilian life, everyday domestic happenings would have done much to cheer up the grey, ice-bound life in Reval.

The early months of 1916 were also lightened for Cromie when the flotilla was offered a much-needed shot in the arm on the engineering front. Because of the frustrations which had resulted from actions at sea using deficient torpedoes, Cromie had much to concern him over the possibility of a similar lack of success once the hunting season opened up again. But for once their lordships back home had paid attention to his reports by sending out Engineer Commander Ernest Mowlam with a team of six torpedo fitters from Portsmouth. How crucial their stay in Reval was can be gauged by the fact that, in 1919, they all received the OBE. To assist them they had the stalwart support of Gunner Samuel Kent, whose inventiveness produced a device enabling a torpedo to be used for practice purposes.[7] The workers in Reval dockyard were naturally unfamiliar with these new British E Class boats and Cromie's crewmen, skilled though they were, could only achieve so much. Another positive arrival, this time to tackle the submarines' battery problems, was the Chloride Battery Company's engineer, Mr McKinnon, together with his foreman.

With the coming of spring in 1916 Francis Cromie began to realise that although Max Horton and Noel Laurence had set an impressive fighting precedent for the flotilla during their year of action, he would now suffer the brunt of the Germans' increased awareness of his enemy at their gates. The Kaiser's navy was about to make use of any technical advance to hand to tackle these British marauders, and that now included aircraft. Cromie had already experienced being shadowed in *E19* by a Zeppelin, and *E1* had even been bombed twice from the air. The enemy soon realised the powerful effect aircraft could have in their anti-submarine missions, and this posed a serious threat. The problem was the Baltic Sea and the clarity of the water. Even at a depth of 90 feet (27 metres) a submarine could be spotted from the air, so something needed to be done. Lieutenant-Commander Athelstan Fenner of *E1* was duly sent aloft in a Russian seaplane to see what *E8* looked like from altitude. His report resulted in a new camouflage design for the boats. This would replace their red anti-fouling paint below the waterline with black, and substitute a dark green for the light green on the upper decks.

Even so, in June 1916 Cromie narrowly escaped disaster in *E19* when a German plane showered no fewer than thirty-four bombs in his vicinity. This attack only served to highlight yet another problem: although *E19*'s crew tried manfully to use her 6 pounder gun against the plane, the weapon, dating from 1897 and, with its barrel worn smooth, was well past its best as Cromie testified after witnessing the shells tumbling through the air.[8]

By his second, undated, despatch of 1916 to Commodore Hall, and following the welcome arrival of the torpedo fitters and the Chloride Battery employees, Cromie seems to have cheered up a little, despite a number of his men suffering with mumps, but he now accepted that *E18* was lost.

> Since I wrote you last large quantities of slops have arrived per SS *Karawak*, *Carrerea* and *Lincarn*, but the shipping agent at Archangel reports one package short on unloading, and from your list I judge it to contain drawers. The boots are on their way and we shall be thankful to get them (officers as well as men). Thank heaven we are getting parcels once more, but I see in an English paper that parcels via Archangel are going to be stopped by the Admiralty for more important war material – could you not arrange that our parcels be allowed to come through? They make so much difference to us.
>
> I am sorry to say that S. Langridge died in Hospital on the 6th of acute kidney disease. We buried him with usual honours in the military cemetery on the 8th, the Padre from Petrograd officiating. The Russians were very attentive and well represented, and most of Reval joined in as well.
>
> There is really precious little for us to do at present beyond the eternal 'stand by' as I have failed to persuade them [the Russians] to let us hunt Fritz off the entrance of the Gulf. They have credited *E18* with that damaged ship[9] and are giving him a posthumous St George, and Langdale and Colson the St Vladimir, and the crew the Silver Cross. I think it is very nice of them as it is not quite within the rules of the St George. Poor H. was so keen on getting it that I know his wife will be really pleased. The Russians

have been genuinely affected by the loss, and we have had many messages of sympathy, including one from the Emperor and a letter from the Minister of Marine.

That year did not follow the impressive pattern of the previous one. Although the Russian submarines had a taste of success when, on 17 May, their boat, the *Volk*, sank three cargo vessels and added to this achievement by actually capturing two German destroyers, the only battle Cromie was engaged in was with his Russian hosts. Admiral Kanin had only one task in mind for the British – that of a last-ditch defence force in case the enemy decided to attack Riga. To Cromie's dismay and annoyance the lacklustre admiral appeared to have some misgivings about the British flotilla, but as he was the Commander-in-Chief Cromie had no choice but to toe the line, frustrating as that might be. On top of these strained relations Cromie's administrative burden seemed to increase day by day, with stores and mail from home frequently getting stuck in a bottleneck at Archangel. Although Murmansk was a port which escaped major ice problems throughout the seasons, the rail link to the harbourage was still incomplete in 1916, leaving only transport by sledge, with all the limitations for heavy equipment which that entailed.

In the tricky area of receiving mails from home, however, the spring of 1916 did throw up an oddity in the annals of the campaign. To begin with, the first mails had arrived via a circuitous route which took in a journey across Canada, but in May two vessels bound for Russia carrying mail were boarded by the German navy, and the letters for the flotilla, among many others, were confiscated. However, they did eventually arrive at Reval – a fact which must have puzzled Cromie as they had been sent to the flotilla from Berlin! Apparently, following extensive scrutiny by German intelligence the hijacked mail had been deemed harmless and the foe had had the good grace to send it on.

Cromie had a close relationship with many of his officers and men. Somehow he managed to find time to pay attention to those little details which could bring a much-needed family atmosphere to the mess decks. An example of this is one of the few private letters from him, written on 1 May 1916 to Lieutenant George Sharp's wife in Ely, Cambridgeshire. The Sharps had just become the proud parents of a new baby girl:

Dear Mrs Sharp,
Many congratulations for supplying a new recruit for *E19*. I suppose at the bottom of your heart you are glad it is not a boy in these days.
   The officers of *E19*, that is Lieut. Mee, Dvorjetski & self are sending a Russian mug and must insist on one name being Tatiana, then her name in Russia will be Tatiana Urieovna, the latter meaning 'daughter of George'. So call her Kathleen Tatiana, in memory of the Baltic and at the wish of her Baltic uncles.
         Wishing you both all health and happiness,
         Yours very sincerely,
         F.N.A. Cromie

In July *E19* ventured out on what was to be a lack-lustre patrol, described by Cromie as 'a very dull and short trip'. But unknown to him, back in Chatham, plans were afoot to send him some company – a further four submarines. On 3 August, up to his neck in accounting problems, he was on his way to thrash out his difficulties with the Naval Attaché in Petrograd, whilst just outside Chatham, on the same day, a quartet of C Class boats were beginning their long and convoluted journey to Archangel. Cromie's life was about to become even more complicated, but not just from an administrative standpoint. Russia herself was beginning to come apart at the seams.

CHAPTER 11

NEW BLOOD

However great the military significance of the Battle of Verdun
may be, the political significance is infinitely greater. In Berlin
and other places they have been wanting 'movement' – and they
will have it.
Hark! under Verdun there is being forged *our* tomorrow.

Leon Trotsky
My Life[1]

The horror of Verdun, almost 1,000 miles (1,500 km) away from Francis
Cromie's struggling outpost in Reval, would seem to have little relevance to the
operation of a few submarines in the Baltic Sea. If anything, what was
happening there between February to December 1916 could be seen as some
sort of pale victory. A German offensive had made initial advances but these
were eventually checked by the French under General Henri Pétain. Despite
renewed German assaults, the offensive by the Allies on the Somme drew off
valuable German troops, and thus the French regained some lost territory.
The cost, however, was enormous. One million men may have been a mere
statistic to the generals, but the repeated tragedy of so many lost lives was to
reverberate across the world. Cromie and his fellow officers knew what this
trench warfare looked like – they had seen it in Galicia. He was as eager as ever
to fight his corner, no matter how insignificant that might be, but the fighting
spirit of his own immediate 'allies' was beginning to run through his fingers like
sand.

The Russian summer of 1916 was a grey and rainy one, with very few weeks
of hot sunshine. On Petrograd's Nevsky Prospekt the international hotels, the
Astoria, the Hotel de France and the Europa, were still doing good business. The
cabarets and theatres were open. Cabs and carriages moved to and fro, their well-
dressed occupants *en route* to yet another soirée, where they would drink their
champagne, smoke their cigars and make facile conversation about the state of
the country and the running of the war. Their forlorn hope was that this was just
another difficult phase in the long history of a mighty nation, and things would
soon return to normal.

Yet each day at the Warsaw Station trains were arriving, their grimy carriages
jammed to capacity with wounded soldiers. The hospital wards were full to overflowing. The price of drugs, from morphine to aspirin, had escalated so much as
to make proper medical care extremely difficult. Thus the shattering reality of

war stretched back from the trenches and onto the doorsteps of those at home. Vast sections of the male population were dead or missing. Children were dying. There seemed to be no respite from all this and little hope in view.

Despite the effect on morale of the loss of HMS *E18*, Cromie's mood in June 1916 had improved slightly. Admiral Phillimore had obviously 'had words' with Admiral Kanin, because Cromie wrote to Commodore Hall that 'Things are going on ball-bearings with the Authorities; the C-in-C taking a personal interest in matters.' His reading of the war on land was perceptive. Although there had been significant advances under General Brusilov's offensive in Galicia between June and October 1916, on some points, as with General Lechinsky's Ninth Army, pushing the Austrians 50 miles (80 km) back to the Carpathian Mountains,[2] Cromie was guarded in his enthusiasm.[3]

> The great push on the Russian SW Front is a live fact and going splendidly; the only fear is that they won't know when to stop, for the railways behind the Russians are bad, and in Galicia simply don't exist. We visited a large portion of this front, and I should be very sorry to be pursued by the bandits we saw in the Russian lines. Their spirit was very good, but impatient: now, of course, they will be quite mad, and very difficult to hold.

Despite the success of the Brusilov offensive, as at Verdun there was a high price to pay – another million men. There was also the logistical problem of hundreds of thousands of Austrian prisoners of war to contend with. As with all wars, and especially with one of such titanic proportions, the drain on the civilian population was just as disastrous as that on the men in the front line. Even in peacetime, the yoke of poverty and near serfdom under which the bulk of the Russian workers toiled was hard enough. But now they faced a multitude of horrors: starvation, the breakdown of the country's infrastructure, the agony of the daily wastage of their loved ones. In the face of such deprivation, and the struggles of the poorly supplied army, the international banks held in their warehouses a third of the country's grain supplies whilst they awaited the inevitable price rises. There were huge stocks of sugar and cotton, all well guarded and ripe for the next speculative transaction.

In hovels and in the streets around Petrograd's Warsaw Station were thousands of starving, bedraggled refugees, crippled soldiers, homeless, poorly clad children and despairing widows, ill prepared for the bitter winter which lay ahead. Already the talk among the thousands of disgruntled sailors, soldiers and workers was beginning to focus on peace. Even officers were overstaying their leave; discipline was breaking down. Barracks in Petrograd which had been built to hold a few hundred men were now crammed with thousands of soldiers, and their mood was shifting rapidly from the gung-ho patriotism of 1914 to seething discontent.

Yet in the grand palaces the crowned heads of the warring nations looked down upon their maps of misery as if they were playing chess. Their romantic notion of the absolute fealty of their subjects is amply demonstrated by such letters as this:[4]

King George V to Nicholas,
September 22nd 1916

My Dearest Nicky

. . . I have recently heard from our friend Mr Anderson, who says 'The Germans realise so far as England and France are concerned that it must be a fight to the finish, on the other hand they still have hopes of being able to detach Russia and are working hard to this end.' What nonsense, they little know you and your people if they think they can make a separate peace with Russia.

Goodbye and God bless you, my dearest Nicky.

GEORGIE

More to the point, how little *either* monarch knew of the Russian people. On the eve of war in 1914 these loyal subjects had fallen to their knees outside the Winter Palace to sing the Tsarist national anthem. It was a dramatic, holy occasion, just the kind of event to bolster the self-confidence of an autocratic ruler and his relatives in Britain. But this image of the bedraggled poor, their raw knees on the cobblestones, heads bowed in magnificent musical harmony, had become well out of date by the summer of 1916. Russia's high society still believed that disintegration on the home front could be thwarted by a military victory. It was to prove a naive hope indeed.

For the time being, the men of the Royal Navy's Baltic Flotilla were still eating reasonably well, still enjoying their daily shot of vodka, courtesy of the Tsar, and at last had some new clothes to wear. Life in Reval had its good points. The British sailors still had the respect and admiration of the population. Despite the limitations of their slim wallets there was recreation, the concert party, the home-from-home camaraderie of the many expatriates in the area, all punctuated by the constant challenge of patrols in the Baltic. Even with its long period of in-activity, this was still a full life. They were fulfilling their mission as Allies and could only stand by in dismay as this strange world they were occupying lurched into darkness. Yet it was the stark contrast of the British Jack Tar's comparative freedom with that of the oppressed Russian sailor which was helping to accelerate the growing atmosphere of dissent in the Russian messes. As the Russian sailor looked on at his British counterpart's superior food, his daily vodka ration and the obvious mutual respect between the Royal Navy's officers and men, the atmosphere of nagging jealousy began to grow. If this was what 'freedom' looked like, then it was time they had some.

The Russian advances under General Brusilov meant little against the five million casualties the army had now suffered. Whilst the newspapers of Moscow and Petrograd kept some kind of media flag flying for 'our brave, courageous soldiers', what opinion did a man like Brusilov hold of his fighting men? Was he proud, optimistic, hopeful? Hardly. As the leaves of autumn 1916 began to pile up, he said to one of his officers, 'In a year of war the regular army has vanished. It is replaced by an army of ignoramuses.'[5] It was hardly the pat on the back an ill-equipped, poverty-stricken son of the Steppes needed whilst freezing to death in a Galician trench. Alexei Brusilov, born in 1853, was a cavalryman of the old school, a tactical genius who had made his name during the Russo-Turkish War of 1877–88. His efforts in 1916 on the south-western front were undoubtedly one of the greatest achievements during Russia's sad involvement in the Great War. But despite his complaints of his 'army of ignoramuses', his pragmatism and tactical skill were matched only by his bold sense of opportunism. This same general of the ignorant masses knew which way the wind was blowing in 1917. He threw in his lot with the Bolsheviks, called for the abdication of the Tsar, and under Soviet rule, became chairman of the commission commanding the Russian armed forces in 1920.

However, during that summer of 1916, the ingrained brutal attitude to the lower orders festered on. Cromie had seen it at first hand on board the *Dvina*. To his credit, he was having none of it.

Ben Benson brought this lofty Russian arrogance into sharp focus. Although still fulfilling his post as *E19*'s telegraphist, he had become much closer to Commander Cromie. As an unofficial secretary and valet, he was always on call, and his diary demonstrates that despite the distance between their ranks Cromie was a man Ben could talk to. One of his duties was to report to the Russian admiral with details of what was being written in the British press. This information would be received by radio, written out by Ben and delivered to the admiral's yacht. On this occasion he had made his way along the dockside in Reval to the yacht. He passed the Russian sentries and began climbing the gangway when he noticed that the admiral was leaving the vessel and was heading down the gangway in his direction. Ben stood aside on the gangway's halfway platform, and as the admiral passed, stood to attention and smartly saluted. The admiral's response was to pause for a moment and, rather than acknowledge the salute, spit full in the perturbed telegraphist's face. He then carried on down the gangway, leaving a perplexed and naturally furious Benson to wonder what on earth he had done to warrant a face full of Imperial saliva. After wiping his face and delivering his despatch, Ben hot-footed it back to the *Dvina* and headed straight for Cromie's cabin.

Cromie was less than impressed. An hour later, after waiting for the admiral to return, he sent for Benson and together they set out for the Russian's yacht. Cromie had a good relationship with the admiral, whose wife spoke good English. Once on board, he told Ben to wait outside the admiral's cabin. He strode in, and in a brave disregard for rank, told the admiral just what he and Ben thought of the disgraceful treatment. To top this off, Cromie insisted that he should apologise – that this telegraphist was *British* – and if an apology was not forthcoming, he would take the incident to a 'higher authority'. After some consideration, Ben was brought into the cabin and the admiral had to face a humiliation which would have been, for such a 'high born excellency' a totally new experience – apologising to a lowly sailor.[6]

During the height of this damp Russian summer, with its 'white nights', when the sun remained in the sky until midnight, the flotilla continued its reconnaissance patrols as Cromie struggled to keep on top of the administrative work. In London, on 31 May 1916, his DSO was gazetted. Another medal for the growing collection. Yet it seems lax of the Admiralty, in retrospect, not to have recognised his worth until a full six months after the Tsar had. But Cromie's request that the Baltic Flotilla should be made an independent command, thus removing the time-consuming process of having to refer all his decisions back to HMS *Maidstone* in Harwich, was granted. On 1 August the flotilla received its independence, but not under the name Cromie had requested, HMS *Baltic*, but as HMS *E19*. To bolster this new status, much to Cromie's relief, the Admiralty had sent him an assistant paymaster, Percy Hayward RNR, to take some of the administrative weight off his shoulders. But what the Commander did not realise, was that despite this apparent relief, his responsibility of command was about to be doubled. Such were the qualities of the various lines of communication between Britain and Russia that even on the day they left England, Cromie had no real idea that new submarines were heading his way. In fact they were well on their way to Russia when Cromie wrote to Commodore Hall on 9 August:

Dear Commodore Hall,
Hayward arrived this morning and delivered your note. I had heard rumours *re*. C boats, but was surprised to know definitely. I think it would be a good thing if you could give me some definite news as to dates of arrival so as to arrange now for the quick assembly of parts. I presume you will send an engineer to oversee the job, as I have not a very high opinion of the native talent on any job new to him, although very excellent when he knows the work in hand.

Commander Cromie, Lt J.R. Parsons RNVR and Rear-Admiral R.F. Phillimore. (*RN Submarine Museum, Gosport*)

This lack of information was embarrassing not only for Cromie but for Admiral Phillimore at Russian Imperial HQ. No one had told *him* that new submarines were coming. In fact Phillimore had even told the Tsar that the opposite was the case.

The four C Class boats could not now take the same risks as the Es and enter the Baltic by the Sound. German anti-submarine activity was at its height and their chances of making it via that route were, to say the least, minimal. The only other option required a triumph of logistics, and that triumph was achieved.

Between Chatham and their destination lay a voyage via sea, land, river and canal of over 4,000 miles (6,500 km). From the Dover flotilla ship, HMS *Arrogant*, Commodore Hall carefully chose four of his best men to command these boats. *C26* would be commanded by Lieutenant Eric Tod, *C27* by Lieutenant Douglas Sealy DSC, *C32* by Lieutenant Christopher Satow, and *C35* by Lieutenant Edward Stanley DSC. With their single petrol engines and only two bow torpedo tubes, their obsolescence made them a poor second to the newer E Class, yet they were the most manageable size of craft available which could feasibly make this complicated, multi-stage journey. It is probably the only journey of its kind in submarine history.

On 3 August with all their hydroplanes, periscopes, batteries and exterior fittings removed, the four boats were towed to Lerwick in the Shetland Isles. In contrast to the tight security net thrown around the mission, which resulted in the Vice-Admiral for Orkneys and Shetlands knowing nothing of their arrival, there remained the bold advertisement of the mission for any passer-by to see – all the crates on board the decks of the tugs were boldly stencilled 'Archangel'. From Lerwick, they proceeded around the North Cape and into the Barents Sea. Here they encountered atrocious weather, and there was some concern when three of the unmanned boats broke free from their tow. Reattaching them to the tugs in violent storms required some brave seamanship. For instance, when *C27* went adrift, it was only a very dangerous leap from the deck of the tug *Hampden* by *C27*'s torpedoman Able Seaman Algy Steel onto the heaving submarine which saved the day. The courageous Algy had to remain alone on board until they reached the anchorage at Yukanski. Eventually, against all the odds, they made it into Archangel on 21 August. Now, ahead of them, lay a journey of 1,386 miles (2,218 km) through Russia's inland waterways to Petrograd.

Compared to the dissolute atmosphere which was increasing elsewhere in the Russian navy, the preparations for the arrival and transportation of the British submarines in Archangel, organised by Captain Roschakoffsky, was a model of logistical planning. The highly experienced Engineer Commander Percy Stocker was in charge of the operation, accompanied by Assistant Naval Constructor George Stantan. Together with four coxwains, four junior ratings and officers from the four boats, they secured the submarines on large barges, which were towed by the paddle steamer *Sealnia*. When one inspects a photograph of these vessels, with their bulk and robust construction, each a dead weight of 270 tons, the immensity of this task becomes apparent, and its ultimate success is a fine tribute to Russian skill and ingenuity. *C26* and *C27* were the first to head out on their journey at 10 p.m. on the night of 22 August. In a hut on their decks, each of the barges accommodated ten Russian carpenters – all soldiers – and the four British coxwains. The following morning, *C32* and *C35* followed on.

The first leg of the trip took them along the River Dvina to Kotlas and then to Ustchuk. Here they entered another river, the Sukhona, where a paddle steamer with a shallower draught relieved the *Sealnia*. Great skill was required by tug skippers in negotiating the shallow waters and sharp bend at Opoke, against very strong currents. By 1 September they had reached Lake Lubenskoe, and then entered the first lock in the Wurtemburg Canal. Over a dozen locks lay between them and the River Sheksna at Topornia. Here the British sailors could see to what use the Russians were putting their thousands of Austrian prisoners of war – they were busily employed building new locks. After colliding with the lock gates, *C35*'s barge sustained serious damage and began to leak. The innovative Captain Roschakoffsky faced up to this challenge by draining the lock completely to convert it into a temporary dry dock so that the barge could be repaired. It was an impressive piece of work. Next came the Novo-Mariinsi Canal, which runs around Lake Bailoe. After many more canals, passing through the region of Lakes Onega and Lagoda, on 9 September, thirty-seven days after leaving their berth in England, the submarines entered the River Neva. It was a remarkable achievement for all concerned, especially in a country experiencing such hardship and tragedy.

Independent command and assistant paymaster aside, poor Cromie now faced new problems. His accommodation space on board the *Dvina* was already limited; he now had to parley with the Russians to make enough space for the influx of new men and officers who would man the C boats. In this he enlisted the help of Admiral Phillimore, who exerted his influence with the Russians. With these preparations under way, on 21 August, just as the Cs had arrived in Archangel, Cromie set out in *E19* for a reconnaissance patrol. Beneath the waves of the Baltic, detached from the rigours of life on board the *Dvina* it must have seemed like a welcome break.

But the arrival of the new boats at Petrograd's Baltic Works was not to be a happy one. Their batteries, transported separately in packing cases, were all damaged. Cromie was not pleased.

> Dear Commodore Hall,
> You will have heard all about the mess up of the C batteries. It seems almost incredible that anyone would pack heavy plates into containers for transit. The whole thing was undoubtedly aggravated by the cases being stowed *loose* on top of the coal in the ships, but that cannot excuse the persons responsible for the packing. I strongly recommend the thoroughness of the Chloride people's method of packing . . .

Problems with batteries took up much of Cromie's time. The ingenuity of his engine-room personnel in cannibalising spares from submarine to submarine in order to keep the boats running was always impressive.

This delay for the C boats had eaten into the time remaining for operations before the winter set in. *C35* did not leave Petrograd for Reval until 18 October. As December approached, *C26* was still in Kronstadt, and to avoid being trapped in the encroaching ice, *C27* needed to be towed to Reval, still minus a complete battery. The Russian Minister of Marine in the meantime had delivered a message to Cromie from the Tsar himself, wherein the Emperor thanked the flotilla 'for all the work you have done'. It seemed a hollow missive to Cromie, who responded to Commodore Hall, 'I am sorry to say we have had but few opportunities this year.' As if things were not bad enough, there were no torpedoes for the Cs; they had been declared 'missing – somewhere in Russia'.

With the icy wind now blowing down the Gulf of Finland and the nights drawn in, Cromie had little to celebrate, apart from the arrival of Staff Surgeon Kenneth Hole as the flotilla's medical officer. It seemed as if the glory days of 1915 could never be repeated. But at least there was some positive movement in the Russian navy, with the removal of the somewhat indolent and uninspiring Admiral Kanin and his replacement as Commander-in-Chief by the infinitely more dynamic Admiral Nepenin. In November another welcome firebrand, Captain D.N. Verderevsky, took charge of the Russian Baltic submarines.

C35 and *C32*, the only two Cs which could operate, were sent to Rogekul in Moon Sound, but after only one patrol they were locked in for the winter as the Baltic began its inevitable freeze-up.

The dark months ahead seemed to have little to offer to Cromie but uncertainty. The Russian successes on land had faded into a series of defeats. In Reval, he was already experiencing difficulties as the dockyard workers began a series of strikes, in demanding better pay, food and conditions. There was a social melancholy afoot which matched the mood of the freezing winter in every aspect. Meriel Buchanan, the daughter of the British Ambassador in Petrograd, moved in those circles of power which were coming under closer scrutiny by the Russian people every day. Certainly no Bolshevik, she nevertheless observed the grim inevitability of approaching calamity.[7]

> And meanwhile the evil tongues continued their gossip, catching here and there a shadow of truth, embroidering on it, and insinuating even more terrible things that were left unsaid. In great shadowed drawing-rooms, in the more intellectual circles, where men with long hair and scrubby beards gathered round tables to discuss profound philosophy over innumerable cups of tea, and in smoke-filled cabarets in the lower quarters of the town – everywhere the slander spread and ripened.
>
> There was nothing bad or vile enough that was not insinuated. The Dark Powers behind the Throne! German influence at Court! The suspicion of a separate, treacherous peace! The power of Rasputin! Infamous stories about the Empress! Scandalous rumours about the Grand Duchesses!

As the saying goes – there is no smoke without fire. Grigori Rasputin was just one of the 'dark forces', and his insistent presence had produced a crazy maelstrom of influence in the Romanov circle which had pushed the Emperor's family into appointing three different war ministers and five interior ministers in the space of ten months. Even on 2 December 1916, just two weeks before Rasputin's death at the hands of Prince Yusupov, and despite all the dark rumours and open dismay at the monk's influence, Nicholas wrote in his diary at Tsarskoe Selo, 'We spent the evening at Ania's talking to Grigori.' Even the Prime Minister, Boris Stürmer, who also doubled as Foreign Minister, owed his position to the so-called 'Mad Monk'. Stürmer, a self-regarding, narcissistic upstart, was universally detested by the diplomatic community. Yet, like many other lackeys around the royal family, he was there because Rasputin said he should be. With a country the size of Russia in the midst of the greatest war in history, this kind of administration meant nothing but disaster.

Grigori Efimovitch Rasputin was living at 64 Gorokhovaya Street, just a short walk from the Admiralty and the Winter Palace. But according to a secret report by the Okhrana, the Russian secret police, his acolytes took him everywhere by car.[8] Many of these people were themselves double agents, reporting back to the Okhrana. It was noted that at each of his meetings with the Empress, when he would often spend time alone with her – hence the 'infamous stories' – he was usually blind drunk. The circle of people observing Rasputin and reporting his movements numbered a staggering 5,000. His libidinous sexual antics, which included talking women into bed with the idea that 'one must sin before one can repent', plus his almost constant inebriation, were reason enough for revolutionary critics of the monarchy to be up in arms.

But it was the ultra-monarchists, those who claimed to have Nicholas's and Alexandra's well-being at heart, who conspired to see Rasputin dead. Prince Felix Yusupov was an attractive young man of twenty-nine who, in his younger days, enjoyed nothing more than dressing as a woman. Married to the Tsar's niece, Princess Irina, Yusupov was said to be heir to a fortune even greater than the Tsar's. Together with a right-wing deputy from the Duma, V.M. Purishkevich, a doctor, a captain of the guards and the Tsar's cousin, the virulently anti-Semitic Grand Duke Dimitri Pavlovich, a plan was laid to kill Rasputin. The resulting murder, on the night of 16 December 1916, still reads like something from a lurid collection of horror stories. Poisoned with cakes and wine laced with cyanide, the monk refused to die; Yusupov's bullets then failed to despatch him. Only after he had been dumped into the frozen Neva did death finally overcome one of the most influential peasants in history.

Yusupov's action resulted in the Grand Duke's exile to Persia, but the cross-dressing Prince got off rather lightly, being sent to his estates in the Crimea. Yet their good intentions in ridding Russia of Rasputin stemmed as much from their fear of the impending revolution as from a regard for their monarch's well-being. But acts such as this were all too late. Rasputin had been infecting the royal family since 1907; the damage had been done.

In Reval the news of Rasputin's death spread among the revolutionary and royalist groups alike to be met with a mixture of delight, some despair, and a little hope. At least someone had done something to shake the Emperor's circle into witnessing how people were thinking. On board the *Dvina*, Cromie's men must have studied the news as if it were the last chapter in a cheap novel. This was a strange place indeed.

Cromie had succeeded in expanding the mess area for his men on board, but at the cost of dismantling the on-board workshops, which were now transferred to the Reval dockyards. On the social front, as Christmas approached, things were really buzzing. Ben Benson and his concert party co-organiser, Paddy Ryan, had landed a week's engagement at the local music hall/cinema to entertain the sailors, the expatriates and the local population, who were still in awe of these blue-jacketed overseas personalities. Paddy and Ben also organised a surprise party for a local English widow, Mrs Potts, which culminated in a rehearsal for the concert party and a loud, enjoyable sing-song. Men travelled ashore to Narva and to Petrograd, for everywhere the British expatriates lived there seemed to be an open invitation for the Navy to enjoy a traditional Yuletide. Paddy and Ben had been saving up their daily vodka ration, which was most welcome at many of the British houses they visited. The vodka was often repaid with whisky and gin – which came in handy for one of Ben and Paddy's concert performances. They did their act inside a huge abandoned gasometer, and as Ben reported, 'Singing in this kind of hall was the most difficult I have ever experienced owing to the terrible reverberation – microphones were unknown at that time!' Francis Cromie, although not a drinker or a smoker, was still a talented and convivial presence at any party. His singing voice was well regarded, he had a neat line in monologues, and he was not afraid to try his hand at the piano.

But as the jollity of the festive season drew to a close, the hard-pressed commander's future was already in the hands of a man living many hundreds of miles away in Zurich, Switzerland. In cramped rooms above a cobbler's shop run by Titus Kammerer at No. 12, Speigelgasse,[9] an intense, bearded intellectual pored over books and manuscripts as he completed yet another political tract, this one entitled *Imperialism, The Highest Stage of Capitalism*, whilst his wife combed the busy shops and market nearby looking for cheap cuts of meat. By the spring of 1917, he would be back in his native Russia, and before long he would face Francis Cromie across his new desk in Petrograd.

Vladimir Ilyich Lenin was coming home.

CHAPTER 12

BITTER WINTER
– SAVAGE SPRING

The dictatorship of the proletariat is a persistent struggle –
bloody and bloodless, violent and peaceful, military and
economic, educational and administrative – against the forces
and traditions of the old society.

The force of habit of millions and tens of millions is a most
terrible force.

V.I. Lenin, *Left Wing Communism*

On sunny days the ice in the Baltic can offer a shimmering vista of beauty which
stretches to a blue-white horizon where it blends with the pale, anaemic winter
sky. A frozen sea defies the imagination. What was once a churning, steel-grey
surface, pushed around by violent winds beneath glowering clouds, a noisy,
living thing, becomes a flat and silent expanse, a temporary continent upon which
lonely gulls plod around, displaying their frustration. Occasionally, where the ice
is thin enough and some commerce needs to pass, an icebreaker will disturb this
pristine silence as it chugs, grinds and cuts a path through the floes. To be on
board a ship passing through an ice field is a lumbering, banging, noisy experience which many sailors confined to more temperate waters may never have to
undergo. But when the sun is not in the sky, and the dirty, low clouds of mid-
winter press down, one is reminded that this is nature's triumph over mere men.
You may call yourself sailors and navigators, but you shall not pass. The lati-
tude and longitude of your chosen location, and the depth of the snowy season,
have combined to deny you your trade. You will stay put until Poseidon decides
the thaw. Meanwhile, on masts and spars, guns and periscopes, the biting frost
and flying snow builds layer upon layer of brittle triumph.

The winter of 1916/17 was a nasty one in many ways, not only in Russia. With
the onset of the ice Cromie's crews had been fully occupied in keeping it from
totally engulfing the boats in the harbour. Using a combination of chipping
hammers and steam, it was all they could do even to keep the recognisable shapes
of their boats visible. It was hard, relentless work, and combined with the engineering challenges of maintaining the boats' mechanical efficiency, ready for
future patrols, it must have seemed a frustrating and futile absorption of time
whilst, hundreds of miles away, winter or no winter, their trench-bound com-
patriots continued to lob shells at the enemy.

December 1916 had been an eventful month. There were changes afoot in the flotilla. On Boxing Day Commander Goodhart (*E8*) and Lieutenants Thorburn RNR, (*E1*) Peirson (*E9*) and Mee RNR (*E19*) left for home. Mee's departure, for reasons which are unclear, would have been welcomed by Cromie. Perhaps it was his ex-Merchant Navy, Royal Navy Reserve status which rankled, although the departing Thorburn was also a reservist, but curiously, Cromie had written to Commodore Hall on 17 October: 'I asked you to change Mee, RNR, *E19*, in whom I have no confidence whatever, although I can bring no definite faults against him.' Sadly, Mee, who had been in the Baltic from the start of the campaign in October 1914, was soon to lose his life in action on board the Q-ship *Willow Branch*.

The continuing popularity of the Royal Navy was well demonstrated when the four officers left Reval. The admiral's band turned out, along with a large crowd of both Russian and expatriate friends, and the British sailors carried the departing officers shoulder-high to the railway station. There was vodka, singing, cheering and jollity, and Ben Benson, as usual, plucked away on his mandolin. Since Horton's colourful departure, this method of saying goodbye to the Baltic had almost become a tradition. Their journey home during that cold winter took them by train through Finland, across Sweden and Norway and then by ship from Bergen to Newcastle.

Poor Goodhart's exit from the Baltic was also to end in tragedy less than a month later. He had been given the command of a new submarine, *K14*, built by Fairfields on the Clyde. Disaster struck on 29 January 1917 when Goodhart joined his good friend Commander Godfrey Herbert to gain some experience in the trials of Herbert's new boat, *K13*. After leaving Govan they sailed into Gareloch. During her final dive the boiler room flooded and she sank stern-first. Goodhart volunteered to attempt an escape through the conning tower. Although Herbert made it, shooting to the surface in a bubble of air, Goodhart hit his head on an obstruction and drowned. He was awarded a posthumous Albert Medal. Such occurrences amply demonstrated that, even when not engaged in action, the submarine life was still a very risky one indeed.

The late arrival of the C boats, the badly damaged batteries and the curtailment of patrols owing to the weather was a cause for great concern. When the Baltic submarines were operational, the men, both Russian and British, were fully occupied. It was a sailor's job to be at sea. To be trapped like this in rigid ice on board an old warship shared with an increasingly disgruntled indigenous crew was a strain Cromie could well do without. As more news came from ashore about food shortages, demonstrations in Petrograd and more casualties at the front, the tense atmosphere in the Russian mess room increased.

There had been a few bouts of illness in the flotilla besides the mumps and a death through kidney disease; as Staff Surgeon Kenneth J. Hole arrived in Reval in late 1916, he found one man recovering in Petrograd from scarlet fever and another recovering from sickness on board the *Dvina*. Until Surgeon Hole's arrival, both the Russian and British sailors had been cared for by the *Dvina*'s Russian Medical Officer, Dr Gomziakoff. Described by Surgeon Hole as 'a staunch patriot and an Imperialist',[1] he had become prey to the first signs of revolutionary fervour among the Russian sailors. Such was their intransigence towards the medic that Surgeon Hole offered to take over the running of the complete sickbay on board the *Dvina*. This was an early symptom for Cromie of the mutinous times which lay ahead. He had cause for concern from home, too. He had received news that, on 28 November, the Germans had sent a plane to bomb London. Six bombs were dropped on Kensington – thankfully some distance from his home in South Molton Street W1, and no one was killed, but it was close enough to worry him. News had also come through of the casualties on the Somme – 600,000 Allied dead and 500,000 Germans, all for the sake of 125 square miles (325 sq km) gained by the Allies.

In December the hapless Romanians had counter-attacked on the Arges river, but were defeated by the Germans at the Battle of Argesil. The following day, 6 December, Bucharest was in German hands. At home Lloyd George replaced Asquith as Prime Minister, and on 12 December the German Government asked the USA to announce to the Allies that it was ready to negotiate peace terms. On 30 December, the German proposals, put forward to the Allies by President Wilson, were rejected.

January 1917 was also an important month for submarine warfare. With the rejection by the Allies of her peace proposals, Germany had to come up with some way of keeping the Americans out of the war. On 9 January, at Pless Castle, Germany's leading military leaders, General Field Marshals Benckendorff and Hindenburg and Dr Bethmann-Hollweg, the Imperial Chancellor, met with Lieutenant-General Ludendorff to discuss the policy of unrestricted U-boat warfare.[2] This was to be a breach of the international maritime law Francis Cromie had been diligently following, which required him to surface, warn merchant vessels and ensure the safe removal and passage of their crews. But it was not something the Germans were afraid of, as the fate of the *Lusitania* had proved on 7 May 1915. The idea of sinking all enemy shipping by torpedo or gunfire without warning was proposed by Admiral Henning von Holtzendorff, Chief of the German Naval Staff. He had estimated that the monthly destruction of 600,000 tons of Allied shipping (mainly British) could bring Britain to her knees in just five months.[3] As Hindenburg pointed out at the conference, 'We would reproach ourselves later if we let the opportunity pass by.' By the spring of 1917, Germany's 100 active U-boats were ready to put this policy into action.

During 1916 the Russian secret police, the Okhrana, had tightened the net around any organised revolutionary party. Any leaders of significance, such as Lenin, were either in Siberia or in exile, as far away from influence as they could be. Leon Trotsky, who was to play an important part in the fortunes of Francis Cromie, was being pushed from pillar to post, first ejected from France to Spain, then on to New York, eventually ending up in a concentration camp in Halifax, Nova Scotia, before finally making his way back to Russia.

It is worth pausing here to inspect Trotsky's slight brushes with both the Russian and British navies prior to his rise to eminence in Petrograd. This was the man, who, as the negotiator of the Treaty of Brest-Litovsk and Commissar of War would eventually sit at the same table as Francis Cromie and Robert

Bruce Lockhart to discuss the fate of the Baltic Fleet. It is a sign of his revolutionary influence, and the fear he engendered in the corridors of the Okhrana, even whilst being shunted around Europe and America, and as the Russian Army were enjoying success under Brusilov in Galicia, that he was as great a *bête noire* in Tsarist circles as his soon-to-be comrade above the cobbler's shop in Zurich.

Whilst editing the Russian revolutionary paper *Nashe Slovo* in his Parisian exile, Trotsky's articles had to pass through the military censor, M. Chasles. Considering that France was one of Russia's allies in the war, it struck Trotsky as odd that although his own articles in *Nashe Slovo* were heavily censored so as not to offend the Russian Embassy, the outpourings of the right-wing Russian military press, which on occasion were extremely disrespectful of their ally, were disregarded. As yet another of his articles vanished under the French censor's pencil, Trotsky recalled:

> At that very time the official organ of the St Petersburg Navy Department was publishing uncommonly insolent articles aimed at the French Republic, sneering at the parliament and its 'sorry little tsars', the deputies. With a copy of the St Petersburg journal in my hand I went to the censor's office for an explanation.

At the French War Ministry Trotsky was met by 'a grey-haired diplomat'. Armed with the Russian navy articles to compare against his own, deleted work, he asked the diplomat what was going on. He was told that the *Nashe Slovo* articles were displeasing to the Russian Embassy. Trotsky reports the ensuing conversation:

> 'But it is precisely to displease them that we write them.'
> The diplomat smiled condescendingly at this answer, as if it were a charming joke. 'We are at war. We depend on our allies.'
> 'Do you mean to say that the internal affairs of France are controlled by the Tsar's diplomacy? Didn't your ancestors make a mistake in chopping off Louis Capet's head?'
> 'Oh, you exaggerate. And besides, please don't forget; we are at war.'[4]

The fact that the Russian navy in far-away Petrograd could take time out to take a side-swipe at the political system of one of its allies demonstrates yet again the hubris of political thought in Romanov circles. Because of Brusilov's sudden rush of brilliance in Galicia, they thought they could display their arrogance in a republic – the very thing they dreaded becoming. And, of course, anyone in the navy reading this material would be reminded of the fact that sailors had been prominent in the 1905 uprising – so take care, the admirals have their eye on things.

Trotsky then had a brief introduction to the British Navy, this time on board a Norwegian ship, the *Christianiafjord*, which he hoped was finally taking him back to revolutionary Russia, only to be stopped *en route* from New York at Halifax, Nova Scotia.

On 3 April [1917] British officers, accompanied by bluejackets, came aboard the *Christianiafjord* and demanded, in the name of the local admiral, that I, my family and five other passengers leave the boat. We were assured that the whole incident would be cleared up in Halifax. We declared that the order was illegal and refused to obey, whereupon armed blue-jackets pounced on us, and amid shouts of 'shame' from a large part of the passengers, carried us bodily to a naval cutter, which delivered us in Halifax under the convoy of a cruiser. While a group of sailors was holding me fast, my older boy ran to help me and struck an officer with his little fist. 'Shall I hit him again, papa?' he shouted. He was eleven then, and it was his first lesson in British democracy.[5]

Trotsky was to spend over a month in a concentration camp before finally leaving for Petrograd, where he arrived with his family on 17 May. The British policeman, Machen, who had instigated his removal by the Royal Navy from the *Christianiafjord* and his arrest and imprisonment, saw the family off from the quay in Halifax. Trotsky was angry, and informed Machen that once he got back to Russia and joined the Constituent Assembly, he would make it his business to bring up the subject of the outrageous treatment of Russian citizens. Machen was unrepentant. 'I hope,' he said, 'that you will never get into the Constituent Assembly.'

In Petrograd, the movements of Lenin's emissaries, well disguised though they were, were carefully mapped. Anyone with a connection to a revolutionary party was in danger of arrest. Yet this carefully orchestrated control had been weakened on more than one occasion by Rasputin's relentless influence on the Empress. Through this influence the Okhrana had been put under the tutelage of Alexander Protopopov, a man whose sanity frequently hovered beneath a question mark. It was unnerving for his tried and trusted agents when they discovered that, during meetings, he would hold much of his conversation with an icon on his desk, to which he referred for help and advice. Even Nicholas himself, despite his autocratic presence, was not informed when the Empress, again on Rasputin's advice, had appointed this same rumoured syphilitic lunatic to oversee the country's food distribution. Nicholas wrote to his wife, 'Our friend's ideas about men are sometimes queer, as you know – so one must be careful especially in nominations of high people.'[6]

Thus the Okhrana's grim reputation was further sullied. Protopopov's administration of food supplies was generally seen as a complementary adjunct to his job as secret police chief – food could be a powerful political weapon. If he held food back, riots would ensue. If riots took place, he could instigate repression on a grand scale. Repression drew revolutionaries into the net. To the nation's growing army of dissidents, all this made a warped kind of sense.

Despite the crocodile tears of the Romanovs and their fawning ministers for the 'great Russian people', the only workable social and economic organisations in the country had been constructed and were run, not by the government's ministers, but by voluntary officials in organisations such as the Union of Towns, which tackled national disease epidemics and dealt with the growing problem of resettling refugees. In the countryside the country councils, or *zemstvos*, were run by liberal landowners to oversee some kind of social service and basic education amongst the peasantry. Their central committee comprised sixteen town mayors, twelve scientists, six engineers and eight doctors. It was the *zemstvos* which were eventually lumbered with the huge task of clothing and feeding the vast Russian army.[7] The government's social inertia was demonstrated following the first German gas attack in the war during May 1915. It was down to the Union of *Zemstvos* to organise the manufacture of gas masks for the army whilst the government offered little but patriotic hot air.[8]

As early as October 1916, the *zemstvos* issued a barbed warning to the government. Although they did not mention the cunning Alexander Protopopov by name, it was clear that he was the target. The warning was blunt and to the point: 'Power should not remain in the hands of those who are unable to resist secret influence and cannot organise the resources of the country.'[9] Protopopov's response was to instruct the Okhrana to pursue the members of the committee, and to ban the union's meetings. This act of gross stupidity could only stoke the fires of revolt. If it was intended to help the war effort, it did anything but, and simply furthered the rumour that the Okhrana chief was nothing less than a closet agent for the Kaiser. With such haphazard political blundering in full sway, spontaneous revolt was assured, no matter how many revolutionaries were exiled.

As the Russian sailors on board the *Dvina* became more familiar with their British counterparts, the obvious differences between the way their country was run in comparison to Britain only served to highlight their growing grievances. Francis Cromie had his ear to the ground. During the months when the boats could not put to sea, he had regularly travelled ashore and, at the British Embassy on the Palace Quay in Petrograd, began to absorb some of the many intelligence reports which were flooding into the building. They began to form a disturbing picture. Already there had been a serious incident in Petrograd at the French-owned Renault works. Four of the foremen had been murdered in the factory by an invading crowd of Russian workers who had risen up under the clarion call of 'No More War!' Increasing prices for what goods and food-stuffs could still be bought had driven other crowds to march through the streets, their red banners fluttering in the frosty wind as they sang the '*Marseillaise*' at the tops of their voices. At the Finland Station troops from the 181st Infantry Division were ordered to disperse such a demonstration, but joined it instead, taking aim at the police. There was some consternation over all this at the British Embassy by November 1916, and as Cromie headed back from Petrograd to face the winter in Reval, he began to wonder how he could keep his flotilla running if the situation became worse. Nearly eighty factories in Petrograd alone had closed their doors as the workers struck in support of the army's demoralised soldiers. Cromie knew that the navy would be next – and he also knew that his prime task was to prevent this rebellion from infecting his own crews.

On 11 March, as shortages of fuel and raw materials brought Petrograd to its knees and bread riots raged, the Chairman of the State Duma, Mikhail

Rodzianko, a staunch monarchist, had been forced to bite the toughest bullet of his career by sending a telegram to his beloved Emperor:

> Most humbly I report to Your Majesty . . . The Government is completely paralysed, and totally incapable of restoring order where it has broken down. Your Majesty, save Russia, humiliation and disgrace threaten. The war cannot be brought to a victorious end in such circumstances, as the ferment has already affected the army and threatens to spread, unless the authorities put a decisive end to the anarchy and disorder. Your Majesty, without delay summon a person who the whole country trusts, and charge him with forming a government, in which the whole population can have confidence. Such a government will command the support of the whole of Russia, which will once more regain confidence in itself and its leaders. In this hour, unprecedented in its terror and the horror of its consequences, there is no other way out and there can be no delay.[10]

Rodzianko and the Duma waited. There was no reply.

CHAPTER 13

THE STORM BREAKS

Never have I seen men trying so hard to understand, to decide.
They never moved, stood staring with a sort of terrible intent-
ness at the speaker, their brows wrinkled with the effort of
thought, sweat standing out on their foreheads; great giants of
men with the innocent clear eyes of children and the faces of epic
warriors.

John Reed, *Ten Days That Shook the World*

The strain of running the flotilla against the growing threat of a full-blown
Russian mutiny was taking its toll on Cromie. He knew that soon, with the thaw,
he could take the boats out to sea again and hopefully relieve some of the pressure from the mess decks. In Reval he was kept busy, not only with the running
of the flotilla, but with much clandestine work ashore. During his short time in
Russia, he had formed many friendships amongst both the British expatriates
and a number of influential Russians. News of his deft handling of the confla-
grations with the increasingly awkward Russian sailors soon spread, and his
position as an unassailable force for fairness, combined with his prestige as a
commanding officer of the Royal Navy, made him a magnet for every worried
Russian who entered his growing circle of friends. It will perhaps never be known
how many men and women he managed to steer from the more vindictive
sections of the rebellion, but he had, in his own words, become 'a kind of Scarlet
Pimpernel'.

But he was exhausted. By mid-March he made a firm decision that a week's
leave at Petrograd's Astoria Hotel would give him a much-needed rest. He could
not have chosen a worse time. The few skirmishes in Reval would be nothing
compared with what was about to happen.

Travelling with Meriel Buchanan, the daughter of the British Ambassador
in Petrograd, who had been staying with friends in Reval, Cromie arrived in
Petrograd on 13 March. He was met at the station by the British Military
Attaché, Colonel Knox, who briefed him on the disturbances, which at the time
Knox considered to be 'quite minor affairs'.

Also enjoying a couple of days' leave in the city was a seaman torpedoman
from HMS *E8*, John Eastman, who had the distinction of being the rating who
had pressed the button which sent a torpedo on its course to destroy the German
cruiser *Prinz Adalbert*. Many years later, as a lieutenant-commander, Eastman
tragically lost his eyesight whilst languishing in a Japanese prisoner-of-war camp

in the Second World War. He eventually moved to Australia, and in the 1950s, on Australian radio, he recalled that day in Petrograd.[1]

> We were on leave in Petrograd on that day, and went into the Opera House. It was nice and peaceful when we went in; there was no sign of anything happening. But when we came out later on, we were amazed to find hundreds of thousands of people, all swarming down the Nevsky Prospekt, shouting, screaming as the Cossacks on their horses charged them, using whips. These people were making for the other side of the city, trying to keep out of the way, but heading also for the gates of the Palace, shouting 'Down with the Tsar!' It all came as quite a surprise for us. We escaped around the back streets and eventually found a policeman, and asked him what was going on. He told us that the people had revolted. There were plenty of bodies laying about – whether they were all dead or not was hard to say. We made our way from there to the British Embassy. There, they told us that we should make our way back to our base at Reval as soon as possible, as the country was 'in revolution'. Although we had travel permits, we couldn't get any trains, everything was in confusion at the station. So we had to return to the Embassy for a couple of days. When we finally got back to Reval, everyone on board the *Dvina* was quite surprised to hear what had been happening in Petrograd. Eventually, on the 17th, it came to us, and we were sent ashore, unarmed, to attempt to remonstrate with the crowd, who had attacked the prison. Eventually they all went to the town square and we all went back to the ship. Everything soon became completely disorganised. There were no public services. We couldn't get burials carried out, the place became littered with filth and rubbish, nothing worked – you just couldn't get anything done. The day the revolution broke out the people broke into the vodka factory and just got drunk. Our own sympathies? Well, we did feel that the peasants had a very poor deal. They weren't allowed to walk on the same pavement as the middle, upper or officer classes. They weren't allowed to go into a restaurant if these classes were in there, and in a theatre they were only allowed into a certain part and had to stand during the interval . . .

As John Eastman and his shipmates were dashing around to the British Embassy for cover, Cromie was arriving in Petrograd for his leave at the Astoria Hotel. A few days later, his leave abandoned, he arrived back at Reval, where he outlined the events in this letter to Commodore Hall:[2]

> We have been through some stirring times lately, and have so far managed to scrape through some very delicate situations without coming to harm. I had just arrived in Petrograd for a week's leave when this revolution started, and saw the worst of it. Foreign officers, especially the English, were at all times civilly treated, and the good nature of the people was marvellous. Of course, one had to walk to get anywhere, but with care one could avoid most of the firing, although it was often necessary to stand in a doorway for a quarter of an hour or so. The whole show started with

bread riots and rather hasty use of the military. Eventually the regiments went over to the people one by one – this led to some very bloody battles between the troops. They made the usual error of opening all the prisons and then burning them, and the Palace of Justice. This of course started the hooligans, who really did the most damage. All officers were disarmed, and those who refused to surrender were killed. During the night I saw many soldiers giving their rifles to the people which added to the gaiety of things. About 1 a.m. the officers' hotel was raided by a furious mob. All the foreign officers, headed by General Poole, collected in the hall, and sent the Russians upstairs and then waited quietly for the mob. They came in brandishing all sorts of weapons, but were quite put off by being met by perfectly calm unarmed foreigners. They were so surprised that they listened to reason, and we all went up about ten miles in the estimation of officers and mob. They insisted on searching one or two rooms then went away. All the ladies present threw themselves on the protection of the English officers. Early in the morning some ass opened fire on the crowd from the roof of the hotel, and in about two shakes they were inside, smashing and firing at everything. Some heroic but foolish Russian officers rushed down and opened fire on the crowd which did not improve matters, and an old general was killed and a lady wounded. Another general was saved by an English officer jerking aside the hooligan's rifle. It was only on the English undertaking that no more firing should take place that they cleared out. A certain amount of looting took place, but the rebel sailors took charge and guarded the place very efficiently. Fortunately, we persuaded them to destroy some 3,000 bottles of wine, but not without some getting drunk.

Cromie also wrote a similar, undated, letter, a private account, to Admiral Phillimore, who by now had returned to England. Although it covers much of the same ground, there are little flourishes which expose the more flamboyant aspects of his character. For instance, after he and the other officers had succeeded in saving the day, he commented: 'Ladies were seven deep around each Englishman, clamouring for protection. Neither Gilbert nor Sullivan dreamed of such situations.'

Cromie could do without vodka or cigars, but as will be seen, the evidence suggests that one luxury he certainly relished was being surrounded by women. By the time the revolution broke out, he had achieved the status of a heart-throb amongst the titled ladies of Reval, and his popularity was soon to bring similar rewards in Petrograd. He was already enjoying the company both in Reval and Petrograd of the twenty-five-year-old Marie Benckendorff, who eventually became the Baroness Budberg. Known to her friends as 'Moura', although she was charismatic and attractive, she was in many ways a mysterious and, by all accounts, a somewhat dangerous woman.

She was born Maria Ignatievna Zakrevskaia in 1893.[3] Her father, Ignatii P. Kakrevskii, was a member of the Ukranian landed nobility. She claimed to have been educated in England, but there is no evidence of this, although she did speak good English. In 1911 she married Ioann (Dzhon) von Benckendorff, who was

Cromie enjoys a sleigh ride with Baroness Budberg (left) and Baroness Schilling (right). *(RN Submarine Museum, Gosport)*

descended from an old-established family of Baltic Germans. As a member of the Russian diplomatic service, at the outbreak of the First World War he held the post of Second Secretary at the Russian Embassy in Berlin. He was eventually murdered by rampaging peasants on his Estonian estate in 1921. Moura then married Baron Budberg, but was divorced after a year.

She appears to have been a woman who kept her options open. She eventually found work at the British Embassy in Petrograd as a translator, where she was close to K.I. Chukovskii, who acted as personal translator to Colonel Thornhill of Military Intelligence. This was an advantage upon which she kept a firm grip. Chukovskii was a personal friend of the writer Maxim Gorky, and Moura soon had her sensuous way with the author, who in turn introduced her into the tangled web of the revolutionary movement.

Moura aimed high in her amorous affairs. In later life she became involved with the great film producer Alexander Korda, and H.G. Wells succumbed to her wiles and completed his autobiography while staying on the Budberg estate in the early 1920s.

In 1917 Cromie appears to have been seeing quite a lot of Moura. How intense this relationship was is unclear, but as Robert Bruce Lockhart, Lloyd George's unofficial envoy to the Bolsheviks amply demonstrates in his memoirs, being married in England did not seem to stand in the way of having a full-tilt affair in Russia. Lockhart had already been hauled over the diplomatic coals for one affair. He described Moura, and his first meeting with her in February 1918:[4]

A Russian of the Russians, she had a lofty disregard for all the pettiness of life and a courage which was proof against all cowardice. Her vitality, due perhaps to an iron constitution, was immense and invigorated everyone with whom she came into contact. Where she loved, there was her world, and her philosophy of life had made her mistress of all the consequences. She was an aristocrat. She could have been a communist. She could never have been a bourgeoise. Later, her name was to become linked with mine in the final drama of my Russian career.

Cromie, our Naval Attaché, was another of her friends, and on his birthday Moura gave a little luncheon party to which we all came. It was during Maslennitsa or Butter Week, and we ate innumerable *bliny* (pancakes and caviare) and drank vodka. I wrote a doggerel verse for each guest, and Cromie made one of his witty speeches. We toasted our hostess and laughed immoderately. For all of us it was almost the last care-free hour we were to spend in Russia.

Lockhart may well have been jealous of Cromie's closeness to Moura, but she probably saw him as a few steps up the information ladder to her handsome captain. Within weeks of the birthday party she and Lockhart were beginning a passionate affair, which probably would not have bothered Francis, as he already had another of his romantic irons in the fire. Subsequent revelations reveal, however, that he should have been a little more cautious about Moura. Such was the duplicitous nature of the diplomatic and intelligence community in which he had been installed, he could hardly have imagined that he was being used. Moura admitted in a letter to Lockhart in July 1918 that her relationship with Cromie consisted of her 'pumping' him for gossip and information and any other titbits around the Embassy.[5] This she was giving to Lockhart – but she was also very close to those supporting the Bolsheviks.

Judging by Cromie's status amongst the Russian sailors at that time, it can be assumed that he was being somewhat modest in his letter concerning the destruction of the wine in the Astoria's cellars. As a teetotaller, it would have been natural for him to persuade the sailors to destroy so much valuable alcohol, but it was also a minor tragedy for the Assistant British Naval Attaché, another Astoria resident, Commander Eady RNVR, who had his new case of whisky smashed. The Astoria Hotel was a well-known watering hole and sanctuary for the foreign military in Petrograd. For Russian ratings, experiencing their first taste of liberation, smashing bottles of what were undoubtedly fine vintages would have been a heartbreaking task in the heat of revolution, yet one which could only have been organised by a man whose air of command left them in no doubt. With many of their fellow Russian officers now disarmed and marched off by their captors into the night to face an unknown, doubtless deadly fate, those remaining in the hotel had much to thank Cromie for.

The following day, after a restless night during which the uprising continued to gain momentum, Cromie decided that a 'holiday' in Petrograd was out of the question – the fate of the flotilla back in Reval lay heavy on his mind. With the city now locked in clashes between opposing factions, he set off with another naval attaché, Commodore Kemp, in an attempt to find some transport back to Reval. His first port of call was the British Embassy, to receive an update on the situation. But getting there was to be a challenge. Together they ran from doorway to doorway, braving the crossfire of various machine-gun posts, and as they passed around the corner of the Nevsky Prospekt to cross the Admiralteyskiy Prospekt on their way towards the Neva Embankment, the two men had to take cover for several minutes as the bullets ricocheted all around them. Counting their blessings, they eventually stumbled through the plate-glass doors into the safety of the embassy on the Palace Quay, just beyond the Troitskiy Bridge, a main artery across the river between the city and the Peter and Paul Fortress.

Here the Ambassador, Sir George Buchanan, informed Cromie that the Tsar had appointed his own 'dictator'. It seemed as if what had been referred to by the embassy as 'quite minor affairs' would soon be dealt with. On 12 March, just as Cromie had been departing for his attempted leave, a Provisional Committee of the Duma had been formed in an effort to take control of the capital.

Upon discovering that his forces had lost their authority in Petrograd, Nicholas had commanded General N.I. Ivanov to select a special force of men from front-line units, with orders to march on Petrograd and restore the government's authority. Satisfied that he had put the wheels of authority in motion, the Tsar decided to return to the comfort of his palace at Tsarskoe Selo, but found the route of his train was blocked. He was then diverted to Pskov, over 100 miles (160 km) south of Petrograd, the headquarters of the northern front. He arrived there on the evening of 14 March.[6]

But the unquestioning loyalty, fear and respect which had kept the Romanovs on their thrones for so long was beginning to crack. The Palace Commandant, Voeykov, accompanying the Emperor, was met by the commander of the northern front, General Ruzsky. But this was no 'hail fellow, well met' encounter. Ruzsky was angry. He eyed Voeykov with some contempt. 'Look what you have done . . . all your Rasputin clique – what have you got Russia into now?' Ruzsky seemed far more aware of the depth of trouble the regime was in than those in the Tsar's entourage. He had maintained contact with the Duma president, Rodzianko, the very man who had sent anguished telegrams to his beloved Emperor, the man who knew that General Ivanov's impending arrival was but a finger in the dyke of revolt which had already burst its banks.

That grim evening Ruzsky attempted to convince Nicholas that only radical concessions to establishing parliamentary rule could save the day. But try as he might, Nicholas could not comprehend the essence of Ruzsky's statement – that 'the monarch reigns but the government rules'. Nicholas's stubborn, obsolete view that it was he who was responsible 'before God and Russia' for the country's fate, and that he could never place his trust in the State Council of the Duma, was to have deadly consequences.

Cromie left the embassy in an attempt to discover how many other officers had survived the night. Somehow he needed to find transport back to Reval before this tide of madness engulfed the flotilla. He arrived at the Hotel de France and there met a group of Russian officers. They outlined a wild plan to seize a loco-motive and drive it down to Reval. But he knew this was a hopeless scheme, and one which could lead to tragedy. As he commented in his letter, 'They were quite mad.' There was, however, news of a train which was due to leave Petrograd for Reval later that day. To get to the station required a dangerous journey of 2 miles (3 km) on foot, through what was now virtually a war zone. He had met up with another British officer named Helmsley, who had set out some days earlier in the vain hope of returning to England, but at the Finland Station, from where he was due to depart, a furious gun battle was in progress. In the confusion he had lost all his luggage. His only hope now was to stick with Cromie, who had, in the meantime, teamed up with a pretty young woman whom he referred to as 'a plucky little lady', the Baroness Schilling. She was an attractive war widow in her early twenties (the Baron Schilling had died early in the war) and was to become a friend to many among the Allied command. Like many of the titled families, the Schillings had residences in various locations, and her house in Reval had, according to Ben Benson, 'become a "home from home"' for many Royal Navy officers. Completing this fleeing quartet was Count Keller, who commanded a Russian submarine division.

Together the four set off through the bullet-sprayed streets, carrying what luggage they had, diving into doorways, hiding in alleys. As they entered Teatralnaya Ploschad, Cromie spotted three Maxim machine-guns mounted on the roof of the Mariinskiy Theatre. Here, in the preceding months, he had been fêted as a gallant ally and experienced the wonders of the Imperial Ballet in the lissome form of Petrograd's prima ballerina, Techechinskaia. But today the glorious interior of the Mariinskiy was not echoing to the thrilling operatic voice of Fyodor Chalyapin, but the incessant chatter of deadly gunfire. They had similar narrow escapes, crossing bridges on the Ekaterinski Canal, ducking the bullets as they hit the stone parapets. For several anguished minutes, as they dashed onwards from doorway to doorway, death was a strong possibility. Helmsley was keen to turn back for the safety of the hotel, but the Baroness was determined to carry on; it would be just as dangerous now to retrace their steps. Eventually, after many narrow escapes, they arrived at the crowded station, where hundreds of sailors were now arriving from their base at Kronstadt to join their new comrades in the uprising. To Cromie's relief, he and his party were shown respect, and remained safe despite the gun battles raging around the station. As usual, he used his forceful charm and authority, and with the help and assistance of the Russian sailors, the party finally boarded the one train leaving for Reval. It had been a close-run thing.

Back at Reval Cromie and the Baroness parted and he headed back to the harbour as fast as he could. To his relief he discovered that the situation on board the *Dvina* was relatively normal. Ben Benson recalled his captain's return:[7]

The first thing he asked me was if I would make him an omelette. That was one of his particular pet things. He could not stand the Russian food and would send for me and say 'For God's sake make me an omelette!' Later, he said to me, 'Pick out another couple of the boat's crew and the three of you follow me when I go ashore. Follow me at a safe distance.' He gave me an address to go to and it turned out to be this Baroness's home. It was a very big house and when we went in his card was on the front door as a kind of safeguard, I believe, against muggers or something. Anyway we arrived and we were met by him and her and shown into a small room off the hall. It contained a single bed, a table and chairs with English papers and cigarettes. There were two dear old souls of servants and they supplied us with coffee and cigarettes. With there being the three of us Cromie said 'Make arrangements among yourselves, I don't mind as long as one of you stays awake all night. We may even find a bed for one of you. I'll leave it to you.'

We tossed for it and I won the toss. I was the odd man out, whether I was lucky or unlucky depends on which way you look at it, anyway, I got a bed for the night. One of these dear old ladies took me upstairs. There were a great number of rooms in the house, and she showed me to a room with a double bed and a bathroom off it. The room had a lot of furniture in it. Being curious I had a look around the wardrobes and they were full of fancy dresses. I imagine they used to have dances in the house at one time or another. When I turned down the bedclothes, I discovered the sheets were black silk. I've never had a more comfortable night's sleep in all my life. In the morning one of the dear old souls brought me up a cup of tea and ran me a bath. I eventually joined the boys and we went back on board again. We only did that for the one night . . .

Ben often accompanied Cromie on his jaunts ashore, and through his memoirs a colourful picture of the captain materialises as an alternative to the disciplined commander and bold mediator. Benson recalled attending a party at the home of an Anglo-Danish couple in Reval. He remembered Cromie to be 'quite a singer at that little do – the song he sang was "Drake's Drum".'

Although there is no suggestion of any impropriety, we can only speculate on what Cromie's sleeping arrangements were at the Schilling residence. No doubt, after their dangerous liaison in Petrograd and the fraught journey back to Reval, the prospect for Cromie of spending a comfortable interlude ashore in the house of an attractive young widow held far more promise than a mug of cocoa and an early 'lights out' on board the old *Dvina*. This choice of a night with the Baroness would seem to hint at Cromie's increasing 'live for the day' pragmatism. His timing was as good as ever, because the ensuing few hours of peace were to be the last on board the old warship.

The time was approaching when he must speak to the men, and not just about war, submarines, torpedoes and all the other minutiae which occupied the overstretched mind of a flotilla commander. This time, somehow, he had to pick his way through the semantics of revolution. Being a skilled submariner he always knew the right moment to take aim. The day he chose, 15 March, was a packed, perplexing day for everyone in the British contingent, and a momentous cross-

142

roads in Russia's history. In the messes on board the *Dvina* the sailors were finishing off their midday meal. It was noted that some of the Russian ratings were missing. Ben Benson and some of his colleagues went up on deck to enjoy a smoke, and noticed that something big was happening across Reval's frozen harbour. There, moored in the ice, were two of the Russian navy's warships. One was the 15,000 ton *Rurik*, the other one of the stars of the forthcoming revolution, the *Aurora*. Suddenly the noise of music struck through the cold air. A brass band appeared on the dockside, and the familiar strains of the 'Marseillaise' drifted across the ice. The curious British sailors looked on as, behind the band, marching in ordered ranks, there appeared a large party of Russian sailors. Since the 'Marseillaise' was banned, Cromie knew that the troubles of Petrograd had arrived in Reval. He immediately ordered the clearing of the lower deck, and had the men muster. It was time to talk diplomacy. 'You will take no sides. Agree to everything and everybody without too much enthusiasm – or criticism. Keep your heads and your tempers no matter what the provocation, and report anything worth reporting to myself or any other officer.'[8]

Ashore, as Cromie spoke, more Russian sailors had begun to join the procession. It would not be long before the civil police would take a serious interest. From Ben Benson's description of what happened next, it is easy to see what an unleashing of pent-up rage this first demonstration was:[9]

> The civil police, who were always armed and occasionally trigger-happy, bore us Britishers no goodwill because of the freedom we enjoyed. They were both feared and hated by the Russian rank and file, service and civilian, and were ruthless in all their dealings. Both the chief of the Reval police and his second in command were similar in appearance and very portly. The chief was notorious for his ruthlessness, but his deputy was known to be more humane. When the trouble started, the chief must have had some warning as he cleared off, leaving his second in command to bear the first clash. The crowds made for the town house adjoining the prison and demanded the keys.
>
> When the assistant chief attempted to remonstrate he was at once overpowered. Believing him to be the chief, the rioters killed him out of hand. I heard later that when the leaders of the crowd discovered they had got the wrong man they recompensed his widow.

Now there was no turning back. The following days saw a series of demonstrations, which Cromie had to watch carefully, whilst all the time reminding his men that they should keep a low profile and not become involved under any circumstances. That night he assembled his crews in the mess and asked for eighty volunteers. The men cast worried glances among each other – volunteers for what? Cromie explained that the British Consulate, which was housed in the same block as the police town house headquarters and the prison, was in danger of destruction from the fire the rioters had set in order to release prisoners. This would be a dangerous mission as he insisted that they would go unarmed, apart from fire-fighting equipment. He soon had his volunteers and they collected every bit of fire-fighting kit they could lay hands on: axes, ladders, ropes, buckets and shovels, and demolition charges. The sight of this well-equipped force of bluejackets marching in neat ranks through billowing smoke and the milling, chanting rioters must have taken Cromie back to his days in China in 1900. As they tackled the blaze, preventing it from touching the British Consulate, Cromie noticed the town's records and prison ledgers being heaved onto a bonfire in the prison courtyard. Much of the archives had already been incinerated, yet Cromie knew that this was Russian business and that neutrality must be observed at all costs. The cells had by now been opened up and a bedraggled parade of ill-kempt, bearded, startled inmates shuffled into freedom to welcoming cheers. Although the rioters had released a fair proportion of ordinary thugs and genuine criminals, most of the men who now joined the rebels were political prisoners.

As random rifle fire cracked all around them, and the odd hand grenade exploded here and there, the British sailors concentrated on the task in hand, and eventually had the blaze under control. It was a near thing. Cromie was relieved to find that the Russians had no argument with him or his men, as they simply expressed the aims of their rebellion – to be free, as the British sailors were. Once the mêlée had died down, the volunteers marched back to the *Dvina*. It was a fine occasion, in that old British tradition, for a good cup of tea, and no doubt the odd slug of vodka. But it was not to be the last mercy mission of its kind.

Over the following days, the Russian officers on board began to fear for their lives – with some justification. The first man to feel the revolutionary heat was the *Dvina*'s Russian paymaster, a man called Darmaross.[10] He was a man, said Benson, who 'certainly must have made a pile with his method of catering'. Perhaps this view was formed from the standpoint of Ben's own rank and his sympathy for his Russian comrades, but the Russian sailors throughout the fleet generally regarded paymasters as greedy contributors to their own under-fed misery.

The hirsute paymaster, with his long black beard, was subjected to a 'trial' by the Russian ratings as the British looked on, powerless to intervene. He was stripped, much of his hair removed, his beard shaved off. He was then ignomini-ously marched off the ship to a chorus of loud cat-calls from the ship's company. He was never seen again on board the *Dvina*, but Cromie's influence during his ordeal once more came to the rescue. Facing up to the Sailors' Committee, he told them that he and his men would not stand by and see murder done. The result was that Darmaross's life was saved, and he left the navy with just one month in prison.

During such events, which were to become regular, the Russians respected the British sailors' neutral attitude. But some episodes were too much for Cromie to bear, and whenever the situation demanded, his bold and authoritative procla-mations of naval law or international wartime regulations came to the rescue. Such an occasion came not long after the paymaster's departure.

By this time, after his frequent visits to Mrs Kinna in Reval, Cromie had got to grips with the Russian language and was able to use it to persuasive advan-tage. A young Russian lieutenant, Boris Miller, acting as one of the liaison officers to the British flotilla, one of the less popular among his ratings, had been

144

singled out as a result of accusations from a member of the newly formed Sailors' Committee. He appears to have been equally disliked by the British ratings. Whatever his sins were, they warranted a similar 'trial' to that of the paymaster. During this procedure the Russian sailors, knowing that their British shipmates held similar feelings about Miller, who was of Anglo-Russian stock, asked the bluejackets what *they* would do with the lieutenant. For Cromie, this was a tense moment; the result would test his faith in his own men. They did not let him down. They cast a glance towards their commander, then back to the Russians, and almost in unison, they said, 'We will obey the orders of our captain.' Cromie then explained, in no uncertain terms, to the Sailors' Committee, that Miller was actually serving on secondment to the Royal Navy, and as such was under his control as Commanding Officer of the Baltic Flotilla. Because of this, the lieutenant was under British discipline. If there was a case to answer, claimed Cromie, then it was his job to deal with it.

It was a breathtaking risk and in some ways a bluff, but it worked. The 'court' decided to adjourn to make further deliberations. Emboldened by this success, Cromie decided to take the risk of using this precious breathing space. Together with another threatened Russian officer, Cromie managed to get Miller transferred from the *Dvina* the following day. Ashore and out of harm's way, he was to survive the war and the revolution, and made an appearance in the Second World War as a wing commander with the Royal Australian Air Force. By another twist of fate, he turned up as Churchill's interpreter when the British Premier visited Stalin. He had much to thank Francis Cromie for on that dark day in 1917.

Yet, almost as if the revolutionary bloodlust had to be satisfied, the man who had brought the original accusations against Miller was made to kneel before Cromie and have his nose rubbed on the deck. He was later exiled to Siberia. Tsarist or Bolshevik, old habits, it seemed, died hard.

Each of the British boats had a Russian telegraphist and liaison officer attached. Whatever their individual leanings may have been, under the watchful eye of the Royal Navy in the shape of Francis Cromie, this status was a strong protection against the fury which was about to rage around them. So far a man had lost his hair, his beard and his dignity. Another was in jail, a further on his way to Siberia. But, like the hapless assistant chief of Reval's police, others were about to make the ultimate sacrifice. The last two weeks of March were the opening pages of an unstoppable catalogue of events against which even the undoubted skills of a mediator such as Francis Cromie would mean little.

After receiving his orders to gather his troops and march on Petrograd, General Ivanov, who was now in Mogilev on the river Dnepr, had opened up a dialogue with the Duma using a primitive telegraph apparatus called the Hughes wire. It was a slow, laborious question-and-answer process, and the answers he was receiving did not bode well for his mission to bring the rebel capital back in line. He asked what food supplies were available. The answer came back, 'None.' Were any railway stations or areas of the city secure? None. What about the police force? It had evaporated. To his further dismay, he discovered that the Duma's ministers had all been arrested by the revolutionaries. Ivanov's hope was that the promised 'loyal troops' who would help to sweep away these problems would be waiting for him at Tsarskoe Selo. His train set off from Mogilev, and at Dno, although he spent a day establishing some kind of order, ever the belt-and-braces military man, he had another locomotive coupled to the rear end of the train in case he needed to head south again.

When he eventually arrived at Tsarskoe Selo, his worst fears were realised. The troops he needed for the job were not there. Only the Fifteenth Cavalry Division had set out, but their train had been stopped *en route*. In any case, the revolution had spread like wildfire. Already the Tsar's troops had mutinied. Officers had been murdered and armoured cars and lorries bristling with rebel soldiers, strips of red flags tied to their rifles, were patrolling the streets.

On meeting the Empress, their short conversation only served to convince him that his mission, even if he could assemble enough men, would be doomed to bloody failure. His second locomotive had been a good idea after all, as he boarded his train and headed south again, this time to Vyritsa. The Tsar's proposed 'dictator', as described to Cromie by Sir George Buchanan, would not be arriving in the capital after all.

In Petrograd, the Duma president, Rodzianko, had been forced to brave a deputation from the new Soviet at the Tauride Palace, formed from workers, soldiers and sailors who had joined the revolution. It was the Soviet's intention that no orders issued by the Duma would be carried out if such orders went against the Soviet, and that the Duma would not attempt to bring out the garrison troops against them. Rodzianko, a staunch monarchist, found this 'rabble' totally alien to everything he had stood for, but he had no choice but to parley. His appeal to them to continue to save the land by fighting the enemy, the Germans, at first seemed to go well, but there was a new appetite for politics afoot which was demonstrated by a sharp response from one of the delegates. He told his comrades that what Rodzianko and his ilk were asking them to do was lay down their lives for a land which belonged to princes and barons. The real question was, he said, would Rodzianko be so keen for them to fight on for 'the land' if it belonged to the people?[11]

Back in Reval Francis Cromie knew that whatever burden his administrative problems had imposed during the previous seventeen months they were to be nothing compared to the difficulties he now faced. The news which spread through the horrified mess decks was stark and dramatic. In Kronstadt, the whole fleet had mutinied.

Kronstadt's strategic importance as a naval base, on Kotlin Island in the Gulf of Finland, had been recognised in 1703 when Peter the Great had built the Kroschlot Fort there. Large ships could not pass through the shallow waters north of the island, whilst a sandbank off the Oranienbaum coast meant that vessels had to sail close to the base. Little passed Kronstadt without the Russian navy knowing about it. Peter also built a large shipyard there, and in 1723 a colony began to form around it, which eventually became known as Kronstadt. The base was no newcomer to revolution. In 1825 the Decembrist uprising was led by a Kronstadt officer, Bestushev. Then came the *Naradnaya Volya* (People's Will) movement. This, too, was secretly led by a Kronstadt sailor, Sukhanov. There had been mutinies at the base in 1905 and 1906, but what happened in 1917 finally changed the Russian navy for ever.

All the admirals were murdered, 200 officers were imprisoned and a further 100 killed. The Commander-in-Chief, Admiral Viren, was killed, his body sliced into small portions and thrown onto a fire in the town square. Even his wife and daughter were murdered. Different factions had formed among the sailors, and bloody skirmishes ensued. At Helsinki, where most of the Baltic Fleet's big ships were based, Admiral Nepenin had been shot in the back to be replaced by a man whom Cromie held in contempt, the opportunistic Admiral Maximoff, who had reinvented himself as a Bolshevik, sporting a red tie and rosettes. The crews of the battleships *Imperator Pavel I* and *Andrei Perzovanny* gave vent to their pent-up hatred and slaughtered their officers. Admiral Nebolsine, divisional commander on board the *Andrei Perzovanny*, and his officer of the watch were killed as they walked along the gangway to report to the Fleet flagship.[12]

On 15 March two members of the Duma also visited Reval, where they addressed the sailors after giving a full report of the conflict in Petrograd. The Jack Tars could hardly suppress their amusement as one of the delegates spoke to them about liberty in an ornate form of English, addressing them as the 'Eengleesh Gentelmanly'. It was a well-meant gesture, but Cromie remained unimpressed. The dockside was crowded with striking workers and sailors who surged forward beneath a forest of red flags and banners. Everywhere the strains of the 'Marseillaise' filled the air. To immense cheering the Russian sailors of the *Dvina* marched down the gangway to join the noisy throng. In the town centre Reval's Military Governor, Admiral Gerashimoff, began speaking to the gathered crowds about keeping order in the hope that they would disperse. Brave or foolish – or both – he made the lethal error of mentioning the possibility of troops being summoned to bring the rabble to order. He was taunted by the screaming crowd – 'And where will you call them from?' – after which he received a severe beating.

Remarkably, the mass naval bloodshed of Helsingfors and Kronstadt was somehow kept at bay in Reval whilst Cromie and his men held their breath. He outlined the situation to Commodore Hall:

> Here in Reval there has been only one murder, but discipline has dis-appeared and the ships are run by Committees of sailors. The real Captain of the *Dvina* is now the man who used to get my bath ready every morning. My position has been most difficult, as to submit, as the Russian officers had to, meant to lose all prestige and respect, and any use of force meant probable murder and international complications. I could not prevent them disarming and arresting all Russian officers on board, but I refused to allow the arrest of Russian officers under my discipline. I offered to hold any inquiry they wished into officers' conduct, but they must treat the English Command with respect, which I would enforce if necessary, but provided they respected my rights I was prepared to act as mediator. On

two occasions my men were approached, but they behaved very well. I am sorry to say one or two weak characters were persuaded to express opinion against a certain Russian officer. I was able to gain enough time to get my one unpopular officer moved out of danger, and preserve others from danger. One ship's officer would undoubtedly have been killed but for us. At one time our position was almost impossible, and the Admiral sent me to the Ambassador to fix up everything with the Government to take over the ship.

Cromie had already made moves the previous year to take over the *Dvina* as a solely British outpost. Even in 1916 he was well aware that Russian discipline was on the slide, and sharing the same vessel with this unruly indigenous crew was hardly conducive to maintaining a disciplined regime. His idea had been to apply to both the Russian and British admiralties to put this plan into operation. Now, more than ever, with dissent, mutiny and murder all around, it made excellent sense to separate the two navies. To Cromie's relief, the Russians agreed to the scheme, but for reasons best known to themselves, their lordships back in England turned it down. Such a move would have been a great help to Cromie in what was undoubtedly his hour of need, but there was no arguing with the Admiralty. In addition to this needless problem, he had been forced by the deteriorating situation to cancel the departure of several of his submariners who were due to go home. At the same time, with the mess decks already crowded, a new batch of crewmen were *en route* to Reval from HMS *Glory* in Archangel.

Day by day the confrontations between Cromie and the Russian sailors' committees increased. At one time they sought to disarm all Russian officers. For an officer to lose his weapon was a great disgrace. It seemed for a grim moment that the horrors of Kronstadt had finally arrived as the sailors, without warning, swarmed into the officers' wardroom and began to fling open the terrified Russian officers' cabin doors. But once more it was Cromie to the rescue, as he moved among them, his clear voice raised in command and protest. Thankfully, his bluster brought their activities to a temporary halt. Thinking on his feet, as usual, Cromie sent for a deputation of what he regarded to be more reliable men from the Reval gunnery school on board the *Peter Veliki*. His judgement of character was proved yet again. The men from the gunnery school debated the disarming of officers with their comrades on the *Dvina*, and won the argument – Cromie's argument – that these officers were under British command and discipline, and the committee usurped his authority at their peril. Yet although the revolvers were given back to the officers, Cromie was well aware that the taking of arms from his Russian colleagues was a central point on the revolt's agenda. Like the increasing practice of removing officers' epaulettes, it fitted in with the general move to bring everyone in the navy down to a similar level – that of the new proletariat. Sooner or later this argument would rear its ugly head again.

Once the more rational comrades had returned to the *Peter Veliki*, what Cromie did next would consolidate his reputation for fairness among the Russians. He talked the confused, deposed Captain Nikitin of the *Dvina* and the other officers into giving the weapons back to the Sailors' Committee; thus it was perceived that Cromie could demonstrate his magnanimity with a mixture of largesse laced with discipline. As many men, from Ben Benson to Vice-Admiral Ashmore, were to say later – the rebel sailors, tough and determined though they were, were no match for Francis Cromie.

Ashore, the country continued to surge forward into the revolutionary unknown. In Petrograd the Soviet had presented the vigorous lawyer and Social Revolutionary Alexander Kerensky with the post of Minister of Justice. Both General Brusilov, whose once victorious forces had descended into open revolt, and General M.V. Alexeev, Chief of Staff and Supreme Army Commander, had joined in Kerensky's call to Nicholas to abdicate. Brusilov's desperate yet respectful telegram of 15 March sums up the growing panic among the military hierarchy: 'It is essential to make haste, to quell the popular conflagration which has flared up and is gaining ever larger proportions, lest it entrain in its wake immeasurably catastrophic consequences.'[13]

Alexeev was in a similar mood: 'Your Imperial Majesty loves our country, and for the sake of its integrity and independence, for the sake of victory, deign to make the decision, which will provide a safe peaceful resolution of the present grave situation. I await your orders.'[14]

Later on 15 March Tsar Nicholas II did indeed abdicate in favour of his brother, the Grand Duke Mikhail. Within twenty-four hours, probably one of the shortest reigns in the history of monarchy was also over, for Mikhail renounced the throne on 16 March. Thus came to an ignominious end four centuries of Romanov rule. Now the power at last lay with the Provisional Government, operating in a shaky alliance with the Petrograd Soviet of Workers' and Soldiers' Deputies. The memory of Imperial Russia had been thrown into what Leon Trotsky was to call 'the dustbin of history'.

At Tsarskoe Selo on the night of 22 March, an engineer officer with a platoon of soldiers exhumed Rasputin's coffin and took it through the darkness to the forest of Pargolovo, where a huge pile of logs awaited. The soldiers broke it open and manoeuvred the decomposing corpse with sticks onto the pyre. It was drenched in petrol and set alight. The fire lasted six hours, and was watched in horror by a circle of several hundred peasant *mujiks*. Thus was the final end of the *Bojy tchelloviek* – the so-called 'Man of God' who had done so much to ruin his own country. As the icy grey dawn broke, the soldiers buried the ashes beneath the snow.[15]

In Reval even the hot flames of revolution could do nothing to melt the stubborn ice of the Baltic winter. Francis Cromie looked out across the harbour at the Russian warships, now bedecked with their scarlet flags and rebel bunting, and then at his own frozen flotilla, their encrusted conning towers lined up alongside the *Dvina*. The snow was still deep on the quay, clinging to the rooftops, the bitter grey sky promising more. This was anything but the mission he had struggled into the Baltic for. It seemed unlikely that those mutinous ships would ever again put to sea against the Germans. His only hope was that, following his lead, when the thaw came, he might inspire the Russian submariners to join his own flotilla,

Alexander Kerensky and
members of the Duma with
Bolshevik sailors.

out on the ocean where he belonged, detached from the violence of Reval's
streets, to keep the war at sea alive.

Soon it would be Easter; the nights would begin to grow lighter, and the spring,
although still only a much-desired dream, might bring a softening of the mood.
Cromie could only wait and hope. His despair in an undated letter to Admiral
Phillimore is tangible:

> My position has been so delicate and, living with a mutinous crew, so diffi-
> cult and injurious that I have, or hope I have, fixed everything to take over
> the ship. How much better if the Admiralty had only done so in the first
> place. I beg of you to help us now, even if I am superseded. This can't pass
> without marking our men. A quarrel may start an international rumpus.
> We have, thanks to an extraordinary winter, a clear month before the ice
> goes, in which to rebuild the discipline of the Fleet, and I am honestly in a
> funk of this spring, as I know for a fact that [German] reinforcements have
> begun to arrive at Riga. . . If we can only get sweepers and miners going,
> the submarines, who are a good lot, will do well, but how can we trust a big
> ship?
>
> The whole show is terribly depressing, and we are all of the opinion that

Renaming the *Dvina* as the *Pamyat Azova*, Easter 1917

the best thing would be all to go home, leaving the boats, but of course that is impossible in present circumstances. If discipline is not restored in a month it is peace for Russia. Cannot you make someone at home realise what an Army or Navy, who kill their officers, is worth?

I have demanded men from the *Glory* for the *Dvina* engine room, and told the Admiralty that we are taking her over. All this with Grenfell's and the Ambassador's advice and by wish of the Russians. Probably I shall be booted out, but am acting for the very best and not solely on my own judgement. Help us if you can. Sorry I am so depressed, but I haven't been to bed before 3 a.m. for a fortnight.

Sadly, Cromie's letter was over a month old before it reached Admiral Phillimore. During that time, any hopes the Royal Navy had of taking over the *Dvina* were to be severely dashed; this old warship meant far more to the Russian revolutionaries than Cromie realised.

CHAPTER 14

HYMNS TO THE HEROES

Probably it was the appearance of our stolid Swedish comrades
that was evoking in us a passionate desire for Illych to resemble
a human being. We cajoled him at least to buy new shoes. He
was travelling in mountain boots with huge nails. We pointed
out to him that if the plan had been to ruin the pavements of the
disgusting cities of bourgeois Switzerland, his conscience should
prevent him from travelling with such instruments of destruction to Petrograd, where perhaps there anyway were now no
pavements at all.

Karl Radek, on Lenin
quoted by Robert Service, *Lenin, a Biography*

As the long-awaited spring of 1917 approached, Cromie and his men saw out the
end of the prolonged, hard winter on board the *Dvina* in an uncertain, darkening
mood. To the Royal Navy's dismay, the Russian Baltic Fleet had all but ceased
to exist as a fighting force. Cromie knew that the Germans were planning reinforcements for a possible move on Riga, yet for the time being he felt utterly
powerless. Discipline among the Russians on board had evaporated. Sailors were
turning up for duty whenever they felt like it, wearing a variety of outlandish
outfits: straw hats, lavender gloves, spats, colourful shirts, in fact anything which
took their fancy. Leave appeared to be taken at any time which suited the crews,
and many sailors simply listed themselves as 'sick'.

To Cromie's dismay, a new set of conditions for service in the new Soviet navy
had been decided upon by the Central Baltic Sailors' Committee, now known as
the Centrobalt. When Cromie and his crews crowded around the notice board in
the mess to read this, they knew at once that their erstwhile allies were not far
from laying down their arms in the war against Germany. The nine points were
laughable to the British:

1. No man to be removed from a ship without the approval of the ship's
   committee.
2. Undesirable officers to be removed at the demand of the committee. Any
   new officers to be approved by the same body.
3. Officers to be elected and promoted by the crew.
4. Work to start at 9 a.m. and cease at 3 p.m.
5. No saluting.

6. Officers and men to have equal rights ashore.
7. All summary punishments to be awarded by a committee of three men and one officer.
8. All matters of routine and internal organisation of the ship to be run by the committee.
9. Food and pay to be improved.

No longer would officers be addressed by archaic forms such as 'High-Born' and 'Excellency'. They would be known now simply as 'Captain' or 'Lieutenant'. How they were going to improve their food and pay was not yet clear.

Of all the forces in this uprising, the Baltic sailors had the highest profile. The severity and servility of their life under Tsarism had engendered a hatred of imperialism which put them in the vanguard of total revolution. To many of these men even the idea of the Provisional Government and the Duma was a limp compromise. They may have been rid of Rasputin, and the Tsar, who now spent his days confined to his palace at Tsarskoe Selo reading the papers, playing puzzles and sweeping snow from the paths, but there was still a long and rocky road to a socialist republic. Although the Duma delegates had managed to visit Reval and make some impression on board the *Dvina*, in Helsingfors the stance of the rebel sailors on board ships such as the *Andrei Pavel* and the *Slava* was so hostile that the Duma representatives dared not go anywhere near the vessels. In Petrograd, much to the chagrin of a large section of the armed forces and the public, Alexander Kerensky was still pursuing the war as best he could.

Kerensky's efforts did not hold much hope for Francis Cromie, however. In fact, despite the minister's tour of the front to keep the war going, Cromie was singularly unimpressed when Kerensky paid a visit to Reval and came aboard the *Dvina* in late April. Writing to Admiral Phillimore from the British Embassy in Petrograd on 4 May he reported:

> Kerensky (Minister of Justice) visited Reval last week and came on board: he is an insignificant-looking little man of 33 and not likely to live long. He spoke to us as well as the Russians: in the latter speech he said 'We have freedom, we hope to have a republic; if we don't, we will earn it, for it is better to lose life than liberty,' . . . which looks like civil war. He urged the continuation of the war, but now the peace party in the ships grows every day, and Russian officers are fearfully depressed, saying that many ships will not go to sea.[1]

Cromie's clandestine voluntary service as a 'Navy Blue Pimpernel' was still in full swing. He had organised expeditions ashore to save people's furniture; found places on trains for many of his friends who had joined the growing exodus from Reval. He had stored money and jewellery for others who knew that, above all, Cromie could be trusted. With armed sentries both on board the *Dvina* and on the dockside, the British crew had to mind their behaviour at all times, and not place themselves under any suspicion. The mutineers had mounted a machine-gun on the bridge, which was constantly trained on the quarter deck. What aggravated Cromie intensely was that this gun belonged to the Royal Navy, and had been purloined from the British stores. What the Russians did not know, however, was that had they attempted to fire it, Cromie had mined its mounting with 4½ pounds (2 kg) of gun cotton which would have been detonated as the first bullet left the barrel.[2] Eventually, after some negotiation, he managed to have it restored to the store locker.

The petty trials of men thought to be less than revolutionary continued apace. One incident nearly provided a spark which would have resulted in full-scale violence between the Jack Tars and the *tovarichki*. One of the British sailors' favourite characters on board was an elderly Russian warrant officer, the *Dvina*'s bosun. The ship's soviet was unhappy with this old man. He had served in the *Dvina* during the first attempt at revolution in 1905, and had not been active in the mutiny on board. Some other trifling charge was concocted against him and, with his history, it seemed unlikely that he would survive the trial planned for him by the Centrobalt. The ship's soviet wanted to make an example of him, but to their dismay he was acquitted and sent to another ship. Against the orders of the Centrobalt, the Reval sailors had the old man brought back on board the *Dvina*. Vice-Admiral Ashmore recorded what happened next:[3]

> Having been disrated, he was sentenced to be imprisoned in Kronstadt. He was thereupon brought on deck, his shoulder badges torn off, and forced to don a canvas suit and a sailor's cap. When his tormentors began to spit on him and were obviously working themselves up to lynch the old man, our sailors, who were standing nearby, waded in and made it clear that any further spitting or violence would earn them a thrashing. What happened to the boatswain at Kronstadt I never heard, but, to my delight and astonishment, when I visited the Russian (Tsarist) consulate in London in 1919, the door was opened to me by my old friend, now employed there as a door-keeper.
>
> In the miraculous fashion in which Cromie could get his own way with those ruthless and irresponsible revolutionaries, he had had him released and had later helped to get him out of the country.

April was indeed a cruel month, especially for Cromie's plans for the Royal Navy to take over the *Dvina*. On Easter Sunday, 15 April, Cromie, forewarned that something special was about to happen that day, gave orders to his men that they should turnout in No. 1 uniform. It would be, he said, 'a day's holiday, but without shore leave'.[4] At the same time, he told them to keep a low profile.

As the first weak rays of the spring sun glanced off the tenacious ice which still gripped the ships in the harbour, the British sailors had barely finished their breakfast when, through the old gun ports on the mess deck, which had been converted into windows, they saw huge crowds begin to assemble on the quay-side. Bands were playing revolutionary songs. There was a definite air of celebration, and following the prolonged tension on board, the carnival atmosphere was welcomed by Cromie and his officers. A colourful array of banners

154

and placards waved in the breeze as far as the eye could see as members of the *Dvina*'s soviet stood on the ship's gangway, one after another, to make speeches. Each oration was followed by thunderous applause as the Jack Tars looked on in wonder.

The ability of ordinary Russians to address a crowd was always a source of amazement for foreigners at that time. The British Ambassador's daughter, Meriel Buchanan, commented:

> Untaught and unread as they mostly are, the Russian peasants seem to have a special gift of speech. I have seen a whole theatre held spellbound while a simple soldier standing on the stage in his dusty, war-stained uniform spoke to them for over half an hour with a perfectly easy flow of eloquence.[5]

The Royal Navy were lucky, for in Francis Cromie, they possessed a captain able to match the Russian orators.

The speeches on this Easter Sunday told of the *Dvina*'s history, of how she was one of the foremost stars of the earlier revolution in 1905. As they drew to a close, with a great flourish drapes which had been hung over the vessel's side were ceremoniously gathered in and her new name was revealed: *Pamyat Azova*. Those British sailors who were now on deck watched as members of the crew and many in the crowd embraced one another – and even the curious Jack Tars received their share of hugs. They were puzzled at first as the ship's large red flag was lowered to great applause, and then replaced as a new naval ensign was unfurled – white, with the blue St Andrew's cross, which sported a black and gold centrepiece of St George and the dragon. Ben Benson, like his comrades, had difficulty at first in understanding what was happening, but he soon pieced it all together.[6]

> At some time, probably in the reign of Peter the Great, a naval ship carried out some heroic work in the Sea of Azov. For this she was Christened *Pamyat Azova* (in memory of Azov) and awarded the St George Cross with the special privilege of flying the naval ensign with the St George emblem as a centrepiece for all time. It is the custom in most navies that when a famous ship is lost or taken out of service her name is handed on to a new ship. I have no doubt that our parent ship was at that time the latest ship to succeed to this custom. In the 1905 revolt the *Pamyat Azova* played a leading role. After the revolt was quelled some of the ringleaders – including Lenin – managed to escape abroad. Many others were executed or sent to Siberia. Among these were some of the *Pamyat Azova*'s officers and men. In addition, the ship was deprived of her famous name and her St George cross and renamed *Dvina*.
>
> Now with her honours restored, it was amazing how the ship's company got busy with pots of paint, scrubbers, etc. In a few days, the old lady seemed to have taken on a new lease of life. So she remained right through the next nine months – anxious months as far as we and our boats were concerned.

155

Cromie was not so impressed with the emotion of the scene; he commented (his exclamation mark) on the exchange of flags 'whilst they played the "Marseillaise" and hymns to the heroes (!) who fell on board this ship in the 1905 mutiny, after they had murdered all their officers.'[7]

It was an odd state of affairs – this most revolutionary of Russian ships, flying not the red flag, but the ultimate imperial ensign.[8] But Cromie's plan to take the vessel over was obviously a non-starter. He was now very anxious that whilst this new wave of something approaching pride among the *Pamyat Azova*'s sailors who, with their paint, spit and polish had temporarily begun to seem like a real navy, he should be able to break out of the harbour as soon as possible and inspire some action. But to his dismay the ice hung on throughout April, keeping the submarines firmly locked in.

Germany's unrestricted U-boat war had begun to bite. In April 1917 430 ships, totalling some 843,549 tons, were lost.[9] The war at sea elsewhere in the world continued apace, yet for all the dash and glory of the Baltic Flotilla's first two years, Francis Cromie faced only frustration and inertia in this land-locked ocean. To the west stood the neutral shores of Sweden and Denmark. To the south-west behind a line which began at the Black Sea and ran up to the Baltic the German forces remained, obstinate and threatening. And now, from his Estonian base right across Russia and into Finland, the military power of Russia had become diluted into a confused morass of anarchic uncertainty. Around him his submarines, the E-boats and the Cs across the Gulf of Finland, stood idle. The revolution, the severe weather, the submarines' mechanical and battery problems, and above all the loss of decisive Russian naval strategy had all combined to deny him the very basic objective which had brought him to this icy region – to wage war against the Germans.

As for the Russian army at the front, the new creed of the revolution, as prac-tised by the Baltic sailors, was taking full effect. There had been a renewed fervour for fighting the war among the soldiers at first. The Provisional Government believed in fighting on for nationalist reasons; the soviets believed that they should support the war in order to defend the revolution, as they feared a German victory would mean counter-revolution in Russia. Of all the political bodies which formed the Provisional Government, only one at this point was promoting peace – the Bolsheviks. Yet the Bolsheviks, although strong in their influence among the striking workers and rebel sailors, had a problem. Their leaders, Lenin, Trotsky, Zinoviev and others, were still in exile. Thus their call for peace had to remain muted – but not for long. Committees of soldiers now dismissed their officers and formed their own rules of engagement. The enemy took full advantage of this growing confusion in the ranks. German planes flew above the Russian trenches and dropped thousands of leaflets, printed in Russian. One such treatise included a transcript of an article from the Berlin newspaper *Nordeutsche Allgemeine Zeitung* of 15 April 1917. Part of it read:[10]

If the Russian people are still obliged to suffer and to shed their blood, instead of dedicating – peacefully and unhindered – all their strength to the widespread development of their newly won liberty, then the fault does not lie with Germany. Who hinders the Russian people from realising their yearning for peace? . . . Their Allies, England, France, Italy and the States adhering to them.

It was not only the Russians who were weary from the war. In France during April civilian unrest spilled over into the army, and by June various mutinies broke out. But the nature of these confrontations differed from the vociferous hatred between Russian officers and men. The lines of dissent were somewhat blurred – French soldiers often discussed their claims with their officers and they saw them in the same role as themselves, victims of this terrible war. The men's claims were similar to those of their Russian comrades many miles away: they wanted to eat better and have more leave, they had concern about the treatment of their families, and above all, they wanted peace. But by the summer of 1917 the French army had a new Commander-in-Chief, Henri Phillipe Pétain. He eventually brought his men back in line, with 3,427 courts martial resulting in 554 soldiers being condemned to death, forty-nine of whom were shot.[11]

At this stage in his career, despite his heavy responsibilities, the rank of Captain was still out of Cromie's reach, although as Commander in charge of the flotilla, he was performing all the duties of a Captain, and more. And apart from the many duties which weighed him down, he was still commanding his own submarine, HMS *E19*. Thus, once action in the Baltic could recommence, he would be expected to also take his boat out to sea, and whatever backlog of work built up on board the *Dvina* would have to be dealt with upon his return. From his letters to Commodore Hall, it is apparent that by this time he had had just about enough of this dangerous juggling act.[12]

> I know very well how much it will displease you, but it is my duty to strongly advise a separate Commanding Officer of flotilla under existing circumstance, and to warn you that it might be *absolutely* necessary, unless things considerably improve in the Russian Fleet in the next few weeks. I am sorry if the above makes you angry, but it is just my plain duty. It is quite impossible for you to realise the delicacy of my present position; it is such that I should not greatly resent a senior officer being sent. Please don't think I wish to shirk my responsibilities even if they are not appreciated; I merely wish to strengthen the English position here.

Without evidence of Commodore Hall's reaction to this cry from the heart we can only speculate on what the Admiralty's response may have been, but what seems plain is that Cromie would have been happy just to put to sea and leave all the red flags, arguments and constant haggling behind him. After the closeness of the violent exchange between the crews over the old Russian bosun, another ugly situation soon developed which Cromie handled with his usual skill.

One of his Russian telegraphists had been openly agitating among the men, against Cromie's expressed orders. This time things got personal between the Russian rating and Cromie – the man threatened him. It was a grave mistake. The agitator, being attached to Cromie's submarines, had been presented with a Distinguished Service Medal, and as he was under British command, he was entitled to a reasonable amount of prize money. As the threats and agitation grew, Cromie decided to act decisively. With the crew assembled, he dispossessed the man of his medal, told him that he had forfeited his prize money, and had him summarily dismissed from the ship. A few weeks later, to Cromie's surprise, the agitator returned and recommenced his belligerence. Cromie demanded of the ship's committee that the sailor be dismissed again, but they replied that he was required on board because of his knowledge of English, to keep wireless communications with Kronstadt. Cromie reported the situation to the Centrobalt and the Fleet Commodore, and gave the sailors forty-eight hours to get rid of the troublemaker. If this did not happen, he warned, he would go to Petrograd and take the problem to the Ambassador and then communicate with the British Admiralty. As if to demonstrate how tepid the Russian discipline had become, the Centrobalt said that they would attempt to *persuade* the rabble-rouser to leave the *Pamyat Azova*. Fortunately, after making several attempts to undermine discipline on the British mess deck, he packed his kitbag and set off on his broadcasting mission to vessels elsewhere in the fleet. For Cromie this was undoubtedly a great relief – an overflow of mutinous propaganda into his own crews was only a slight possibility, but a dangerous one for all that.

Whilst the stresses and strains of life on board the *Pamyat Azova* continued to grow throughout late April and early May, in Petrograd the greater fortunes of the revolution had turned a significant corner and received a new transfusion of intellect and political purpose. For the prosecution of the war, and the *raison d'être* of the British flotilla, this was to prove a major shot across the bows.

In Zurich in January 1917 Vladimir Ilyich Lenin, now ten years into his exile from Russia, had addressed a meeting of students where he gave a lecture on the failed 1905 Russian revolution. 'We of the older generation', he told his young audience, 'may not live to see the decisive battles of this coming revolution.'

However, in the middle of March, one day in their cramped apartment above Herr Kammerer's cobbler's shop, Lenin's wife Nádya had just finished washing the pots from their lunch when the door burst open and a Polish Bolshevik M.G. Bronski, breathlessly exclaimed, 'Haven't you heard the news? There's been a revolution in Russia!'[13]

Now Lenin faced the same seemingly insurmountable problem as Trotsky was encountering across the Atlantic in Halifax – how to get back to Russia. Neither the British nor the French would issue what they considered to be dangerous international socialist exiles with passports. But if the revolution was to succeed in the way Lenin thought it should, and be the spark which would ignite an international proletarian uprising, he knew that he and his fellow exiles, all of whom had devoted their lives to this very moment in history, had, by any means possible, to get to Petrograd and fight for the reins of government.

The new Provisional Government was a mixed bag of loose alliances and warring factions. At its head, as Prime Minister, was an aristocrat, Prince Georgy Lvov. To Lenin, Lvov's presence at the helm represented the uphill struggle his own philosophy would have to face if he returned. The Duma itself had only existed since 1905 as a neutered form of lacklustre parliament, a sop to the people of Russia handed down by the Tsar to placate the first revolution. It had continued to function with little positive effect, purely at his whim. Only one of the six main parties who quarrelled daily at the Tauride Palace, the Bolsheviks, possessed the ultimate revolutionary zeal and extremism to follow Lenin's own carefully planned path to an international socialist world. But the distant fountainhead of inspiration and knowledge for those in Petrograd who actually knew of his existence was stuck in Zurich and had done little more than write some very stirring pamphlets and articles in *Pravda*. But like Trotsky, it was the power and influence of his ideas which sent a shudder through the ranks of the right-wing Octobrists, led by Alexander Guchkov on behalf of the land and factory owners. And Lenin had no time for the Constitutional Democrats, known as the Cadets, led by Pavel Milyukov. It was Milyukov who had sent telegrams around the world to Russian consuls to order them not to help in any way to repatriate Lenin and his internationalist comrades. The Cadets favoured a parliamentary monarchy and were firmly in favour of carrying on with the nationalist war.

The remaining three parties had all been instrumental in their own extremist ways in bringing about this new tidal wave of change in Russia. The largest was the Social Revolutionaries. Led by Viktor Chernov, they included in their ranks Russia's huge peasant population. Their platform was 'all land to the peasants' and they believed that the war should be continued in defence of the revolution, and not as an offensive conflict. The Mensheviks, led by Julius Martov, were also 'defensists' in the war argument, and followed a moderate programme of demo-cratic socialism. They were particularly loathed by Lenin. However, together with the Left Social Revolutionaries, he knew that they could be brought into his camp with some tough persuasion. This churning, Petrograd-based mass of political indecision needed licking into shape if the impetus of the uprising was to be maintained, and if heads were to be knocked together, then Lenin was the man to do the knocking.

But first he had to reach Russia. He discussed various plans. One was to go home by plane, but he dropped this. During his life on the run and in exile, he had adopted many disguises and aliases, and toyed with a similar ruse to get home. He proposed the idea that, using forged Swedish passports, he and Grigori Zinoviev might travel home as two deaf mutes (to cover their lack of Swedish). But the ever-vigilant Nádya pointed out the potential folly of such a scheme: 'You'll fall asleep and see Mensheviks in your dreams, and you'll start swearing and shouting 'Scoundrels, scoundrels!' and give the whole ploy away.'[14]

It was the leader of the Mensheviks, Martov, who first came up with the idea that Lenin might come home if the Germans allowed him to travel through Germany in exchange for the release of a significant number of Austrian and German prisoners of war. But although Lenin thought this was the best method, Martov withdrew. The old Tsarist supporters in the Provisional Government were still keen on an aggressive war with the Germans and the last person they wanted to see was Lenin. Even many of the socialists outside the Bolshevik party were far from keen to see this firebrand return. They were all too busy juggling with their own political agendas and knew that the powerful presence of Lenin would certainly be a cat among the Petrograd pigeons.

Thus Lenin pursued the plan himself, and with the aid of yet another Menshevik, Nikolai Chkheidze, Chairman of the Petrograd soviet, finally convinced the German Ambassador in Switzerland that he and his stranded revolutionaries should be allowed to travel via Germany to Sweden. This suited German policy at the time; the vacillating fighting spirit of the Russians on the eastern front because of the uprising, combined with the further perceived political destabilisation Lenin might cause in Petrograd, could only make life easier for the Kaiser in his prosecution of the war.

There were over thirty exiled revolutionaries, led by Lenin, on board the famous sealed train which left Zurich on 9 April 1917.[15] They were adamant that under no circumstances could rumours be spread that they were in the pay of the Germans. They each bought their own tickets throughout the journey. They travelled across Germany, and after being held up in a siding at Berlin for a full day, eventually arrived at the Baltic port of Sassnitz. Here they boarded the ferry, the *Queen Victoria*, to cross the Baltic to Trelleborg, in Sweden.

Coincidentally the stretch of ocean now being traversed by the founder of the Soviet Union had been Cromie's happy hunting ground when he had lurked there in HMS *E19* almost two years earlier. The *Queen Victoria* sailed over the spot where Cromie had despatched the *Svionia*, travelled a few miles west of similar sites, such as that of the *Lulea*, and skirted close by the sunken wreck of the German cruiser *Undine*.

After Trelleborg, it was on to Stockholm, where the neutral Swedes treated the party to a sumptuous breakfast against the backdrop of a huge red flag. Lenin was fêted by the mayor of Stockholm, Karl Lindhagen, after which Karl Radek, his Polish socialist comrade, insisted that Vladimir should smarten himself up a little before attempting to take over the Provisional Government. He took the hobnail-booted Lenin to a department store and kitted him out with some new clothes and a decent pair of shoes. From Stockholm they travelled by sledge into Finland, where a slow-moving train took them back into Russia.

Across the water in Kronstadt the news spread among the Bolshevik sailors – the legendary Lenin (although still unfamiliar to many men) was returning. It would be a source of historical pride for the Baltic fleet if they, in the vanguard of the revolution, could be there to meet him.

On the border, just half an hour away from Petrograd, the train was boarded by the moderate Bolshevik Lev Kamenev. With him was a rough-looking peasant – Josef Stalin. Kamenev was excited, and pleased to inform Lenin that there was quite a reception awaiting him in the capital. Lenin, however, was more concerned with some politically off-message writing Kamenev had been publishing in the pages of *Pravda*. Whereas everyone around him wanted to indulge in the sense of romantic, historic occasion, Lenin remained cool and practical. For him every minute, every second, was part of the political process. There was no time for nostalgic nicety. History was something one got on with, it was not for pausing over and celebrating.

On the platform at Petrograd's Finland Station two smart units of Baltic sailors were lined up in their best uniforms. Outside on the station concourse

The C Class submarine depot at Rogekul. *(Ashmore Collection)*

The frozen harbour at Reval. *(Ashmore Collection)*

The C Boats in the winter of 1916–17. Note the steam coming from the boat on the right. Steam pipes were fed into each boat to keep them heated. *(Ashmore Collection)*

thousands of banner-waving people had gathered; soldiers in their grubby uniforms, sailors, workers, peasants, and the curious from every class and political party. Searchlights flickered across the sky and over the station façade. It was 11.30 p.m. on 16 April as the red and black locomotive number 293 steamed to a halt alongside the platform, which was bedecked with red and gold arches. The Kronstadt sailors snapped to attention. Lenin's one concession to the gravity of the moment was to remove his familiar workman's cap and replace it with a more statesmanlike bowler hat.

As he pushed open the carriage door and stepped onto the platform, the waiting band struck up with the 'Internationale'. There may have been many people there who had never seen this architect of revolution before, to whom Vladimir Iylich Lenin was still an enigma. But on that platform stood many faithful Bolsheviks who, like him, had suffered long and hard for their convictions with years of imprisonment and exile. The power of this evening squeezed tears onto cheeks from eyes which had seen too much of the suffering Tsarist Russia had to offer. The feminist Alexandra Kollontai stepped forward and presented him with a bouquet of roses. In the special station rooms which were usually reserved for the Romanovs, Nikolai Chkheidze, Chairman of the Petrograd Soviet, the man who had helped to bring this prodigal politician home, gave a speech about the need to defend the revolution both internally and externally; in effect, outlining the need for the continuation of the war. Lenin was having none of this as he fiddled with his bouquet whilst looking up at the ornate ceiling decorations of a dead imperial past. The first people he spoke to were the Kronstadt sailors. He greeted them as 'the advance guard of an international proletarian army'. Oblivious to the political scene as it was in Petrograd at that moment, Lenin told the navy that their government under Prince Lvov had deceived them. 'The people need peace, the people need bread, the people need land. And they give you war . . . The war of imperialist brigandage is the beginning of civil war in Europe . . . The hour is not far away when . . . the people will turn their weapons against their capitalist exploiters . . .'

He strode on through the station with Kamenev in his wake, and marched through the main doors into the waiting masses. The cheers were deafening as the waiting crowd surged forward and hoisted him onto their shoulders to deposit him on the turret of a waiting armoured car. From that vantage point, with the searchlights purloined from the Peter and Paul Fortress flashing over the fluttering red and gold banners, he gave his first speech to the Russian people on Russian soil in ten years.

The shock waves of this epicentre of energy and emotion would soon be felt by those who thought that Russia might settle down to some kind of parliamentary democracy. But despite this auspicious return, Lenin's long wait for power still had six months to run.

Back in Reval Cromie had even less to celebrate when he learned that the dynamic Rear-Admiral Vederevsky, a former commander of submarines and a very capable administrator, had been replaced by the commander of the battleship *Sevastopol*, Captain Vladislavoff. Vladislavoff knew nothing about submarines and was without war experience. For Cromie, this all served to convince him that nothing but madness reigned all around him. The only consolation was that, as new Chief of Staff to the loathsome Commander-in-Chief, Admiral Maximoff, Vederevsky might instil some much-needed common sense into the Fleet.

With the ice beginning to break, and the war ostensibly still being fought, albeit in a reduced fashion, it would soon be possible to put to sea again. Soon, the four C boats based in Rogekul would be ready to operate in the Gulf of Riga. *E8*, *E9*, *E1* and *E19* were made ready for action. Cromie crossed his fingers for a good summer's hunting.

CHAPTER 15

THE SUMMER OF DISCONTENT

> Finished a long analysis of the revolutionary movement. Tried
> to give it a fair view but the position is so unclear and so uncer-
> tain that any attempt at prophecy is difficult. It seems impossible
> that the struggle between the bourgeoisie and the Socialist
> elements or proletariat can pass off without further bloodshed.
> When this will come, no-one knows. The outlook for the war is
> not good.
>
> Sir Robert Bruce Lockhart
> from his diary, Petrograd 23 March 1917

It was time to move, time to plan new strategies, time to re-engage the enemy.
Francis Cromie had only one hope, and that was a slim one. It was that the
Provisional Government's increasing bombardment by Bolshevik ideals could be
kept on hold. Throughout the fleet, although the rebellion had taken full effect,
there was still no clearly defined political philosophy other than that of a
confused notion of 'freedom'. The sailors' committees were as yet not totally
infiltrated by Bolshevik propaganda, although its growing presence was there for
all to see. If anything, the mood among the sailors veered more towards the black
flag of anarchy. Whilst the Provisional Government's professed aims were still
to wage war on the Germans, either for nationalistic reasons or, as in the case of
the Mensheviks and Social Revolutionaries, as a defence of the revolution, there
was still a chance that the Baltic Fleet might return to something like a fighting
force. Yet Cromie's vista was a bleak one. With the Russian command structure
demolished, with most of its officers either imprisoned or murdered, with stokers
and ordinary seamen now striding the bridge alongside captains who held
appointments only by their favour, this was a navy in complete disarray. Only
the Russian submarine arm promised a slight ray of hope.

On land, the Russian army faced similar problems. If the Germans decided to
launch a major offensive on the front, the Russian lines would undoubtedly
crumble. If this happened, Cromie's base at Reval was in real danger.
Everything he needed to fight on was hanging on the strained thread of Reval.
All his repair workshops had now been moved ashore in order to convert space
aboard the *Pamyat Azova* into accommodation areas for his increased crew. All
the flotilla's torpedoes, stores and submarine parts were housed in sheds on the
dockside.

In early May intelligence reports provided the chilling news that the German navy was already back at sea, reinforcing its minefields, its U-boats checking the limits of the ice fields in order to distribute yet more mines. Cromie was worried. If the Germans could steal such a march, and if their armies overran the Russians and attacked Riga, then they would be into Estonia, and Reval would soon fall. With this in mind, he opened up a new strategy.

First he requisitioned a Lighter and into this he moved all his stores and torpedoes. Then he held his breath for the big move. He used all his diplomatic skills of persuasion with the Centrobalt and the vacillating Admiral Maximoff to persuade the Russians to let him take the *Pamyat Azova* to sea and transfer her to the Finnish port of Hango. Helsingfors at first seemed a better base of operations, but Cromie knew that the Finnish capital was a hotbed of Bolshevik activity – moving there was literally a frying-pan-into-fire situation. Meanwhile, to his relief, the Russian submarines had ventured out into the Baltic in an attempt to attack German shipping, but with no positive success.

As the month of May progressed and the ice slowly began to break, another party of British sailors had been settling in after coming out from England to join the flotilla. They had left Liverpool on board the Wilson Line steamer *Oslo* and sailed via Belfast, Romanoff (Murmansk) and then by train to Petrograd. With this party was Able Seaman Jefferys, whose diary has thankfully survived. Although he claims not to be 'a poet', his entries do open a small window on life for the ordinary seaman with the flotilla:[1]

18.5.17. Have had two hours sentry in our boats. It's Sunday, a glorious evening, and I am just watching the setting sun. All around is ice, broken up of course. Not a ripple on the water. It reminds me very forcibly of home, and of Sunday evenings I have spent by the old church at Lavenham. Am firmly resolved to go there again as soon as the opportunity occurs, and to take (-?-) with me. I know she will appreciate it. That is the one thing the war has taught me, to appreciate old England; it is a paradise compared with this benighted place. There's an old German proverb that runs, 'Blessed is he that hath the home longing for they shall return', and with average luck I'm going to. There are rumours flying around that we are to be shifted to another base. Well, a change is as good as a rest – perhaps. We shall see.

Jefferys had only completed his submarine training in February that year, and his boat, *E1*, was to be the sick child of the litter, with her continuing history of breakdowns. He reports that her nickname had become 'the Wallflower'. Jefferys too was soon in trouble:[2]

22.5.17. Had to see the Captain today for playing cards on the mess deck; after some argument we had to stand over and were eventually stopped three days' leave and a month's privileges. Eight of us all told. Cards are not allowed in Russian ships, so we are not allowed to play, merely out of courtesy to the Czar, but he is no longer, so what matters it? But after all an order must be obeyed.

11.6.17. Where we are now, Ganga as it is in Russian, or Hango in Finnski, is a great improvement on Reval. Very quiet and pretty, and quite a small place. I do not know how long we are staying here, but hope it is for the summer. The Russian sailors don't seem to like the idea of being here at all. I would like to shunt the lot of them out of it, none of them are any good, a crowd of ignorant scallywags. The trip from Reval here was very interesting. Navigation was very difficult as there are a great number of islands *en route*. It took us about ten hours. Marvellously pretty those islands looked in the early morning sun. Got under way at midnight. Now it does not get dark at all, merely dusk between ten and twelve. We made a stop of two days at Lapwick, another very pretty place, nothing more than a village. Plenty of fishing but we were unfortunate and caught the magnificent sum of nil. The Wallflower left yesterday morning at 2 a.m. on a ten-day trip to Bornholm. After ten hours running the engines refused duty and we had to come back. They've dished us up and we do a trial run tomorrow. Hope it will prove successful.

16.6.17. But after all our hopes have been dashed to the ground. The Engineers branch has been at work all this week. I don't believe the boat will ever be any good. It's a rotten shame. We have the finest skipper out here and he's just dying to do something.

20.6.17. *E19* and *E9* returned today. Nothing doing! We did a trial run, but I do not know the result definitely. Think it proved successful, if so we leave on Saturday. I'm no fervid patriot and sometimes think I would like to stop in harbour all the time, but after all one must do something to justify one's existence. Even if we do one trip it'll be something.

The C boats were still at their berths over 50 miles (80 km) down the coast south of Reval in the tiny hamlet of Rogekul, situated in the Moon Sound, which runs between the Estonian coast and the islands of Osel and Dago. Compared to the livelier urban atmosphere in Reval, Rogekul had little to offer Cromie's men. During 1915 and 1916 the town had transformed into an advance base for forces protecting the Gulf of Riga. Moon Sound had been extensively dredged to deepen the channel there. But for a British sailor, far from home in the inhospitable Baltic winter, the place had little in the way of recreational facilities compared to Reval. There were no cinemas, theatres or sports grounds, and no canteens for the men to visit. Yet at least the heat of political propaganda was less in evidence there, and after their long trip overland and the ensuing engineering problems, there was plenty of work to do on the boats to get them ready for action.

If the Germans attacked, the the Gulf of Riga would be the place. The Russians knew that the only force capable and reliable enough to defend the gulf was the Royal Navy. As an area to defend, it had certain advantages. Its narrow entrances were protected by batteries of 12 inch (30 cm) guns. There were substantial Russian minefields, which, if they came, the Germans would have to sweep in advance, and because of those big guns on shore, this could only be done at night. Even then, the enemy would have to face the Russian destroyers. But the Gulf of Riga was still a liability and Cromie knew he had to concentrate on it.

May Day, which was to have socialist overtones for decades to come, had never been celebrated in Russia. But although the Russian Julian calendar was thirteen days behind that used in the West, on 18 April (1 May in the rest of the world) the housebound Tsar Nicholas, writing in his diary at his palace at Tsarskoe Selo, noted that the rebellion which had deposed him had instituted a new tradition: 'Abroad it's the 1st May today, so our blockheads decided to celebrate with street processions, musical choirs and red flags. Apparently they came right into the park and placed wreaths on the tomb.' [3]

Cromie also noted the passing of May Day in Reval, where the now familiar huge flag-waving processions took place, which, to his disgust, included a number of Austrian prisoners of war. The night before, several arrests were made of what were thought to be German agents who had been plying Russian sailors with drink, preaching against the government and inciting the murder of their officers. It seemed very clear that there was to be no let-up of the political tension.

As to the return of Lenin, he could only watch. Cromie's letter to Admiral Phillimore from the British Embassy in Petrograd dated 4 May demonstrated that, hero though Lenin was to his Bolsheviks, for the rest of the politicians the jury was still out.[4]

> Here in Petrograd Lenin, the Socialist, has a fair following, and I have just seen three or four thousand in procession with peace banners. But yesterday there was a demonstration at last in favour of the Provisional Government; curiously enough they met a Lenin procession in the Nevsky and passers-by ran to avoid the fight, *which did not come off.*

In the countryside, from Estonia to the north of Petrograd, violent confrontations were taking place between titled landowners and angry, impatient peasants over the distribution of land. There were murders, arson attacks and regular pillaging of country estates. Many of the Baltic nobles were leaving their manors, escaping to wherever they could in order to avoid arrest. Here we have the first mention of the possibility of an organised opposition to the rebels, as Cromie reported that the nobles 'are supposed to be organising a counter-revolution, because they are drawing their money from the banks'.

On 9 May Cromie visited the Russian Admiralty for a meeting in Petrograd. As he entered the building and when he left he noted that shooting was still going on in the streets. After dodging the bullets he travelled back to Reval with little cheer. The meeting had not been a good one. His hopes for an upturn in the Russian navy were dashed when he learned that the renowned Admiral Alexander Kolchak had turned down the offer of the post of Commander-in-Chief of the Baltic Fleet.

Perhaps if the Russian Imperial Navy had possessed more officers of Kolchak's calibre at the outset of the war, the embittered rupture in relationships between men and officers would have been less extreme. Until his posting to the

Black Sea in June 1916, he had earned a brilliant reputation for his skills in mine-laying deep into German waters. A man with no political ambition or acumen, despite his powerful disciplinarian stance this staunch Russian patriot was noted for his warm relationship with both his officers and ratings. He was an inventive strategist and was one of the first admirals to recognise the potential of naval aviation, using seaplanes in the Black Sea Fleet for bombing missions and recon-naissance. As the tentacles of the uprising of 1917 began to reach the fleet in June Kolchak had to face the committees of sailors and workers as his colleagues in the Baltic had. They had boarded his flagship to inform him that the officers were to be disarmed. Kolchak was known for controlling his emotions, but on this occasion he lost all patience. He had already been accommodating to the rebels in many ways, and retained a kind of neutrality which had enabled him to stay in command. But he assembled his crew on deck and let rip with a caustic lecture on naval discipline and war, and outlined his disgust at the notion of being disarmed. He ended his vociferous speech by unsheathing his sword, which had been presented to him for bravery during the Russo-Japanese War, saying, 'The Japanese left me this sword when we evacuated Port Arthur – and I will *not* give it to *you*!' He then tossed the invaluable golden weapon into the sea, and resigned his post on the spot. At the time of his resignation, Kerensky was Minister for War, and called the disillusioned admiral back to Petrograd to explain himself. During his train journey he met Admiral James Glennon of the US Navy, who invited him to America. The Provisional Government, against his expectations, let him go. Yet Kolchak returned with a vengeance to fight again in the Civil War. He was defeated ultimately by his growing brutality and imperial ambition. His ultimate fate, after many failed military and political adventures, was to be shot by the Bolsheviks on 7 February 1920.[5] Had he continued in service and taken control in the Baltic, then perhaps Cromie's life would have been made a little easier. But it was not to be.

By mid-May the sea was fully open at last and Russian mine-laying and mine-sweeping got under way. Cromie had now been granted permission by the Admiralty to stand down as commander of the submarine *E19*. The boat's new commander would be Lieutenant George Sharp, until then *E19*'s First Officer, and he soon took Cromie's old command into action in the Baltic off Libau, where he managed to fire two torpedoes at an unescorted German transport ship. Unfortunately, both missed their mark. Lieutenant-Commander Vaughan Jones in *E9* also came back from a trip with some disturbing news. Not only had he come across trawlers fitted out with a new device – hydrophones – but he had experienced what was subsequently to become the dread of all submariners – for the first time, depth charges had been used in the Baltic.[6]

Although this new arrangement freed Cromie to carry out his extensive duties in Reval and Petrograd, and was some form of acknowledgement of the strain he was under by the Admiralty, his requests for a senior officer to come over and take command had fallen on deaf ears. His problem was his rank – although in his bearing and his skill he was every inch a Captain in everyone's eyes, in ranking terms he was still small fry amongst the captains and admirals he had been dealing with so far. His hoped-for move to southern Finland in the *Pamyat Azova* was to be kept on hold for a while, and in the meantime, the problems with the mutinous crews continued. After a night ashore in the theatre, some British sailors were insulted by a Russian sailor, who was arrested by the Reval police. Cromie had to force the ship's committee to dismiss the man.

Events which could have been dealt with swiftly and decisively under strict naval discipline were now the subject of long debates followed by ballots. This was to test his patience almost to breaking. Yet with the new Russian order, it was the only way to stay alive. When a British officer, Lieutenant-Commander Vaughan-Jones, was out walking with his Estonian girlfriend one night, he had insults heaped upon him by a passing Russian sailor, who quite cockily latched on the the lady's free arm. The officer, keeping his temper, asked two passing Russian sailors if they would take their comrade away. To his relief, they did, but minutes later the offender returned and slapped both the woman and the officer. The crowd in the street still held the British in some respect. The enraged officer grabbed the miscreant in a stranglehold, holding him at arm's length, until the crowd took him off his hands. The following day, a special guard arrived on board the *Pamyat Azova* from the nearby warship *Bogatir*. In their charge was a terrified prisoner – the offender from the previous night. He was forced down onto his knees in front of Cromie and the British officers, made to apologise, and then given a sentence which, despite his misbehaviour, was extreme – twelve years in Siberia. Although Cromie was impressed that bad behaviour could still be punished with such discipline, he was also wise enough to realise that if news of the severity of this sentence spread through the already jealous Russian mess decks, it could only stoke up anti-British feeling. In a characteristic display of compassion and diplomacy, Cromie argued with the men for a long time, and finally sent the victim, Vaughan-Jones, over to the *Bogatir* to argue for clemency for his attacker. The man's sentence was then considerably reduced, which enhanced yet again Cromie's reputation for understanding and fairness.

But his problems with political agitators were far from over. After despatching two such trouble-makers, he got rid of a third, but as in the other cases, eventually the man reappeared on board the *Pamyat Azova*. The committee convened to discuss whether or not the wayward comrade should stay or go; a ballot was cast against him after Cromie spoke to the crew for over two hours, finally resorting to bluff, refusing to take responsibility for 'all sorts of vague things that would happen'. Again, Cromie won the day – the man was dismissed from the ship.

In Petrograd the internal wranglings of the Provisional Government, struggling on the one hand to keep some kind of order and on the other to keep the country on a war footing, continued under the watchful eye of Lenin. On 1 May Milyukov, the Foreign Minister, sent out a note reaffirming Russia's loyalty to her allies, and pledged not to make a separate peace. For the next three days protests against Milyukov raged. The soviets were a thorn in the Government's side, but like Lenin, they could not be ignored. On 10 May Prince Lvov decided to ask them to join the Government. Five days later, Alexander Guchkov, the Octobrist Minister of War, and Milyukov both resigned.

169

Across the Neva from the British Embassy at the other end of the Troitskiy Bridge stood the big white house of Petrograd's favourite ballerina, Techechinskaia. But she was no longer at home. This former mistress of Nicholas II had been ousted and now a huge red flag flew from the roof. For the British in their Embassy, who were in sight of this new development, it was a provocative reminder that despite Lloyd George's efforts Lenin was back, for this was where the Bolsheviks had set up his camp. Meriel Buchanan recalled: 'Every night lights blazed from all the windows, every day crowds surged all around the house, while, from a little kiosk at the corner of the garden, Lenin spoke to them, inciting them against the war, against the government, against the Allies.'[7]

On 17 May, another train was rapidly approaching the Finland Station. Like Lenin's, it stopped at the border of Belöostrov, where a delegation from the United Internationalists and the Central Committee of the Bolsheviks stepped on board. They were there to greet another Titan of the revolution – Leon Trotsky. After finally being released from his incarceration in Halifax, he had sailed on a Danish steamer and, like Lenin, crossed Sweden. At the Finland Station in Petrograd the crowds were out again. After a decade in exile, Trotsky, a freer man with his emotions than his self-controlled comrade Lenin, was overwhelmed with the reality of it all; the banners, the bands, the gathered workers, soldiers and sailors – everything he had worked for during his life seemed to be there on the concourse outside the station:[8]

> And when they suddenly lifted me into the air, I thought of Halifax, where I had had the same experience; but this time the arms were those of my friends. There were many banners around us. I noticed my wife's excited look, and the pale disturbed faces of my boys, who were not certain whether this was a good or bad sign; they had already been deceived once by the revolution . . .
>
> Even my wife and I shared a bit in the bewilderment of our boys in the streets of Petrograd at hearing Russian and seeing Russian signs on the shops. We had been away from the capital for ten years. When we left our oldest boy was only a little over a year old; the younger one had been born in Vienna . . .
>
> The soldiers sang revolutionary songs as they marched, and sported red ribbons on their tunics. It all seemed as incredible as a dream. The tram cars were full of soldiers. Military training was still going on in the wider streets. Riflemen would squat to charge, run a distance in line, and then squat again. War, the gigantic monster, was still standing behind the revolution, throwing its shadow upon it. But the masses no longer believed in the war, and it seemed as if the training were going on only because no one had thought of stopping it. The war had become impossible, but the liberals (Cadets) had not yet begun to understand that, nor had the leaders of the so-called 'revolutionary democracy'. They were mortally afraid to let go of the skirts of the Entente.

With Milyukov and Guchkov having resigned, Prince Lvov now knew that his Provisional Government needed to broaden its base – the Bolsheviks and

Hango, Finland in the summer of 1917. *(Ashmore Collection)*

Tennis at Hango. *(Ashmore Collection)*

Mensheviks had great influence but until this point had not actually held any portfolio. At 2 a.m. on 18 May the Provisional Government became a coalition government which now included the more radical elements of the Mensheviks and the Bolsheviks. Kerensky became Minister of War, Mikhail Tereshchenko took over as Foreign Minister. The Social Revolutionary leader, Chernov,

171

became Agriculture Minister, and two Mensheviks, Matvei Skobolev and Irakli Tsereteli, took the ministries of Communications and Labour respectively.

On his frequent visits to the embassy on the Palace Quay, Francis Cromie would sometimes witness all this political traffic from the balcony overlooking the embankment. As Lenin and Trotsky's influence seeped into the new political atmosphere, the feeling against the British began to grow. But as yet, as spring had turned into summer, perhaps only a third of the city's population were firm Bolshevik supporters. There was a broad, confusing political menu to choose from. Thus many other citizens still regarded the British way of life as something to aspire to, and mixed groups of revolutionaries, although still crowded beneath the ubiquitous scarlet banners, would often draw to a halt on the Palace Quay, and Sir George Buchanan would appear on the balcony, give a short speech about democracy and liberty, accept thunderous applause and then retire back to his diplomatic chores. As an exercise in public relations, it seemed worthwhile.

At last the much desired move to Finland happened. Cromie was glad to leave the turmoil of Reval behind, but both he and his men were also leaving many friends and a social life which had done much to alleviate what was a very un-settling year. *E8*, *E9* and *E19* sailed over to Hango, with *E1* staying behind in Reval to complete repairs.

The four C boats passed the summer patrolling the Gulf of Riga, calling in occasionally at Reval or Hango to carry out repairs. Although they lived daily in expectation of running into the enemy in the gulf, the Germans failed to make an appearance. But Russian disorganisation at this time was almost as big a threat as the enemy. One hot afternoon in late June, HMS *C32*, commanded by Lieutenant Satow, took a tow from a Russian icebreaker to Reval for repairs. As a precaution, the submarine and the icebreaker had with them an escort of twelve trawlers. As the Reval breakwater came in sight, the icebreaker suddenly exploded. Minutes later, one of the trawlers blew up. To his horror, Lieutenant Satow realised that the Russians had taken them into a *Russian* minefield. He hastily brought all his crew up on deck, leaving Lieutenant C.A. Kershaw[9] below to run the motors and thus take them as carefully as possible into port. It was a nasty experience.

The Russian submarines *Bars*, *Gepard*, *Vepr* and *Volk* had attempted to score some action in late May, but their lack of success was tragically underlined when the *Bars* failed to return. The fact that they had gone out at all was a relief to Cromie, but a further effort in July was to have an even more tragic result. Completed in the Petrograd shipyards from parts sent over from Canada, the Russian boat *AG15* made the fatal mistake of diving with a hatch open. Only eight of her crew were saved, with eighteen losing their lives. But it was the loss of another of these vessels, the *AG14*, at the end of September, which caused the most grief for Cromie and his men. She was commanded by Lieutenant-Commander Otto von Essen, the son of the late Commander-in-Chief. Otto had been extremely popular and a good friend to Cromie, right from his early days in 1915 when he served as Russian liaison officer on board *E9* with Max Horton.

172

In a navy with most of its reliable officers murdered or imprisoned, Cromie could ill afford the loss of such a friend and ally.

In July Cromie received some good news at last. Admiral Maximoff's bumbling inefficiency had finally put him out of favour with the Provisional Government. The result was the elevation to Commander-in-Chief of his Chief of Staff, the ex-commander of submarines, Rear-Admiral Vederevsky.

But whenever Cromie received good news, there was always almost enough bad news to blot it out. On 16 July the Bolsheviks organised huge demonstrations in Petrograd. Their theme was 'All Power to the Soviets' – and an end to the war. But this was a firecracker which had been lit far too early and both Lenin and Trotsky knew it. It had been hastily organised by the party's Central Committee. Lenin had been feeling ill, exhausted by the constant round of lengthy meetings and speeches since his return to Petrograd. To preserve his health and recharge his batteries, he had gone to rest to the Finnish village of Neivola. Early on the morning of 17 July Maximilian Savelev, sent by the Bolshevik Central Committee from Petrograd, came knocking on his door.[10] Lenin was none too pleased to have his recuperation interrupted, and even less pleased with Savelev's news that the big demonstration in Petrograd was about to be put down mercilessly by troops ordered by Kerensky. Already in several skirmishes between Cossacks and workers blood had been spilled.

The atmosphere was heavy with danger and there was real fear on the streets. Prince Lvov was about to throw in the towel as premier, with Kerensky ready to take control of the Provisional Government. Lenin found that he had no choice but to go back to Petrograd. He arrived back in the capital and hurried to his headquarters around midday. There he found a large group of Bolshevik sailors from Kronstadt – like many of the other Bolsheviks milling around the building, they thoroughly expected that his arrival heralded the end of the Provisional Government and a Bolshevik takeover. He was asked to speak, but turned on those present, saying, 'You ought to be thrashed for this!' The crowd were stunned – they had thought that such an uprising would be just right for their prodigal leader. But Lenin had an uncanny knack for timing – and he knew that this was the wrong time. After speaking to the crowd, he finally won his argument. The following day, after much fighting and many deaths, the demonstration was called off. But there was an unpleasant aftermath. Kerensky, who had ordered a new offensive on the front against the Germans, ordered an enquiry into the Bolshevik's finances. The newspaper *Zhivoe slovo* went to press on 18 July with the story that the party was financed by the Germans, and that Lenin was a German spy.[11]

Trotsky was arrested and imprisoned, and arrest warrants were issued for Lenin, Zinoviev and Kamenev. Lenin once more had to go into hiding. Together with his two comrades, he decided to disguise himself and retreat to the village of Razliv, on the coast of the Gulf of Finland. There they would hide in a hayloft until the heat was off. Zinoviev and Kamenev wore wigs as a disguise. But before he left Petrograd, Lenin took the opposite course – he decided his beard and moustache would be shaved off. The man who acted as the Bolshevik barber was one Josef Stalin.

Cromie watched all this political drama with a degree of dismay – first he had a reliable man running the Russian navy, and then, suddenly he didn't. During the July uprising Kerensky ordered Admiral Vederevsky to back the Government against the Bolsheviks by sending some 'reliable' destroyers to the capital. Vederevsky was not whole-hearted or quick enough with his response, and although he did rustle up some naval support, Kerensky was suspicious of the admiral's leanings and had him imprisoned. When Cromie received the news he was dismayed; surely, before long, the Russian navy was going to run out of admirals.

Vederevsky had been the very man, a submariner, who might have inspired some new initiative among the Baltic Fleet. 'Good news – Bad news' seemed to ping-pong back and forth so much that Cromie's letters during this period swung from relief to despair at every turn. Yet to everyone's surprise, Kerensky, having scared Lenin out of town and imprisoned Trotsky, felt confident that his July offensive in the war could be pushed through smoothly now with the Bolsheviks temporarily marginalised. Thus emboldened, he released Admiral Vederevsky, and this time gave him the job of Minister of Marine.

Back in Britain July was also a trying month. In a debate in the House of Commons on the 24th MPs were disturbed to discover that the war was now costing Britain a staggering £7 million per day. On the 31st the Third Battle of Ypres began, with the Allies losing 250,000 men to gain 5 miles (8 km) of territory.

As for Kerensky's new Russian offensive, despite the beating drums and the flag-waving, it was doomed to failure. The lines in Galicia between the Russians and the Germans had remained so static for so long, that weeds, corn and flowers had begun to grow in no man's land.[12] The Germans, having helped Lenin on his way back to Russia, had taken the opportunity to sit back in their trenches and let the peace propaganda of the Bolsheviks do the work of bullets and shells. They could afford to just watch the Russians across no man's land without firing a shot, and the Russians took this as a welcome break. Thus, when Kerensky's offensive opened up on 18 June, the first two days at first looked every bit as impressive as Brusilov's advance of the previous year. Several miles were gained, and then, to their officers' dismay, the Russian soldiers simply stopped fighting – and those units in the rear, who, under normal circumstances would have been sent up to reinforce the advance, stayed put.[13] Between 18 and 28 July, the German and Austrian forces in East Galicia drove the Russians back. For Kerensky, who had taken over the Government from Prince Lvov on the 20th, it was a disaster.

Cromie still had hopes that Riga would survive. Kerensky had managed to find enough of the tough, no-compromise Baltic sailors, those who still believed in fighting the Germans, to form volunteer naval parties to join the Russian soldiers at Riga. The idea was that their fighting spirit would rub off on the soldiers.

The new regime at Hango, where the flotilla was now based, was less politically stressful for Cromie. Here they had a sub-depot ship, the *Mitawa*, a large transport, but he was still having to be vigilant, and now had serious money problems.[14]

Many ships, including us, sent in resolutions condemning the new Russian advance as a very bad policy. However, relations between the two crews here has improved vastly since our stay at Hango. I have had to kick out many new Russian telegraphists to avoid further trouble and nip a new propaganda in the bud, but I hope for peace again now.

I have been rather out of touch with the political situation lately, but things between Russia and Finland are nearly at a deadlock. Finland refuses to accept roubles, and they get enough marks to pay the fleet. For this reason the Russian sailors have been without pay for six weeks and have to return to Reval. There is practically a boycott of all Russians, and you change marks for less than 1.30 mark = 1 rouble officially, but no one accepts; whilst before the Revolution the value was 2.16 marks = 1 rouble.

At least the day-to-day running of his submarines kept his mind focused on the war, but there was little in the way of success. And as the summer rolled on, more storm clouds formed on the horizon.

Flexing his muscles as Prime Minister, Alexander Kerensky, embittered by the failure of his offensive against the Germans, sacked General Brusilov, the army's Commander-in-Chief, and replaced him with General Lavr Kornilov. Kornilov was strongly in favour of carrying on the war, and as the son of a Siberian Cossack and a well-regarded 'man of the people' Kerensky hoped that there was still a chance through this new man to pump some enthusiasm back into the trenches. French intelligence agents had warned him that the Bolsheviks were planning another coup. On 25 August he ordered Kornilov to find some 'reliable' troops to move on Petrograd. Kornilov began by forming a plan of destroying the Soviet and disarming the politicised regiments in the capital.

He ordered the Third Cavalry Corps from the Romanian front, with two Cossack divisions and the Savage Division – who were Caucasian Muslims – to the town of Velikie Luki, halfway between Moscow and Petrograd. The Savage Division, it was hoped, would have no qualms about shooting down Russians. But Kerensky had bitten off more than he could chew. Kornilov's moves soon had the rabid support of the moderate elements in the Government, and it dawned on Kerensky that knowledge of the plan would soon plunge him into more trouble with the soviets, the Bolsheviks and the other radical elements, all of whom he had been carefully juggling to maintain in some kind of political equilibrium. He also had some doubts – which were well founded – about whether Kornilov's forces had the will and the numbers to achieve the plan. But Kornilov was becoming popular with all those government elements which longed for the removal of the Bolsheviks. Kerensky's star began to descend. In the end, he could neither support Kornilov nor appeal to the Bolsheviks without losing his own kudos and position. But ever the opportunist, he remained as tight-lipped as he could and waited a while – just in case Kornilov might pull things off.

It was a bad gamble. Kornilov had moved his men into position, but the attempted move on Petrograd was a shambles – and the Bolsheviks were aware of what was planned. Rail lines carrying his forces to the capital were cut. As for

Star of the revolution – the cruiser *Aurora*

The former British Embassy, St Petersburg

the fearsome Muslims, he had overlooked the fact that the Bolsheviks had Muslims, too. A congress of Muslims had been meeting in Petrograd, and members bravely volunteered to go and convince the Savage Division of the futility of their mission. The Savage Division's train had been derailed by a bomb twenty-seven miles outside Petrograd. The fast-talking delegates from the Bolshevik Muslims soon had the Savage Division under the red flag. Not many miles behind them in Luga, the Third Cavalry Corps soon also began to abandon their mission. Agitators had blocked the tracks, whilst Bolshevik speakers opened up long debates with the troops, convincing them that their move on Petrograd was not needed – there were no riots to put down in the capital. They were all 'comrades' and should stick together. It was a powerful brew, and it worked. The red flag was hoisted yet again.

Thus, in another desperate move, Kerensky now fired Kornilov. This destroyed the Provisional Government's remaining credibility because those who hoped for the war to carry on had seen Kornilov as a last hope.

The clean-shaven Lenin, now in hiding in Helsinki, where he was living in the house of the city's Chief of Police, Rovio – himself answerable to the very government which had put out a 200,000 rouble reward for Lenin – began to look upon the political shambles presided over by Kerensky as a ripening plum, just about ready to pick.

But yet again, he was waiting for a catalyst. It had already been provided before Kornilov's mission had got under way, and it was the one thing Cromie dreaded the most.

On 3 September, the Germans had taken Riga.

Lenin's locomotive at the Finland Railway Station, St Petersburg

Lenin's statue in the gardens at the Smolny Institute, St Petersburg

CHAPTER 16

WATERED WITH BLOOD

During September and October the possessing classes were
awaiting the outcome as a hopelessly sick man awaits death.

Autumn with *muzhiks* is the time for politics. The fields are
mowed, illusions are scattered, patience is exhausted. Time to
finish things up!

The movement now overflows its banks, invades all districts,
wipes out local peculiarities, draws in all the strata of the
villages, wastes away the considerations of law and prudence,
becomes aggressive, fierce, furious, a raging thing, arms itself
with steel and fire, revolvers and hand grenades, demolishes and
burns up the manorial dwellings, drives out the landlords,
cleanses the earth and in some places waters it with blood.

Leon Trotsky
History of The Revolution, Vol. III

In Hango, Cromie was the first to feel the immediate heat generated by
the abortive Kornilov coup. The Bolsheviks, assuming with some reason that the
attempted coup had come close to a re-establishment of the old order and the re-
emergence of the officer class, decided to strengthen their position – especially in
the Baltic Fleet.

The Sailors' Committee confronted Cromie, producing an order that they had
put out to the whole fleet. All officers were to sign a declaration that they would
now take orders from the Centrobalt above orders from the fleet's Commander-
in-Chief. Cromie had to think quickly, but he knew what his duties were. He
made it clear to the sailors that he had been placed under the command of the
Baltic Fleet's Commander-in-Chief by his own Admiralty. Thus all the officers
under his command, including Russian officers and ratings who reported to him,
were directly answerable to him and the British Admiralty. It was a powerful
argument. He added that Russian politics could not, under any circumstances,
get in the way of the Royal Navy's submarines in their operations against the
Germans. They were, he said, the common enemy – and Britain was at war with
them, hence his presence in the Baltic.

Once more he won the day. The committee backed off and conceded his points.
But he was lucky. Four Russian officers on board the battleship *Petropavlosk*, a
vessel renowned throughout the fleet for its revolutionary credentials, questioned
the legitimacy of the committee's new order. Their argument was that the fleet's
Commander-in-Chief had been appointed by the Provisional Government, and

they obeyed his orders. They were ordered ashore and shot in the back as they descended the gangway.

When the Germans finally made it through to Riga, the Russians at first put up significant resistance, denying them total occupation of the city. But the line was not held for long, and after twenty-four hours Riga was theirs. The detachments of Baltic sailors sent to put fire in the soldiers' bellies had had some effect, but it was not enough. By this stage in the war the use of air power had become more widespread, and the Germans ruled the air in the Gulf of Riga and had deployed a new tactic – aerial mine-laying.

Despite this bad turn of fortune, at least Cromie's men now had a tangible enemy on their doorsteps. They no longer had to look for Fritz; he was here. Now the C boats had something in the Gulf of Riga to really get their teeth into. Two German mine-laying submarines, the *UC-57* and *UC-78*, had arrived in Riga. The enemy was becoming more audacious by the hour.

Both *C27* under Lieutenant Douglas Sealy DSC and *C26* commanded by Lieutenant Eric Tod now became involved in the nerve-racking task of mine reconnaissance. They took great risks in picking their way through the mine-fields, checking the swept channels, going in very close to the port of Riga itself. Lieutenant Sealy reported to Cromie on the sheer contempt the Germans were now showing the crumbling Russians.[1] From his vantage point in the darkness on board *C27* one night he watched in dismay as the German planes dropped over 200 bombs onto the Russian forts on the islands at the mouth of the Gulf. There seemed to be very little resistance from the ground. One night the enemy hit the jackpot by striking an emplacement of four 12 inch (30 cm) guns at the southern end of the island of Osel, where a bomb found its mark on a munitions dump. The explosion which followed killed or wounded 100 Russians.[2] With such a success to bolster their growing confidence, the Germans could feel easy about their impending attack on the Gulf.

Cromie was having further discipline problems in Hango. Food was also becoming a difficulty. His supplies were running low and often the boats were having to put to sea on emergency rations. With all the other stresses and strains, this was not the best atmosphere to ensure a good fight. And a good fight was, by this time, just what the Jack Tars were spoiling for with their Russian counter-parts, with whom they were beginning to lose all patience. On 27 September, Cromie outlined his concerns about food and the violent atmosphere to Admiral Phillimore:[3]

We are out to a bean for food until I get stuff from England. As usual they have promised everything for the last three months, and I stuck it till the boats had to go to sea relying on their emergency provisions for all dry provisions, and then gave a week's notice for closing down except for four day trips. Even Admiral Stanley[4] has not moved them from the promising stage. I don't think he cares for his position, finding it somewhat more diffi-cult than he anticipated. I am afraid of this winter as the Adm. submarines wants us to winter in Helsingfors, and I feel sure, apart from the food and repair difficulties (workshops being full of big ship and TBD work) that we shall have trouble with the men in a town where most of the amusements are closed, where they have no friends, and the very worst of the Russian Fleet to fall out with. You see the 50,000 odd sailors run Helsingfors, and our men begin to show their contempt for the Russians too openly to please me, and I fear the long idle evenings and the discontent there will be over food. I carry no weight in Helsingfors, whereas in Reval I have the town behind me, the credulous populace believing that we stand between them and destruction by the Fleet; also there are only a couple of thousand sailors wintering there and we get most provisions we wish. It was a great mistake not giving us our own ship last year, and we are no means out of that wood yet.

Peace is not far off our end of the world unless foreign troops are brought in. Kerensky is more or less doomed, and peace talk is more and more common. The whole show is very disheartening.

It did not take long for the cauldron to boil over. Just over a week after his letter to Admiral Phillimore, Cromie had to arrange to have a man sent home for ninety days' imprisonment. He was to be accompanied on the trip by Lieutenant Tod of the *C26*. Tod's command would now be taken over by Lieutenant Basil Downie, a man who was to play a significant part in the remainder of the Royal Navy's Baltic episode.

The miscreant who had overstepped the mark was a stoker, Bertie Baxter. He had lost his temper with a Russian sentry and thrown a punch at a quartermaster, whom he had tried to disarm. Cromie was annoyed that this was the fifth such incident in a month, and sending a man home was a much-needed display of discipline which also struck the right chord with the Russians.

By the second week in October, Francis Cromie's weariness becomes more evident; he wrote to Commodore Hall:[5]

> Have you yet considered relieving me? I am not applying for it, but I am ready to go. I get on all right with the powers but can't stand this navy as a whole, since the revolution, also I don't look forward to a more or less idle winter for English and Russians to fall out in. Tereshchenko, Minister for Foreign Affairs, suggested I should become Naval Attaché, but I think I nipped it in the bud; anyway I look to you for protection if this goes any further.

As events began to unfold, this seems a curious paragraph. As a respite from the myriad problems Cromie faced whilst on board his submarines and the *Pamyat Azova*, his frequent trips to Petrograd were becoming very precious to him. It is not certain at which point it happened in 1917, but at one of the many soirées he inevitably attended in Petrograd and at the diplomatic functions which were still being held at the embassy, he had met a beautiful young girl in her early twenties, Sonia Gagarin. Known as Sophie, she was to play a major role in deciding his future.

The Germans, much to Cromie's disgust and the Russians' shame, now had most of the waters he had so diligently patrolled to themselves. On 2 October they launched Operation *Albion*, a major amphibious assault on the islands of Osel, Dago and Moon. At the same time, they heavily attacked the Russian warships in the Gulf of Riga. Cromie's E boats had patrolled off Libau for some time and sent in reports of the massive build-up of German warships. Yet despite this, their efforts had gained little, as the Russians seemed totally unprepared. Perhaps it was the many other problems in their fleet, the miserable internal wrangling, the shifting tide of politics, the constant change-over of commanders-in-chief. But Cromie was bitterly disappointed by their stunned inertia. As far as he was concerned, he had done his job, provided them with the intelligence, and their response was to crumble in the face of the enemy. And the Germans were now perilously close to Reval. Another source of dismay for Cromie was that there were no Russian submarines operating in the Gulf of Riga, only two British boats: Lieutenant Sealy's *C27* and Lieutenant Satow's *C32*.

It only took seventeen bloody days for Moon, Osel and Dago to fall, and even Rogekul, which had been the C boats' base, now had to be evacuated, with all the remaining Russian ships escaping to bases in the Gulf of Finland.

Lieutenant Downie on *C26*, Lieutenant-Commander Vaughan-Jones on *E9* and Lieutenant Fenner on *E1* were all in Hango. Once ready for sea, Cromie despatched *E9* and *C26* on a mission to see what damage they could do to the Germans. *E9* tried unsuccessfully to attack two large escorted transports, arriving back in Hango empty-handed. Lieutenant Downie on *C26* bravely ventured into the Irben Straits, and after arriving to the south of Moon Island, made an attack on two König Class battleships. Sadly, the torpedoes missed, his range of just 300 yards (275 metres) being too close as his tinfish passed under the German ships. But he had another problem: operating in very shallow water he ran aground. His only option was to surface, but following the failed attack the Germans now knew that there was a British submarine in the vicinity. As *C26* broke the surface, a blistering volley of shells hit the sea all around her. He immediately dived again. The water was so shallow it barely covered the conning tower. As the angry Germans criss-crossed above him, Downie was forced to wait for a nerve-racking two hours as *C26* was lambasted with depth-charges.

He surfaced again, in the hope of making a dash to deeper waters, but was soon spotted again by prowling destroyers and had to dive quickly, jamming his hydroplanes and fouling the propeller on an anti-submarine net. Another merciless bombardment ensued, with depth-charges shaking the boat. Riddled with leaks, his crew's nerves in tatters, Downie's only option now was to lie on the bottom until, under cover of darkness, they might get under way again. But the submarine was barely seaworthy by now. When darkness fell he blew tanks and surfaced, delicately manoeuvring the stricken boat through the deadly clusters of new mines laid by the Germans. His hope was that they could reach Pernau, which, to the best of Downie's knowledge, had not yet been taken by the enemy. Thankfully, his hunch was right. The following day a battered *C26* limped into Pernau. For his determination and courage, Basil Downie was awarded the DSC.[6]

Lieutenant Sealy was navigating the Irben Straits in *C27* on 16 October when he spotted four battleships, five transports and a brace of destroyers. His first attempt, an attack on the battleship *König*, failed. Sealy went deep to reload and then made ready for his next target, a German minesweeping flotilla's parent ship, the *Indianola*. One torpedo from 800 yards (730 metres) did the trick, hitting the *Indianola* amidships. Sealy rapidly dived, and within minutes, the depth-charges began to reverberate through the boat. She remained undamaged. After waiting, there seemed to be a lull, and he risked surfacing again. To his horror he found he was surrounded by German ships. Once more *C27* plunged to the seabed and this time received the pounding of her life as the depth-charges shook and rattled the boat. Jets of water spurted everywhere as the leaks began to multiply. It seemed to Sealy and his crew that the end was surely at hand.

But eventually things became quiet again. After tense hours of waiting in the wet darkness, spent making repairs and pumping out his flooded bilges, he brought her to the surface. The problem now was how to get home – the only realistic route was through the Irben Straits. But strewn as it was with both Russian and German mines, it was too great a risk. Yet through his binoculars Sealy spotted a hopeful sight. The stricken *Indianola* was still afloat, kept so by trawlers lashed to either side. Although he had one torpedo left, Sealy decided against using it. He knew that the Germans would be taking the *Indianola* back into the open Baltic and away for repairs. Her lashed-on escorts would know their way through their own minefields. Sealy decided to follow her. Thus *C27* got through the swept channel and back into the open sea, thanks to her crippled victim. But although she made it back to the Finnish coast, *C27*'s troubles were not yet over. They ran into thick fog, and when it cleared, Sealy discovered he was in the middle of a Russian minefield. His only option was to hold his breath and pick his way inch by inch through the danger. His luck held, and he arrived battered but safe back in Hango.

Meanwhile, poor Lieutenant Satow in *C32* had not had such luck. On the evening of 13 October, a minefield had got between him and an intended target, forcing him to call off his attack. He headed off across the Gulf to Moon Sound and again found the enemy, a four-funnel cruiser. But he was interrupted whilst preparing to fire as a German seaplane, able to spot the lurking silhouette of *C32* through the clear water, began showering her with bombs. Satow took the boat to the bottom, deprived of his target. Later that day he tried again, against a large transport escorted by three trawlers. He fired two torpedoes but was forced to dive as the second one was being unleashed. Submerged, the crew heard two explosions, but his target, the netlayer *Eskimo*, was undamaged.

He was now in deep trouble, as the tremendous depth-charge attack which followed put out all of *C32*'s lights, and caused many dangerous leaks. Worse still, his compass was broken. When darkness thankfully came, Satow surfaced, but now, with no compass, he knew that it was sheer folly to attempt to brave the minefields through his only escape route, the Irben Straits. Unlike Downie, Satow decided not to take the risk of sailing into Pernau, which he thought would be occupied by the Germans. A passage through the heavily mined and patrolled Moon Sound was out of the question. His decision was to get his crew safely ashore in an attempt to break through the German lines and make it to Reval on foot. As for his boat, he decided to scuttle her. As 21 October dawned, he beached *C32* in Vaist bay, west of Pernau, set explosive charges and scuttled her. It must have taken poor Satow's breath away when the party staggered into Pernau to discover that the Germans had not taken the town – and there, in the harbour, lay *C26*, awaiting repair.

Cromie was furious when the hapless lieutenant finally arrived back at Hango. In a dry comment in his letter to Admiral Phillimore he wrote, 'Satow also bagged a transport, but got so tickled that he had to finish off his own little fish and join the Cossacks.'[7] A submarine lost in action was one thing, but one needlessly scuppered was a cardinal sin.

Such was the conclusion of the Battle of Riga. It was a sad coda, an example of what the Russians were up to whilst their allies were risking their lives. The Russian crew on board the flotilla's depot ship in Rogekul had all deserted, and on their departure had stolen all the British sailors' belongings and made off with the Royal Navy's stores. No wonder Cromie despaired. It was with some justified bitterness that he read the Russian version of the campaign in an ornate manifesto from the Centrobalt which, for the Royal Navy, beggared belief:[8]

> Attacked by superior German forces our fleet perishes in the unequal battle. Not one of our ships evades the struggle, not one of our sailors goes vanquished to the land. The slandered fleet fulfils its duty before the great Revolution. We vowed to hold the front firmly and guard the approaches to Petrograd. We keep this vow. We keep it not at the command of some pitiful Russian Bonaparte who is ruling by the mercy of the long-suffering of the Revolution. We go into battle not in the name of carrying out the treaty of our rulers with the allies who have bound with chains the hands of our Russian freedom, we go to death with the name of the great Revolution on lips that do not tremble and in the warm hearts of the fighter. We send you a last flaming appeal, oppressed of the whole world!
>
> Lift the banner of insurrection! Long live the world of revolution! Long live the general peace! Long live socialism!

On 19 October Francis Cromie's titanic efforts in the Baltic were finally, belatedly, recognised by the Admiralty, and he was given the rank of captain. But even then, it was a disappointing promotion, as he was only to become 'acting' captain. Undoubtedly, he deserved the rank proper. Some weeks later in a letter to Admiral Phillimore, he wrote: 'Many thanks for your congratulations, but as it is only an acting rate I hope to receive them once more. You have no idea what a difference a fourth stripe makes out here.'[9] His standing among the Russians – and the ladies who frequented the British Embassy – was raised a significant number of notches with the extra gold braid. As one of his contemporaries recalled:[10]

> From then on Cromie's dashing figure was to be seen everywhere in his famous uniform overcoat with the astrakhan collar, now enhanced with the

Captain's shoulder straps, the white enamel and gold of his St George Cross gleaming as it dangled, Russian fashion, from the lapel of his jacket as he strode aboard the flagship at Helsingfors to beard the all-powerful Centrobalt or brushed confidently past the lounging sentries at the Ministry of Marine in Petrograd on the way to demand support for his exiled flotilla.

Ashore in Petrograd Kerensky had continued to twist and squirm in every direction in an attempt to stay in control of the Government, but his days were numbered. In the countryside bloody confrontations between land-hungry peasants and obstinate estate owners were raging. The Bolsheviks were watching, waiting.

Unknown to Kerensky, Lenin was back. Wearing a selection of theatrical wigs and using various aliases, he finally arrived in Petrograd at the end of September posing as a Finnish pastor of the Lutheran Church.[11] From his hiding place on Serdobolskaya Street close to the Finland Station, he was soon directing operations with the Bolsheviks, sending a stream of letters and instructions via his hard-worked messenger. Knowing he was in constant danger, he had few visitors other than Nádya, his wife. On 17 September Kerensky had released Kamenev and Leon Trotsky from prison. Two days later, for the first time, the Moscow Soviet showed a majority on a Bolshevik vote. On 6 October the Petrograd Soviet elected Trotsky as its Chairman. Two days later a new coalition government was formed.

Lenin was frustrated by his clandestine existence and knew that letters and scribbled notes were no substitute for face-to-face argument if he was to lift the Bolshevik Central Committee onto a new plateau of the revolution. Thus on the night of 23 October the staunch atheist, still disguised as a Finnish preacher, braved the dangerous streets of Petrograd and made his way to the flat of Galina Flaxerman, the wife of a Menshevik left-winger. Twelve of the Central Committee members were there, and Comrade Yakov Sverdlov opened the meeting with a report on the current situation. It was perhaps one of the most important in Russia's history. It had a lighter side – the Bolsheviks could hardly contain their amusement at Comrade Vladimir's ecclesiastical appearance, and as a regular, somewhat concerned wearer of fake hair, he had a habit of constantly patting the toupee to his head.[12]

What Lenin had to say filled the committee with dread, but his determination, his timing and decisiveness bombarded them for over an hour. It was time, Lenin said, for insurrection. The Provisional Government could well be planning to hand over Petrograd to the Germans. This was Kerensky's weakest hour – the moment had arrived for the proletariat to take control. The hours of heated debate, fuelled by countless cups of tea from the constantly bubbling samovar, passed, and as the grey dawn of 24 October lurked behind the heavily curtained windows, a vote was taken. Lenin's motion for insurrection was won by ten votes to two, with Kamenev and Zinoviev abstaining.[13]

Within the next few days, old Russia was to be swept away for ever.

CHAPTER 17

THE VOLCANO

Revolution is not a dinner party, not an essay, not a painting,
nor a piece of embroidery; it cannot be advanced softly, gradually, carefully, considerately, respectfully, politely, plainly and
modestly.

Mao Tse-tung

Writing to Admiral Phillimore on 29 November 1917, Francis Cromie made one
of his characteristic understatements. 'We are on the top of a jolly little volcano,
and at least shall not have a dull Christmas.' The volcano had already erupted
three weeks earlier on the night of 6/7 November.[1]

On 25 October the Petrograd Soviet established a Military Revolutionary
Committee. The talk of a coming insurrection began to spread as a low whisper
throughout the capital. The first signs for the British came on Saturday
3 November, with the arrival at the embassy on the Palace Quay of a group of
cadets from the Petrograd military school, who informed the Ambassador that
they had been sent by the Government to guard the building. The Buchanans
had been preparing for a trip to England, but this had been put off from 4 to
8 November. Meriel and the other ladies in the embassy hastily organised beds
for the cadets.

Sunday passed quietly. At a luncheon in the embassy on Monday the 5th,
Foreign Minister Tereshchenko told the guests that he was perfectly confident
that, should the Bolsheviks attempt anything, the Government could handle it.
Sir George Buchanan was not so sure. There was a suppressed edginess about
the Russian guests which no one could quite put their finger on, and their casual
confidence was not entirely convincing. It was to be the last time the Buchanans
would see the tall, suave and clean-shaven Tereshchenko.

After a quiet afternoon, a sense of foreboding developed when, at six o'clock,
the Ambassador received a telephone call. It was a warning of a large Bolshevik
demonstration which was to take place during the night. Apparently there was
talk of cutting off the electricity supply at 8 p.m. Soon afterwards one of the
cadets arrived with odd news; his colleagues who had been appointed as a guard
for Tereshchenko had been told that they should not defend him during the night.
If they were approached by an armed party seeking the Foreign Minister's arrest,
then they should not resist and give him up. Sir George despatched a member of

his staff to warn Tereshchenko. Meanwhile, in the fine old British tradition – be prepared – the embassy staff set about preparing candles and torches for the expected blackout.[2]

Everyone waited nervously, peering from the windows at the street outside and the nearby Troitskiy Bridge. Things seemed normal. In fact, as the evening wore on, nothing happened. The lights continued to burn, there was no demonstration. The Buchanans retired for a somewhat uneasy sleep.

In the grey, cold hours before dawn of Tuesday, 6 November, Kerensky went into action. The print shop of the newspapers *Soldat* and *Rabochy Put* were attacked by a squad of cadets, who smashed type and machinery, then closed the doors, sealing them with wax seals. He was upstairs in the Winter Palace, from where he could see his troops taking up positions on the strategic bridges across the Neva.

In August 1917, the Petrograd Soviet, dominated by the Bolsheviks, had moved to the Smolny Institute in the north-eastern sector of the capital from the nearby Tauride Palace, which had been chosen as the venue for the Duma in 1905. The Smolny had been built in 1806–8 as the Institute for Young Noblewomen. Its takeover by the Bolsheviks could not have provided a more extreme contrast to its original use. Now its lights blazed nightly, as armoured cars and other vehicles bristling with revolutionary soldiers, sailors and workers came and went at all hours. In the Smolny's lofty halls endless debates and meetings hammered out the future path of Communist history. John Reed, the American journalist who witnessed the revolution, described his first visit there in his epic account, *Ten Days That Shook the World*.[3]

> The long, vaulted corridors, lit by rare electric lights, were thronged with hurrying shapes of soldiers and workmen, some bent under the weight of huge bundles of newspapers, proclamations, printed propaganda of all sorts. The sound of their heavy boots made a deep incessant thunder on the wooden floor . . . Signs were posted up everywhere: 'Comrades: For the sake of your health, preserve cleanliness!' Long tables stood at the head of the stairs on every floor, and on the landings, heaped with pamphlets and the literature of the different political parties for sale . . .

Like Lenin, Trotsky too had a sense of timing. On the night of 7 November the Bolsheviks called the Second All-Russian Congress of Soviets at the Smolny. With everyone in place in Petrograd at one time, this was a perfect night to stage a coup. The congress did not get under way until 10.30 p.m. because Lenin was waiting impatiently for a report from the Military Revolutionary Committee's forces, who had been sent to take over the Winter Palace, where Kerensky and his ministers were still in session.

As Lenin and Trotsky waited for the congress to open, they retired to a room off the meeting hall. This was to be their only chance of snatching a few minutes' sleep – neither man had slept for at least twenty-four hours. Earlier that day, as he pulled the strings of the coup together in the office of the Military Committee, Trotsky had asked Kamenev for a cigarette. After three puffs, he had fainted. He realised that he had not eaten for forty-eight hours. In the dark of the empty room, the two architects of Communism lay side by side on the floor on a blanket, their heads on pillows, their bodies covered with an old carpet.

There was little of the romantic in Lenin, but the sheer significance of this evening, his exhaustion, and this stolen moment of nocturnal meditation with Trotsky briefly raised the iron curtain of his self-control. He asked Trotsky about the way he had organised the Red Guards, the soldiers, the workers, the determined Kronstadt sailors. In the dim, flickering twilight from the cars arriving and leaving outside, Lenin gazed momentarily at the high ceiling of this room once frequented by his gilded, titled enemy, and gave way to something approaching emotion: 'What a wonderful sight: a worker with a rifle, side by side with a soldier, standing before a street fire!'[4]

Their attempt at rest was short. Lenin's sister, Ilyanova, burst into the room. The congress had opened and Trotsky was needed – he had to make a speech. There was much confusion. Few realised that, as the congress was meeting, an insurrection was surreptitiously being carried out in the capital. But although the Winter Palace was under siege as the congress progressed, it was not finally taken until just after midnight. Yet Trotsky was confident enough that his days of planning would be successful. The telephone exchange, the post offices, the railway stations, the State Bank, government buildings and all other strategic points would all be in the hands of the Bolsheviks by the following day. Kerensky had finally overstepped the mark, and by now, over at the Winter Palace, surrounded by Red Guards and Bolshevik sailors, he knew that his number was up.

When Captain Ericsson of the cruiser *Aurora* was ordered to sail her up the Neva to her strategic mooring by the Nicholas Bridge (now the Lieutenant Schmidt Bridge), he told the ship's committee that he was unsure of the soundings in that part of the river. He feared grounding his ship. It was a responsible attitude for a ship's master, allowing for the fact that he was living in a fragile alliance with his Bolshevik crew, existing on a knife-edge. His sailors lowered boats and rowed up the Neva as far as the bridge, taking soundings. They established that the water was deep enough. Ericsson was told that if he did not take the *Aurora* up the river, they would. The fearful captain obliged, as a last act of naval responsibility. Having brought her safely to her historic berth, he resigned from the navy.

At 9.40 p.m., an hour before the congress opened at the Smolny, the *Aurora* fired a shot which served as a signal for the assault on the Winter Palace.

In the meeting hall at the Smolny the atmosphere buzzed as the 600 delegates limbered up for what was to be a momentous series of speeches and arguments. The Social Revolutionary Fedor Dan had realised that the conspiracy was in full swing and was challenging the Bolsheviks to form a coalition with his party and the Mensheviks. Trotsky took the stand:[5]

We have been forging, openly, the will of the masses for an uprising. Our uprising has won. And now we are being asked to give up our victory, and come to an agreement. With whom? You are wretched, disunited

187

individuals; you are bankrupts; your part is over. Go to the place where you belong from now on – the dust-bin of history!

Whilst all this drama was taking place in Petrograd, Francis Cromie was plunged further into the doldrums in Hango. For a brief while, due to the inexplicable disappearance of the Russian navy's commander of submarines, Commodore Vladislaveff, Cromie had been in charge of all submarines, Russian and British. Vladislaveff, ominously, was never seen again.

The flotilla's accommodation problems had suddenly become acute. The atmosphere on the *Pamyat Azova* had become unbearable, yet rather than live in what he called 'a half small mess deck full of bugs, and four terribly smelly cabins' on board the *Europa*, a temporary sub-depot ship, men had opted, reluctantly, to live on board the submarines. It was not a comfortable life, especially for the ratings. Flotilla surgeon Kenneth Hole recorded his views of Hango:[6]

> Our boats had another depot ship for a short time, the *Europa*, but she was so indescribably filthy that the men lived in the submarines and the officers ashore . . . Hango is a small seaside town in Finland and quite different to anything we have seen before. The first thing that impressed me was the extraordinary cleanliness compared with Reval. All the countryside around is covered with pines, somewhat irregular but rather flat and monotonous. The coast is full of little bays and inlets studded with small pine-covered islands. The town itself is quite small and before the war was the main exporting town for butter. On the quays were the remains of big stone buildings and refrigerators which had been blown up at the commencement of the war as it was considered a favourable spot for a German landing. The town was a favourite watering resort and contained many large hotels, these, however, with one exception, are shut. Casual visitors, owing to the difficulties with the food supplies, were not allowed and only actual inhabitants allowed to remain. Amusements for the sailors were limited. We were given the use of the town football ground, canoes could be hired and there were two cinematographs. The greatest difficulty was the language question. Practically all the sailors spoke some kind of Russian and here it was nearly useless, only Swedish being spoken. For the officers there were three excellent tennis courts and during the month of June we thoroughly enjoyed ourselves. There was absolutely perfect weather and with the 'white nights' we could play games until 10 p.m. and after that go out in canoes . . .

With the summer over and the winter now opening up with a vengeance, and an imminent move to Helsingfors ordered by the Russian Commander-in-Chief, the nights seemed to be drawing in to make one big darkness, full of wrathful surprises. Once again Cromie visited Petrograd and the Ministry of Marine, and after calling at the embassy, heard the blood-curdling news. With the Bolsheviks' seizure of overall power, what would this now mean for the Baltic Fleet? The situation seemed hopeless, but there was still hope that Kerensky might pull something off.

On the morning of 7 November, with most of his ministers no longer around him, and the telephone to the Winter Palace cut off, Alexander Kerensky, after months of political and military juggling, was now left with only one option. He had already ordered what he hoped would be loyal troops to assemble in the south at Pskov, where the headquarters of the Commander-in-Chief, Northern Front, were situated. His hope was that with enough reliable force he could turn back the Bolshevik tide.

He was accustomed to rushing around the Petrograd district in a fast car. This was the way he left the capital on this day of defeat. Together with the Minister of Trade and Industry, Konavalov, he went on foot across the Palace Square to the office of the district military staff. There it was decided that he should leave Petrograd and head south to meet his troops. Much propaganda was made later about Kerensky's escape from the city under the protection of the American flag. Kerensky told it thus:[7]

At the last moment, just before the acting commander of the Petrograd military district, my adjutant and I left, some officials from the British and US embassies arrived on the scene and offered to drive us out of the city under the American flag. I thanked the Allies for their offer, but said that the head of the government could not drive through the Russian capital under the American flag. As I later learned, however, the car turned out to be useful for one of my officers who could not fit into my own car. It drove a distance behind us.

As the days following the coup passed, the Buchanans, unable to leave for their trip home, were as far away from tea and crumpets in their London drawing room as ever. Destroyers from Kronstadt were now on the Neva, within sight of the British Embassy, described by Meriel as 'grey, vicious-looking shapes on the grey waters, with guns bristling in all directions.' Often in the embassy, around the dinner table, they had joked about such dim possibilities as Trotsky becoming a government minister. He was now Foreign Commissar in the new Soviet government.

By 16 November it was obvious that Kerensky's much-vaunted counter-attack was not going to happen. The power of the Bolshevik creed in the ranks had put paid to that. For now, Kerensky and all he stood for were eclipsed by Lenin's long and lasting shadow. Robert Bruce Lockhart, who was then Acting Consul-General in Moscow, knew Kerensky well, and summed up his plight.[8]

Caught between the cross-fires of the Bolshevik Left which was screaming peace at every street corner and in every trench, and of the Right and of the Allies, who were demanding the restoration of discipline by Tsarist methods, he had no chance. And he fell, because whoever had tried to do what he did was bound to fall.

One of the Bolsheviks' first moves to settle the war situation was to seek an armistice. Cromie had always feared this, and as the news spread that the new government in Petrograd had begun to make such overtures, it was plain to the flotilla – Bolshevik Russia was no longer Britain's partner against Germany.

On 13 November Lieutenant Downie, after waiting weeks in Pernau trying to repair *C26*, finally made it back to Hango in time for the move to Helsingfors. His crew's inventiveness had done much to get them there. He did, however, have the sterling assistance of Engineer Lieutenant Stanley Jackson,[9] whom Cromie had sent over to Pernau. He had even constructed a Heath-Robinson wooden pulley to drive the main petrol pump.

Together with the old *Pamyat Azova* the seven remaining British submarines transferred to Helsingfors for the winter. It was a worrying time for Cromie, and the men were now experiencing more and more antagonism with the Russian sailors. They had the victory of their revolution to strut their pride with. The camaraderie of 1915–16 was a thing of the past. Propaganda had given them a new view of the British navy – it was a navy of old imperialist ideals, a navy of capitalism. The only bright patch on the horizon for the British was that, after Reval, which, although they had been entertained there, was rather primitive, and Hango, which was small with few facilities, Helsingfors was Finland's capital. Here, despite the political convulsions, there was still some kind of working civic machinery. The wide streets were clean. Good restaurants and international hotels flourished. There was entertainment, theatre, cinemas. But there was also the Russian Baltic Fleet.

Acting Captain Francis Cromie, after over two years of trying to fight a war in the most difficult conditions, was now in command of seven submarines with little in the way of a support infrastructure, and over 200 bluejackets with nothing to do. The hard question had to be faced – what should become of the boats?

Various ideas were put forward. One was that they should try and leave the Baltic as they had entered, through the Sound, heavily protected by Russian destroyers. But with the change in the political wind this seemed unlikely, and in any event, it would be close to suicidal with the Germans now ruling the area. Max Horton was consulted on the matter and agreed that any attempt to leave the Baltic would be futile. Another idea was to sail the boats into Swedish waters, then sink them. The crews could then be taken ashore as shipwrecked mariners, thus avoiding internment, and pass through Norway on their way home. On 29 November Roger Keyes, Director of Plans at the Admiralty put forward the tough yet realistic proposal – bring the crews home, and sink the submarines in deep water.

Cromie looked at his boats in Helsingfors Harbour as the winter snow began to fall and realised that they were no longer a fighting force. It would have been easy to imagine that his grand adventure was over, but he knew in his heart it was not. We can only speculate on the inner, private mental anguish he was now experiencing. Gwladys, his daughter Anthea and his mother were almost distant memories. He had not seen them since the summer of 1915. Despite his tenacity, strength and ability, like all men living on the edge of calamity and possible death, he needed a safety valve, an alternative to the constant grind, the political wheeling and dealing, and the challenges of keeping those boats afloat. Like his colleagues he could have consumed limitless amounts of vodka, or chain-smoked. In an environment where these habits were not only common, but encouraged, it is amazing he avoided this solution. But the recreational safety valve which kept him sane, and reminded him that, at thirty-six, he was still a man, and a virile one at that, was Russian women. There had been Moura Budberg, and the Baroness Schilling. But it was the beautiful twenty-five-year-old Sonia Gagarin who filled his later days in Russia.

One cannot judge by today's so-called 'civilised' standards the adulterous behaviour of a handsome naval officer, far from home and in constant danger in the midst of war and revolution almost a century ago. A few rungs up the social ladder, where Cromie no doubt aspired to be, and especially in Russian society, the practice of having an extra-marital liaison was as common as membership of a golf club is today. War provides the scenario, the opportunity. Russian women, no matter what their class, were human in the same way as British wives were in the face of such temptations as a handsome GI in the Second World War.

The Gagarins were an old, titled Russian family. Prince Andrey Gagarin, Sonia's father, had bought land in the nineteenth century from the estate of Elizabeth Novostiev in the Pskov district, and built a beautiful neo-Georgian mansion there, Holomki. Cromie had no doubt met Sonia through her brothers, Lev, Peter and Sergei, who were officers in the Tsar's army.

On his early forays into Russian society, Cromie met and was impressed by many of these dashing young nobles, who, even then, in 1915–16, seemed to the more prosaic British officers like characters from some Bohemian fairy tale. For Cromie, with his comparatively humble background, this was a different world, but a world in its final twilight. It is doubtful if at home he could ever have mixed at such a level. Although, like Russia, Britain was a land where blood, titles and

Holomki, the Gagarin's mansion at Pskov. *(Graham Harrison)*

property still defined a man's place in society, Russians of less than noble breeding could still rise in the ranks through sheer grit, determination and bravado. The failed hope of the Provisional Government, Lavr Kornilov, was such a man: the humble son of a Siberian Cossack who, by his tough, ruthless determination had clawed his way through the ranks to become one of the Tsar's most respected and feared generals. Some of those who knew Cromie say that he loved Russia. He certainly picked up the language quickly enough. But it was perhaps a romantic love for a mythical world which was already slipping into legend after the first revolution of 1905. The Bolsheviks, bent on creating a new, monochrome workers' Russia, offered to Cromie none of the colourful romance of the old.

There is no direct evidence of any impropriety in Cromie's relationships with women in the Baltic campaign. And even after so many decades, it is fair to say that what transpired was his own business. But his relationship with Sonia revealed another dimension to his character. The inner Cromie, whom we may never really know, pulls back the corner of a heavy curtain during his final months to reveal the possibility, had he survived, of a totally different conclusion to his time in Russia.

The early days in Helsingfors were not as fraught as Cromie had expected, but food problems still made his life difficult. He had been informed that stores had arrived at Archangel, yet he was loath to send a detachment to find them. All the boats needed extensive overhauls, and at this point, as no definite decision had been made as to their fate, he was still determined to look busy by carrying out what maintenance he could. But spare parts and their transit from England were subjects of constant aggravation. At one point a spare propeller for one of the boats was found dumped in the bushes alongside the Petrograd–Murmansk rail track. Crates either did not turn up, or, as often as not, arrived damaged or pilfered.

By now, with Lenin in control, the Russian Sailors' Soviet had dispensed with any pretence of naval diplomacy between themselves and the British command. A new arrogance had developed, and it manifested itself in one of the most potentially explosive situations since 1915.

Cromie had put the extra kudos the rank of Captain gave him to good use. He had regularly met Vederevsky, who was now Minister of Marine, and had become a familiar visitor at the British Embassy in Petrograd and the Astoria Hotel. His meetings on board the *Pamyat Azova* in Helsingfors were more often than not confrontations, but if the Sailors' Committee had developed a 'party line' he could match this with a mantra of his own. On one occasion, he had to go to great lengths to make it clear yet again to the Centrobalt that he could never submit totally to their control because he only recognised the power of their Commander-in-Chief, but said, 'Yet I am always willing to work alongside you all against the common enemy.' Perhaps even he was amazed at times that he could, as a lone representative of a foreign navy, still pull off these triumphs and go down the gangway in an atmosphere of goodwill, rather than being shot in the back, which some members of the Centrobalt would have wanted.

But the crisis came in December 1917. Flushed with their revolutionary victory, the Sailor's Soviet came up with a plan to take the battleships to sea, sail to Kiel in Germany and there fraternise with the enemy in an attempt to spread the doctrine of revolution. This prospect filled Cromie with horror. Although the new government had definitely put feelers out for an armistice, the idea of the very vessels Cromie was working with in Helsingfors leaving port with no aggressive aim, simply to meet the Germans on a friendly basis was the proverbial red rag to a bull.

He issued instructions one morning for all the officers of the flotilla to attend a meeting in his cabin. They knew it was important, because he had placed an armed sentry at the door. Once assembled, he opened the proceedings in a cheerful manner. Lieutenant Ashmore recalled Cromie's mood:[10]

> Sitting at his desk, calmly and cheerfully he told us in crisp, trenchant phrases of the situation that had arisen and his determination to scotch the proposals of the committees. His plan was in keeping with his determined and forthright nature. If the Russian move was finally agreed upon, he intended boarding the flagship, accompanied by engineer Lt. Jackson and a signalman. There he would confront the ship's committee and any officers who still had authority with an ultimatum. Either his engineer officer must be permitted to put their main engines permanently out of action, or, at a pre-arranged signal, our boats, by then lying off in readiness, would torpedo the battleships one by one. While we were digesting the boldness and implications of this plan, Cromie dismissed us. 'You will go to your boats now and prepare them for action', he said.

Fortunately Cromie did not need to put the plan into action. As the submarines made ready for sea, he decided to pay one more visit to the Sailors' Committee. It was perhaps the most difficult act of persuasion he had yet had to face. Although he avoided outlining his plan, he made an emotional appeal to the still smouldering embers of Russian patriotism. In any case, he told them, his own flotilla and his men would soon be going home. The two navies, despite all that had happened in Russia, had managed to retain some level of sensible dialogue. It would be a shame and, perhaps, an insult to the British effort, to the sailors whose different way of life they had at one time so aspired to, if the last memory they had of their Russian shipmates was of them cavorting with the enemy, who even now were planning to overrun their country. The committee deliberated as Cromie held his breath. Again, he won. They abandoned their fraternisation project. but he had not finished. He told them that soon, 200 of his men would be leaving Russia. Could he have a guarantee of their safe passage from Petrograd to Murmansk? With handshakes all round, he got it.

With this dark episode out of the way, as ever, the next challenge arrived on Cromie's desk. On 4 December 1917, the Finns declared independence from Russia, and demanded that all Russian forces should leave Finland. This was to have a grim effect on the mood of the Russian sailors. Tensions came to the surface again, and the British, counting the days to going home, had had quite enough of the petty arguments and jealousies. Cromie often repeated his exhortation that they should, at all costs, ignore any intimidation or provocation. But a Jack Tar with a drink in him is not the kind of man to turn the other cheek. When two British ratings were attacked in a café and stabbed whilst enjoying a peaceful coffee together, the atmosphere became explosive. Able Seaman Jefferys commented upon the difficulty of keeping cool under such provocation: 'This affair was the result of trying to hold to our principles. Had the lads tried to defend themselves in the first place, probably it would not have been so serious. We are always being told to try and avoid trouble, keep temper, etc., but the other people will not count ten.'[11] Cromie was more scathing: 'How I hate these foreigners. On a word they will use a knife. If you dare show a crowd of them the business end of a bayonet, they would soon skip.'

At long last, with incredibly inept timing, the flotilla's much-needed stores, after being caught up at various points in Russia for so long, had arrived. Cromie's dilemma, however, was that he now had enough food and materials to see them through six months, yet at the same time the final instructions had come from the Admiralty to send the majority of his men, around 200 officers and ratings, back to England. They were to travel by train on an epic journey from Petrograd to Murmansk, and from there back to Britain by sea. The supplies now took on the nature of currency for Cromie – and would also be used as a further example of his thoughtful, compassionate approach to those in Russia who had helped him survive the risky ride of the past two years. In a fund-raising exercise he first sold large quantities of food and other materials to local shops in Helsingfors, and made sure that all his British friends and contacts in the city, and in Petrograd, received their share – especially food. It was a much-appreciated gesture. His next task, now that he had the Centrobalt's guarantee of their safety, was the thorny one of arranging for a train to take his men to Murmansk.

As the heavy snow began to fall, Cromie cast an eye over the seven submarines berthed alongside the *Pamyat Azova*. He could not have realised it at that moment, but his own career as a brave submariner was already passed. He could no longer make any sense of his presence in this cold, distant land. During four years, he could count the days he had seen his own wife and family on the fingers of his hands. It was a poignant end to a campaign which had begun with so much promise and glory.[12]

> These are sad times and mighty difficult to keep the peace. I wish one need not. So we struggle along looking after our 'friends' instead of our enemies. The local Governor-General cannot read or write; the practical C-in-C was a stoker; the Second Marine Minister was ship's cook on the *Bayan*, and after some words the Baltic Committee graciously 'rendered up control of th English Flotilla'.
>
> The Gerrards[13] will probably come home soon, as nearly everyone is clearing out. Most estates in the south and in Estonia are looted, and Russia as a nation no longer exists.

CHAPTER 18

A SAILOR'S FAREWELL

What splendid surgery! You take a knife and with one masterful
stroke you cut out all the stinking ulcers. Quite simply, without
any nonsense, you take the old monster of injustice, which has
been accustomed for centuries to being bowed and scraped and
curtsied to, and you sentence it to death.

Boris Pasternak, *Dr Zhivago*

As the Bolsheviks laboured to make a silk purse from the pig's ear which was
the Russia of December 1917, a strange twilight world of black market wheeler-
dealing had begun to develop behind the zealous revolutionary pride.

No doubt it was this spiv's world of stolen goods, requisitioned property and
purloined stores which enabled Cromie to pull off so many bartering deals using
his Admiralty supplies, often with people he would have dearly preferred to
shoot. He had a bold and daring assistant in these transactions, the giant, no-
nonsense Assistant Paymaster, Kenneth Baker RNR.[1] The comrades only had
to take one look at this mountain from Winnipeg in Canada to realise that there
would be no serious haggling allowed. The money raised was to be used to pay
the flotilla's wages. Food had become very scarce and so many commodities had
now escalated so much in price as to become like gold to many. Three-year-old
British officers' jackets could be had for a princely £3, and there was no shortage
of customers. Cromie commented that 'there was almost a fight for old boots at
£1 per pair'.

Yet although he realised the nefarious nature of the dealings he had, without
choice, entered into, he still retained a laudable sense of decorum and duty to his
country. Evidence of this came when he was approached ashore by a deputation
of Helsingfors businessmen who were adherents of the White Russians. The
White Russians derived their name from the royalist opponents to the French
Revolution. The French royalists were called the Whites after adopting the
white flag of the French Bourbon dynasty. They had had their fill of their capital
being patrolled by Bolshevik Red Guards, who relied on the back-up strength of
the 50,000 Baltic Fleet sailors. The Whites had a plan. They estimated that they
had enough force of their own available in Helsingfors to 'deal with' the Red
Guards in the city – but only if the Bolshevik sailors could be prevented from
going ashore whilst the planned pogrom went ahead. Cromie, they hoped, would
be just the man to be able to arrange some naval order to keep the unruly
rebels on board ship for a night. With this in mind, he was made the staggering

personal offer of £50,000. In the Royal Navy, the businessmen saw what Cromie referred to as 'the bogey policeman of the Fleet'. But he knew he had to turn this offer down. Such a move, however tempting, on his part, especially on the eve of going home, could easily wreck the hard-won understanding he had with the Centrobalt, and certainly remove the guarantees of safe conduct for those men who were eager to go home.

But if £50,000 was a lot of money in 1917, £5 million was several kings' ransoms. This was their offer for Cromie's submarines, which the Whites knew would be of no further use to the Royal Navy. Yet Cromie's main concern was that, with the Germans approaching fast, the vessels might fall into their hands. One cannot but ponder over the possibilities accepting this money could have given Cromie. Had he been an avaricious opportunist he could well have expanded his romantic Russian dalliance and retired a very rich man to some remote paradise. But he avoided the temptation of entering a fairy-tale world. He turned the offer down, of course.

In Petrograd all manner of thievery and other assorted criminality was rife. Meriel Buchanan wrote of the night when a band of soldiers broke into the wine cellars at the Winter Palace.[2]

> The Preobrajinsky regiment, whose barracks were next door, tried at first to put up a feeble resistance, but very soon joined in the general plunder themselves. All during the night the orgy continued, and several encounters took place between drunken bands of soldiers and sailors, and from the Embassy we heard the constant sound of firing all down the Quay and the Millionaia . . . Soldiers in huge motor lorries drove up to the Palace and went away, their motors full of cases of priceless wine. Women, their arms full of bottles, could be seen trying to sell them to passers by in the streets. Even the children had their share of the plunder, and could be met carrying a bottle of champagne or perhaps some valuable old liqueur . . . Even as far down the Quay as the Embassy the air was infected with the reek of spirits, and everywhere drunken soldiers lay about, broken bottles littered the streets . . . the crowds in some instances scooping up the wine-stained snow, drinking it out of their hands.

It all seemed a world away from Cromie's successful efforts at the Astoria Hotel when he had the wine supplies destroyed. But despite Meriel Buchanan's worthy indignation, these were simple people plagued by war at the tail-end of centuries of privation, poverty and ill-treatment. That they should seek some solace in a massive cellar full of fine wine bought, in the final analysis, with the sweat of their brows for the privileged elite, is understandable.

The anarchy was to continue for some time as the new government bedded down. It was no longer safe to go out at night in Petrograd – even in a car, which could be halted and requisitioned by Red Guards at their whim. Anyone wearing decent clothes could be stopped and divested of their garments and belongings. It was a tough time to live through.

As the flotilla's final Christmas approached, ashore the Finns waited patiently to see if their ultimatum to the Russians – that they should respect their newly announced independence by taking the Baltic Fleet out of Helsingfors – would be honoured. But the Centrobalt was in no hurry.

It was a Yuletide of mixed emotions for the men of the flotilla. There had been glory, adventure, frustration, anger, danger and disappointment. None of these men could have predicted the nature of this unusual mission when they had left England. More so than any other theatre of war, the fulfilment of their duty was dictated by ice and darkness, in a country so strange, so alien in many ways, that the memory of it all would haunt them throughout their lives. The men on mainland Europe had had the very worst that the war could throw at them, yet they did not have the added problem of revolution. But now the sailors were standing by for the expected order to get their kitbags packed. Perhaps there would be peace in the New Year. As far as the Royal Navy in Helsingfors was concerned, peace had already arrived. As early as 3 December a Russian delegation had arrived at Brest-Litovsk to plan a ceasefire, but on the same day the British government had refused to recognise the Bolshevik regime in Russia. Meanwhile, the rest of the world had been fighting on. The British had taken Passchendaele in November. On 9 December Allenby had entered Jerusalem. The Americans, who had declared war on Germany on 6 April 1917, had declared war on Austria on 7 December. There seemed no end of the misery in sight. The commonly held view of 1914 that 'it'll all be over by Christmas' had failed to predict *which* Christmas that might be.

But for now, Ben Benson and Paddy Ryan had their last Christmas concert party to plan. With the knowledge that home and some well-earned leave was on the horizon, it was to be an enjoyable one. Yet for Ben, who had become close to Cromie, there was an edge of sadness. Cromie held the industrious and able telegraphist in high regard. In fact, the previous year he had attempted to steer him up to officer rank, almost without Ben realising. There had been a busy meeting in the officers' wardroom and the Naval Attaché from Petrograd was present. Ben was a little puzzled because he was called away from some maintenance work to Cromie's cabin that day, and found himself amidst the higher ranks, feeling rather self-conscious as he was still wearing his boiler suit. But he soon found himself engaged in conversations with first the Attaché and then the other officers. As an intelligent, humorous man, Ben was soon at his ease and, among those present, the feeling was mutual. The following day, Cromie called Ben to his cabin again.[3]

'You know, Benson,' said Cromie, 'you passed for an officer yesterday.'

I said 'Passed for an officer? What do you mean, sir?'

He said 'That little bit of business that went on while you were waiting for me – that was your examination for an officer. What do you think of it?'

I told him I wasn't interested in being an officer for various reasons, but the main reason was that when the war was finished I wanted to get out of the navy if I could. He said that I could probably get out whether I was an officer or not. He asked me what the other reasons were. I told him I could not be bothered at the way officers used to talk in those days, especially in the 'big' navy – 'Wa! Wa! Wa!' He hoped that it didn't apply to him. It didn't apply to the majority of submarine officers – they seemed to be different chaps altogether. They had to live amongst us and we had to live amongst them, and we always seemed to get on very well together, but in big ships it is quite different. Anyway, I refused the offer and he called me all the BF's he could lay his tongue to and told me that he would not recommend me if I didn't want it.

One has to admire Ben's obstinacy in some ways. No doubt he would have made a fine officer (he was, in fact, commissioned as Boatswain A/S RN in May 1945), but perhaps he enjoyed his vantage point from his rank as telegraphist and jack-of-all-trades on board. He was a working-class lad, talented, full of fun and a shrewd observer of everything which went on around him. In 1939, he submitted a fascinating poem to the Admiralty as a 'suggestion for improving the Asdic efficiency during the Battle of Britain'. The first verse gives us a clue to his naval outlook:[4]

> Sing a song of sailing on the ocean blue
> Able Seaman Winterbottom, lots of jobs to do
> Never gets a minute, doing what he's told
> Bosun's Mate and flunkey, Captain of the hold.
> Clearing up the mess deck, winding up the clocks,
> Polishing the brightwork, dobeying his socks,
> 'Show a leg' to 'Pipe down' outlook's pretty ruddy,
> Can't be intellectual, got no time for study.

On New Year's Day 1918 Cromie assembled the crew. A wave of relief spread through the ranks as they listened to his words. 'Gentlemen, our job with the Russian Admiralty is finished. Get your kits packed forthwith – but we might have a long wait before leaving.' Some days later Benson went along to Cromie's cabin to find his captain sitting at his desk with tears in his eyes.[5]

> I enquired of him whether he was ill, but without speaking he showed me a signal just received instructing him to remain in Russia as Naval Attaché in charge of the British Embassy in Petrograd. Sir George Buchanan, the Ambassador, had already left for home.
> 'Help me unpack, please, Benson. I hope the rest of you will be getting away as soon as the special train arrives.'

This episode in Benson's memoir warrants closer inspection. Cromie seemed unhappy about not going home – indeed, he shed tears. Ben's informative and entertaining record has an unfortunate tendency, being written many years after the events, of slipping backwards and forwards in time, and many of his stories are not dated. The mention of Cromie sitting in tears comes in the same paragraph as the passage about him assembling the crew to tell them they were going home. If Cromie's tearful revelation to Ben of the signal instructing him to stay actually occurred in early January, as Ben's memoir suggests, then his captain's tears, although genuine, may not have flowed because he was not going home; his emotions would have been in turmoil for other reasons. His command was being dissolved; despite his interests in Petrograd, the company he had enjoyed – that of his officers and men – was about to evaporate. In any case, we know from his letter to Commodore Hall, dated 2 December 1917, that he knew he would be staying in Russia weeks before he told Benson. It is a curious letter.[6]

> I did my best to persuade Admiral Stanley to remain so as I might see the end of the extraordinary crisis in this Fleet, but he did not approve, so I got as far as being tied up waiting for the train when I got a wire saying the Ambassador had applied for me to remain as temporary Attaché, as the present man is only RNVR. This is the very billet I asked you to protect me from when the late Minister of Foreign Affairs suggested it, but rather than see our interests left to a RNVR, who has no knowledge of naval matters, I am willing to stay till a more competent person is found. But it is a position I cannot afford when I have to support a family and my mother out of my pay. Therefore I earnestly ask you not to abandon me for ever to the backwaters of diplomacy, even if the Admiralty do approve. I want to get home and I want to stick to submarines, and I hope to get home as soon as the peace terms are settled.

This letter and Ben Benson's memoir have thus far been enough to convince those naval historians who have included Cromie in their works that he was a severely homesick, reluctant diplomat. His letters to both Commodore Hall and Admiral Phillimore seem to support this. There is evidence, however, to suggest otherwise.

In 1936, Sir Samuel Hoare, Viscount Templewood, whom Cromie had met in Russia in 1916 when the former was heading a special intelligence mission, published a memoir of his time in Russia entitled *The Fourth Seal*. When the review copies were sent out, one of the recipients was Admiral Sir Victor Stanley KCB, Cromie's superior in Russia. Stanley took slight exception to Hoare's nineteen-page chapter on Cromie. His letter is worth repeating here in full.[7]

From Admiral Hon. Sir Victor Stanley KCB
73 Upper Berkeley Street
London W1.

January 5th 1937.
To Sir Samuel Hoare.

Dear Sir Samuel,
I have been reading your book, *The Fourth Seal*, with interest as I know many of the people whom you mention, having lived in Russia for three years as Naval Attaché and having been out there during the war. But I am writing to point out an error with regard to Cromie.
  I pass over his somewhat irritating remark which you quote from a letter of his, as I am the Admiral to whom he alludes as having 'faded away at

the critical moment'. As a matter of fact I had been obliged about that time to go to Archangel. I arrived in time to make all the arrangements for evacuating the submarine crews by way of Archangel (which took some weeks owing to the difficulty of getting a train from the Bolsheviks). I eventually saw them off at the station in St Petersburg.

Cromie, gallant officer though he was, never could see beyond his own immediate horizon. But it is the paragraph about Cromie's disdain at being appointed Naval Attaché to which I take exception. The facts of the case are as follows:

When it was felt that we could do no more good with the submarines there was danger of them falling into the hands of the Germans. I was directed by the Admiralty to make arrangements for their destruction, evacuation of the crews, etc. I was to come home myself. By the time all this was done we were out of communication with England.

Cromie, who I believe had romantic reasons for not wishing to return home, came to me and asked to be allowed to remain in Russia 'to see the thing through', as he put it, remaining till the end of the war.

I told him I could not possibly allow this, as not only were submarine officers urgently required in England, but that his duty was to go with his officers and men, and that there could be no question of any further naval work in Russia, with the exception of that up at Archangel.

However, a few days after this the Ambassador, who was himself going home, sent for me and said that Lindley, who was remaining as Chargé d'Affaires, did not like to be left without any naval man and asked whether I could not have someone sent out. I immediately thought of Cromie and sent for him.

I said, 'I could not do what you asked the other day, but an opportunity has now arisen which does now make it possible for me to allow you to remain. I will take it upon myself to appoint you Naval Attaché, if that suits you.' Cromie jumped at the idea and so it was arranged.

I need hardly say now, in light of subsequent reports, I sincerely regretted what I had done, but I was only meeting his wishes and his end could not have been foreseen.

Yours sincerely,
Victor Stanley.

This all makes the story rather confusing. Cromie's first mention of the possibility of becoming Attaché came as early as 10 October 1917 in his letter to Commodore Hall. According to this, the job was suggested by the then Russian Minister for Foreign Affairs, Tereshchenko, and Cromie told Hall, 'I think I nipped it in the bud; anyway, I look to you for protection if it goes any further.' By 2 December he was expressing his dismay to Commodore Hall about being appointed, yet at the same time complaining that he had failed in trying to persuade Admiral Stanley that he should stay behind! Yet, if he wanted to stay, what post did he expect to fill? It seems obvious in some of Cromie's letters that he had a less than perfect regard for Stanley – thinking that he did not care much for his position' and that he 'faded away at the critical moment'. One could argue that Stanley's letter to Sir Samuel Hoare was a chance to 'get back' at Cromie, but by 1937 he had been dead for almost nineteen years, so there seemed little point.

Sadly, there is no evidence existing of Cromie's relationship at that time with Gwladys and his family back in London. But it is worth considering that the taut political tightrope he had been walking for over two years, and the sheer weight of responsibility in running the flotilla, had by then placed him almost in some kind of Russian fantasy world with Sophie Gagarin's elite circle. No doubt one part of his heart did yearn to come home, but the attractive elements of his stay in Russia sought to make him wish to extend the dream just a little longer. His letters to Commodore Hall and Admiral Phillimore, therefore, could be seen in some ways as playing to the gallery. When writing to the Admiralty, Cromie was the naval officer incarnate. Had his personal letters and diaries survived, we might have discovered his inner thoughts. Sadly, for even an approximate insight into these we only have the words of those who were with him in Russia. If Admiral Stanley is telling the truth, then Cromie's 'romantic reasons' must have been common currency. Distance is no barrier to rumour – it would have got back to Cromie's wife eventually.

One thing is certain, according to Cromie's existing descendants, there was much bitterness after his death. The source of this bitterness is unclear, but this aspect will be examined later, and may well explain certain matters at the end of this story. But there is evidence to suggest that Sophie Gagarin was certainly serious about Cromie. When not enjoying the summers at Pskov, the Gagarin family stayed in Petrograd in rented apartments. After 1910 they had an address at 30 Angliiskaya Nabernaja ('English Embankment'). Sophie had separate rooms, and her own entrance in the courtyard in Galernaja Street, number 29. Considering that she lived only a short walk from the embassy, it is surprising to learn that, after the revolution, she actually moved to live in the British Embassy building itself. Perhaps it was a safety measure, but this was where Cromie spent his final months, too.

The embassy building had a long history as a centre for diplomacy. Several European and Scandinavian countries had used the building since 1724. At the time of the revolution, the site was owned by the family of Prince Saltykov. It was left to his heir, the Princess Saltykova. The princess married Prince Obolensky, with whom the building is still strongly associated today – his picture hangs in the hallway. Part of the embassy site was still the Obolensky home in 1918. The Obolenskys were related to the Gagarins; Prince Obolensky was Sophie's mother's brother, and Sophie, after 1917, lived in the building with her cousin, Anna Alexeineva Obolensky. (The key to this connection was the latter's daughter, Masha Davies-Obolensky, who now lives in England and put me in touch with the current Prince Gagarin.)

Thus Francis Cromie had every reason to spend as much of his time in the embassy as he could. Sophie was there, just a few rooms away.

On 15 December Trotsky had sent a note to all the Allied embassies, informing them that he was seeking peace. The Germans were soon on the scene to parley, and when Admiral Kaiserling and his staff descended on Petrograd a whole hotel was placed at their disposal. A further gesture towards the desired peace was the release of a number of German and Austrian prisoners of war, who now roamed Petrograd's streets freely.[8]

The Buchanans, whose expected voyage home had been delayed since November, now had 8 January as their departure date. Four days earlier, on the iron-grey morning of Thursday 4 January 1918, in the thick snow on the quayside at Helsingfors, 150 of Cromie's officers and men stood in neat silent ranks. At their feet stood their kitbags. Some carried parcels, souvenirs of an unforgettable chapter in their seagoing lives. In this poignant moment, they could glance across the harbour at their submarines. For the previous few days they had cleaned, painted and polished the craft so that they looked brand new, as if ready for some other burst of action. But this was simply a proud act of naval discipline and respect, one which may have served to remind the now slovenly Russians of the pride they had once taken in their own vessels, a pride which would take many years to return in the Red Fleet. Lieutenant Ashmore recalled the scene that morning:[9]

> I shall always remember my last sad inspection of *C35*, my first and treasured command. The crew had cleaned and polished her to the last moment. Spotless deck cloths[10] were spread on the deck. The brass work glinted brightly. I was never prouder of any ship and it was bitter gall to be leaving her to such a doubtful fate. *E1*, in which I had spent so long, was in a similar perfect order. It was with a sad heart that I turned to leave with my men for the station.

The British boats had only one short voyage left to complete, one which, gladly, these silent men on the quayside would not have to take.

Cromie brought the men to attention. Within seconds, they were on their way to the station, and from there to Petrograd, ready to catch a train for Murmansk. It was, like all the rail travel ahead of them, to be an uncomfortable, lengthy journey. The trip from Helsingfors to Petrograd alone which, under normal circumstances, took twelve hours, on this occasion stretched to over thirty-six. As some glanced over their shoulders they could take one last look at the funnels of the old *Pamyat Azova*, the vessel on which so many of their memories had been made. Although the Centrobalt did not know it, her days were also numbered. The sombre tone of the departing Jack Tars was punctured on the orders of Cromie himself, who went with his men to the station to see them off. Ben Benson was the chosen instrument.[11]

> As we marched along to the station carrying our various items of luggage – I was carrying my mandolin – Captain Cromie came over and said to me 'Strike up a song'. I shall always cherish the last handshake with him when he said 'It may not be long before we meet again, Benson. Thanks for all your help. When I get home, get in touch.'

Thus through the wide, snowy streets of Helsingfors a lone mandolin rang out as accompaniment to 150 pairs of marching naval boots, as the Finns looked on at this odd spectacle as the 'bogey policemen' of the Baltic Fleet made their final exit.

Twenty-two ratings had volunteered – some having to be 'persuaded' – to stay behind as a care and maintenance party in Helsingfors to oversee the destruction of the boats. The man in charge of this detachment was Lieutenant Basil Downie, assisted by Artificer Engineer Gerald Wilton RNVR, highly regarded by Cromie for his skills as a Russian interpreter, and Assistant Paymaster Kenneth Baker, RNR. The coxswain of the party, Petty Officer William Johnson, was, like Cromie, a veteran of the early submarine service, having survived the near disaster of the *A4* when she was almost lost in 1905. Sadly, he was to lose his life on board the last British submarine to be lost in the Great War, the *G7*. The men left behind were perhaps the toughest of the tough – and now, as such a small group in the oppressive atmosphere on board the *Pamyat Azova*, they needed to be.

Crumpled and tired after spending almost two days in their cramped carriages, the returning sailors now had another long, cold, depressing wait at the Finland Station in Petrograd. On Monday, 8 January, Britain's Ambassador Sir George Buchanan and his family, along with various officers from the embassy, were also due to depart from the same station. The contrast between the imminent journeys home of the two parties could not have been starker. First, the Buchanans:[12]

> Then to the bleak, dirty Finland station, the loitering, staring soldiers – a company of Red Guards jostling everybody out of their way as they slung down the platform – the little crowd of people who had come to see us off, shivering in the icy cold, stamping their feet to try and keep warm – the jerk and rattle of the train, the shrill scream of the frozen wheels, as at last it started.
>
> Thanks to the kindness of the station master we had managed to secure a sleeping-car to ourselves and the seven English officers travelling with us, and having taken food with us we were fairly comfortable and the day passed quite quickly.

Because of their more elevated status, the diplomatic party were to travel back via Sweden.

For the Royal Navy, however, what lay ahead was not a sleeping-car, but a ten-day journey to Murmansk in an old bone-shaker of a train which, although the carriages were thankfully heated (as Ashmore commented, 'or we should have died in the bitter winter cold'), possessed no other amenities at all. For the ratings, Able Seaman Jefferys recalled that in a space approximately 30 feet × 12 feet (9 × 3.5 metres) thirty-six men had to share a carriage in which there was no sleeping accommodation. Fortunately, the grim privations of life on board a submarine would have prepared them for this, and at least there was a bonus – they were going home. The officers fared slightly better, each sharing a two-berth compartment with a petty officer. Oddly, the train included a restaurant car – but with neither food nor crockery! Fortunately, with ample stores, the men soon organised a cooking rota, and meals along the route were prepared using the party's mess gear. Another problem was that the train had no interior lighting. Fortunately, the sailors had managed to take along a small stock of candles, but these had to be severely rationed. In an environment where it became dark at four in the afternoon and remained so until ten the following morning, this made for a depressing prospect. However, as Ashmore recalled, 'The lack of light was perhaps not of itself so great a hardship as it might have been, as we had nothing whatsoever to read.'

All afternoon on that freezing Monday the men sat and waited for the permit to proceed. At the opposite platform they could see the Buchanans' more luxurious train, and many probably wondered who was lucky enough to be riding in that particular carriage. Cromie arrived at the station as the permit to leave finally came through. Lieutenant Ashmore's words describe the scene better than any.[13]

> Now we saw his distinguished, debonair figure passing down the train shaking hands with us, saying a few cheerful words to each of us. I think all felt as I did – that we were in the presence of a remarkable character whose like we would not meet again. I know there was a lump in my throat as the train pulled slowly out and we waved goodbye to the solitary figure, somehow pathetic, for all his self-confident air of flourish. Perhaps we had some premonition of the heroic death awaiting him in the land we were leaving.

Soon, as the slow-moving train rattled along the track in the early darkness, a pall of melancholy settled over the travellers. It was hard playing cards with one candle. Some sang songs, others tried to make themselves comfortable, propped up against kitbags, wrapped in their greatcoats to enjoy their only luxury – a pipe or a cigarette. Rating John Eastman told how the train would stop each night:[14]

> We went by a very lonely route which avoided all the cities. Things went well until we reached a place called Petrozadovsk. We bedded down for the night as the engine was a wood-burning thing – it went out at night and started again in the morning. The next morning when we got up we discovered that our engine had been pinched. Further, we were between two camps – an Austrian prisoner of war camp and a German prisoner of war camp. It seemed to us that the Russians intended to intern us as well. A train came along and we crossed the line and stopped it. We were then surprised to hear an English voice shouting 'Hey! What the hell do you think you're doing, stopping our train!?' It was an English colonel who had been given orders to get out of Russia. But we took his engine and shackled it onto our train – and we proceeded on our journey – but we were very careful to guard our engine at night so that nobody else pinched it.

It may be that the 'colonel' to whom Eastman refers was, in fact, a Major Babbington, as mentioned in Ben Benson's account of the same journey. It is hard to say in which direction the other train was going, as Benson referred to the track as a single line – so the other train must have been bringing up the rear, although as they were at Petrozadovsk, with its twin prisoner-of-war camps, perhaps the line there ran to two tracks with sidings. Earlier in his memoirs, Ben recalled a trip in the Baltic on HMS *E19* with Cromie when they stopped to pick up two distressed deserting German sailors in a lifeboat. In an odd turn of events, in the middle of Russia's massive sprawl, they were to meet again.[15]

> It was a one-line railway which had been built, I believe, by a British officer, I think his name was Major Babbington. He had the job of being the transport officer at Murmansk. In the early days he had started off with reindeer sledges and then he eventually got this railway going. He was on the train with us and used to give us lectures about the whole story. There were several prisoner-of-war camps along this railway, where we would get wood fuel for the engine and for our fires and water for the water tanks.
>
> We met the two German chaps – they were in one of these camps and were very pleased to have a yarn. Some months before we left one of the chaps on our boats had picked up a little black dog and trained it up to do little tricks. We would put an onion under a little enamel basin and throw it along the mess deck and this dog got the way of getting the onion out. He loved an onion, and it used to be amusing to see him eating it, tears running down his face all the time – a very funny thing. Well, the sailor who had adopted this dog was bringing it home with him – whether or not he would have got it ashore I don't know. The train used to stop now and again – sometimes for hours, others just a few minutes. Everybody used to jump out and get a bit of exercise. On this occasion everybody jumped off – including 'Chauny', the dog – who was looking for a tree. He was called Chauny as this was the Russian word for his colour – black. Suddenly the train started up again and everybody got back on board – but Chauny was missing. It was still daylight and we looked out of the windows – and there was Chauny running after the train. The communication cord was a piece of rope that ran the full length of the train but when somebody pulled it the rope broke and the train didn't stop . . . Poor little Chauny got further and further behind. We never heard any more of him – he was probably caught by a bear.

The days rolled on into the colder, frozen wastes of northern Russia. Lieutenant Ashmore played endless games of chess in his compartment with Lieutenant Sealy. Occasionally their attention would be distracted as the train would grind to a halt owing to massive snow drifts, yet within minutes hordes of Latvians or Chinese would appear, as if from nowhere, frantically shovelling away the snow to clear the track.

As if to highlight the success of the proletariat over the bourgeoisie, whilst the British sailors, who had worked hard and risked their lives for the Russians, were crammed thirty-six men to a carriage, the Bolshevik able seaman who travelled with them as escort enjoyed the luxury of a whole carriage to himself.

There was a brooding threat of danger along the line too. Many of the Austrian and German prisoners were now free to roam the countryside. They were ill equipped for the Russian winter, and mostly starving. Although the carriage containing the naval party's stores was constantly well guarded, there was at least one occasion when a determined attack by foraging Austrians had to be fended off. One incident also filled Lieutenant Ashmore with horror.[16]

> An English Army colonel who spoke fluent German and Russian was taking passage with us. When he berated a German soldier for not saluting his uniform, there was a loud protest from the Russian bystanders that the custom of saluting had been abolished. Without a moment's hesitation, the colonel slashed the German across his face with his riding switch. Not only did the German spring to attention and give an immaculate salute, but the Russians shouted in delight and admiration, 'That's right, Colonel – hit him again!'

When Cromie had first been given the green light to send his men home, the Russians had allowed him a mere fourteen days to accomplish the task. They arrived in Murmansk, crumpled, cramped and tired, with only a day of the deadline left. There at the quayside lay their final transport home, the armed merchant cruiser, *Andes*. But it was to be, in many ways, a frosty, seagoing extension of the grim trip the lads had just made overland. In peacetime the *Andes* was a liner, equipped not for the rigours of the Arctic circle but for the tropics! Ashmore was dismayed to find 'mess decks and cabins like ice-boxes' and a 'vast, bleak saloon in which two electric radiators of doubtful efficiency strove in vain to dispel the frost in the air'.

As the sailors finally found enough space – a cold one at that – to stretch their legs and were relieved at not having to constantly guard their belongings, they may well have looked forward to a well-earned drink in the ship's bar. They were disappointed. The *Andes* had been waiting in port for the party for so long that her officers had drunk the bar dry. Ashmore puts a fitting coda to this chapter: 'Life had reached its lowest ebb. The gale of wind and pouring rain which greeted us on arrival at Greenock was as nothing after this nadir in our fortunes.'

CHAPTER 19

POSSESSION DENIED

All men dream: but not equally. Those who dream by night in
the dusty recesses of their minds wake in the day to find that it
was vanity: but the dreamers of the day are dangerous men, for
they may act their dream with open eyes, to make it possible.
This I did.

T.E. Lawrence, *Seven Pillars of Wisdom*

With the greater part of his force now gone, Francis Cromie threw himself into
his new job as a diplomat. To his dismay he was discovering that although the
post held some kudos, his wages hardly seemed to reflect this. One of his first
letters in January 1918 as Naval Attaché was to his new superior, Admiral
Reginald Hall, Head of Naval Intelligence (not to be confused with Commodore
S.S. Hall of the Submarine Service). Cromie was now entering the deep end of
the navy pool. Until now he had only dabbled, albeit successfully and in a somewhat amateur capacity, in the murky world of espionage and undercover work.
Although it seems obvious from his letters that he was not altogether happy
mixing with the British military 'spooks' in Petrograd, he was to be drawn
inevitably into their net in the coming months. To all intents and purposes,
Francis Cromie had become a secret agent, whether he liked it or not.

Admiral Reginald Hall, later to be knighted, who went under the nickname
'Blinker', was probably one of the most powerful men in the history of naval
espionage. The American ambassador in London, Dr Page, wrote: 'Hall is one
genius that the war had developed. Neither in fiction, nor in fact, can you find
any man to match him. Of the wonderful things I know he has done, there are
several that it would take an exciting volume to tell. The man is a genius . . . All
other secret service men are amateurs by comparison.'[1]

Cromie would have to work hard to serve such a man, yet apart from a wealth
of information on the Germans' demarcation lines in the Baltic and Arctic, his
first transmission to Blinker ended on a more prosaic note.[2]

I understand that the peace salary of the NA was £365 from Admiralty and
£800 from FO; at the present moment, when a joint costs 70 roubles, I shall
be worse off than in my last job unless I get a flat for nothing, as heating
will cost about 1,000 roubles per month. Living is not less than six times
peace rate, and we get only 3½ times the number of roubles per pound. Of
course I shall not be able to entertain very much on the peace footing. I

understand I am here only for a short time, but should it become desirable for me to remain, I beg of you to consider a reasonable increase on the peace salary.

The kind of intelligence services we have come to know today, such as MI5, MI6, Special Branch, etc., were, at the outset of the First World War, the military establishment's very small and rather poor relations. But nothing more fulfils a spy's existence than war. During peace, there are scruples to observe. Your information is collected and logged, filed for later. But in war, the game is on and the gloves are off; the secret agent becomes all important – what he discovers, the information he sends back, could save or cost millions of lives. At the time Cromie came under the watchful eye of Blinker Hall, the Admiral was presiding over an increasingly powerful department, with fingers in a number of international political pies.

To illustrate the growth of the intelligence community, it should be noted that at the opening of the war, Special Branch had just seventy members; by the time of the Armistice in 1918, it had 700. In 1914 MI5 had around twelve members; by the Armistice it employed 844, with a further 1,453 men and women working as censors on letters and telegrams at the Post Office.[3] Much of the increase in clandestine information-gathering was not particularly because of the German threat. What was worrying the crowned heads and governments of Europe was the growth of the revolutionary movement. Fighting the Germans – or the French, or anyone else – was simply an alternative to cricket. The Empire expected to have a scrap every few years. But revolution and its attendant industrial unrest was a threat to the comfortable social order and required extra special attention.

Already in Moscow, preparing to work with Cromie in Petrograd, was a man who was destined to go down in the annals of espionage as 'the Ace of Spies' – Sydney Reilly. Reilly was in Russia for MI6 and had no doubts about who his own 'enemy' was in the Great War.[4]

> Gracious Heavens, will the people of England never understand? The Germans are human beings; we can afford to be even beaten by them. Here in Moscow there is growing to maturity the arch enemy of the human race . . . At any price this foul obscenity which has been born in Russia must be crushed out of existence . . . Peace with Germany? Yes, peace with Germany, peace with anybody. There is only one enemy. Mankind must unite in a holy alliance against this midnight terror.

It is doubtful that Francis Cromie would have fully agreed with Reilly's view of the Germans in January 1918, and his experience of the 'foul obscenity', mainly through the sailors' committees, although extreme, never drove him to such paroxysms of hatred. Cromie was a man who assessed the immediate situation as it affected him and his men and acted accordingly. It might well be, as Admiral Stanley later commented, that Cromie 'could never see beyond his own horizon', but there had been enough on that horizon for any man to tackle.

* * *

In Helsingfors on board the *Pamyat Azova*, the absence of Cromie's strong refereeing presence was making life difficult for Lieutenant Basil Downie. The twenty-four remaining men of the original flotilla force felt isolated, and the bullying arrogance of the Russians began to make their lives hell. They at least knew that they would soon be going home, but the pettiness on board and the explosive atmosphere was a strain poor Downie, only two years into his rank as lieutenant, could well do without. But over two years of Cromie's boldness and determination had rubbed off on Basil Downie. He was determined to follow his captain's example.

The rumours of a full British stores locker spread through the ranks of the Russian sailors, but Downie was ready for them. The pilfering of Royal Navy stores had become a constant threat, so with engineering assistance, Downie had the steel door handle to the locker wired up to the electricity supply. Sure enough, one dark night the Russians sneaked below to raid the supplies, but the agonised bellowing of one of the culprits, unable to loose his grip on the handle as the voltage coursed through his body, sent out a firm message to the comrades. The attempt was not repeated. Further dark threats were insinuated, almost melodramatically: a display of wires and alarms clocks loaded aboard the submarines with the rumour spread through the Russian mess decks that, should the British sailors have any bother from the Russians, they had each submarine wired up on a time charge and the ensuing explosions would sink not only the boats but the *Pamyat Azova*. Despite the Centrobalt's revolutionary confidence and cocky truculence, they knew from experience that the Royal Navy had a propensity for action above mere words. Thus, Downie's Cromie-esque posture kept the would-be marauders at bay.

As for the Finns' declaration of independence, at first this had been accepted by the Bolsheviks on 31 December 1917, but Josef Stalin persuaded the Petrograd Soviet to alter the terms of the independence. This was followed by the Bolsheviks' assistance to the Finnish left to establish their own power over the country. Under the terms of the Armistice, Russian forces should have been withdrawn from Finland, but this was not to happen quickly – and in any case, the Red Fleet was by now iced in, so there was no chance of a naval withdrawal.

Cromie visited Downie as often as he could when calling on the Centrobalt at Helsingfors. He was still a submariner at heart, and when writing from the embassy in Petrograd to Commodore Hall he dropped his guard:[5]

> I have just returned from Helsingfors where everything remains quiet as far as we are concerned, although other things are disturbed enough. Fortunately I have a big pull with the Central Balt and was able to squash an embryo pogrom of officers. I am much disturbed at this enforced 'change of horses' at this critical point in my career, and I assure you this place is not of my seeking, as I once asked for your protection from it last summer. However, at present I can be of some use, but when this crisis is over I want to get back to my legitimate job.

Downie was now finding it increasingly difficult to cash navy bills, and with the currency situation worsening all the time, had no choice other than to continue Cromie's black marketeering. As he had up to six months' stores in hand and knew that soon the care and maintenance party might get the final order to destroy the boats, and then go home, he took the risk of selling off surplus clothing and tobacco at profitable rates in order to keep the crew paid.

Over at the British Embassy in Petrograd, Cromie, used to the practicalities of running ships and submarines, organising crews and all the other logistical planning his post had required, soon found that the way the laid-back, gentlemanly intelligence services and diplomats ordered their lives was a mystery. By February he was already giving his opinion on the matter – wanted or not – to Admiral Hall.[6]

Having more or less settled down in my new job – which by the way I have not yet been appointed to – I would like to make a few remarks which strike me as a new hand. Probably my ideas will appear idiotic, but I must plead ignorance of the inner workings of my new job.

First is the extraordinary amount of duplication of work due to the overlapping of departments; I refer to NA, AA, Gen. Poole and Boyce. It strikes me that this is principally due to a lack of combination and contact between these departments, resulting very largely from a professional as well as personal jealousy. This sounds ridiculous in these times, but I assure you from personal experience it is true. Having expressed my intention of discussing a question with Gen. Poole, I was asked why I did not act for myself and take what kudos there was. I don't think this spirit leads to the best result, and I have taken it upon myself to interchange all news with Boyce, which I find is very a valuable aid to sizing up the true position.

I was so struck with our lack of co-ordination that I inquired into the French methods; there I find that General Nicelle is head of a large organisation where the heads of the departments report to him at 4 p.m. every day, from which short conference he is able to properly appreciate the situation and issue directions to the various departments as to policy, information etc., required. With us I find there is no head to direct different departments as a homogenous organisation, much less direct their policy. Each wanders along, more or less indifferent to the policy and ignorant of the work of its neighbour. I would earnestly suggest that Gen. Poole be appointed the chief of commissions under the Ambassador, so as to direct the efforts of all departments on a definite plan and eliminate these petty jealousies: NA and AA to be included. That such ideas will raise a storm of abuse and protest I fully realise, but being unbiased and only a bird of passage, it won't hurt me very much.

Of course, Cromie was no stranger at the embassy by this time, but his boldness in criticising the working methods of his colleagues – especially to Admiral Hall, the Head of Naval Intelligence – after only a month in the job only demonstrates just how precocious he could be at times. It seems doubtful if holding up the French as an example of efficiency to the grandees at Whitehall would have won him many friends. This said, he probably had a point. His naval background in submarines ran on close-knit teamwork. Without it, as the Russians had frequently proved, the job fell to pieces. After his long struggles with the sailors' committees, the last place he expected to find petty jealousies was here, in his own embassy. Yet the various military attachés and intelligence agents living in the twilight world of Petrograd in 1918 often acted independently, and as the year progressed, Cromie discovered that, for him, the navy way of doing things was a thing of the past.

He continued:[7]

> The present situation in Finland is asking for us to put our fingers in – but we spend thousands in propaganda – one party wants to aid the Red, another wants to remain neutral, yet there is no direction! Of course I keep outside political and SS[8] work of any sort, because I should lose the trust of the Fleet if they found me doing anything of that sort. However, I lay all my information before those concerned to telegraph home, and only handle those things I consider my job, but this does not happen with every department. This may sound very incoherent, but I beg of you to give the idea due consideration in view of the French success in this matter.
>
> I should very be much obliged for information as to my salary, etc., so that I can make financial arrangements – at present I allot £25 per month to my wife's account, the remainder I wish paid into my account, Lloyd's Bank, Portsmouth, but I cannot find out who I should communicate with.

Money again. It seems astounding today that a man would move from submarine captain to diplomat and then have to puzzle over what his salary was, and indeed, where it might be coming from. On the other hand, it might be hasty to assume that Cromie's pleas to Admiral Hall over money went entirely unheeded. The record of clerical staff at MI5 in London shows that a Mrs J.G.C. Cromie started work there on 11 March 1918 and stayed until 4 September. There is then a break in her employment and it recommences on 1 October, but there is no indication how long she stayed after this.[9] So, did Blinker Hall do his new chap in Russia a favour and give Gwladys a job? It would seem so.

The inevitable peace deal between the Germans and the Bolsheviks had not received the hoped-for response from Berlin. When the first delegation got back from Brest-Litovsk, in Trotsky's words, 'bringing with it the monstrous demands that Kühlmann had submitted on behalf of the Central Powers',[10] Trotsky was chosen to go to Brest-Litovsk in an attempt to stall matters and get a better deal. 'To delay negotiations,' said Lenin, 'there must be someone to do the delaying.'[11]

Considering his boldness as a revolutionary, Trotsky did not relish his visit to Brest-Litovsk: 'I confess I felt as if I were being led to the torture chamber. Being with strange and alien people always had aroused my fears; it did especially on this occasion. I absolutely cannot understand revolutionaries who willingly accept posts as ambassadors and feel like fish in water in their new surroundings.'[12]

The negotiations dragged on and the less than satisfactory treaty, from Russia's point of view, was finally signed on 3 March 1918. Trotsky and Lenin had fervently hoped that as a backdrop to the negotiations the beacon of their own workers' uprising would be the signal for the rest of Europe's proletariat to rise up and make the revolution the international cause their carefully worked-out theories had predicted. It was a forlorn hope. Not only did Russia, through Brest-Litovsk, lose 90 per cent of her coal fields, all her Baltic ports except Kronstadt, the Black Sea Fleet plus the extensive granaries of the Ukraine, it was also the major spark which was to ignite the Russian Civil War. Yet Trotsky's response to the situation was stark and succinct: 'no war – no peace'. For the Germans, to the horror of Francis Cromie, it meant that without the Russians as belligerents, they could now consolidate and add to their Russian gains. And for the struggling new Naval Attaché Brest-Litovsk contained an additional condition to which he was never going to agree – the seven British submarines at Helsingfors were to be handed over to the advancing German forces. The Admiralty had hoped that as long as Helsingfors remained in Finnish or Russian hands the boats would be safe. Peace would mean that at some future point they could be saved and brought home.

Finland's parliament was fairly balanced between left and right, and furious debate had not resolved the thorny question of how the country would deal with the Germans. The right wing had been pro-German throughout the war, and had even sent Finnish volunteers, the 27th Jäger Battalion, to fight along-side the Germans on the Baltic front.[13] After the Finns declared independence in December 1917, a workers' militia had been formed to fight against any proposed alliance with the Germans. Fighting had broken out in January between the growing contingents of White Russian forces and the Reds in Helsingfors. The militias seized the capital, and although the Whites were defeated and driven out of the city, they formed a front north of Helsingfors which stretched from the east to the west of Finland. The Finnish Minister for Foreign Affairs, Yrjo Sirola, met young Lieutenant Basil Downie and confirmed that the protection of the flotilla would continue. All that Downie could do was carry on his barrow-boy activities, selling boots and tobacco, and keep the care and maintenance party ticking over.

Cromie's confusing workload continued to increase. Before, he'd had sub-marines, revolution and the Germans – now he had Bolsheviks and the Germans, plus a third element to contend with – the White Russian forces. The Finnish White Guards, supported by counter-revolutionary Russians under General Gustav Mannerheim, launched an offensive to dislodge the Reds. Gustav Mannerheim had been one of the Tsar's most efficient officers, and had served under Brusilov. He was in an awkward position. Whilst he was vehemently anti-Bolshevik, he was certainly not pro-German. His mission in Finland was to uphold her independence, not see the country become yet another German province. These three diverse forces, the pro-Soviet left, the right, which was awaiting German support, and Mannerheim, who appeared to have no time for either, provided a confusing backdrop for the Royal Navy. But after three years in Russia, Cromie, and apparently also Downie, had learned how to pick a careful path between these factions and use whatever support each could offer to the navy's advantage. Already the German Baltic Division, under General von der Goltz, delayed by the winter ice, was now rapidly approaching Hango. This promised to be the death-knell for the flotilla, and Cromie knew it was time to act. The submarines, he said, would not fall into German hands, so the plan to destroy them was about to be put into action.

The boats were prepared for sea as the ice began to break up in late March. Time fuses and demolition charges were laid, and the Russian liaison officers agreed to support Downie in taking the boats out of the harbour when the fateful day arrived. Cromie arrived in Helsingfors from Petrograd on 3 April with the shocking news that the Germans were coming ashore in the flotilla's old summer quarters along the Finnish coast at Hango. Immediately, he issued Downie with the order – 'Destroy the boats.'

As he looked out over Helsingfors harbour at the shattered ice in the weak sun of the dying winter, Francis Cromie had the satisfaction, since becoming a diplomat, of knowing that his efforts with this deadly little collection of submarines had been a real pain for the Germans. He had written to Commodore Hall from Petrograd in February:[14]

> I had some most gratifying news from Admiral Altfata, one of the Russian peace delegates at Brest Litovsk, who informed me that the Hun Admiral Hoppmann told him in private conversation that the English Flotilla was a constant anxiety to them in the Baltic, in fact the only one, and that the Huns had organised and constantly kept at sea a special force to deal with these 'pests'.

Cromie agreed that although they had done less material damage than he had hoped for, they had 'given the Hun furiously to think'. In fact, as early as 1915, after Max Horton's string of successes, Prince Henry of Prussia had addressed his U-boat crews, who were then operating in the Gulf of Finland: 'I consider the destruction of a Russian submarine will be a great success, but I regard the destruction of a British submarine as being at least as valuable as that of a Russian armoured cruiser.'[15] But now they would be destroyed to spite the Germans rather than to please them.

To get the boats out of the harbour for scuttling in the Gulf required the services of an ice-breaker. Although, in Downie's official report, he made small mention of local difficulties, his bold dealing with last-minute Russian procrastination provides ample evidence that Cromie's legendary bravado had rubbed off on him. Both the captain of the dockyard and the tug-master were unwilling, for whatever reasons they could cobble together, to organise the release of a tug and an ice-breaker. Downie shrugged his shoulders and, telling the Russians that he 'fully understood their difficulties', expressed his regret, therefore, that he would now be forced to blow up all the submarines – and the barge full of torpedoes – right there in Helsingfors harbour, with all that event's attendant destruction to the area and the ships moored there. The dockyard captain was alarmed, and said, 'Well, perhaps tomorrow the ice-breaker will be available.' Downie was already walking away. 'Sorry. That will be too late.' Within seconds, the captain called him back. 'We'll have the ice-breaker ready in half an hour.'[16] The destruction, which was neither quick nor easy, is best told in Basil Downie's own words.'[17]

I have the honour to report that on the 3rd April 1918 official information having been received of the landing of German forces at Hango, 100 versts west of Helsingfors, I proceeded to carry out the destruction of the Baltic Submarine Flotilla. Sometime previously, the greater portion of stores including propellers, clutches, battery gear etc., had been loaded in the barge used as a torpedo store and workshop.

News of the German landing was received at 11.30 a.m. A little difficulty was experienced in obtaining the services of any ice-breakers, but this was overcome by threatening to blow up the boats in the harbour. All Russian officers who had been attached to the British S/M Flotilla, and who were then in Helsingfors offered their assistance in the destruction of the Flotilla.

At 1.15 p.m. I proceeded to sea in *E1* followed by *E9*, *E8* and *E19* in charge of Russian officers, leaving a small party behind for the destruction of the stores which were left in the dockyards; big armatures, etc., which it had been impossible to transport into the torpedo barge.

A point 1½ miles south of Grohara Light with a depth of 15 fathoms was decided on for the destruction of the boats. The charges used for destruction consisted each of two Mark VIII warheads with a 20 lb dry gun cotton charge as primer. Three of these had been placed in each boat, one forward, one aft and one amidships. These were fired electrically, the timing arrangements consisting of an ordinary alarm clock fitted so that when the alarm bell rang contact was made and the firing circuit completed.

E19, *E1* and *E9* were destroyed, but owing to the refusal of the ice-breaking tug to remain at sea any longer after the second failure of the clock in *E8*, this latter boat had to be left out for the night. At 7.00 a.m. the following morning, April 4th, I proceeded to sea in *C26* followed by *C35* in charge of a Russian officer and ice-breaking tug towing the torpedo barge. *C27* was left behind in accordance with the wishes of Captain F.N.A. Cromie, RN, who considered it advisable to retain one boat until the last moment in case of any trouble arising with the Russians. *C26* was secured alongside *E8* and the two boats were blown up together. *C35* was secured alongside the torpedo barge. Two attempts were made to blow them up, but each time the clock failed and the tug refusing to remain out any longer, we had to return to harbour without completing the destruction.

A party had been left ashore for the destruction of 40 torpedoes stowed in the Russian S/M salvage ship, *Volhoff*. The swirlers and sinking gear of these torpedoes were removed, they were blown through with 1840 acid and afterwards smashed up with a sledge hammer.

The following morning, April 5th, *C27* was taken out to sea and as the German troops had been reported only 20 miles away, it was decided that there was not time to chance a failure of the clocks, and therefore the two boats, including *C35*, were sunk in 15 fathoms.

About 3 minutes after the sinking of each boat a big explosion occurred, the water being thrown up about 12 feet. this, presumably, was the exploding of the battery.

As the ice was considerably less thick than previously and the difficulty getting away in the tug therefore considerably less, I considered it safe to use a 15 minute Bickford fuse for the torpedo barge. This worked satisfactorily and the barge and all torpedoes and stores on board were completely demolished.

At 6.00 p.m. the same evening officers and crew left Helsingfors by train for Petrograd, the Germans at that time being reported only 5 miles west of the city.

Downie had planned everything well and had anticipated that getting his men away from Helsingfors and up to Murmansk, probably not by the usual route via Petrograd, with the Germans rapidly advancing, would be just as much of a challenge as destroying the boats. With this in mind he had concocted an ingenious plan for the party to lie low in a farmhouse close to the front in the hope that the White forces would overtake them, thus providing them with the freedom to travel to neutral Sweden and then on to Britain. As there was a British merchant ship in the harbour, and his men required civilian passports to make such a journey, Downie persuaded the master of the vessel to sign on each of his men as crew members. The helpful captain then took the contingent to the Swedish and Norwegian consulates and explained to the consuls that he wished to repatriate these 'crewmen'. Had this strategy been carried out, it would have resulted in a complex journey, but the Germans' bad luck was to be Downie's salvation. Von der Goltz's troops had suffered a delay, enabling Downie to make a dash for the station in Helsingfors where there was a possibility that the party might still make it by train to Petrograd. He was lucky – but boarding the train was a desperate experience. Downie had to use all the force, bluff and bluster he could to get his men on board. Bayonets were fixed and two Bolshevik sailors had to be forced from the carriage. Sentries were placed at either end to prevent anyone else invading their valuable space. This was their one chance of going home, and nothing would stand in their way.

Cromie, in a conversation with Downie some days earlier, had intimated that he, too, was considering getting out of Russia whilst he had a chance. The suggestion was that he might join the care and maintenance party on their trip home.[18] Cromie's new job working from the British Embassy had put him under constant scrutiny and he had a growing band of enemies. As captain of the flotilla his task was relatively straightforward and his various accommodations and dealings with the Centrobalt were understood. But by the spring of 1918 he was already associating, by necessity, with characters from the intelligence community who would always remain under suspicion from the Bolsheviks.

Cromie put in an appearance at Helsingfors station, but to Downie's dismay he had changed his mind about leaving Russia. As Cromie said a last farewell to the final remnants of his gallant force, Downie pleaded with him to take this opportunity to get out. It is hard to imagine what was going through Cromie's mind as he waved his final goodbye. Perhaps the image of Sophie Gagarin was there. His excuse for remaining was that there were three British-owned merchant ships still docked in Helsingfors, and that, rather than see them go to the Germans, he was about to destroy them – on his own. Downie offered the help of the care and maintenance party in the endeavour. After all, to every man in that railway carriage, Cromie was a hero and they would have willingly helped him in this one last act of the war they were still duty bound to fight. But it was not to be.

Downie's party arrived in Petrograd on 9 April. The reports of the destruction of the submarines and the party's departure from Petrograd in the London *Times* has a suitably jingoistic flavour:[19]

END OF THE BALTIC SUBMARINES
SEVEN SUNK OFF HELSINGFORS
RETURN OF THE CREWS

The following Admiralty communiqué is issued:

The seven submarines of the Royal Navy which remained in Russian waters were destroyed by order during the five days from April 3 to April 8, 1918, upon the approach of German naval forces and transports to Hango (South-West Finland). None of the ships fell into enemy hands.

The guns at and near Hango had already been dismantled; and upon the appearance of the German forces the Russians retreated from the vicinity, after blowing up their own four American submarines. Four British submarines of class E were taken outside the harbour of Helsingfors on April 3, blown up and sunk. Three C boats were demolished between that day and April 8. Their crews were duly removed to Petrograd.

BLUEJACKETS IN PETROGRAD

PETROGRAD, April 9 (received yesterday)

Yesterday evening the Russian public passing along the Neva Quay in front of the British Embassy building were very much attracted by the unique sight of a party of British sailors preparing to escort several cartloads of baggage and naval stores to the Nicholas railway station.

These were bluejackets, about 30 in number, who had been obliged to destroy their submarines last week in Helsingfors in order to save them from the Germans. They were homeward bound by way of the Murmansk railway, and were taking with them provisions for a month or more. They had loaded rifles slung across their shoulders or laid on their knees as they sat upon cases of Australian 'bully' beef and biscuits, ready against any hooligan attempt at expropriation.

216

There was a free and easy manner about them, even a jaunty air, which seemed to defy the squalor of the Russian surroundings, and which were quite out of keeping with the melancholy aspect of Petrograd and its dirty, unkempt inhabitants. They had made good use of the 24 hours spent in comfortable quarters in the Embassy mansion to wash and rig themselves out afresh, and they turned out spick and span as if on parade. The spotless blue of their dress, and the shine on their shoes, the only polished footgear seen here on any soldier or sailor for many a long day, presented a glaring contrast with the grey untidiness of the undisciplined soldiers and sailors of the Russian Republic, with their mud-begrimed boots, who stopped to look on with gaping astonishment. The half-starved natives cast longing eyes at the abundance of toothsome rations which these Jack Tars were guarding so jealously, and well it was they took this precaution, for sudden raids by marauders are now of almost daily occurrence.

This departure of the British naval contingent from the Baltic, which is now completely under the control of the Germans, marks the last scene and the end of Great Britain's active help to defaulting Russia as an ally in the war.

One of the most ridiculous tit-bits published here in this connection, and which afforded much amusement to the submarine crews, was a story about the 'heroic' suicide of one of their officers who was so much affected by the loss of his boat that he sang 'Rule Britannia' and then shot himself.

And so Downie's 'jaunty' contingent marched off for their five-day ordeal by rail to Murmansk and then home on board the transport *Huntsend*.[20]

Like the earlier return of their comrades in January, the trip was not without incident. The party this time shared their train with an elite gathering of fleeing diplomats. On board were the ministers of Portugal, Belgium and Greece and their legation staffs, plus the French military mission. The rest of the train was filled with other fleeing refugees who had been well placed or rich enough to buy their passage out of a Russia they no longer recognised. As an interpreter to accompany his party, Downie had taken along his Russian liaison officer, Sub-Lieutenant Victor Geyseler.

Geyseler's authoritative presence proved to be an advantage three days into the journey when a somewhat officious commissar boarded the train. They had already suffered many halts, with their attendant inspection of papers and passports, but in this instance the commissar decided that the sailors' papers were 'not in order'. He immediately ordered the party to return to Petrograd so that the matter could be further investigated. Using that mix of bluff and bluster to which the Royal Navy had become so accustomed to in Russia, Geyseler faced up to the awkward commissar and issued him with a stern warning – these sailors were *armed*, they had no more business in Russia and they were going home whether he liked it or not – and a return to Petrograd was out of the question.[21] The commissar retreated to think things over, and as if by magic, the incorrect paperwork was suddenly deemed to be in order.

As if this obstacle were not enough, the train was brought to another halt by a section of track, over half a mile long, which had collapsed. Fortunately, their luck held when another train was sent down from Murmansk. Everyone on board had to disembark with their luggage and stagger the distance to join the new train.

Finally walking up the gangway to board the *Huntsend* must have been a great relief. Victor Geyseler, upon arrival in Murmansk, had serious, and no doubt justified, concern over his future as a Russian naval officer now that his cordon of protection was about to sail away. Thus he took the opportunity to get out of Russia and sail to England on the *Huntsend*. Yet there was an odd coda to the story, as related by Ashmore: 'Reaching London at last, Downie and Geyseler alighted on the platform at King's Cross together. Turning a moment later to speak to the Russian, Downie found, to his astonishment, that he had vanished. Never again, from that moment did he see or hear anything of the young Russian.'[22]

And so, for the 200-plus men of the Royal Navy's Baltic Flotilla, the epic adventure of war and revolution in a country of exotic extremes was finally at an end, apart from the further escapades of their captain. Looking at Basil Downie's innovative efforts between Cromie's move to the embassy in January and the destruction of the submarines and the return home, one might have expected he would have been honoured by the Admiralty. A note was passed on 26 May 1918 to the Naval Secretary and Commodore Hall recommending an honour, but Hall's handwritten comment on this read:[23]

> It is advised that Lt Downie received the D.S.C. for his services in the Baltic as recently as 26 April 1918. The preparations for blowing up were made entirely by Lt S. Kent (then the gunner-T of flotilla) who bought clocks and improvised the time fuses etc.
>
> The above is not intended to detract from Lt Downie's successful execution of the duty of carrying out the destruction, for which he was retained; but in view of his recent decoration perhaps a letter from the Admiralty would be considered sufficient.

Francis Cromie was now alone in Helsingfors, with the advancing Germans only a few miles from the city. Whatever Downie had felt as he had watched Cromie's poignant figure from the departing train, it was mirrored by the man himself, when he wrote to Phillimore on 2 May: 'It gave me the hump to see the last remnants of the little force I was so proud of (and not without reason) steam cheering and laughing out of the station whilst I remained alone.'[24]

Ahead of him lay a task which would normally require the help of at least a dozen seamen. To the Germans' angered dismay, his seven British submarines were in their final resting place at the bottom of the Baltic. This submerged bit of Britain's fighting fleet was about to be joined by three merchant ships. His men might have gone, but Cromie knew he could still be a thorn in the Germans' side – and his war with 'the Hun' was far from over.

Above, left: Sonia ('Sophie') Gagarin at Holomki, the Gagarin mansion at Pskov *c.* 1912–15, with her father's self-portrait on the table.

Above, right: Sonia and her eldest brother, Lev, an officer with the White Army who died from typhoid at Constantinople after the revolution.

Right: Sonia in 1904.

Below, left: The current Prince Andrey Gagarin, St Petersburg 2000.

Below, right: Vladimir Milosevsky's pencil sketch of Sonia Gagarin.

CHAPTER 20

SOLITAIRE

> I can't write about the general exodus of Allied Embassies; it was
> too sickening to see the last shreds of our prestige being thrown
> to the dogs; that it should have been led by the British and organ-
> ised by their military advisers made me lose my temper.

Letter from Cromie to Admiral Phillimore, 2 May 1918

According to the records,[1] there were just four British merchant vessels deliber-
ately sunk in the Baltic by their crews between 1914 and 1918. Three of these went
to the bottom courtesy of Francis Cromie. The odd one out was the SS *Toledo*,
1,159 gross tons, owned by the Leith, Hull & Hamburg Steam Packet Co. Ltd.
According to one source[2] this vessel was reportedly blown up by her crew to avoid
capture on 5 October 1917, 1½ miles (2.5 km) east by north of Dago Island. It
appears that the *Toledo* had been requisitioned by the Soviets as a transport for
the Russian navy. Considering that at this time Cromie's C boats were operating
close by at Rogekul, one wonders what became of her original British crew –
perhaps the Royal Navy rescued them, but they do not feature in the flotilla's
records. However, the three other ships do, and dramatically so. In July 1916,
after the Battle of Jutland, over 200 British ships left the Baltic, where many had
been tied up at Kronstadt and Petrograd. How they got home, considering the
vigilance then in force by the German navy, is another question.

But not every ship made it. When the 1,834 ton SS *Cicero*, owned by Hull's
Wilson Line, left Hull on 13 July 1914 she was bound for Sweden and then the
Baltic ports on one of her regular voyages. Hull has always had strong connections with the Finland/Russia trade. Her captain, William Henry Pinchon, was
accompanied on this trip by his wife, Eliza Boston Pinchon. They were a strong,
hardy couple and spent much time at sea. Eliza had been married twice and given
birth to ten children, not to mention having several miscarriages. But the poor
lady had lately become subject to heart attacks, which is hardly surprising. What
happened on that trip, therefore, was barely conducive to poor Mrs Pinchon's
health.

As the hostilities of the Great War opened up in the Baltic, the *Cicero* was
intercepted by a German submarine. On the surface, the U-boat opened fire in
an attempt to get Captain Pinchon to heave to. A shell came through the pantry
cabin bulkhead and created quite a mess. Thus humbled, Captain Pinchon
decided that discretion was the better part of valour and invited the German

skipper on board. The U-boat captain apologised for the trouble, and here the information on the movements of the *Cicero* dries up. What we do know is that Mrs Pinchon became so ill after this attack that the vessel was escorted to a German port and she was put ashore, only to be spat upon by civilians. Eventually, she was repatriated through the Netherlands. How the *Cicero* came to be in Helsingfors in 1918, after being captured by the Germans in the opening weeks of the war, is a mystery. There is a three-year gap in the archive, but Captain Pinchon did leave a hand-written statement, dated 17 September 1918:[3]

Captain Pinchon and the Chief Engineer (who were the only representatives of the owners in charge of the vessel) left the *Cicero* on March 16 1918 at (1) Helsingfors, as ordered by Captain Cromie, RN, acting for the British Ambassador, because the Germans were approaching Helsingfors. The vessel was then in the inner harbour fast in the ice. She was loaded at Helsingfors with Agricultural Machinery, with the intention of taking them to (2) Petrograd. The Swedes then took charge from Captain Pinchon, with the intention of moving the vessel to Sweden and Christiana (3) when practicable and handing her over to her owners when at Christiana. Later on (perhaps a month after) the Chief Engineer Mr Scofield received a letter from one of the senior British submarine men[4] stating that, in order to prevent the Germans getting possession of the vessels, the submarine men had blown up the submarines and also the *Cicero* and the British steamer *Emilie* (McCormicks) of Leith – adding that they had all got safely home, the *Emilie*'s Master, Chief Engineer and Second Officer having come home with Captain Pinchon and *Cicero*'s Chief Engineer. The vessels were moved into the outer harbour at Helsingfors to be blown up.

(Signed) W. H. Pinchon

How Captain Pinchon and his men had occupied themselves between 1914 and 1918 we may never know. It has been suggested that the *Cicero* may have eluded the Germans and taken refuge in neutral Swedish waters, or was employed as a courier of sorts between Petrograd and Helsingfors.[5]

There is no doubt about her fate, however, and that of Cromie's other two victims, the *Emilie* and the *Obsidian*. Cromie's taking of the latter almost seems like a Spike Milligan plot for the *Goon Show*. On 8 April, whilst the care and maintenance party were waiting in Petrograd for their train, Cromie rose early to put his three-ship destruction plan into action. It is obvious from Captain Pinchon's report on the *Cicero* that, as ever, Cromie had planned well ahead and had these transports in his sights for some time. He had spent the intervening weeks arguing his case to commandeer the vessels with whoever might stand in his way – 'liquidation, evacuation, transport committees, sailors' unions, and God knows what', as he put it. The Germans were also on the case – with their usual efficiency, long before they reached Helsingfors, they had circulated a leaflet threatening severe retribution for anyone sabotaging ships, and offering rewards if vessels were handed over. Thus it was almost impossible to find any real seamen to help him in his mission. He went, therefore, to the Officers'

Employment Bureau, where he found five army officers who were willing to help out. After eventually receiving the necessary documentation from the local commissar to take over the vessels, he set off for the harbour, dressed in civilian clothes, accompanied by his quintet of bemused officers, none of whom would have recognised a shackle from a samovar.

This was not going to be easy. As they arrived on the dockside to board the *Obsidian*, Cromie was confronted by a squad of armed men, who were adamant that he could not have the ship. To everyone's amazement, Cromie brushed past them, strode up the gangway, walked along the deck and lowered the Russian flag. He took from his pocket a somewhat ridiculous Union Jack handkerchief, attached it to the flag halliard and hoisted this miniature emblem of the empire to flutter bravely in the stiff Baltic breeze. He then turned to face the guards. 'We are now under the *British* flag, and in a *neutral* port, and I will not admit *foreigners* aboard this ship. If you wish to guard the vessel, then do it from the jetty.' Everyone burst out laughing, to his credit Cromie included.

'This little comedy', he wrote, 'put us all in a good temper, especially as I had papers and they had none.' He then despatched one of his army officers back to the commissar's office to rustle up 'half a dozen terrorists' to enforce his orders. The ship's guards became somewhat perturbed at this, and at this bold man's obvious determination. The ensuing conversation revealed to Cromie why the men were so reluctant to part with the ship. It was not so much the bulk of her cargo – torpedoes – which they would regret losing, as a consignment of clothing, in particular a large case of trousers. Having become of late something of an expert in the international currency value of trousers, Cromie quickly made the guards an offer – the ship, in exchange for a pair of trousers apiece. Such were the simple, heartfelt needs of the time that the offer was eagerly taken up. Crowbar in hand, Cromie descended into the hold, got the men's sizes, and with the flourish of a denizen of Savile Row presented each eager customer with his chosen goods.

Cromie now faced the difficult task of firing up the ship's boilers. In the engine room he had to act as chief stoker and show two of the officers what to do. With the other three on deck, he took up the gangway, cast off, and ran up to the bridge. It took some time to crash through the ice, and as the *Obsidian* made her slow headway out of the harbour, another threat loomed – a tug came alongside with twenty heavily armed men on board. Their leader asked Cromie what the hell he was up to, and told him they intended to board. He took from his pocket a slightly comical small .22 pistol and waved it in one hand, with his documentation in the other. 'This is a an English ship in neutral waters – any firing or boarding by force of arms is an act of piracy – we are not in Russia! I will kill the first armed man who sets foot on board! I have *my* papers here – where are *yours*? I do not believe you are anything but *pirates*!' The men then threatened to tow him back into the harbour. Cromie was adamant. 'If you try it, I will sink this ship right here in the channel and so shut in the remaining ships!' He looked around – his trouser customers were looking anxious.

The stand-off continued, so he played for time, offering to wait ninety minutes where he was whilst the 'pirates' went ashore to get papers which would cancel his. But he warned them that if they returned with a larger force, he would blow the ship up anyway. Perhaps it was because of the ostentatious display of his St George Cross – still a powerful military emblem in Russia at the time – on his civilian jacket which made the tugmen think twice. Yet they did return, with the instruction that the torpedoes must be unloaded before he could destroy the ship. This accomplished, on 9 April Cromie took the vessel out beyond the harbour and scuttled her, returning to shore in her jolly boat. To his dismay the rest of the trousers and everything else on board had been pilfered the night before, but Cromie prevented things getting worse by holding fifty looters at bay with his 'toy pistol'.

His next two conquests were less fraught affairs. Also on 9 April, this time accompanied only by a journalist and a university professor, he put paid to the 1,635 ton *Emilie*. Long before these ships were sunk, Downie's men had been on board, under great threat from the Russians, to put warheads in place to blow them up. The following day, the slightly comic trio boarded the *Cicero*, only to discover that the battery and one of the detonators for the warheads had been stolen. Yet somehow, Cromie managed to improvise; the *Cicero* went to the bottom.

As Cromie bade goodbye to his helpful newspaperman and the elderly academic, for both of whom this had been a great adventure, he could hear the sound of artillery outside the city. Always adept at keeping friends in most of the warring factions, he was now reasonably popular with the Reds for sinking the ships, and not without friends among the Whites of the Mannerheim persuasion, one of whom now gave him the tip-off that he had only one chance of a train leaving Helsingfors before the Germans arrived. On the night of 10 April, with only hours to spare, his train finally pulled out of the station headed for Petrograd.

His day-to-day existence was to be a trial. With many of the staff gone, his position in the embassy, whilst not exactly solo, left him without a diplomatic mentor of the calibre of Sir George Buchanan. This would be a crash course in diplomacy, but his enforced training through his continuous struggles with the Centrobalt had been a good grounding. In many ways, because of his energy and capacity for hard work, Cromie acted almost as Britain's ambassador, not that the Foreign Office would ever regard him as such. Despite his few embassy companions, it was a lonely job in a dangerous atmosphere.

There was some comfort to be had, however. With Sophie Gagarin living in the same building, just a few corridors away, his recreational outlet was assured. Yet times had changed for the worse since the Buchanans had flown the coop. Supplies were low, and with the escalating poor exchange rate, Cromie's concern over living conditions was growing.[6]

Intrigue follows intrigue, bribery is worse than ever, and food is dreadfully scarce, with nothing but riots to look forward to. Prices are: suit, 1,300 Roubles, boots 350, serge 80 for 28 inches, butter 22 R. funt[7] – seldom found. Bread not obtainable, but lucky to find at 30 R. funt, jam unknown, sugar fought for at 25 R.funt. Eggs 2 R each, potatoes 15 R. funt. Meat (mostly horse) 11–15 R. No dish at a restaurant less than 2 R, smallest cab fare 5 R . . . this, mark you, with all the banks closed, house property and ships nationalised. If you need money you must pay ten per cent to the Commissar. We split our submarine supplies between Helsingfors and Petrograd colonies, and I lost most of my little store *en route*, having to leave all my heavy gear at Helsingfors. Heaven knows how I am going to come out of this affair as I don't even know my salary. Such military people as have crept back to Petrograd now have a daily allowance of 70 R. I have not had a letter this year or a parcel since September, and I would be deeply grateful if you could pull the necessary string; the French get theirs regularly, and I am sure someone could arrange things to go to Murmansk very frequently. One thing is sure – we have got to be fed from home or clear out.

The political situation in Russia had continued as a series of increasingly dangerous twists and turns. As the Allies began to form a fuller picture of Lenin's new republic, they were not liking what they saw. Lenin always feared the possibility of Allied intervention against the new regime, but in these early months he sought another option – to use the Allies to defend vulnerable parts of Russia against the rapacious Germans.

Robert Bruce Lockhart was thirty when he returned to Russia in January 1918. The previous year he had been an energetic young acting Consul-General in Moscow, but was called home in the autumn of 1917 after an adulterous affair with a French woman, Madame Vermelle. The affair itself was little different from those many diplomats of the day were enjoying, but with one exception – Madame Vermelle was Jewish. Anti-Semitism, as most writing of that time will reveal, was more or less an institution. It did not 'do' for a British consul to philander in such a manner.

At first, Lockhart had a fairly open mind on the Bolsheviks. He was frequently frustrated by what he saw as the stupidity of his own government back in London, who refused to take Lenin and Trotsky seriously. Although British through and through, he none the less saw the Bolsheviks as the coming power in Russia, and as such better to deal with than ignore. As his brief sojourn in England towards the end of 1917 drew to a close, his face-to-face reports of the situation in Russia at the Foreign Office and with major politicians of the day soon had Prime Minister Lloyd George taking this young man more seriously. He called him to a meeting and asked him if he would return to Russia as the head of a mission to establish unofficial relations with the Bolsheviks. During 1917 he had already met Cromie on various occasions and was familiar with most of the major Russian politicians.

He arrived back in Petrograd to commence his new job on the evening of Wednesday, 30 January 1918. On 12 February he dined with Raymond Robins, the head of the American Red Cross mission. Discussing Trotsky, Robins made the classic remark: 'Trotsky is a poor kind of son of a bitch – but the greatest Jew since Christ.' During the coming year, Both Lockhart and Cromie were to see much of Leon Trotsky, and be similarly impressed.

His 'no war – no peace' attitude at the conclusion of the Brest-Litovsk Treaty meetings had given way to a period of acute military and political confusion which the Germans were now ruthlessly exploiting as they advanced ever closer to Petrograd. The Bolsheviks were forced to make a difficult decision. Rather than remain in the path of a German advance, they would move Russia's capital from Petrograd to Moscow. For the Allied ambassadors who had remained, this German advance was a threat which could only be faced by evacuating their embassies at the end of February to a town over 300 miles (480 km) north of Moscow, Vologda.

Vologda was a vastly different environment from the hustle and bustle of Russia's two major cities. It was a quiet town with a preponderance of churches. Conditions for the diplomats lacked much of the grandeur and dignity they had enjoyed before. In an old, requisitioned clubhouse the Brazilian Chargé d'Affaires and the Siamese Minister shared accommodation with the American Ambassador, Francis.[8] M. Noulens,[9] the French Ambassador, was living in an abandoned schoolhouse. In true American style, Francis, an ex-St Louis banker approaching eighty, had his negro servant make up a golf links for him on a nearby field so that he could play a round every day, whilst in the evening he played poker.[10] As the troubles raged in Moscow and Petrograd, these distant diplomats thus enjoyed a quiet country life where the food was better and more plentiful and the commissars were thin on the ground. Although these ambassadors were officially instructed to have no dealings with the Soviets, to Lockhart their remoteness was a cause for some concern. 'It was', he said, 'as if three foreign Ambassadors were trying to advise their governments on an English cabinet crisis from a village in the Hebrides.'[11] But political intrigue was still rife, as Vologda seethed with anti-Bolshevik plotting, an example of which was the League for the Regeneration of Russia, which was to play an important role in setting up a White government in Archangel, with the help of the British.

But there were others who remained in Petrograd and Moscow, with whom Cromie was now working. Amongst these was the Consul, A.W. Woodhouse, and the military mission of General Poole in Archangel was represented by Captain Schwabe and Major McAlpine. Cromie's Naval colleague was Engineer Commander Le Page. And of course there were the Secret Intelligence Service men, sent out from London by Admiral Reginald 'Blinker' Hall, who, by the spring of 1918 was determined to find any opportunity he could to bring down the Bolsheviks. Of these agents perhaps the peripatetic Sidney Reilly was the most famous, along with Commander Edward Boyce RNVR. In Moscow Lockhart was not entirely solo; he had with him Captain George Hill, known as Agent IK8, who headed an intelligence operation for Military Intelligence at the War Office, Captain William Hicks, Edward Phelan, Edward Birse, and the elderly Sir Oliver Wardrop, who had taken over Lockhart's old job as Consul-General. There were typists, passport clerks and still the odd servant here and there, and many of the British commercial community who had made the brave decision to stay on would frequent the embassy on occasions. And, of course, there were the inevitable journalists, such as Victor Marsden of the *Morning Post* and the *Manchester Guardian*'s Arthur Ransome. Ransome was an interesting character, made more so by his close relationship with Lenin and Trotsky's associate, the ebullient Karl Radek, whom Lockhart was to describe as 'our chief delight among the Commissars'. Ransome, who spoke good Russian, went on to marry Trotsky's secretary, Evgenia Shelepin. The couple eventually lived in the Lake District, where, in 1930, Ransome completed his classic children's book, *Swallows and Amazons*.

Despite the awful conditions prevailing in Petrograd and Moscow, there were many other shady international characters moving in and out of the various embassies and legations, yet in some way Francis Cromie seemed to stand apart from them all. It may have been because of his unfamiliarity with this strange world of diplomacy, which contrasted with the more pragmatic, practical approach essential when running a submarine. And Cromie had unbending agendas, plans which he had formed long before his elevation to Naval Attaché, such as his determination that the Baltic Fleet would not fall into German hands. He had, in many ways, tried to stand aside from politics, and his views on the Bolsheviks were coloured by his experiences in Reval and Helsingfors on board the *Pamyat Azova*. He respected men for their ability and their willingness to listen, rather than their political beliefs. He had almost as much mistrust of the Whites as he had of some of his Red associates, but now he was working for Admiral Hall, and the wind was beginning to blow him in a new direction. As an obedient servant of the Crown, he would go with it.

His secret dealings had become complex. He had become involved in spreading anti-German propaganda amongst the sailors of the Baltic fleet in Kronstadt in an attempt to prepare the way for the fleet's destruction should it become necessary. Many of these men hailed from Estonia and Latvia, which were now under German occupation. At the same time, he was consorting with the Whites, helping them in their struggles against the Reds. During May he paid visits to Moscow with Lockhart to meet Trotsky to discuss, among other subjects, the fate of the fleet. Trotsky knew that his ailing strategy was only leading to one thing – more of the very war he had been trying to get out of. Lockhart's diary entry for Wednesday 15 May illustrates the all-round frustration:[12]

> Went with Cromie to see Trotsky about the fleet. Trotsky said war was inevitable. I therefore asked if he would accept Allied intervention. He replied that he had already asked the Allies to make a proposition. I then said that if the Allies would come to an agreement on this point, would he give me half an hour to discuss things. He said 'When the Allies come to an agreement it is not half an hour but a whole day that I would give.'

Cromie was also involved in evacuating large cargoes of precious metal from any location threatened by the Germans. He was operating in a strange netherworld between opposing forces and ideas. To him the situation was simple – he was still at war, as a naval officer, with Germany. He might not have his submarines, but any act which could damage the enemy was, to Cromie, worthwhile. Moving everything of value from their path was one of his top priorities.

Day by day he bargained and cajoled to find barges and lighters upon which to load his booty. Examples of his work in this area are found in his letters to Admirals Phillimore and Hall. They also show how that Cromie's charm with the ladies was in full swing, too: 'Now I have organised the evacuation of 6,000,000 poods[13] of metal by water since the railways are blocked, but a Commissar came from Moscow and knocked it on the head; however we got at his lady secretary and are merrily at work again.'[14]

> We have daily trouble with evacuation, but have got round the lady secretary (temporary wife of the Commissar) and have proved our organisation to be the only one working. The main obstruction comes from Moscow and the nationalisation of all craft. However, we have obtained six tugs, and have 300,000 poods of copper ready to leave when the ice-run is finished. We work with the French, and have just pulled a Yankee into it. Capt. Schwabe, British Military Mission, and Mr Alardi, French Commerce, are the hard workers. I merely instituted the barge idea, and they use my name to get papers or deal with sailors' unions. Somehow we have kept going in spite of the number of committees and meetings.[15]

Here we see Cromie's innate modesty once again; he 'merely instituted' the barge idea, and deflects any praise for what was undoubtedly a huge task on his part – getting hold of the copper at all – onto Schwabe and Alardi, who without Cromie's pulling power with the Bolsheviks could have done little.

Even at this stage of the war, like Lockhart, Cromie could still find some sense in recognising the Bolsheviks if the battle against Germany was to continue.[16]

> We need definite and strong action as a reply to German aggression, and I believe it could be done with the approval of the masses if we recognise the Bolshevik enough to get a fair and open start. The matter of transports is an endless question, taking up endless time, and really needs a special officer; . . . Le Page is an excellent worker, but I cannot tell him off for transports as I seem to spend all day with interviews and meetings . . .

He finished on yet another anguished note on the perennial problem of money. Although he was, by this time, involved with massive sums in his various dealings with international officialdom, his own financial situation was still unresolved:

> The thing I hate is financial responsibility. Please don't think me very mercenary on account of the official application for allowances in lieu of fixed salary, but the position is really becoming untenable without private means to fall back on. The whole situation is critical and so wavering that it is impossible to give a definite view of facts even if one could separate them from fiction.

With his huge, dangerous and varied workload, it seems a wonder that Cromie had any time left for other speculative ventures, yet it appears that he did. It is obvious that apart from his prowess as a navigator and submarine commander, he was a fast learner in the world of commerce. Although the Bolsheviks were the avowed enemies of capitalism, there was, apparently, still some leeway in the north at Murmansk for an impressive exercise in international business speculation. A document in the Public Record Office[17] shows just how important Cromie was to a large gathering of international speculators in plans to set up the Russo-English Dockyards and Shipbuilding Company there. This endeavour included shipbuilding and repair workshops, various bought, leased and chartered vessels, plus the intention to become involved in the fishing industry. It already had at its disposal 1,100,000 roubles in March 1918. Cromie was offered a seat on the board, and agreed to join. This may explain his curious comments to Admiral Hall concerning a Russian vessel named the *Fluor*:[18]

> I have dismantled the *Fluor* and am sending her to Archangel; but the tug in question is the devil, so I arranged a sale of one laid up and took up the full mortgage in my name, keeping entire control in lieu of interest; this avoids the navigation law and, in case of a row, I can transfer this private mortgage to an Anglo-Russian Co.

No doubt such a facility would be invaluable in the event of Allied intervention, which at that earlier juncture in 1918 would have been considered a supportive act against the Germans, rather than what it eventually became, a counter-revolutionary campaign.

In Cromie's ever-darkening world of intrigue and double-dealing, money – and lots of it – played a very important part. And to finance some of his more grandiose schemes, such as the possible destruction of the Baltic Fleet, along with a similar concern he had with the Black Sea Fleet, he was to be trusted with ever larger sums. As the mood in Britain began to shift from mere intervention in Russia as an anti-German project to a pro-White, anti-Red plan, Cromie's pivotal position came to be recognised as more important. The day before he and Lockhart met Trotsky in Moscow, the following telegram was despatched to Consul Woodhouse in Petrograd:[19]

> Very Urgent and Secret: FOREIGN OFFICE MAY 14TH 1918 7.30 p.m. Please hold at immediate disposal of Captain Cromie 1,500,000 roubles from embassy or other available accounts. Lockhart has been asked to facilitate in any way possible your operating on these accounts. You should take any steps open to you to make the money available to Cromie when he wants it. He will advise you as to rate at which he will require the money. He may be able to help you in overcoming obstacles on part of bank officials. If you have any difficulty in satisfying Cromie's needs in full, advise us immediately.

Lockhart received a similar message in Moscow instructing him to 'do anything in your power to facilitate Woodhouse . . . This is much more important at the moment than transfer of funds to Moscow.'[20]

In a meeting with Lenin, Lockhart tried to discover what the new leader of Soviet Russia's attitude was to the Allies. He told Lockhart that if the Germans did come and attempt to install a bourgeois government, then the Bolsheviks would fight even if they had to withdraw to the Volga and the Urals – but they would fight on their own conditions, and not become a cat's paw for the Allies. Lenin said that if the Allies understood this, then there was an opportunity for co-operation. He was pleased that Lockhart had decided to stay on, and guaranteed his safety and would grant him a free exit when he wished to leave. He was ready to accept Allied military support whilst the German threat existed, but his acute political acumen surfaced icily as Lockhart left: 'At the same time I am quite convinced that your government will never see things in this light. It is a reactionary government – it will co-operate with the Russian reactionaries.' Lenin was right. Lockhart's mission was doomed. The world looked a different place from the safety of Whitehall – these troublesome Bolsheviks were surely nothing but an evil rabble. The level of understanding in the Cabinet offices, where no one could even speak Russian, of what was going on in Russia was abysmal. Baron Edward Henry Carson, who was First Lord of the Admiralty in 1917 and went on to become the leader of the Irish Unionists and founder of the Ulster Volunteers, had probably never even heard of Karl Marx when he asked, as a member of the War Cabinet, 'Can someone tell me the difference between a "Marximalist" and a Bolshevik?'[21] And, of course, it was still believed in London that both Trotsky and Lenin were German secret agents, as it suited their purposes. Such was the pitiful situation at home with which Lockhart had to contend.

What was referred to as 'the Russian Question' by the Allies had, for the armchair generals, only one solution. As early as March 1918 the subject was debated in London between the prime ministers of Italy, France and Great Britain. Their conclusions were wired to the United States, and the following day, 16 March, Britain's Foreign Secretary, Arthur Balfour, said that in order to prevent the Germans from occupying Russia 'there is only one means – Allied intervention'. Soon after, Allied troops went ashore in Murmansk from the American cruiser *Olympia*, the French cruiser *Admiral Aube* and the British battleship *Glory*. On 5 April 500 Japanese marines landed at Vladivostok – much to Trotsky's anger – to be followed by other foreigners, including the British and Americans. Of course, it was all done under the pretext of waging war against the Germans and defending Allied interests, such as stores and ammunition dumps. But it gradually became a convenient smokescreen to hide the ultimate intention of bringing down this upstart workers' republic, and reinstating the kind of government capitalism was used to dealing with.

The landings may have constituted a dramatic signal to the Russians on both sides of the political divide, but they soon lost momentum – with the massive campaigns in full swing in Western Europe it was impossible to siphon off more valuable forces for what was still a political adventure.

Trotsky had been busily building up the Red Army to face the German threat. A number of ex-Tsarist officers had rejoined the ranks after accepting that Bolshevism was the new Russia, like it or not. Discipline, after two years of dissolution, was slowly making a comeback. Perhaps there was an opportunity to reopen the Eastern Front, if the Allies were willing to help. There had been a thin strand of Allied policy which allowed for the possibility that, given adequate assistance, Trotsky's new-style army might be worthy of support. In March George Hill, who was working closely with Lockhart in Moscow, had been offered to Trotsky, to whom he was to report direct, as an Allied adviser, and even had the title Inspector of Aviation.[22]

But as Trotsky, firebrand, man of action, planned, becoming ever more strident in his military outlook, Lenin was looking inwards at the socialist philosophy he had spent so much of his life developing. The eventual consequences of Lenin's meditation were to be calamitous.

The Czechoslovak Legion, some 40,000 strong, had become stranded on Russian territory following the signing of the Treaty of Brest-Litovsk.[23] It was formed of Slovaks and Czechs who had originally fought, somewhat reluctantly, for the Austro-Hungarian army, and had been taken prisoner earlier in the war by the Tsarist army. The Bolsheviks, now with their 'no peace – no war' scenario, had no further use for them, and had given them permission to travel to France so that they could fight on against the Central Powers. But the only route open to them was east, across Siberia, North America and then across the Atlantic. They were well armed and well disciplined, and strung out in the first gruelling stage of the journey along the length of the railway line between Siberia and the Volga River. The Allies, still seeing a chance to join up with Trotsky's growing Red Army (conscription had now been introduced), suddenly realised the value of 40,000 well-equipped troops, already on Russian soil. Urgent messages were sent to the Czech commanders that any of their forces still west of the Urals should immediately alter their plans and not go east, but north to Archangel, where they would be met by General Poole's forces. They would then all join up with the Russians and head for Vologda, and from there west to reopen the front against the Germans.

But Lenin had thought things over. The results of regional elections throughout Russia in the spring of 1918 had not been good for the Bolsheviks. There were also many organised factions and political groupings, with as many agendas, all chipping away at Lenin's power. An alliance with the Allies might play into this growing opposition's hands, for with an Allied presence on Russian soil it might not take long for the thrust of the revolution to be reversed – and the thought of a return to some form of coalition government, after coming this far, was an anathema to Lenin. Now he had thousands of armed Czechs in the heart of Russia thinking they were about to join the Allies, who had promised them that they would free Czechoslovakia from Austro-German rule. They must be disarmed. As Commissar of War, Leon Trotsky was about to earn his stripes.

The Czechs, now regarded by Lenin as being in league with the Allies against Soviet Russia, revolted, taking over part of the Trans-Siberian railway, and were eagerly encouraged and joined by every counter-revolutionary group in their path. This was one of the grim opening chapters in the bloody civil war which was to rage for the next two years.

*   *   *

The atmosphere for Cromie and Lockhart now took a turn for the worse. There was a new, dark mood of suspicion. The Bolsheviks were more vigilant and began to double their guards on important buildings. Bolstered by the news of the Czechs in Siberia, the Bolsheviks' enemies, both left and right, began taking chances. Volodarsky, the Commissar for the Press in Petrograd, was murdered on 21 June. There was still a strong desire to restart the war against Germany. The Germans had reopened their embassy and on 6 July their Ambassador, Count Mirbach, was assassinated by a man named Blumkin, a Social Revolutionary who lived in the same hotel as Lockhart.

Cromie was now plunging deeper and deeper into his clandestine work, and there was a price on his head from the Germans, who were still smarting from his escape from Helsingfors and the destruction of the merchant ships. There is a break in his letters from 17 May to 26 July, but there is a secret cypher telegram during that period which demonstrates the keenness for Allied intervention and the workload under which Cromie was labouring.[24]

> From: Naval Attaché Petrograd.   Date 24.6.18   Allied Cypher No. 1: 202. Following from Vinegradeff our chief agent.
> Business men in contact with Germans state latter do not intend to advance or permit the Finns to advance on Petrograd until allies make a definite north as Germans find they can gain more by political intrigue than by their offensive which they now seem to regret. If Germans make first move the Press will probably be pro-ally but it is organised by Germany to agitate against an intervention on the part of the allies. Germans do not now wish to seize fleet by force but hope to gradually obtain possession by Germanising Russia. This is probably in progress judging by the way in which Russian sailors are leaving while Estonians remain. If allies do not intervene Germany hopes to gradually obtain all she requires by intrigue but she thinks the Czech-Slav affair the first step of allied campaign. The success of the movement appears to afford satisfaction to a large section of populace. I now give extracts from V's written report original of which will be forwarded later.

>> (begins.) If destruction of fleet is to be assured real action in the Kors Fjord must be undertaken. You hope to get Russian material to back you up, if you do not wish to lose this possibility you must go on, if not, it will be too late and all is lost. Every day Russia becomes softer and weaker and by herself is worth nothing but with an outside impulse may be re-born. If you do not come Russia will turn to Germany whom she sees approaching slowly but surely.
>> Russia's future will be decided not in years and months but in weeks and days. If you do not come you lose, if you come later than a month you will find only wadding and sand and will need too many of your own forces. You have our sympathies now but lose them every hour by your indecision and you lose even more, Russia's faith in England. If your strength is not a thing of the past you must move

Felix Dzerzhinsky Head of
the Cheka

Leon Trotsky

Tsar Nicholas and King
George V

Vladimir Ilyich Lenin

233

on and move quickly. When you move you will start much agitation against England you awake all who are friends, if come too late you lose these friends with faith in England. All your losses are German gains is much worse than hostility. I regret this letter but I must say it, I feel the moment critical and possible result irredeemable. You do not know Russia and you do not understand (not you personally) the moment. (Ends.)

From personal observation and that of my staff the above is only too true. England's great prestige in Russia is falling daily and that of Germany ascending. Russia has been led to expect intervention in the north (but this idea has not been propagated from this office) and is building her hopes on it. I submit with all respect and perhaps lack knowledge that the present apparent indecisive policy is doing more than anything else to ruin England's present and future prestige and will undoubtedly affect future relations between the two countries. Intervention on a thorough scale is the only thing that will save the situation and Russia, and I repeat that force raised locally cannot be relied on unless each unit is stiffened by at least 25 per cent allied troops.(Ends.)

During that period Cromie had come into contact with some very clever and extremely dangerous people. Whilst Lockhart, from Moscow and Petrograd, still insisted to his government that they should talk to the Bolsheviks, he was mainly ignored. In London opinion was changing. A new banner was being unfurled – the Bolsheviks had to fight the Germans, or they had to be brought down, and that meant exactly what Cromie was pleading for: intervention. Bringing the regime down was to be no easy task, and required the special services of a multi-talented *agent provocateur* to light the fuse. Lloyd George now consulted C – the Head of the Secret Service, Captain Mansfield Cumming. Was there a man who could precipitate the destruction of Lenin's government? Cumming had no doubts. He would be an agent code-named ST1 – Sidney Reilly. As April 1918 drew to a close, Litvinoff, Lenin's representative in London, was duped into issuing Reilly with a special pass for Russia. As Lockhart and Cromie struggled to keep some equilibrium between the Allies and the Bolsheviks, ST1 was on his way from Murmansk to fulfil his role as a spanner in their delicate works.

Lockhart said of Cromie, 'He was a gallant and extremely efficient naval officer, but was without experience of political work.' The latter part of this statement was, sadly, about to be proved true. On 26 July Cromie wrote to Admiral Hall: 'There is some danger in having so many irons in the fire, but I think I have enough friends to get me out even if it comes to flying.' He was about to involve himself in one risk too many.

CHAPTER 21

THE STING

A Russian only understands a big stick and a big threat,
anything else is taken for weakness. One must not forget that
one is *not* dealing with a European, but with a cunning and cruel
savage who is servile enough when you have a stick in your
hand . . . The Hand that feeds this people will be the Master of
Russia, in spite of any military force that may be sent against it.

Letter from Cromie to Admiral Hall, 14 August 1918[1]

The late summer and autumn of 1918 were Cromie's busiest time since his arrival
in Russia. Since the assassination of the German Ambassador, Mirbach, suspicion of Allied intentions had reached fever pitch. Although the murder had
been carried out by Russians, its intended effect was to push Russia back into
the war. This, too was the Allies' aim. The search was thus on for any 'dirty tricks'
and subversive plotting among the Westerners who still frequented the various
embassies. Bolshevik suspicions were not without foundation. But whatever
clever schemes the slick, over-confident Allies could come up with through their
own secret services, the Bolsheviks could easily match.

Russia's long tradition of secret police forces had not died out when the infamous Tsarist Okhrana had been disbanded. Far from it. After the Bolshevik
coup in November 1917 a section of the dissolved Military Revolutionary
Committee was retained. It went under the title of the 'All Russia Extraordinary
Commission to Fight Counter Revolution', and became known by the abbrevi-
ated form of its Russian name, Chresvynhainaya Kumissaya, Cheka – also,
rather aptly, the Russian word for 'linchpin'. It was run by an eight-man
committee, chaired by Felix Dzerzhinsky. Dzerzhinsky, a Pole, had spent fifteen
years in the Tsar's jails, and knew more than many of his comrades about the
inner workings of the Tsar's secret police. Now he had his own force to operate.

His first task was to tackle bourgeois saboteurs, drunken mobs and the general
banditry which had ensued since the Tsar's abdication. From his headquarters
in a large house, formerly an insurance company office, on Moscow's Lubyanka
Square, Dzerzhinsky, known because of his uncompromising stance as 'Iron
Felix', had, by the summer of 1918, put together a ruthless network of skilled
agents and *agents provocateurs* to tackle what the Bolsheviks referred to as the
'hydra of counter-revolution'. Mirbach's assassin, Blumkin, had himself been a
Cheka agent, but he wanted Russia back in the war. The murder of the German
Ambassador was to be the catalyst for this, and was timed to coincide with

an uprising by Blumkin's party, the Left Socialist Revolutionaries. Although the uprising took place following the murder, and even resulted in the rebels taking the telephone exchange, it was soon put down by the Bolsheviks, and all the Socialist Revolutionary delegates to the Congress of Soviets were quickly arrested. The Cheka, which over the years became the OGPU, the NKVD and, ultimately, the KGB, was in tight control of Bolshevik security in the summer of 1918. With the civil war now under way, wherever the Cheka found pockets of counter-revolutionary resistance to Lenin, it was ruthlessly put down. In Yaroslavl, 200 miles (300 km) north of Moscow, the local Cheka executed 350 White Guards. In Moscow in April Cheka agents assisted by Red Guards raided every building controlled by the Anarchists, who had been such a nuisance amongst the sailors of the Baltic Fleet. Thirty were killed and 600 arrested.

Iron Felix, with his high intelligence and impeccable manners, was none the less a wily, cunning and ultimately humourless man. In Petrograd the Cheka also had a strategically placed headquarters in the centre of the capital at 2 Gorokhovaya Ulitsa, opposite the Admiralty Gardens. Moisei Uritsky, regarded as repulsive by those who knew him, was the Cheka chief in Petrograd.

By the time of Cromie's final letter from Russia, to Admiral Hall, dated 14 August 1918, the Cheka were watching him closely, and it is obvious that he was in some danger. 'Affairs have reached some sort of climax here, and I am afraid we shall have to clear out as best we can in order not to hamper the Expedition by becoming hostages.'

With the Czech Legion in revolt, several White generals throughout Russia leading their armies against the Red Guards, Allied troops at Archangel and the Germans ignoring the Brest-Litovsk Treaty and carrying out operations as usual, Trotsky and Lenin had their hands full. Whilst they were still wondering quite what the Allies' intentions were, they were taking no risks over their suspicions that they were planning a full-scale operation in conjunction with the White offensive in an attempt to bring down the Soviet government.

Lockhart and Cromie knew by the end of May that intervention against the Bolsheviks, as opposed to assisting them against Germany, was probably on the cards. Yet Cromie travelled to Moscow twice between 15 and 23 May, still desperate over both the Baltic and Black Sea fleets. Trotsky was still friendly. He saw in Cromie and Lockhart two men who had a more sensible grip on what was happening in Russia. But if the Soviet Commissar for War had known the contents of the cypher telegrams Lockhart was receiving daily from the Foreign Office, both Lockhart and his handsome companion would have been in danger. And now, hidden under various disguises, there was Sidney Reilly, Lloyd George's secret weapon, already beavering away behind the scenes with his almost Napoleonic one-man plan to bring Lenin down and install a new government. Lockhart knew that the wind had changed against him, and his hopes of making Whitehall see sense had been dashed. Letters from his wife contained disturbing reports that he was considered to be a 'pro-Bolshevik' and that there were rumours that he might be recalled.

The final realisation of his situation came at Vologda, where he had gone on 26 May at the request of the French Military Attaché, General Lavergne. Like

Lockhart, Lavergne believed that any intervention by the Allies in Russia could only take place with the agreement of the Bolsheviks, and had written a report to this effect. His counterpart at the Italian Embassy, Romei, took a similar stand. But Lavergne was answerable to his somewhat hawkish Ambassador in Vologda, Noulens.

For Lockhart's first twenty-four hours at Vologda Russia was hardly mentioned. After playing cards all night with the elderly American Ambassador Francis, and losing his money, Lockhart, although he found the American amusing and charming, wrote rather tersely in his diary: 'Old Francis doesn't know a Left Social-revolutionary from a potato.'[2] Apart from the politically illiterate Francis, there was the Brazilian Ambassador, whose proud claim was that he never did anything if he could help it, except sleep by day and play cards at night. The only diplomat there who had any firm political knowledge or conviction was M. Noulens. Over lunch the next day Noulens discussed Lavergne's report with Lockhart. At first everything seemed fine, until Noulens announced an amendment – that if the Bolsheviks would not agree to intervention, then the Allies would intervene without their permission. Lockhart's heart sank at this point. He had been hoping to have Romei, the Italian, along to support Lavergne's views, but, as he was to discover, he had not come to Vologda because of pressure from Italian headquarters. Lockhart described his feelings:[3]

> I was in a corner. If I refused to agree, M. Noulens would go ahead with his own policy. He would carry the Italians, the Japanese, and even Francis with him. If I consented, at least I should escape the stigma of having stood out against the united opinion of all the other Allied representatives. I capitulated.

When Lockhart got back to Moscow he found a telegram from Cromie waiting for him, requesting him to come to Petrograd immediately. He arrived there on the evening of 28 May and went straight to the embassy. With Cromie was a British army officer, McGrath, who had come down from Murmansk where he had arrived with General Poole's mission. It is hard to say what Cromie's reaction to McGrath was, but Lockhart was relieved to discover that the intervention plan was not very far advanced; there was no definite policy yet, and would be none until Poole had completed his report and sent it to England. It seemed like a breathing space, but something did disturb Lockhart. Poole, it appeared, was very keen on intervention, and Francis Lindley, who had been Chargé d'Affaires in Petrograd, was on his way back to Russia. This was bad news for Lockhart, and he interpreted it as a lack of confidence on the part of his government in his ability. It was also annoying that he had learned it, not by a diplomatic despatch, but in passing from a visiting army officer. No doubt he told Cromie of his meeting with Noulens and the possible consequences. And if intervention was going to happen one way or another, Cromie knew now that his usual zeal and energy would be required to ensure the success of the mission.

Back in Moscow, at a meeting with the Soviet Foreign Minister, Chicherin, Lockhart revealed his shift in policy; he tried to get around it by saying that, by attempting to disarm the Czechs, the Bolsheviks were helping the Germans, and if they continued to interfere in the Czech Legion's progress, this would be considered as a hostile act against the Allies. The Bolsheviks listened to him in silence. What he had said almost proved their suspicions – the Allies were looking for a fight and the Czech business was a green light for intervention. His carefully nurtured relationship with Trotsky was over. Lockhart's credibility had been wiped out.

On the night of 17 July, Lockhart received a message from Karakhan, a commissar at the Bolshevik Foreign Office. Tsar Nicholas II had been executed at Ekaterinburg. Lockhart was the first person in Russia to release the news to the rest of the world.

But the British government was capable of coming up with surprises of its own. Both Cromie and Lockhart were amazed when, on 22 July, a situation only Gilbert and Sullivan could have dreamed up developed in Moscow. A four-man British economic mission, sent out by a department in Whitehall which obviously had no idea what was going on in their own building, arrived in the city to discuss the possibilities of trade relations with the new Bolshevik government!

As these four hopeful commercial leaders arrived in the capital, up in Vologda the Allied embassies were hurriedly packing their bags to escape to Archangel. Two days later, after a decidedly cool reception from the Bolsheviks, the quartet of would-be traders landed on Cromie's doorstep in Petrograd, whilst the Allied embassies were hot-footing it across Russia to find a passage home.

On 2 August General Poole's force landed at Archangel. The rumours spread around Russia – several divisions had landed, thousands of troops. In fact it was more like 1,500: a British battalion, consisting mainly of men unfit for service in France, a French colonial battalion, some Royal Marines and fifty American sailors.[4]

At some time early in August, Cromie received two visitors at the embassy in Petrograd. They were young Latvians who gave their names as Bredis and Schmidchen, members of the Latvian guards regiment. Cromie took them into his office and scrutinised them carefully. At first he was on his guard. The Latvian regiments were among the Bolsheviks' most potent fighting forces, and had acted throughout the revolution as Lenin's Praetorian Guard. Cromie was puzzled as to why these two men should visit him. The thought of assassination may have crossed his mind, but there were any number of chances to bump him off outside the embassy. And, in any case, he was undoubtedly shadowed wherever he went.

Schmidchen remained silent as Bredis began to talk. Their own country Latvia, he said, was suffering under German occupation. They, the regiment, wanted nothing more than to go home. They had supported the Bolsheviks and fought for the revolution, but this fight for the Russians could not go on for ever. They had heard of General Poole's landing. If the Allies, as they expected, were to win the war against Germany, then they felt that they would be happy, because they felt that Latvia's fate would be in safer hands. Because of this eventuality, the two men said that the Latvian regiment did not seek to fight against General Poole's forces at Archangel. But they were worried that in the event of intervention, they might be shot at by Poole's forces. They wanted their position made clear, and hoped that Cromie could arrange it so that they would not be attacked. Cromie was impressed. These men had to be very brave to come to him like this. What was more, if Poole and the steadily increasing White forces could get the Latvians on their side, they could be a formidable addition to the anti-German thrust Cromie was hoping for. His first thoughts were of Lockhart. He asked the men to wait whilst he wrote a quick letter. He addressed it to Lockhart, and handed it to Schmidchen, telling him to call on Lockhart in Moscow, who might be able to take the matter further.

On 15 August Schmidchen and Bredis arrived at Lockhart's Moscow flat. He was having lunch at the time and his servant told him that there were two 'Lettish' (as the Latvians were then called) gentlemen at the door. Lockhart invited them in. Like Cromie, he was on his guard. They announced that they had been to see the Naval Attaché in Petrograd, and he had given him this letter. Lockhart recognised the handwriting immediately.[5]

> The expression that he was making his own arrangements to leave Russia and hoped to 'bang the dore before he went out' was typical of this very gallant officer. Above all, the spelling was his. No forger could have faked this, for like Prince Charles Edward, Frederick the Great, and Mr. Harold Nicolson, poor Cromie could not spell.

Lockhart was careful not to give them any further encouragement. He sympathised with their reluctance to fight with the Allies, but told them that he was not in direct contact with General Poole, although he might be able to arrange something. He asked them to call back the next day. At this point Lockhart had had enough of his stay in Russia and was well advanced with his plans to go home. He discussed the Latvians' plea with the French Consul-General, M. Grenard, and General Lavergne. They saw no harm in letting the Latvians themselves send an envoy to Poole. Lockhart duly wrote a letter of introduction for them to take to Archangel. The next day, Schmidchen and Bredis returned, this time in the company of a man they said was a colonel in their regiment.

Colonel Berzin looked every inch the military type: square-jawed, clean cut, and, as Lockhart later described him, 'with hard, steely eyes'. The story of their disaffection and the feelings of their Latvian comrades was repeated. Now the redoubtable Sidney Reilly enters the scene. This time Grenard, the French Consul-General, and Reilly were present at the meeting. Colonel Berzin expanded his two comrades' original story. He told the Allied gathering that his troops were ready to rise against the Bolsheviks, and with their help, everything 'could be arranged in five to six weeks'.

As Reilly was staying on in Russia, Lockhart suggested to the Latvians that they deal with him. All their negotiating could be carried out, said Berzin, in a safe house in Moscow which they could provide. Reilly soon went to work and raised 1,200,000 roubles to finance the coming uprising. This he eventually delivered to Berzin.

Since his arrival in Russia, Reilly, with Lockhart's assistance, had been busy.

Moura Budberg

Robert Bruce Lockhart

Sidney Reilly

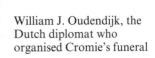

William J. Oudendijk, the
Dutch diplomat who
organised Cromie's funeral

He had been moving vast sums of money which were going to the anti-Bolshevik White armies of Savinkov in the north-east, and in the south Alexeiev, whose army of Cossacks was fighting the Reds south of the Don River. His commercial acumen was impressive; he would make friends with well-placed bourgeois Russians who would provide him with thousands of roubles, against which Lockhart would organise promissory notes in sterling, payable at London banks. He also worked closely with Captain George Hill, Agent IK8. Hill was almost as colourful a character as Reilly – devious, with nerves of steel and fluent in Russian. The spy Kim Philby described Hill years later as 'Jolly George'.

Reilly already had two aliases: one as Mr Constantine, a Greek businessman, another as Mr Massino, a Turkish merchant. Of course he had all the correct documentation for these mythical characters. He would board a train from Petrograd to Moscow as Constantine, who would then vanish, and become Mr Massino in Moscow. Massino would travel back to Petrograd, and similarly vanish, to become Constantine again. Reilly was an expert in disguise, and his command of languages got him out of many scrapes. His real name was Sigmund Rosenblum, and he had been born in Poland to a well-heeled Jewish family in 1874. Much of his life is shrouded in mystery. He married into an Irish family after moving to London in the 1890s, and used Reilly, his wife's father's name, for his British documents. But, according to some sources, he had as many as eleven different passports and 'a wife to go with each'.[6] He was devious, and an expert in killing his enemies by either shooting, throttling, stabbing or even poisoning. He was sexually attractive and had a string of mistresses. He was also an amazing escape artist. On one train journey between Moscow and Petrograd, the Cheka boarded the train to look for him. Reilly saw a Russian sailor go into the train's toilet. He forced his way in, knocked the sailor out cold, stripped him of his uniform and dumped his body through the window onto the track. Wearing the Soviet sailor's clothes, he then volunteered to help 'his comrades', the Cheka, look for the elusive Sidney Reilly. Both Winston Churchill and Mansfield Cumming, head of the Secret Service, regarded him as their most inventive and formidable agent. Not long after arriving in Petrograd he took on yet another alias, arranged by an *agent provocateur* friend who had infiltrated the Cheka. Using a genuine Cheka pass, he also became 'Comrade Relinsky'. As such he could get into many places, such as the Moscow Opera House and various theatres, and scare the life out of any inquisitive Bolshevik who stopped him.

But even Sidney Reilly was not perfect. Even the best agents can be prone to the enemy's trickery – such is the nature of intelligence work. Schmidchen and Berzin were a bright ray of hope for Reilly: 'The Letts . . . they were foreign hirelings. Foreign hirelings serve for money. They are at the disposal of the highest bidder. If I could buy the Letts my task would be easy.'[7]

Indeed it would have been easy – if the Latvian trio had been who they claimed to be. In fact, they were three Cheka *agents provocateurs*. Their nationality was Latvian, but 'Schmidchen' was actually Yan Buikis and 'Bredis' was Yan Sprogis. Berzin was probably the colonel's real name, but as to whether he was a Latvian guard is doubtful. The 1,200,000 roubles Reilly had handed over went straight into the Cheka's coffers, and the so-called 'safe house' had been provided by the same organisation.

Felix Dzerzhinsky was enjoying a spot of leave from Cheka HQ. He was in no hurry. He could savour the results his men had achieved, and by waiting just a little longer, they might well reveal more of their plotting against the Bolsheviks. He now had more than enough rope to hang these imperialist scoundrels with – and he could sit back and enjoy the spectacle.

Reilly blundered on. On 28 August he caught a train with Berzin to Petrograd where he had been promised further meetings with anti-Bolshevik Letts. Some reports say that he met Berzin in Petrograd when he arrived, but whichever is the case, it seemed to the 'ace of spies' that all his plans were coming together nicely. But two unexpected calamities lay immediately ahead.

On Friday, 30 August, Moisei Uritsky, the head of the Petrograd Cheka, was assassinated by a military cadet. For the enemies of Bolshevism at large, this was bad enough. But the day was not over. In Moscow, Lenin received the news of Uritsky's death. His sister, Maria Illinichna, disturbed by the assassination in Petrograd, begged him not to step outside the Kremlin.[8] But Lenin was Lenin – he had speeches to make, at the Corn Exchange and then at the Mikhelson factory. After several hours of rallying the workers, he walked back to his car. On the way two peasant women harangued him about the difficulties they were having selling their grain. He briefly paused to discuss the problem, then resumed his journey to the car. Two shots rang out. Lenin was hit in the chest and the neck by two bullets fired by a young woman, a Social Revolutionary named Fanya Kaplan.

Reilly, Lockhart and everyone else in the Allied diplomatic community could forget their schemes. As for Captain Francis Newston Allen Cromie, DSO, RN, the sunset of 30 August 1918 was the last one he would see. The Terror was about to begin.

CHAPTER 22

BLACK SATURDAY

It is difficult to overestimate the effects of this intervention at a
time when Russia's revolution was regarded as a defeat for
morality. She lay, an apparently mortally wounded dinosaur, as
huge and impracticable as a prehistoric animal which had, by
some fluke of nature, survived into modern times. Now the
vultures were settling on her warm body, and finding her flesh
to their liking. It is even more difficult to overestimate the effect
when the dinosaur rose unexpectedly, shook the vultures off,
and struck them clumsily. The landscape was full of feathers.

Sir Peter Ustinov, *My Russia*

The events following the assassination of Uritsky and the attempt on Lenin's life
have, over the decades, inspired millions of words. The general consensus is that
the fledgling Soviet state, having nothing to lose but its beleaguered power,
lashed out in an orgy of bloody terror which its opponents regarded as death
throes.

The wounded Lenin, bleeding profusely from the neck and chest, had been
bundled into his car by his chauffeur, Stephan Gil. Gil was streetwise enough not
to race to a hospital – if there had been assassins at the factory, this might well
have been part of a bigger plot, and the enemy could well have the route to the
hospital covered. He drove straight to the Kremlin, but it was the early hours of
Saturday 31 August before two surgeons finally arrived to stabilise the patient.
He did not die, but it had been a close call.

Cromie's life during August had taken several dramatic turns. The news of
General Poole's landing at Archangel had reached Moscow on Sunday 4 August.
The following day, the British Consulate was surrounded by a group of armed
men. Everyone was arrested except Lockhart, Hicks and Wardrop. Perhaps
Lockhart escaped because extending his freedom of movement allowed him to
keep on plotting – and the Cheka were keen for this one busy bee to lead them
to the hive. Lockhart still had his pass, too, originally issued by Trotsky. But
there were restrictions – he was unable to leave the city.

When Cromie heard of the arrests at the consulate, he gathered his staff and
instructed them to be vigilant and to take no risks. They would all lie low for a
while to see if the crisis would pass over. It was still, at this late stage, unclear
what the intervention force's plans were. Perhaps the air would soon clear. In
the meantime, his only concern was the advancement of his plans to blow up the

Baltic Fleet. Soon, even this scheme would have to be put on hold as he became more embroiled in wild military plotting of an even grander scale.

The embassy was being watched. Those with flats outside the building, including Cromie, had to move quickly, and often under the cover of darkness, to get home. There was no telling who might be spirited away in the night for a Cheka grilling – and if someone was arrested, in the small hours, alone, the embassy could only speculate as to where he was. One member of the embassy staff, Andrews, had almost been taken, but managed to walk past his opponents, unsuspected, to the embassy car wearing a chauffeur's uniform. Cromie's flat had been turned over whilst he was out, so he decided to move to a safe house. But as Reilly had discovered after another narrow escape, safe houses in Petrograd were not always what they seemed. Two nights after his flat had been raided, a group of Cheka agents burst into Cromie's new 'safe' address (it is not known where this was) looking for him. As they clambered noisily up the stairs, Cromie threw open the window and escaped over the rooftops. This was hardly the life one would expect for a British diplomat.

From then on the embassy staff, Cromie included, decided to sleep in the embassy building. It was no longer safe to leave the sanctuary of what had become their diplomatic cocoon. Cromie issued instructions for the destruction of any sensitive paperwork in the building. He had ceased keeping any records or a diary, lest they be captured. There was constant talk of making a break for it, of going home. Those who remained in the building had given themselves a name – the 'Last Ditchers'. Yet Cromie still feverishly worked away at his plots and schemes; his act of 'banging the dore' was still in rehearsal.

In the midst of all this tense danger, he was once again to have strange visitors. At this juncture, to say 'the plot thickens' is an understatement.

The Allied landing had given the opposing factions in the civil war both hope and dread in equal measure. Many of the White forces, strung out from the Don to central Russia, were inspired by a mixture of motives; some wanted the old Tsarist Russia back, others wanted some kind of liberal democracy, some would consider collaboration with the Germans,[1] others were socialist yet wished to carry on the war, and a common thread running through most of the factions who were not pro-German was the possibility of a tie-up with the Allied forces to achieve their aims. But to Trotsky and Lenin, they all shared one damning characteristic – they were the bourgeois enemies of their new philosophy, bent on destroying the Bolshevik government. From the Soviet point of view, the Allied presence on Russian soil was a calamitous rallying point for these enemies, yet despite the recent introduction of conscription and the slow return to discipline, Trotsky's new Red Army was not quite ready yet for major battle honours. Thus the vipers in their midst, the despised diplomats and agents of imperialism, still at liberty in their *cordon sanitaire*, now became the focal point of hatred and suspicion. In short, the job of Allied embassy official in Russia in August 1918 was not one of diplomacy's choicest appointments.

At the beginning of August Cromie was visited by a man called Sabir, who stated that he had been a lieutenant with the Commander-in-Chief of the Baltic Fleet, Admiral Shastny, who had been executed as a counter-revolutionary by

Trotsky the previous month. He gave as a reference a man called Mr Dick.[2] He was kept waiting for a while in the entrance hall, to be joined a few minutes later by a character calling himself Steckelmann.[3] Cromie appeared, and Steckelmann produced a letter of introduction, which he showed to Cromie. It was from Lockhart.[4] They then revealed that they were White Guards, and offered their services. Sabir said that he was now the commander of a mining division. Cromie, rather rashly it appears, quickly came up with an idea that they could blow up the Ochta railway bridge, which joined the Nicholas Station to the Finland Station. This, Cromie said, was in case of a German advance from Finland.

Cromie seems to have been following his full interventionist agenda by now, as he advised Steckelmann and Sabir that his wish was to unite a number of Russian organisations to work together under British instruction, and that he would guarantee that the parties thus brought together would be 'genuine'. Steckelmann and Sabir seemed quite in favour of this, and began to outline the impressive help they could offer. Steckelmann claimed that he had at his disposal 60,000 White Guards in Finland, and that the railway, telegraph and telephone officials were all in his pay. At any given moment, he claimed, he could disorganise the whole traffic, and throw open the frontier to Poole's forces. In the meantime, this would paralyse the German forces in Finland, as Steckelmann claimed he could organise railway strikes, etc., and the next stage of the operation would be his White Guard army joining up with Poole's force, to march on Petrograd. As if to bolster up the claims of the Latvians, Colonel Berzin, 'Schmidchen' and 'Bredis', he went on to tell Cromie that he had 25,000 Letts in Russia available, and at the given command, they would 'assemble at a settled point, thus bringing the force up to 80,000'. Sabir then threw his hat into the ring with the claim that he had the Petrograd situation under control. His contribution would be to capture all the armoured cars manned by the Bolsheviks, and that he had the night guard in his pay, with a battalion of White Guards officers ready to seize the armoured cars at the right moment.

Cromie mulled over the information. The two men had told him that they were both members of the same 'Finnish organisation' (there is no evidence of what this 'organisation' was). It is easy to accuse Cromie of naivety in his dealings with these men, and the letter from Lockhart remains a mystery. As to whether or not all this subterfuge had passed through the grubby hands of Sidney Reilly is debatable, but Reilly always spread his bets around so it is possible that he may have been involved. In a perfect espionage world, if such a state exists, and had Cromie possessed the necessary expertise, he would have been wise to check these men carefully. If he had had the staff available they could have been shadowed. Which White Guards were they attached to? If they had so many crucial operatives 'in their pay', who was supplying the funds? But the thing Cromie lacked more than anything was time. The Allied troops had landed. The civil war was no longer a threat – it was happening around him. If Steckelmann and Sabir were who they claimed to be, then what a glorious coup for Cromie – perhaps he had a victorious vision of Poole's forces marching into Finland, then onwards, unopposed and into Petrograd. And who would have been the architect of this victory? Captain Francis Newton Allen Cromie DSO RN, holder of the Russian

Orders of St George, St Vladimir and St Anne. But such speculation is perhaps unfair. Cromie, all the evidence shows, was nothing if not modest. He was doing his best for his country, as he had always tried to do.

Cromie's next move was to arrange a secret meeting of leaders of various counter-revolutionary groups at the Hotel de France in Petrograd. He would introduce them to Sabir and Steckelmann. One of those invited was to be General Nikolai Yudenich, who within a year would be threatening Petrograd with his forces and would almost succeed in cutting the rail link between Petrograd and Moscow, to be stopped only by Trotsky's rapidly acquired prowess as a military leader. Who actually turned up at the Hotel de France during the second week in August in unclear, but Steckelmann did not appear, leaving only Sabir in attendance. The two men had been away, apparently, 'inspecting their various posts, etc.', but one would have thought that, having done most of the talking at the embassy, and with such an important plan being formulated, Steckelmann would have made the effort. Or was there someone expected at the hotel who might have recognised him?

The two men then vanished off the scene for a couple of weeks, ostensibly 'inspecting their posts' again. The next time Cromie met them was Saturday 31 August, when they would be cast in a very different light.

During late July and early August there was another burst of organisation by Cromie, evidenced by the following telegram forwarded to Sir Mansfeldt Findlay (who held the distinction of being the tallest man in world diplomacy) at the British Legation in Christiania in Norway:[5]

No. 2726 2.15 p.m. August 8th 1918
Following from Petrograd for Senior Naval Officer,
Murmansk and General Poole.
(Begins) Colonel Spiranski sent by Bolsheviks as Chief of Staff for Pavodsk region is an officer of Chaplin's[6] organisation and well known to me. He will arrange points for passing recruits to the North and will command Brigade mentioned by Milcont as wishing to turn over to us on arrival at the front. I attach great importance to this affair and am in touch with local draft officers that this Brigade will be sent to Betvodsk. I have refused offer of destroyers on Lake Ladoga as we cannot give them any base unless we invade Finnish territory and would have great difficulty to supply them. If a small base can be formed at Perchguba or Brukoba both close to station Medvieja, I can organise a small naval force on Lake Onega. At present I am in touch with bullet proof motor boats 12 knots with sufficient kerosene for 80 hours which should leave this week ending 28th July towed by tug to complete repairs. They will keep in touch with Gillespie [7] at Vologda and are prepared to go anywhere. There are also four petrol boats 25 knots but sufficient petrol is not obtainable. Both classes carry 75 millimetre gun and one maxim. Am trying to raise armed tugs for same purpose. Many contact and drift mines are now being sent to Perchguba and Archangel. If naval co-operation on River and Lake desired please inform me giving proposed bases and detailed plans. (Ends.)

It is not certain who Colonel Spiranski was, apart from a White spy, and this telegram may have been sent after the visit of Buikis and Sprogis, the Latvians, as Cromie says, 'I am in touch with local draft officers', which could be the phoney Lettish guards.

There had been another promising contact, too. In mid-August Cromie had heard the news that an officer named Kovalenski, of the Finnish Dragoons, was organising a courier service to link up the White forces in the Vologda area with Poole's forces in the north. He was taking with him two messages, in cypher, which he would conceal in true spy style in the collar of his pet fox terrier. Kovalenski was, apparently, in some way connected with Sabir – apparently he was the only man apart from the agent H.T. Hall who knew about the messages in the dog's collar. But Kovalenski never made it to Murmansk or Archangel. Two hours before he was due to leave, he was arrested by the Cheka. Their first question was, 'Where is the fox terrier's collar?' Sadly, there would be no way that Cromie could have learned of this arrest, or of Sabir's involvement. If he had known, then perhaps the necessary alarm bells would have rung – Sabir was not to be trusted. But Cromie by now was working flat out to pull all the threads of a combined Allied and counter-revolutionary advance together. He had thrown caution to the wind, and like a gambler, placing his last five pounds on a hopeful treble, his eyes were not on the horses but on the winning post. When he mentioned in his letters having 'so many irons in the fire', one has to imagine a pretty large fireplace.

At 3.30 a.m. on 31 August 1918 Lockhart was roughly shaken from a deep sleep in his Moscow flat. After receiving the news of the attempt on Lenin's life, he and a fellow member of the British Mission, Captain William Hicks, had sat up until 1 a.m., discussing their possible fate in hushed voices. Here another conundrum surfaces. Lockhart did not allude to the possibility, but Reilly could well have been involved with Fanya Kaplan's failed act of assassination.[8] Like many secret agents of the time, Reilly was a law almost unto himself. He lurched from one hermetically sealed pocket of opportunity to the next to advance his plans. An example of his 'act first – think later' nature came on the night he arrived in Moscow. Going straight to the Kremlin, he banged on the door, and asked to see Lenin. Lenin was out. He was greeted by Vladimir Bonch-Brouevitch, Lenin's close friend. He told him that he had been sent out from England by Lloyd George, who was not satisfied with Bruce Lockhart's reports. Knowing that this could be embarrassing to Lockhart, the Bolsheviks wasted no time in letting him know about the audacity of this new envoy, of whose arrival HMG had omitted to tell Lockhart. When Lockhart was introduced to Reilly the following day, he gave him a roasting.

Reilly did not have much connection with Dzerzhinsky at the Cheka, but both he and Lockhart knew Iron Felix's number two, Jacob Peters, quite well. Like Reilly, Jacob Peters was something of an enigma and became more so during the three decades after the revolution. Although born in Russia in 1886, he had gone to Britain in 1909 where he worked in the clothing industry as a steam presser. He was involved in the siege of Sidney Street on 3 January 1911, when the police fought with anarchist terrorists. Three anarchists burned to death in a fire, and Peters himself was arrested, suspected for a time to be one of their notorious leaders, 'Peter the Painter'. He was acquitted in the subsequent trial, but there is evidence to suggest that he became a Scotland Yard informer, and possibly a spy for the Tsarist Okhrana. He married an English woman, Miss Freeman, in 1913 and in 1917 was sent back to Russia by the revolutionary London Russian Delegate Committee. From then on he appeared to be a committed Bolshevik.[9] He spoke excellent English, and had been in England so long the accent had begun to dominate his Russian. The wily Reilly, as one of the many weapons in his armoury, was not opposed to using blackmail. He knew of Peters's dubious past and was blackmailing him in an attempt to raise a coup against Lenin.[10] Thus it is possible that either Reilly or Peters, or both, were behind the failed attempt on Lenin. Perhaps Peters had also feared that, with the ferocity of the civil war and the Allied landing, the Bolsheviks' days were numbered. Most importantly, between 6 July and 22 August, Dzerzhinsky had been on leave – Peters was controlling the Cheka during that time.

On Lockhart's rude awakening that morning, he looked directly from his pillow into the barrel of a gun. He was surrounded by ten armed Cheka agents, and their leader, Mankoff, ordered him to ask no questions but to get dressed. The room was ransacked. Within minutes he was being driven with his fellow prisoner, Hicks, to the Cheka headquarters on the Lubyanka. There he was interrogated by Jacob Peters.

Peters produced the pass Lockhart had issued to Berzin, Sprogis and Buikis. 'Is that your writing?'

Lockhart claimed diplomatic immunity and refused to answer, as he did also to the questions 'Where is Reilly?' and 'Do you know the Kaplan woman?' He was taken back to his cell.

There in the darkness he realised that in his breast pocket he was carrying the most important and incriminating piece of evidence – his secret notebook. He said in his memoirs. 'It contained figures, and, if it fell into Bolshevik hands . . . they would say that the figures represented movements of Bolshevik troops or moneys I had spent on fomenting counter-revolution.'[11] He did not say, however, what the figures *did* represent, and of course he had been moving vast sums of money around, so he was right to be worried. What he did next was in every way in the classic John Buchan British tradition of a fine young gentleman caught in a hole – he asked to go to the toilet. With two guards standing over him, he finished by tearing the pages from the book and using them as toilet paper, an act which attracted no suspicion at all from his captors. Thus the crucial secret figures were flushed into Moscow's – and history's – sewers.

Hicks and Lockhart sat in silence in their cell until, at six in the morning, a black-haired, silent woman was brought into the room. They believed that this was, in fact, Fanya Kaplan, and that she had been placed in their cell to see if there would be some recognition between them. But silence reigned. She was later taken away and shot. At 9 a.m. they were visited by Peters, who told them that the Bolshevik Foreign Minister, Chicherin, had protested at their arrest. They were free to go.

After arriving back at the flat, which had been thoroughly trashed by the Cheka, Lockhart discovered that his mistress, Moura Budberg, had also been arrested. After a shave and a bath he dressed and set off to find the American Red Cross representative, Major Wardwell, who might be able to help in securing Moura's release. On the way he called at the Dutch Legation, to see Mr Oudendijk, another diplomatic colleague. The Dutch Legation had also been raided. But what Oudendijk had to tell Lockhart on that fractious Sunday morning plunged him into despair.

Saturday 31 August was to be a special day for Francis Cromie. If he could keep on juggling all the balls in the air for just a little longer, and if his various plans fitted together, he would pull off a victory equal to Lawrence of Arabia's assault on Aqaba. Poor Francis, however, was not juggling with balls – these were hand grenades. Steckelmann had telephoned to say that 'the time for action is ripe and cannot be delayed'. Agent H.T. Hall had taken the call and asked him how long it could be postponed; Steckelmann said two days at the maximum. He added that it was important to get in touch with the 'other organisations' at once. He suggested that Cromie and others should meet him and Sabir at the Hotel de France. But that seemed too risky to Hall – he suggested that they come to the embassy. A time was agreed – 4 p.m. Hall told Cromie of the arrangement, and Cromie immediately despatched him to find General Yudenich, who was holed up at an address near the Nicholas Station. Yudenich was not at home, having gone to the Dutch Legation. Hall came back and told Cromie, who then sent his assistant, Andrews, with a chauffeur in the Embassy car to fetch the general. As Cromie was instructing Andrews, Steckelmann and Sabir arrived. Cromie ushered them into the anteroom next to the ambassador's quarters, where they sat with Hall. Sabir suddenly got up and made for the door. Hall asked him where he was going. Rather curiously, he replied, 'My organisation has detectives posted outside and I am going to tell them to keep a sharp look-out.' On his return, Cromie took Sabir, Steckelmann and Hall into Le Page's room, and they began to talk.

During the night of 30/31 August the horrendous reflex action resulting from Uritsky's murder and the attempt on Lenin rippled through Moscow and Petrograd like shockwaves from an earthquake, their epicentres in the Lubyanka and at Gorokhovaya 2. There were shootings: many estimates suggest a figure of at least 600 deaths, but the real figure may never be known. Over the coming days the prisons would be full to overflowing, so much so that barge-loads of the arrested could be seen travelling along the Neva *en route* to Kronstadt's grim gaols, never to be seen or heard from again.[12] The flats of Allied diplomats and their legations and offices were raided. Yet for the moment, the British Embassy on the Palace Quay in Petrograd remained unscathed. There was a tense, brooding silence on the quay, broken only by the sporadic sound of gunfire across the darkened city and as the occasional armoured car or military truck rumbled past, bristling with the black silhouettes of a moving forest of bayonets. It is doubtful whether the 'Last Ditchers' slept much that night.

Despite the danger, like the mad dogs and Englishmen they were, not everyone chose the sanctuary of the embassy building. Ernest Boyce, of Military Intelligence, had gone to his flat that night. Cromie's assistant, Commander Le Page, had gone around to Consul Woodhouse's flat to relieve the tension with a few vodkas and a game of bridge. In defiance of the danger all around them, the two men decided to walk the short distance back to the embassy. It was a rash decision. They were bundled into a car by Cheka agents just after midnight, only a few yards from the embassy. Their non-appearance on the Saturday morning was a mystery to Cromie, but little did he know then that the two men were *en route* from a grilling at Cheka headquarters to a cell across the river in the Peter and Paul Fortress.

There are about thirteen different versions of what transpired on the Palace Quay during the afternoon of Saturday 31 August 1918. Some, such as the press reports in *The Times* and *Pravda*, are unreliable owing to florid political and journalistic licence. Other versions appear in various books, such as Robin Bruce Lockhart's *Ace of Spies*. Like many of the other versions, this also over-gilds the lily of what was already a major drama. An image has also emerged over the years from those few authors who touch on Cromie's demise as a lone diplomat, bravely representing his country in an almost empty embassy. Of his bravery and capacity for work there is no doubt, but on the day in question he was far from alone, as there were thirty-three people in the building with him, not allowing for Le Page and Consul Woodhouse, who were otherwise engaged.

One of the most frequently quoted reports of what happened is that of a young Anglo-Russian nurse, Mary Britnieva. There are some anomalies in her version of events, however, which stem from the fact that although her account is some-times regarded as a first-hand report, it is not: she was definitely involved in the events of that day, but she was not at the embassy. Her account is nevertheless packed with information and is always a good starting point. Whatever their political positions (which were naturally anti-Bolshevik, and, sadly, often anti-Semitic, a prevalent sickness of the time), what comes across in the intermittently fine writing of Meriel Buchanan, Mary Britnieva and other British women in revolutionary Russia is a sense of outraged honesty. Their husbands or male partners were mostly involved, either by their military positions or secret deal-ings, in the ghastly intrigues which led to the British débâcle, so their own reports are perhaps often circumspect, made to fit a military or Foreign Office expecta-tion. But not the women; they reported what they saw from a more pristine, emotional viewpoint.

Mary Bucknall married a Russian surgeon, Dr Britnieva, in Petrograd in March 1918. They worked at the old Palace Hospital, where they lived 'over the shop' in a pleasant apartment. Many of the well-bred daughters of the British diplomatic and commercial community living in Russia, including Meriel Buchanan and Florence Farmborough,[13] somewhat laudably gave their services as nurses at the start of the war. The Tsar was our ally, and it was a worthy occu-pation to tend to the sick and wounded of his forces. Mary had a sister who was nursing the troops in southern Russia, and three brothers, two serving in regi-ments in France and one who had been with the Naval Armoured Car Division. In August 1918 her brother, George, was attached to Cromie's staff, where he had been retained to wind up the Armoured Car Division's affairs. Their father, George Bucknall Senior, had extensive business interests in Russia. His connection with Cromie and the embassy was crucial.

Ever since the outbreak of the revolution in March 1917, Cromie had become a reliable conduit for the safe-keeping of British money and valuables. Mr Bucknall, like other expatriates, had been forced to deposit a considerable sum of money and other valuables totalling in excess of £50,000 with Cromie at the embassy because of the Bolsheviks' closure of the banks. By all accounts the Bucknalls, with their servants and cooks, were still living reasonably well, and this living standard had to be maintained. George junior and his wife Nathalie were at first living in the last hotel in Petrograd which had not been nationalised, the Medved. Most of the others had become workers' and soldiers' lodging houses, much to the chagrin of the smart set. But George's closeness to Cromie was attracting the attention of the Cheka, who were shadowing everyone in the Medved, which was becoming rather irritating for the Bucknalls. Mary and her husband offered them temporary accommodation in their hospital apartment at the less suspicious Palace Hospital, which is where they were living at the end of August.

On Saturday the 31st George was due to travel down to Peterhof, where he was responsible for some motor boats owned by the embassy. He was a careful man, used to the force of arms after almost four years of war. He never went anywhere in Petrograd in those days without his two revolvers, a large Smith & Wesson in his hip pocket and a small Browning which he kept hidden for back-up in his waistcoat. On that Saturday morning Nathalie was overcome with a sense of foreboding about the guns, which was to save her husband's life. She begged George not to take the pistols out with him. After much pleading, she was relieved when he agreed and left the weapons with her. She also had an inexplicable sense of dread, according to Mary, and insisted that she accompany George. They set off for the embassy where he would discuss the motor boats with Cromie, intending to return later for lunch, which was set for 12.30. Nathalie had friends in the building, such as Miss Blumberg, the passports clerk, and various other secretaries, with whom she could chat whilst waiting. After their visit they would go back to Mary's for lunch, and then head for Peterhof.

Elsewhere in the city, at about the same time George Bucknall was getting ready to go to the embassy, Sidney Reilly, unaware of Lockhart's and Hicks's arrest in Moscow, and still brimming with enthusiasm for what he believed to be his imminent Latvian uprising, arrived at Ernest Boyce's flat. Reilly gave Boyce the full details of the interlocking subterfuges and his dealings with the Letts, and outlined the possible timetable of events over the next twenty-four hours which might spark the counter-revolution. Boyce was not wholly enthusiastic, but knew that things were moving fast. Although he told Reilly that the whole plan was 'extremely risky', he agreed it was worth a try. Boyce's idea was to dovetail Reilly's Lettish scheme into Cromie's advanced plans, so he told Reilly that he would go around to the embassy, collect Cromie and bring him back to the flat by 3 p.m. for a council of war. Reilly knew he had to keep a low profile. On his night-time journey earlier in the week from Moscow he was questioned and his papers checked, but as usual his false documents were so good the Cheka agents on the train did not realise who he was. But now it was daylight in Petrograd. He had already risked the journey to Boyce's place, and he was not going to tempt providence any further.

At the Britnievas' hospital apartment the time for lunch slipped by without any sign of George. At 1 p.m. Mary received a call from him. He seemed guarded and gave the impression that all was not well. He said the trip to Peterhof was off as 'there had been some happenings'. They would have to skip lunch, but would return at about five o'clock. Mary reported that George and Nathalie had left the Palace Hospital in a car driven by their chauffeur, Vasiuk, at 10 a.m., so they could easily have arrived at the Embassy well before noon. George's phone call back to the Britnieva apartment was said by Mary to have been received at 1 p.m., so if this is the case, one would imagine he had made the call from the embassy. But Nathalie's signed statement[14] opened with the words, 'I came to the Embassy at 4.15 p.m. with my husband, George Bucknall, in the car with the chauffeur, Vasiuk.' In fact, upon arrival at the embassy in the morning George left Nathalie in the car outside whilst he went in to see how long Cromie might need him. The first thing Cromie told him was that Le Page and the Consul had gone missing. After twenty minutes George raced back down the embassy stairs and climbed into the car, taking over the wheel from Vasiuk. He drove at break-neck speed to the only place he knew where he might discover what had become of Le Page – Bolshevik headquarters at the Smolny Institute.

There was no recognisable gendarmerie or police force in Petrograd at this time. Not only were the Cheka a threat, but banditry was at its height and robbers thought little of murdering victims and pushing them into the Neva. Perhaps someone at the Cheka knew something. What force of law and order existed emanated from the Smolny. George knew a commissar at the institute with whom he had struck up a working relationship in the previous months. But as he entered the building, the commissar in question was descending the stairs. He looked George in the eye and shook his head. Something was afoot; something was happening, but George could not put his finger on it. It was probably from the Smolny that he made the telephone call to Mary, which explains why he sounded so guarded. The 'happenings' he spoke of were still not clear to him at this point. They arrived back at the embassy. By this time Boyce had arrived to announce to Cromie that Sidney Reilly was in town.

At seven that night the Britnievas ate their dinner alone. Mary was by now very concerned, and tried to telephone the embassy. To her surprise, there was no reply. She telephoned her parents. Her mother said that she had better come over; she seemed very perturbed. At her parents' house, Mary heard what had happened. Mr Bucknall senior had walked to the embassy to withdraw some cash and had arrived on the Palace Quay at approximately 4.15–4.30 p.m. As he walked around the corner from the Suvrovskaya Ploschad onto the Palace Quay he saw a large number of cars drawn up outside the embassy. Armed soldiers and civilians were standing about in groups. Suddenly he recognised George and Nathalie's car, alongside which stood Vasiuk, the chauffeur. Their eyes met. Vasiuk made an almost imperceptible motion with his head. Mr Bucknall took it for what it was – a warning. Instead of approaching the embassy, he walked on to the Troistkiy Bridge, then stopped to look back. A large number of armed men were pouring out of the embassy doors.

Mr Bucknall could hardly believe what he was seeing, yet it was obvious that the embassy, a piece of British territory protected by international law, had been raided by the Bolsheviks. That night Mary's parents packed everything valuable or dangerous and stayed in the house of a friend, a Finnish merchant. They were wise to do so; when they returned they discovered that the house had been raided by the Cheka. Letters, papers and documents were taken. Fortunately, they had not found the Chartwood safe hidden behind the panelling in Mr Bucknall's study.

To form some kind of an accurate picture of what happened in the embassy after 4 p.m. we have three accounts to rely upon. One is that of H.T. Hall, another is Nathalie Bucknall's statement to Consul Bosanquet, and the third is George Bucknall's account given to his sister, Mary, which is included in her book about her life in Russia.[15] The latter was written sixteen years after the event, but her account does seem to tie up with the others, although there are still some inconsistencies.

At approximately 4 p.m., Cromie sent Andrews to find General Yudenich. He was now in Le Page's room with Hall, Steckelmann and Sabir. Sabir, we will recall, had been outside to inspect his 'detectives' and keep them on their toes. Hall claimed to be a civilian[16] and on Nathalie's statement he was listed as 'accidentally in the Embassy'. If this was so, he was in the room with major players in secret events, and must have been in the building for some time, as he reported that Cromie had, an hour before Steckelmann and Sabir's arrival, taken Le Page's revolver from the drawer and placed it in his pocket. This ties in with the fact that Cromie's own loaded revolver was discovered back at his flat two days later. It seems amazing that the Cheka did not take it in their raids, and even more surprising that Cromie did not have his own gun with him at the embassy. Confusingly, Hall's report was written in the third person:[17]

> [Sabir] had been away for about three or four minutes, and on his return, Cromie, Hall, Steckelmann and Sabir went into Le Page's room, sat down, and started talking. After about seven or eight minutes a car was heard in the yard behind, and at the same time the door of the room was tried by someone. Hall thought it would be Yudenich. Cromie got up and looked out into the yard, and Hall got up and opened the door, saw a man with a revolver levelled at him, and shut it again quickly. At the same time Cromie said 'Don't open the door', pulled out his revolver (Le Page's) from his hip pocket and said, 'Remain there and keep the door after me.' He then opened the door, levelled his revolver and said 'Clear out, you swine', and advanced along the passage driving the man before him.

Meanwhile, another drama was unfolding on the landing at the top of the staircase. This is what happened according to Mary Britnieva, as told to her by George Bucknall:[18]

> After his return to the Embassy from Smolny, he had been engaged on a report that Captain Cromie was preparing for the Admiralty on the events

of the previous night and of that morning. There was also the usual routine work. At a few minutes before four o'clock he was alone with Captain Cromie in the Naval Room. The telephone rang and the clerk told my brother that a letter had been brought to him and was in the Chancery. The Chancery was situated on the same floor and to reach it one had to traverse the large landing at the top of the first flight of the grand staircase. My brother got this letter and came out again into the corridor. He had not quite reached the landing and had stopped to read the letter just beyond a dark recess which was on his right where a couple of telephone boxes were installed. He had the letter in one hand and the penknife that was attached to his watch chain in the other when he sensed rather than saw something in front of him. He looked up and there in front of him stood a man in a dark slouch hat who pointed an automatic pistol at him and immediately yelled 'Hands up!' At that moment a number of shots rang out and the man dodged off behind my brother. A second later another man came up from behind my brother's back and held a pistol a few inches from his face. My brother said this fellow was very agitated and his finger was almost twitching on the trigger, so that he felt sure it would go off at any moment. Simultaneously something cold was pressed against my brother's neck, just behind his right ear, and he guessed it was a pistol held by a second man. My brother's hands, in one of which he still held the letter while from the other his chain and watch dangled, were raised above his head. The man behind him shouted, 'This is the one that has been shooting.'

Suddenly my brother remembered the incident at breakfast [Nathalie's request re the pistols]. He quickly said 'You can convince yourselves at once that I have no arms at all.' This created a diversion which probably saved my brother's life as the fellow in front of him was so obviously nervous that my brother is sure that in another instant that finger of his would have twitched him into eternity.

Bucknall was then searched. For a while the intruders thought he had perhaps ditched a gun in the dark recess by the phone boxes. One of them searched, using lighted matches to penetrate the gloom.

Across the landing Bucknall could see the corridor leading to the ambassador's quarters and the naval and military rooms. To his right he could see halfway down the staircase. A man, revolver in hand, was ascending the stairs. At the same time, Bucknall was horrified to see Cromie, steadily advancing along the opposite corridor towards the landing.[19]

My brother realised to his horror that Cromie was going to meet the man at the angle just as he reached the stairs. *Captain Cromie was certainly not carrying a revolver or a pistol.* [Author's italics]

My brother fluttered the paper that he was holding in his hand in an attempt to catch Captain Cromie's eye to warn him to go back, but Cromie never looked up and in a second he had run right into the man. They looked at each other for a moment and then Cromie thrust the man aside and started running down the stairs. At that instant my brother was pushed through the door that led to the Chancery. He heard a great deal of shooting as he crossed the threshold.

Nathalie Bucknall's timing in her testimony seems slightly at odds with Hall's and Britnieva's. She put their arrival at the embassy at 4.15 p.m. and said that everything was quiet until 4.45 p.m. However, whilst George was upstairs with Cromie, Nathalie was on the ground floor in the passport office talking to the passport clerk, Miss Blumberg.[20]

> At 4.50 I heard very loud and harsh voices. I went out into the small room between the passport office and the entrance hall and found the door closed and heard shots upstairs and terrible screams. I opened the door into the entrance hall, and saw the hall porter Matvei looking up the stairs, and when I asked him what was the matter he begged me to hide. I jumped back into the small room leaving the door partly open. I saw several people rushing down the stairs, probably Embassy servants, and go into the rooms opposite where the hall porter lives. When the hall was empty I ran back towards the hall porter, and at this moment I saw several Red Guards running down the stairs with Captain Cromie in front. I ran back into the small lobby, quickly shut the door and saw through the hole in the door Captain Cromie fall backwards wounded on the last step. I saw two Red Guards rush past Captain Cromie, who was then lying on the stairs, calling in Russian, 'Stop him . . . stop him . . .'
>
> They went out into the street and then returned and rushed back up the stairs and disappeared. All the time there was firing.

Just prior to this drama, upstairs in the chancery the raiders had assembled their victims. Most of the embassy staff were stood around the room at gunpoint, their hands raised. Boyce was standing by a filing cabinet, faced by a glowering Red Guard who had a pistol trained on him. The door burst open and a man backed in, firing his gun into the corridor repeatedly. Suddenly he fell to the floor, clutching his stomach. 'Comrades! Comrades!' he cried, 'I've got a bullet in my stomach!' One of the Guards turned around. 'Silence, comrade. Silence!'

Downstairs Nathalie watched as more Red Guards trooped through the entrance hall. One of them violently kicked Cromie's supine form. Upstairs loud voices could be heard, shouting, 'Come out of the room or we will open machine-gun fire on you!' It seemed obvious that not all the staff had yet given in.

Suddenly, Nathalie and the terrified Miss Blumberg realised that the entrance hall was empty. They nervously pushed open the lobby door and ran into the hall and across to Cromie. He was covered in blood. As Nathalie bent over him she noticed his eyes flickering and his lips move slightly, but there were more voices at the top of the stairs. The two women ran back to the lobby. After a while they decided to emerge, Nathalie taking off her overcoat so as to pass for an embassy clerk. Miss Blumberg went back to Cromie and bent over him, but Red Guards appeared again on the staircase. The women were soon surrounded and forced up the staircase at gunpoint. Nathalie tried to remonstrate in Russian but was pushed violently from behind with the words 'Oh . . . speaks *Russian*, eh? Here on a friendly visit?'

They were thrust into the chancery. By now everyone in the building was under arrest. They were frisked for arms. By the chancery door Nathalie noticed a body on the floor. Each person's pockets were emptied, wallets and jewellery taken, and all items were each put into a large envelope with each prisoner's name written on the face. The Chief Commissar, Hillier,[21] entered and announced, 'Two of our men have been killed. The Consulate has now been taken by the Red Guards in the name of the law and of the Soviet government.' Miss Blumberg was thinking of Cromie and asked if she could take him some water. The commissar refused. 'He can lie there – we've no time to look after him!' A call was sent out for sailors to come from nearby destroyers to seal up the embassy and set up a guard around the building. They were also ordered to arrest anyone passing in the vicinity of the embassy. The commissar asked who had been in the room from which shots had been fired. At this point Andrews had returned to the embassy, without General Yudenich. One of the guards said that Andrews had been in the room. It seems doubtful, but a loaded revolver was produced as evidence. The embassy chaplain, the Reverend Lombard, was marched in. He requested that he might go and attend to Captain Cromie. He was violently refused. The hall porter, Matvei, was pale-faced and shaking, a revolver pressed to his neck. The commissar bellowed at him: 'The embassy will be searched from top to bottom. If you refuse to open any door, you will be shot!' Sailors had appeared in the building and began the search. Soon, everyone was marched down the stairs and had to retrieve their overcoats for a long walk under guard to the Cheka headquarters at Gorokhovaya 2. Outside the sky had turned a dark grey and a steady drizzle was falling.

As they all filed into the entrance hall to find their coats the women wept and the men stared in stunned disbelief at the crumpled, bloody figure which had been pushed across the marble floor and now lay under the hall window. The dark hair, the finely chiselled features of a handsome, brave and gallant man were still there for all to see. But the grand and dangerous planning of that menacing summer had climaxed in this ultimate tragedy. Captain Francis Newton Allen Cromie DSO RN, master submariner, hero of the Baltic, the dynamo who had kept this far-flung outpost of the Empire buzzing with life and activity, was dead.

The staircase on which Cromie was shot in 1918. (*Graham Harrison*)

CHAPTER 23

THE AFTERMATH

I was serving in submarine *L6* on the Bay of Biscay patrol.
During an organised press message by radio from our parent
ship HMS *Ambrose* in Plymouth I learned of Cromie's death.
Had it been my own brother I was reading about [by Morse
code] I would not have felt it more.

Ben Benson,
Memoirs of an Ancient Submariner

If Sidney Reilly's counter-revolution had been a success, his plan was not to kill
Trotsky or Lenin, but to divest them of their trousers and parade them through
the streets of Moscow and Petrograd before locking them in prison. He saw this
as a more potent method of destroying their credibility than allowing them to
become martyrs for the Bolshevik cause. One might ask, if this was the case, why
it has been suggested that he and Jacob Peters may have been behind Fanya
Kaplan's failed assassination attempt on Lenin. The answer probably lies in a
very comical comment on Reilly by a keen researcher on the period,[1] that 'Sidney
Reilly was so bent he had to put his pants on with a corkscrew'. Whereas there
is little doubt as to Reilly's prowess and ability as a spy, one only has to read his
own interpretation of events to realise that he had spent so much of his life as an
agent, double agent and *agent provocateur*, and existed in so many different iden-
tities, that his views and plans changed several times each week, along with his
passports. After Lockhart's and Hicks's arrest in Moscow, Reilly had escaped as
usual. But the Cheka did manage to round up no fewer than eight of his
mistresses. Few of them had much idea why they were being arrested, and
without fail each one claimed to be his legal wife. The ensuing squabble, which
began when they were all confined to one cell, loudly arguing amongst themselves
as to which of them was his *real* wife, must have provided the Cheka with hours
of entertainment. Yet this was the bizarre and fantastic life Reilly lived. His
version of reality shifted from hour to hour.

For instance, Agent George Hill's official report on the events of 31 August,
as mentioned in the previous chapter, had Reilly waiting at Boyce's flat whilst
Boyce went to the Embassy to bring Cromie. All the reports worth considering
put the raid on the building at between 4 and 5 p.m. Not Sidney Reilly. His narrative said that he had telephoned Cromie on the Saturday morning to summon
him and was awaiting his arrival in a café run by one Serge Sergevitch Balkoff,
a place where he had met Cromie on previous occasions:[2]

Not like Cromie to be unpunctual. My feelings may be imagined, as I waited there. In my mind I went over the happenings of the last two months, my high hopes and their ignominious sequel. I had been within an ace of becoming master of Russia . . . With a whirr and a cling the little clock on the mantel struck recalling me with a start from my flight of mental rhetoric. A quarter past twelve and Cromie not there. I dared not wait any longer. Balkoff, comrade though he was, was probably suspect. But it was imperative that I should see Cromie that day.

I decided to risk a visit to the British Embassy. It was a dangerous move, of course, both for the Embassy and myself. But I had brought it off successfully before. The street was clear. I stepped out . . . In the Vlademirovsky Prospekt I met some men and women running. They dived into doorways, into side streets, anywhere. There was evidently a panic. What had happened? Then suddenly the cause was revealed to me. A car shot by, crammed with Red soldiers, then another, then another. The Cheka was out. I quickened my pace, and was almost running, when I turned into the street where the British Embassy maintained a precarious oasis of civilisation in the midst of the waste that was Petrograd. And this is what I saw:

In front of the British Embassy was arranged a line of bodies – the dead bodies of Bolshevik soldiers, Four cars were drawn up opposite, and across the street was drawn a double cordon of Red Guards. The Embassy door had been battered off its hinges. The Embassy flag had been torn down. The Embassy had been carried by a storm. That line of Red bodies told that the garrison had sold the place dearly.

Suddenly a voice addressed me by name, and I looked round to find myself looking into the face of a grinning Red soldier.

'Well, Comrade Relinsky, have you come to see our carnival?'

'I have longed to see this sight,' said I sweetly, 'but, behold my usual luck. I ran all the way, and I am too late. Tell me, comrade, what happened?'

The man was one I had met fairly often in my guise of Comrade Relinsky of the Cheka, and he proceeded with the greatest gusto to tell me what had been happening whilst I was awaiting Cromie at Balkoff's.

The Cheka were endeavouring to find one Sidney Reilly, and had actually raided the British Embassy in the hope that he would be there.

In the Embassy were some forty British subjects with Woodhouse at their head. When the raid took place Woodhouse had rushed upstairs to the upper room, where they kept all the Embassy papers, which he proceeded to destroy as fast as he could. Meanwhile, the gallant Cromie, a Browning automatic in each hand, had held the stairs against the Red horde, and had emptied both magazines into them before he had fallen, literally riddled with bullets.

This flight of fanciful conceit is riddled with as many holes as Reilly says Cromie was. First, he arrived at the embassy at least three hours before the raid actually happened. The row of dead bodies is fantasy. Of the three Russians shot in the raid, whether by Cromie or not, only one, Yanson, was killed, with Sheikman and Vortnovsky seriously wounded, according to the report in

259

Isvestia.[3] Reilly also said that Woodhouse ran up the Embassy stairs – an incredible feat, as he was either under interrogation at Cheka headquarters, or across the river in a cell at the Peter and Paul fortress. There were not 'forty British subjects' in the building. Of the thirty-three people listed at the end of Nathalie Bucknall's statement[4] who were in the Embassy that day, six were Russian subjects, four of whom worked as clerks or typists and were released, and four members of the Swedish Red Cross whose offices were in the same building. Of course, in true Tom Mix style, Cromie had not one but two Brownings. According to *Pravda*, the raiders had no problem entering the Embassy's ground floor, so Reilly's account of the front door 'battered off its hinges' only serves to demonstrate what a grotesque world he lived in. One can only speculate what his bosses in England, Mansfield Cumming and Lloyd George, must have thought of his reports, if they contained just a fraction of the imagination of the above. Little wonder they formed such an increasingly black view of the Bolsheviks. And of course, the raid was nothing to do with anything else but the search for the famous 'Ace of Spies' himself, such was his over-inflated ego. If nothing else, he would have made a good action novelist.

But what *was* the raid about? The names Steckelmann and Sabir do not appear on the list of those arrested or released on the day. To try and make sense of this, we have to return to H.T. Hall's account.[5] According to him, when Cromie had gone to the door with Le Page's pistol and driven the gun-toting intruder along the corridor, he had told Hall, 'Remain here and keep the door after me.' At this point Hall's report is confusing. We cannot tell if he was in Le Page's room or outside in the corridor, but he then said that he 'heard a shot and found Steckelmann and Sabir with their revolvers out, after which several shots were fired'. According to Hall, who ended up with the rest of those arrested in the Peter and Paul Fortress:

> Sabir was removed from Peter and Paul prison about a week after our arrest under suspicious circumstances, as his name was not called out as usual, and he passed Hall's cell in silence. Hall saw him and he looked well fed and happy. He had in the few days of his imprisonment sent in letters to Hall asking him what he thought of affairs, and stating that Steckelmann had been taken to Moscow and shot.

This seems highly unlikely, unless, of course, one subscribes to the view expressed by some writers that Cromie was killed by German agents or a Russo-German raiding party. The Germans were offering 100,000 roubles for Cromie's head, so any bounty hunter willing to take the risk would have been attracted. Neither the Germans nor the Bolsheviks wanted the prospect of Allied intervention. And if 'Steckelmann' was the man's real name, it has more of a German ring to it than a Russian one. If Steckelmann was working for the Germans, could it be that Sabir was his Bolshevik contact, and that once Steckelmann had served his purpose, he was indeed not allowed to go back to wherever he came from, but shot by the Bolsheviks to cover any tracks? It seems as if Sabir was 'arrested' as a ploy to plant him in the Peter and Paul so that he might continue gathering information from his fellow prisoners, hence the internal letters to Hall. This may explain why he was released early and looked 'well fed and happy'.

And if Steckelmann and Sabir were armed and firing, whom were they firing at, and why were they not bundled into the chancery with the other captives? Hall did not say what he did or what his location was when they drew their guns. Was it they who shot Cromie? Who was the man Cromie bumped into on the stairs? To the innocent observers, such as Nathalie and Miss Blumberg, anyone in the building who should not have been there was regarded as 'Red Guards'.

But Sabir is the key. It was he who, shortly after arriving at the Embassy, went back outside to check his 'detectives'. It looks highly possible that he was first making sure that Cromie and Boyce were in the building before giving the green light for the raid.

There are several versions of the raid on the embassy which usually list the number of men shot by Cromie to be two or three. Robin Bruce Lockhart, R.H. Bruce Lockhart's son, in his biography of Reilly, *Ace of Spies*, offers a cinematic version of Cromie's death. With this much colour, it is little wonder that his book was turned into a successful TV series: 'The gallant Cromie had resisted to the last; with a Browning in each hand he had killed a Commissar and wounded several Cheka thugs, before falling himself riddled with Red bullets. Kicked and trampled on, his body was thrown out of a second floor window.'[6]

The second-floor window is an interesting touch. There are the two pistols again, and the body 'riddled'. According to the woman who prepared Cromie's body for burial, the doctor's examination revealed that two bullets had entered Cromie's head at the back, one of which had stopped in the forehead.[7]

After the raid the assembled prisoners had been marched to the Cheka head-quarters on Gorokhovaya. The women, including Nathalie Bucknall, were placed in a crowded room with thirty-five other female prisoners. Among those already there she met the relatives of the student, Kanegisser, who had carried out Uritsky's assassination. Even his old grandmother, in her mid-eighties, was in for interrogation. The prisoners were surprised to see that many members of the French diplomatic mission had also been arrested. The British prisoners were asked which political party they belonged to: 'None,' they replied. Rumours spread throughout the building that the male prisoners were about to be shot because of the Allied forces in Murmansk. However, such an act on top of violating an embassy might well have been one act of retribution too many; the men were not shot.

On Sunday morning at 11 a.m., most of the women were released. The men were eventually taken to the Peter and Paul Fortress, where they spent a very uncomfortable thirteen weeks before their final release, which was accompanied by an order to leave Russia within forty-eight hours. During their incarceration, the prisoners were eventually allowed food parcels. This enabled an illicit communication system to be set up using a particular brand of sardines, Amieux Frères. The tins had a double lid. By removing the outer lid, small messages could be inserted in the cavity, and the clip-on lid reattached. Return messages were smuggled out by a peasant woman employed on the Peter and Paul Fortress staff. The Britnieva family paid her well for her services.

At home, the outrage at the embassy failed to make the front pages, but never-theless warranted the lofty indignation of the fourth estate. For one journalist, the whole event could have been quite a scoop. He was Victor Marsden, corre-spondent of the *Morning Post*. Unfortunately, he was in the embassy on that fateful day and had joined the prisoners in their plight. The press reports gave two interpretations of the event. *The Times* of 5 September said:

BRITISH ATTACHÉ MURDERED
A PETROGRAD OUTRAGE
'RUSSIA TO FIGHT THE ALLIES'

Bolshevist troops have attacked the British Embassy at Petrograd, forced an entry and killed Captain Francis Cromie, the Naval Attaché, whose body was afterwards barbarously mutilated. The Russian version of the revised peace treaty with Germany recently negotiated at Berlin, states that Russia agrees to fight against the troops of the Allied Powers in Northern Russia.

The outrage at the Embassy took place on Saturday last, and followed the publication by the Soviet Government, on August 29, of a decree ordering the arrest of all British and French subjects between the ages of 18 and 40.

Immediate reparation and the prompt punishment of those concerned in the attack have been demanded by the British Government, and M. Litvinoff, the Bolshevist representative in Great Britain, and members of his staff have been placed under preventative arrest until such time as all British representatives in territory under Soviet control are set at liberty and allowed to proceed to the Finnish frontier free from molestation.

Captain Cromie, who was appointed Naval Attaché on January 10 this year, made a gallant attempt to defend the Embassy, and killed three of the Soviet soldiers with his own hand before he was struck down. His corpse was treated with the worse indignities, and permission to say prayers over his body was refused to an English clergyman.

The embassy papers were sacked and wholly destroyed.

On 9 September the same newspaper gave the Russian version of events.

BOLSHEVIST STORY OF THE ATTACK

A SEARCH FOR DOCUMENTS

AMSTERDAM, Sept. 4 – The *Pravda*, as quoted in a Moscow telegram, gives the following details as to the 'search' of the British Embassy in Petrograd. Forty persons, the majority of whom were English, were arrested. The reasons for the arrests were that the Moscow authorities had received an important report regarding the connection of various counter-revolutionary organisations with the British Government and the British Embassy. As the main thread of the conspiracy organisations led back to the British Embassy detectives were sent to Petrograd to investigate.

Commissioner Hillier was instructed to carry out the search and the arrests. It was reported that discussions between the counter-revolutionaries were to take place, and M. Savinkoff and M. Filonek were supposed to be hidden in the Embassy. Accompanied by a detachment of scouts, M. Hillier proceeded to the British Embassy, the lower parts of which he succeeded in entering without resistance.

When, however, the party entered one of the rooms on the first floor, shots were fired, killing one of the scouts and wounding another. M. Hillier went with a detachment of scouts into the next room, where he arrested a person whose identity is unknown. The fight in the corridor continued, however, and the scouts were obliged to fire where the Naval Attaché, Captain Cromie, was killed. Policemen then entered the Embassy and arrested 40 persons, one of whom was Prince Shashkovsky.[8]

It is further alleged that weapons and compromising documents were found. Great importance is attached to the search. – *Reuter*

There are two further Russian versions of the raid worthy of inspection. One, dated 2 September – very close to the event – appeared in the Petrograd *Krasnaia Gazeta*,[9] and one in a 1995 book on the Petrograd Cheka by Vasilii Berezkhov.[10] The *Gazeta* article stated that Commissar Geller (Hillier) led a ten-man Cheka party to raid the embassy as the Cheka had reason to believe that Savinkov (Savinkoff) and Filonenko (Filonek) were hiding there. They were not. The timing is slightly different as the raid was said to have taken place at 5 p.m., and those comrades wounded were listed as 'Borisenko', who became 'Bortnovskii' (translated into English from *Isvestia* as Vortnovsky) and 'Shenkman' who became Sheikman. The man killed, Yanson, was listed as 'Lison'. The report did not actually state who shot Cromie.

Berezhkov's book revealed Geller (Hillier) to be an ex-Social Revolutionary and one-time member of Kerensky's police force. Both accounts link him to Savinkov, and the suggestion was that Geller was chosen to lead the raid as he would be able to recognise and identify Savinkov. Geller admitted to much confusion as the shooting went on in darkened rooms and at the top of the stairs, and also admitted that it was he who shot Bortnovskii (Vortnovsky) 'by mistake'.

For Geller the raid, generally regarded by his superiors as a complete mess, was to have a bad result. He was expelled from the Cheka after being discovered to be an associate of smugglers and speculators. One of his nefarious contacts was Boris Borisovich Gol'dinger, who had done much business with the British and had been arrested on suspicion of being a British spy, but was freed soon after Uritsky's assassination. Gol'dinger then offered the Cheka information on certain British agents which included a man named John Merrett and a mysterious 'Gillespie'. The latter turns out to be Sidney Reilly yet again, under one of his numerous aliases. Oddly enough, neither Merrett nor 'Gillespie' were arrested, but Gol'dinger remained a full member of the Cheka. Both Geller and Gol'dinger were shot by the Cheka for various misdemeanours on 10 January 1920.[11]

What the Red Guards did at first with Cromie's corpse is open to question, but it did end up at the Smolny Institute, probably after a short stay at the Lutheran Church off the Nevsky Prospekt. It seems obvious that no one was quite sure what to do with him. Even the Reverend Bousefield S. Lombard, the embassy chaplain, who had married Cromie's sailors, christened their offspring and been such a close companion to Cromie during those difficult months, was languishing in prison. There were no Allied diplomats left to manage the situation. Within three days of the raid Lockhart was back inside the Lubyanka in Moscow, rearrested.

And so this bloodstained legend, cold and dead, Captain Cromie, lay in a rough wooden box on a trestle in the heart of his enemy's headquarters. The Cheka decided that he would be buried at night, like a common criminal, in an unmarked grave.

Cromie deserved a better exit from his world than that, and a charismatic man like this had more than his share of friends in Petrograd beyond the Allied community. In this rabid atmosphere of civil and international war, subterfuge and revolution, the neutral non-combatants in the Dutch, Swedish and Danish legations must have seemed like strangers to many, but they knew enough of their colleague Francis Cromie to ensure that their brave friend would meet his maker in style.

CHAPTER 24

THE LAST SALUTE

Call him on the deep sea, call him up the Sound.
Call him when ye sail to meet the foe;
Where the old trade's plyin' a' the old flag's flyin'
They shall find him ware and wakin', as they found him long ago!

Sir Henry John Newbolt,
'Drake's Drum'

William Jacob Oudendijk was a short, stocky Dutchman of forty-four. In a world of diplomats of varying quality, from the downright indolent to the highly active and talented, he reigned at the pinnacle of the latter in Petrograd. He had been born in Kampen, Holland, in 1874, and his broad academic talent aligned with his gift for languages soon saw him join the ranks of the Dutch diplomatic service.[1] By the time he had reached thirty, he was fluent in kuo-yü, the language of northern China. He had many diplomatic missions under his belt in such far-flung posts as Tehran and Peking. He was soon to become fully fluent in Russian, and spent his first stretch as Dutch Ambassador in St Petersburg between 1907 and 1908. When war broke out, then revolution, the Dutch government knew that the tricky position of retaining a neutral legation in Petrograd could be held by just one man – William J. Oudendijk. He was not without his faults, and like Lockhart and many other men of his position at the time, anti-Semitism rears its ugly head in his memoirs.

Oudendijk arrived in Petrograd early in 1917, just before the March uprising. It was a good day for the British, as in September 1918 the brave Dutchman was the last taut thread upon which England's dignity hung. Were it not for him, the remains of Captain Francis Cromie would have shared the anonymity of the other estimated 8,000 victims throughout Russia of the Terror of September 1918. Thankfully, the Dutch Minister left a well-written memoir behind after his demise in 1953.[2] From this we can experience something of the poignant atmosphere of Cromie's makeshift funeral.

The day after the embassy raid Oudendijk called a meeting of all the diplomats in Petrograd who had not been imprisoned. Two British officials, Bosanquet and Kimmins, had managed to escape arrest in Petrograd and had taken refuge in the Dutch Consulate. Oudendijk's main supporters were the Swiss, the Belgians, the Danes and the Swedes. It was decided that he would deputise for them all, and he paid a visit to Chicherin, the Bolsheviks' Foreign Minister. They met at the Metropole Hotel. Chicherin liked to give himself a 'proletarian' look

265

by dressing badly. Oudendijk described him in a 'shabby, dirty badly cut tweed suit, filthy sweater and high collar . . . He looked as if he always slept in his clothes.' Chicherin listened to Oudendijk's bitter complaints about the arrest and detention of the allied diplomats. Chicherin replied that the Dutch, more than anyone, ought to be sympathetic to the revolution. Had not Oudendijk's country had to struggle for her freedom and independence, too? The Dutchman was having none of it. The argument rumbled on to an unsatisfactory conclusion. Similar confrontations took place with L.H. Karakhan, Chicherin's assistant at the Bolshevik Foreign Office. Oudendijk warned Karakhan, who sat toying with a huge revolver, that the Russians' barbaric behaviour would stand them in bad international stead for the future. There would be a price to pay for Cromie's murder.

However, like the diplomat he was, Oudendijk did make an offer to mediate in an attempt to get Litvinov, the Soviet representative in London, released from prison, where he had been immediately placed when the news of the Embassy raid had reached Whitehall. After several hours of argument, Oudendijk received permission for Cromie's body to be removed from the Smolny, from where it was taken to the tiny English church on the Palace Quay.

Other diplomats suggested that now that they at least had a chance to bury Cromie, perhaps it ought to be done quietly, at night, to avoid any demonstrations or hostility. The Dutchman was outraged.[3]

> Having spoken as I had to the Government in Moscow of the scandalous and criminal way in which the authorities in Petrograd had behaved by attacking with armed bands a foreign Embassy placed under my protection, by imprisoning foreign officials and citizens and by killing a foreign naval attaché who, in the execution of his duty had defended the Embassy against lawless trespassers, I could not give my consent to have that officer buried like a criminal. I was determined on giving Captain Cromie the funeral that befitted a hero, and I was going to make it as elaborate as the drab conditions of Petrograd, already cowering under the fearful blows of the Red Terror, would allow me to do.

In different circumstances, the priest at such a funeral would have been the British Embassy's own chaplain, the Reverend Lombard. But as we have seen, he was languishing in a cell across the Neva in the Peter and Paul fortress. Lombard appears on the evidence to have been, as his calling required, a compassionate man. Earlier in the war, he had been tending to the spiritual needs of the sick in Petrograd's English hospital. There he met a patient, an intelligent young Russian girl called Frances Wagner, who spoke good English. The surgeon in charge had asked Lombard if he might be able to find her some work among the British commercial community. But as the revolution broke, the confusion and uncertainty which spread through the expatriate businesses made this impossible. To his credit, once she had recovered from a serious operation, Lombard took Frances Wagner on as his secretary.

As she was one of the few individuals to remain at liberty, it fell to her to carry out the sad and unpleasant task of dealing with Cromie's body. Her long letter to Lombard written in early October 1918, halfway through his incarceration, is a sad document.[4] On Monday, 2 September, she had visited the Dutch embassy, where the fugitive Mr Kimmins asked her to prepare the English Chapel to receive Cromie's corpse. At six that night Oudendijk went in a borrowed motor hearse with his secretary, van Niftrik, the Danish Minister, M. de Scavenius, and the Belgian Ambassador through pouring rain, to the Smolny. As they slid the rough wooden coffin into the hearse the Red sentries looked on balefully as the rain splattered their shoulders from a black sky above. It was a slow, melancholy drive to the little chapel by the Neva.

The men solemnly shouldered the coffin into the chapel and placed it on a trestle. They stood around it for a few moments. The cook and servants from the chaplain's quarters, all of whom had known Cromie from his regular visits, and who had enjoyed his friendship, filed in and stood in tearful silence with these well-bred men from countries they knew little of. Oudendijk announced that he had organised a proper coffin which would arrive the following morning. After a few more minutes of silent contemplation, the party left and the chapel was closed for the night.

In the morning, Kimmins telephoned Frances from the Dutch Embassy to tell her a doctor and a nurse were coming to examine the body and help her to prepare it for burial. She wrote:[5]

> I and little Jenny got everything ready in five minutes and brought in a basin with water and soap and all the necessary things. Then the doctor began to undress the body to examine the pockets.
>
> In the pockets was found: a silk handkerchief, a little baby's glove, nine roubles in stamps, the leather from his watch, but not the watch, and a piece of Indian rubber. That was all that we found. I put all that in an envelope and brought it afterwards to the Dutch Embassy. Not a single paper was in his pockets. Captain Cromie's face was just as it always was; his lips tight together, but otherwise he had not changed at all. His hands were together and on his right hand on the top there were three little black marks, the Doctor saying that he had probably hit something hard. Two wounds he had, high up in the back of his head and one bullet had stopped in the forehead which the Doctor took out. Then he was washed and I gave a pair of clean pyjamas of yours and a pair of clean white socks, because nobody had tried to get his things. Then the same suit and same trousers in which he died we put on as Mr Kimmins and Mrs Oudendijk had ordered and told me to. All that was covered with blood and dirty. I am shivering while I think of it.

Frances had pleaded with someone to attempt to retrieve Cromie's uniform from the embassy, but the building had been sealed by the Cheka. Thus he had to be buried in the civilian suit he had been wearing on the day of his death. To Frances, it seemed unforgivable: 'I do not know how officers are buried in England, but here they are buried in their uniforms. But I think that nowhere

267

they are buried in dirty clothes covered with blood – unless it is on the battle-field.'[6] Her touching outrage seemed justified, but in a sad way, perhaps Cromie had been on his last battlefield on that black Saturday afternoon.

Acting on instructions from Mrs Oudendijk, Frances then braved the fearful streets of Petrograd and headed for Cromie's flat to retrieve any belongings of his which might have escaped the Cheka raid. Surprising though it seems, one of the items she retrieved and sent to the Dutch Embassy was his loaded Browning revolver. Later that day it was returned to her at the chapel, wrapped in a brown paper parcel with a note from Mrs Oudendijk instructing her to throw it into one of Petrograd's canals. She decided against this and later gave it to the Swedish Consul, Mr Langenfeld. Judging by the tone of her letter, Frances does not seem to have had much time for the Dutch, despite their efforts to see Cromie off in a decent way. The Dutch, conscious that they might be raided again, were reluctant to have an unregistered loaded weapon found in the building. This was seen by Frances as timidity: 'The Swedish Embassy I was sure was not afraid to have it there.'[7]

The funeral was arranged for Friday, 6 September at 10 a.m. Oudendijk had tried everywhere to find a White Ensign with which to drape the coffin, but without success. A Russian lady, however, Mrs Artysmovitch, managed to find a Union Jack. On the day of the funeral Frances had a choice between attending or going into Petrograd to collect what food she could to send in a parcel to the Peter and Paul for the Reverend Lombard. She chose the latter.

There had been a problem over who should take the service in the absence of the Anglican minister. Oudendijk wasted no time in contacting the Presbyterian minister in Petrograd, the sixty-one-year-old William Kean. Kean, born in Rothesay in 1857, had spent much of his life tending his flock in St Andrew's Church, Alexandria, Egypt.[8] To be asked to don the surplice of the Anglican Church may have seemed an unusual request but his Christianity was broad and accommodating. He had an affinity with sailors, too: his son, Dallas, had been a Merchant Navy captain and had lost his life at sea in 1915. Kean stayed in his Petrograd parish to the end, helping the city's British residents. He was to die there in December 1918.

None of the British diplomats who remained free were able to attend. If they had left their sanctuary at the Dutch Embassy, they would have been in danger of being captured. But the tiny church was filled to capacity, none the less. It would probably have warmed Francis Cromie's heart to know that the congregation was dominated by women: French women, Danish and Swedish, British wives, Russian women who had known the intrepid sailor, the wives and friends of the Swiss, Belgian, and other legations, all joined together to make sure that Petrograd would witness what they had thought of this man. As to whether his beloved Sophie Gagarin was there, we do not know, but according to the current Prince Gagarin, it is highly likely that she would have joined the cortege.

The funeral service opened to the sad accompaniment of Handel's 'Dead March' from the opera *Saul*. The tiny church had perhaps never contained as much moving grief as it did that grey morning. Eventually, to Chopin's 'Dead March', the Union-Jack-covered coffin was placed on the hearse, the only flowers to break the symmetry of the flag being a large wreath in the name of the British Admiralty, which had not actually come from their lordships – Oudendijk had ordered it himself. Behind the hearse came a large carriage bearing the dozens of floral tributes which had arrived from all over Petrograd. Oudendijk and the Dutch Consul, Mr van der Pals, walked solemnly behind the hearse. Behind, the long, slow procession of women and men, many of them almost strangers who had, in some small way, been touched by Cromie over the previous months, wound its way in silence. They were flanked on both sides by furtive, glancing men who were impatient with the slow progress of the crowd. They were used to loud and noisy, fast-flowing demonstrations of a different emotion. These were the agents of the Cheka, ambling along like carrion crows to see if there were still pickings to be had among the grim faces of the mourners.

It was a long walk, about a mile and a half (2.5 km), to the Smolensky Cemetery on Vasilievskiy Island. Then, as the cortege turned in the pale autumn sun to begin crossing the Nicholas Bridge, something happened – something almost as moving as the funeral, an event which defied the notion that Bolshevism had completely sullied Russia's soul.

The Smolensky Cemetery, Vasilievskiy Island, St Petersburg.

Moored along the River Neva were three destroyers of what was now the Soviet Navy. The indolence and indiscipline among the Red sailors which had so depressed Francis Cromie was still evident. Accordions were being played, whilst around the deck the sailors lounged, smoking, drinking, enjoying the company of their women. Some among the procession cast glances at this sight, which at first added to their sad and angry silence. Then a group of sailors on the first destroyer walked to the rail and looked. The music stopped. Other sailors joined them. As the cortege drew closer, the sailors on the other destroyers did the same. Then, like some rapid rewind of a film, taking these men-at-arms back to a discipline they had long forgotten, the Red sailors began to line up along the decks, in neat ranks, their caps in place. More men came from below, until the destroyers' crews, as if engaged in some grand naval review, were all at attention.

There was a silence broken only by the shuffling feet and the rumbling wheels of the hearse across the cobbles as the Red navy realised whose coffin this was. Someone had said 'Cromie', someone on those decks, perhaps more than one man, knew that Captain Francis Newton Allen Cromie DSO RN had fought by their side, argued their case, shown compassion, patience and fairness. He had not passed open judgement on their uprising. He had remained, as they hoped to remain, devoted to his own navy to the last, a force the equity and integrity of which they, in their former imperial misery, had once aspired to. *En masse*, in defiance of the scornful looks of the Cheka men, they saluted, and remained at the salute as this dead Englishman, like them, a sailor, passed across the water for the last time.

In the leafy, vast expanse of the Smolensky Cemetery the cortege came to a halt in the Lutheran quarter. Oudendijk recalled the scene:[9]

> At the cemetery we stood in sorrowful groups round the open grave. The English took up a position behind their priest; the diplomats stood together as did the foreign military officers. Then Dr Kean impressively read the service for the burial of the dead. The coffin, covered with the Union Jack, was slowly lowered into the vault, and we all joined in the Lord's Prayer.
>
> Then I pronounced a short address. This was certainly not an occasion for much verbosity, so I stepped forward and said:
>
> 'On behalf of the British Government and of Captain Cromie's family, I thank you all, especially the representatives of the Allied and neutral powers, for having assembled here to pay your last respects to Captain Cromie.
>
> Dear friends, we have all known Captain Cromie as a real friend, as a British gentleman, and as a British officer in the highest sense of the word.
>
> Happy is the country that has sons like Captain Cromie! May his splendid and beautiful example inspire us till the end of our days.'
>
> The Bolshevik detectives watched the proceedings at close quarters. M. Odier, the aged Swiss Minister, gave expression to his sympathy for the late Captain Cromie who had died for his country.
>
> I directed that the Union Jack should not be removed, but should remain

covering the coffin of the brave Englishman resting from his labours in his lonely grave in that foreign country in whose defence he had fought and by whose ungrateful, murderous sons he had been brutally slain.

When the enormous slab of stone had been placed over the vault and the numerous wreaths and bunches of flowers laid on top of it, I removed all the ribbons with inscriptions and the name card attached to them, and later forwarded them to his widow at home. Dr Kean, Mr van der Pals and myself were the last to leave the cemetery; even the detectives had gone. There had been little for them to detect except to witness the grief of many for a brave man and a faithful friend.

CHAPTER 25

A SORT OF SHADOW

The pride of all the Baltic,
The terror of the foe,
The joy of the Russian Ladies –
Well, that is us, you know.

Able Seaman Wingrove, HMS *E19*[1]

Smolensky Cemetery, St Petersburg, June 2000

And so the end of Cromie's story is here, somewhere beneath my feet; not under the angry sea, not made from the vicious blast of depth-charge or mine, but here, in this tree-lined plot of forgotten land among the untended headstones and grim mausoleums of other men and women. They, too, had come to Russia in answer to some call, long before his birth. Their monuments stand silent and vandalised.

Over there lie George and Mary Wylie – who were they? Heinrich von Storch, President of the Academy Wissenschaftes, born 18 February 1766, died 6 November 1835. Lidia Berlin, 13.11.1880–1.5.1909. Friedrich Theodor von Schubert 1758–1825. Graves upon graves. Above the canopy of the ubiquitous poplars the sun beats down on this fine summer afternoon. Below the sorry scene is dappled by the shade of waving branches. The breeze brushes the leaves, somewhere birds sing. My colleague, the photographer Graham Harrison, and I are still almost breathless from our first brush with Russia. The Nevsky, where I was attacked by Gypsies, saved only as I crumbled beneath a rain of fists by Graham, his tripod held aloft with deadly threatening intent. The cruiser *Aurora*, already a relic of yet another political system come and gone. The immensity of the Winter Palace and the sheer historical ambience of that massive, cobbled square. And the melancholy, glistening beauty of the softly flowing Neva, that gun-metal stretch of water, a rolling, liquid history of struggle, tragedy and triumph.

And there was the old British Embassy, today the St Petersburg Academy of Culture and Arts. Within its walls, the bright and hopeful young staff, Thatcherites to a man and girl, stood drop-jawed as I told them that here, in this beautiful building, murder was done. The Principal, the tall and elegant Galena Varganova, took us up the grand staircase. There were still chips in the marble where – dare we imagine – the bullets of 31 August 1918 ricocheted into history. We had arrived at a time when the meticulous restoration of the building to its 1918 condition was almost complete. Cromie's naval room had gone, but the glorious chancery and the ballroom were still there, sparkling in their white, blue and gilt glory. Yet but one man in this new seat of Russian learning, the elderly Assistant Principal, knew about that fateful Cheka raid. Who did he think killed Cromie? Who did he think Cromie shot at? We waited for the translation.

'Perhaps', he mused, 'it is as I have heard it. Perhaps Bolshevik sailors, who entered from the other entrance on the Millionya, were firing through the building indiscriminately. I had heard that they may have shot some of their own Cheka comrades.'

I talked to Miss Varganova about Lenin, about Communism. Like all modern Russians, she steered me off the subject. It is past. We are building a new Russia. Subject closed. I asked to be left alone at the top of the staircase. Yes, after all the months of picturing the entrance hall, the passport clerk's office, all the late nights thinking my way through that mental floor-plan, it all fitted. I looked down the steps towards the ornate glass entrance porch, and imagined Cromie running, three steps at a time, the shots ringing out. Then the crack and splinter of bullet into bone as he fell, backwards, at the final step. It all seemed like a film set, but this was real. This was where it started, and this was where the end came.

That night, as Cromie no doubt often did, Graham and I dined in the old Russian splendour of the Literature Café on the Nevsky Prospekt. The Russian chicken and the beer were excellent. The Literature was Pushkin's favourite haunt. A statuesque contralto in a vivid blue dress sang Gypsy songs to the accompaniment of a fine pianist on a grand piano from an alcove flanked by Doric columns. It was unbearably sweet and nostalgic; one need not be Russian to be almost moved to tears.

We had not found Cromie's grave in the sad wilderness of Smolensky. Sure, there were graves with anchors, the odd ship here and there. But the cemetery records were destroyed in the 1970s – the records for this, one of the most legendary burial places in Russia. In Cromie's day brass or copper nameplates graced the fascias of many of those tombs. That such valuable metals should not survive in a city which has suffered so much is not surprising. But we knew he was there, somewhere, beneath the weeds, beneath the undergrowth of eighty years of neglect and indifference. Had we not always had an embassy here? Was his name not remembered long enough for some junior diplomatic servant to be sent with a spade and a bunch of roses every now and then? Too much to ask, I suppose.

Perhaps we had walked over him several times. And even if we had found him, my original, far-fetched notion of providing him with a new headstone now seemed futile. The Smolensky Cemetery is a focal point for drunks and drug addicts. They gather in grubby circles in openings between the trees, vodka bottles at their feet, and like their cardboard-boxed comrades around the world bark at one another in unintelligible grunts through stained teeth. They looked at the two dazed Englishmen, possible gift horses, and shouted at us for kopeks. One offered to help us. 'Cromie? Cromie? Come – I show you where . . .' Of course, he had no idea what we were talking about – he simply wanted us to himself to do a little solo begging. We sent him packing through the trees. Someday, we might find the captain. But it was not to be on that trip.

The next day we learned more of Cromie and Sophie. We had an invitation to lunch – not just any lunch, but lunch with a Russian prince, Andrey Gagarin.

We had met Prince Gagarin twice during our week in St Petersburg. In the eight decades since the Romanovs vanished from the map of monarchy, one would imagine that the old-fashioned bearing and formality associated with titled families would have been scorched away under the blow-torch of Stalinism. Yet this notion dissolved on our first visit, on a balmy June evening, just two days into our trip. It was simply an introduction. Andrey was pleased to meet us, but he insisted that he required the best part of a day to reveal his information. Still, even though there seemed a touch of reluctance when we contacted him for the first time on the telephone that night, we simply had to make use of the time we had and steal an hour of his evening. He was the linchpin of the week. He had only existed in cyberspace – it was almost as if we wanted to prove that he existed.

The Gagarins, Prince Andrey and Princess Tina, lived on the sixth floor of an apartment block in a shady courtyard off the Rubinstein Ulitsa. We left our taxi and studied the street map. We were in the right place. I rang the entryphone bell and a rich voice told us to come up. 'I am sorry, but the elevator is not in service.'

When we entered the lobby it was dark and cool. Like everything else of its age in Russia, this apartment block looked as if it had seen better days. And yet, one asks, when *were* those 'better days'? Was it pre-revolution? What was St Petersburg like when it was new? Was this a pristine habitat in the 1930s? A conundrum. Coats of paint and adequate lighting do not seem to figure in urban Russia – surviving day to day takes precedence over such frippery.

The staircase wound around an ornate lift shaft the like of which England has not seen for decades, a baroque cabin with a single, 20-watt light bulb and wrought-iron concertina doors. If only it had worked. It was a long, sweaty walk to the sixth floor. We found the ancient door, lofty panelled oak, and pressed the bell.

Andrey was a square-set, virile-looking man for a pensioner: firm features, square jaw, a good head of silvery hair. His eyes could only be described as Russian. If this sounds vague, there is something in a mature Russian's eyes, something honest, something which says 'delighted to see you' and something faintly tragic. They are the eyes of people who have seen hardship on a grand scale.

Our introductory meeting was brief and polite. Tina, a stocky woman with brown hair, was less ebullient than her husband, but instantly made us feel welcome and at ease. The reason Andrey could not spend much time with us on this first night was that he had Russian guests – but Russians who lived not in St Petersburg but in California. They were broad-chested, bearded men, reminiscent of photographs of Tsarist officers. They were smartly dressed in jackets and ties. And they wore the two-headed eagle emblem of the Romanovs as little badges on their lapels. The language in the room slipped in and out of broad Californian and a bassy, resonant Russian. They were relatives, émigrés from over the sea, and Graham and I realised that we should not be there. This was Russian business.

'Friday, gentlemen, we will lunch,' said Andrey, 'and now you know where I am it will be easier for you. Friday morning I will give you all the time you need, and tell you the stories of Sonia Gagarin and Captain Cromie.'

Friday arrived. Our lunch date. We were due to fly home late in the afternoon. This time, the lift was working. At 10 a.m. we were once more in the Gagarin apartment. The glass doors onto the balcony were open and the June sun cut across the room in a warm swathe, flecked with the floating, cotton-like detritus from the poplar trees. It floated in the air like snowflakes; the Russians call it *topol.*

There were portraits on the wall, men and women of an older Russia. They looked down like pages from a story book. The furniture was classic, solid, old, made by craftsmen probably long before this apartment existed. A bureau, a tall French-styled china cabinet, comfortable old sofas.

Andrey's father lost his life during Stalin's purges. He was brought up by his mother, and his academic ability led finally to his appointment as a science professor, specialising at one time in laser technology at St Petersburg's State Technical University's Russian-American High School of Management. Now, in his retirement, he is a busy man, his time spent in his study on his computer, keeping tabs on the many international émigré strands of the Gagarin dynasty. He is a man proud of his heritage. I made the *faux pas* of asking him if the Gagarins had any connection with the Romanovs.

'Ah . . . the Romanovs! They were only around for three hundred years. The Gagarins go back eight hundred. We are much older, you see – and no, not connected, definitely not.'

For two hours we sat enthralled as he brought up on screen the Gagarins *circa* 1914–18: handsome young men in Tsarist uniforms – Sergei, Lev and Peter. And then there she was – their sister, the delicate and beautiful Sonia Gagarin, 'Sophie', the girl who stole Cromie's heart. We saw her aged twelve, then as a teenager, then at twenty-five. There was a sketch of her by the painter Vladimir Milosevsky (1893–1976). I looked at Andrey's eyes, then at the sketch – that look was the same: dark, almost tragic, yearning. There was a picture of the Gagarin mansion at Pskov, Holomki. It was tall, white-pillared, reminiscent of a plantation owner's mansion in Carolina or Georgia. Today, the Gagarins retain only one slender strand of ownership on the estate – they are allowed to travel to Pskov every year to collect the honey from the beehives there.

But I was looking at the clock and itching to know about Cromie and Sonia. What about the affair? Was it well known? Slowly, the evidence began to appear. Andrey began: 'After the revolution the family had to struggle to keep hold of Holomki. The Gagarins, and especially Sonia, had many artistic friends, artists, poets. We had to find a way of holding on to the mansion whilst at the same time pleasing the Bolsheviki, who were taking land and houses everywhere. Sonia's three brothers joined the White armies. They fought the Bolsheviks. Lev died of typhoid in the White army near Constantinople. But everyone else stayed behind and Sonia helped to turn Holomki into a kind of sanatorium, a rest and re-cuperation home for young poets and artists, those who had been sympathetic to the revolution. Many men fell for her at this time – and they knew of her love for Captain Cromie. There was jealousy. They had met in St Petersburg. Some of the artists and poets who knew of this relationship mentioned it in their works . . . Here is a short extract from a memoir by the painter Vladimir Milosevsky.[2]

> Stories of Sophia Andreevna were covered with some kind of sadness or carried with themselves a sort of shadow. Maybe, this year she was living in the past. The tragic romance with the English officer, who commanded a submarine which was attached to the Russian Fleet . . . after October,when the Red Guards wanted to penetrate the English Embassy, he stood in the doorway, wanting to hinder the armed soldiers. The result of this was clear – he was lifted on their bayonets!
>
> The story of this was well known in Petrograd. I have forgotten his surname. I didn't want to ask questions and stir up painful memories in her heart. She had mystically conversed with her hero, who was sitting in his submarine under the water. He had sent her his own messages from under the water, also mystically! The epoch then was not at all materialistic. They spoke in the most serious manner, that Rasputin was the Devil, the incarnation of the Devil.

This suggests that Sonia and Cromie met in 1916 or 1917, when he was still in command of *E19*. He had always been a regular visitor to the embassy. A telepathic love affair? It seemed so mystical, so strange. Andrey scrolled the screen down and more Russian text came up. He continued: 'Here is a short extract from the draft of a proposed novel by the writer Yevgeny Zamiatin. Zamiatin was a famous writer. Gorky helped him to leave Russia in 1930, and he died in Paris in 1937.'[3]

> Nothing dies . . . and Sonia does not understand it – it is difficult – then at once and already continues his thoughts. And they climb up to God knows what heights. The Prince [Gagarin] shakes his head, 'Oh!' and, feeling embarrassed, says 'But what daughter of mine is this?'
>
> An Englishman – a submarine officer. Somehow it came about that he and Sonia fell in love. Only . . . on that very day they captured Grisha . . . in the English Embassy and they killed him . . .
>
> Only Grisha knew, no one else. And in one letter from prison wrote, 'But here I sit, quiet, as under the water . . . Good.' And Sonia understood.
>
> Somehow Pet'ka sniffed this out. That one gave him a pen-knife. One day he brings it and clumsily gives it to Sonia.
>
> 'Here, you have no knife. Take it.'
>
> The story of Grisha was fortunate: it helped to endure the death of Cromie.

The proposed novel, *Oaks*, was never published. As it was a work of fiction, we can take it that 'Pet'ka' and 'Grisha' were invented characters. But for Grisha's real identity, Prince Gagarin offered a fragment of a poem by the painter Mstislav Dobujinsky (1875–1957), one of many Russians who managed to emigrate to the USA along with composers such as Rachmaninoff and Stravinsky and fellow artists such as Nicholas Roerich and Sergei Hollerback. He had a son who was working in Paris in 1992. He appeared to be yet another of Sophie Gagarin's keen admirers, and apparently wrote this poem to her after being imprisoned following the revolution:

> He was a noble comrade,
> The Son of Smoky Albion,
> He was a seaman without fear
> The hero of Baltic battles,
> He could just laugh
> And could be the child like her.
> He didn't dream
> And didn't try to be better than he was.
> He came back often
> To his submarine
> And he created fairy tales,
> Under the water – for her.

Apart from an almost indecipherable document written in what is claimed to be his own hand, I have no other provenance for this. Yet it throws a light, albeit a pale one, on the type of people Cromie mixed with in his off-duty hours. We have to remind ourselves that Cromie too was an artist. His talent may not have been in the Dobujinsky or Milosevsky mode, but his artistic side is not in question. This was a man who played the piano, who could give inspiring, impromptu speeches off the cuff. Ben Benson told us of Cromie's stirring rendering of Newbolt's 'Drake's Drum'. This dizzy, Bohemian world of Russian artistic passion would have provided a heady alternative to the petty 'sins' of his British colleagues – alcohol and tobacco.

After a busy morning of collating this information, with Graham Harrison cataloguing and copying the various sepia pictures of the Gagarins' past, we were seated in the dining room. Tina brought us tasty Russian bread, fine sausage, salad. The one item of luxury was a silver kettle of hot water, accompanied almost ceremonially by a silver tray on which was presented an open jar of Nescafe. We used our spoons judiciously. The whole meal, sitting in that sunlit room, was a delicious memory, topped off with small Russian cakes upon which we spread delicious honey brought from the Gagarin estate, Holomki. We packed and ordered our taxi to the airport, shared warm goodbyes. Somehow, we knew that we would one day return.

At the airport we drank vodka and mineral water. It had been a tiring but fulfilling week. Four hours later, as the plane swooped through the rain over Heathrow, it all began to seem like an exotic dream.

CHAPTER 26

EPILOGUE:
THE PRICE OF A LIFE

68 Twyford Avenue
Acton
London W.3.

Sept. 18 1918

Dear Sir George Buchanan,
   I am writing to ask you to take up your cudgels on my behalf. I have
written to the Foreign Office to ask what compensation they intend to give
me and mine. I have a letter from my husband dated Jan. 1/18 stating that
he had just had a wire from you asking him to stay on as Temporary Naval
Attaché – this was on the eve of his return home. My husband and I had
no private means, so it leaves me in a pretty bad position. My husband's
life was certainly sacrificed for the FO as he was over there for technical
Naval duties.

Awaiting your reply, Believe me,
Yours sincerely,
Josephine Cromie.[1]

We do not know how much Gwladys (who signed her letters as 'Josephine') knew
of her husband's life in Russia. Perhaps the story of Sophie Gagarin had not
reached her. By the tone of her letter to Sir George Buchanan it seems that she
actually believed that her husband was about to come home on 1 January. He
had every opportunity to, according to Admiral Stanley. If his letters home had
survived, we might have been able to assess Cromie the husband and father. But
they have been destroyed, so we can only guess at what he told Gwladys. Yet
there is one poignant reminder of his home life which cuts through all the
intrigue, suggested adultery and dark dealings of those final months. It comes in
Frances Wagner's letter to the Reverend Lombard – the baby's glove she found
in the dead Cromie's pocket. Was it a souvenir of his other life? Did he carry it
as a talisman from another existence, a world he had almost forgotten?
   One might imagine that, when Gwladys was asked if she wanted her husband's
body to be brought home for burial, she would have agreed – having a proper
funeral at home for one's spouse would close the circle of grief. There would then
have been a grave, a focus for mourning, and a memorial for the future. But she

told the Admiralty to leave him in Petrograd.[2] It seems as if things had not gone well for the Cromie household in London since Francis's departure in 1915. His mother's remarriage to the ship-owner John Lennard had not provided for her as well as she had expected, for he had died some time before the war broke out. His fortune appears not to have given much in the way of a legacy, and the Cromie family – Mary Lennard, Gwladys and Dolores – were still living in Mary's house at 44 South Molton Street during the war. But now we see Gwladys in the less salubrious climes of Acton. The correspondence during the three months following his death bears a tragic similarity to that of the other Mrs Cromie, Francis's stepmother, following his father's death in Africa. Of course, in the armed forces of the time, bravery and sacrifice, although admired, paid few dividends if you were of the wrong class. Medals were fine things to pin on your uniform, but they were useless for keeping your widow and children. Gwladys's simple, honest admission that the Cromies had 'no private means' could result in only one response from the grandees of Whitehall – 'Tough luck.'

David Beatty, who, as Cromie's commander, had sent him ashore with the Naval Brigades at Tientsin in China in 1900, had reached the rank of Rear-Admiral by 1910. But his climb up the social ladder had had an acceleration the like of which a middle-class boy like Francis Cromie could only dream of. In 1901, then aged just 31, he married a wealthy American divorcee and extremely well-connected socialite, Ethel Tree. When the honours were handed out after the war, in 1919, Beatty became the 1st Earl Beatty, with an award of no less than £100,000. Roger Keyes, another of those who had served with Cromie in China, had to struggle on after the war with the title of 1st Baron Keyes of Zeebrugge and a mere £40,000. And poor old Jellicoe, the hero of Jutland, who, like Cromie, had entered the Navy as a cadet on board the *Britannia,* was forced to make do with a viscountcy and £50,000.[3]

In a letter to the Foreign Secretary, Balfour, also on 18 September, Gwladys vents her anger on another point: 'Another thing I should like to draw your attention to is the fact, that all the dreadful details of my late husband's murder have been used as political propaganda, without any consideration whatsoever for the feelings of his family.'[4] Some things never change.

Her friends, some of them with influence, took up her case, and several wrote letters to the Admiralty and the Foreign Office, including Lady Acland of Torquay, who pointed out that, in her opinion, Cromie had after all been Britain's *de facto* ambassador in Petrograd. Charles R. Burk weighed in from the Carlton Club in Cadogan Square, apparently to little effect. Lord Stopford wrote, as did the Royal Club for Officers Beyond the Seas in Pall Mall. But the Foreign Office did not see Cromie as 'one of theirs'. An internal memo written two days after Gwladys's letter states:[5]

> Captain Cromie was paid out of Navy funds, so any compensation to his widow must come from the Admiralty; reply accordingly; and add that while we should desire to show every consideration for the feelings of his relatives, we think we should be doing his memory less than justice if we had withheld from the public the details of the heroic way in which he met

his death or attempted to minimise the foul outrage committed by the Bolsheviks.

That last line speaks volumes. Here was Europe coming to the end of the most disastrous war ever. Russia was in revolution, and there was growing social unrest in Germany and France. The British Labour Party and the trades union movement were on the rise. Even America had large socialist groups looking to Petrograd and Mocow for inspiration, and John Reed's despatches from Russia were providing it. The aftermath of a war is usually a dangerous time for any government – and any idea that Bolshevism was something to aspire to had to be nipped in the bud. Cromie may not have made all the front pages – the horrendous death toll on the Western front put paid to that – but his demise was a fine example of the 'foul outrage' of Bolshevism. Gwladys was right to complain – her husband *was* used for political propaganda.

The Foreign Office studied the letters of support for Gwladys and in true Whitehall style, a memo on 25 September states: 'Please see annexed letter from Lord Stopford. Is it anything to do with us? If not, can you tell me to whom application ought to be made?'[6] The initials are indecipherable. The football was kicked around Whitehall for some time, some correspondents suggesting that the Secret Service ought to provide an extra sum of compensation, but that it was becoming unlikely that any provision could be made for Cromie's mother, Mrs Lennard. Always the language attempts a positive note: 'Secretary of State Mr Balfour is most anxious', etc.

By 19 December 1918, Gwladys's campaign had pushed the Foreign Office to this, the final letter in the file:[7]

19th December 1918

Dear Sir Ronald Graham

Mrs Cromie has already been granted by the Ministry of Pensions the highest rate of pension and gratuity that can be given under their scales to the widow of an Officer of this rank killed in action. The actual award was as follows:

A pension of £200, and a gratuity of £602. 5s. 0d to Mrs Cromie.

A compassionate allowance of £24 a year, and a gratuity of £200.15s. 0d for their child.

Whilst we are most anxious to do everything that is possible in this case, it seems very difficult to ask the Treasury for a special grant in addition to these awards. It would be placing the case on a higher footing than the most heroic case of a death in action, and although no member of the public would be likely to suggest that this particular case was being treated too generously, it might undoubtedly lead to a demand for equal treatment in many distressing cases in which Officers have died heroically in action, leaving their families poorly provided for.

So far as I am aware, the most recent case in which special action was publicly taken to make provision for the widow and dependants of a Naval Officer over and above that ordinarily allowable under the regulations was the case of the late Captain R.F. Scott, the Antarctic Explorer. In that case it was decided to treat the death for the purpose of the pension scale, as if it had occurred in action, and, in addition, the Prime Minister gave an assurance to Parliament that all the relatives of Captain Scott and those who died with him would be put in as good a position as if the deaths had not occurred, to redeem which promise certain additional grants were subsequently made.

So far as rates of pension and allowances are concerned, Mrs Cromie has already been similarly treated. As regards additional allowances, it must be borne in mind that the Scott case happened in a time of peace, when the event assumed an importance in the public eye that no single incident can possibly possess in wartime, and I doubt very much whether it would be practicable for a government to adopt a similar attitude now in any individual case however distressing.

In a recent case in which a Naval Officer died under somewhat tragic circumstances, after having done exceedingly good service for the Foreign Office, you arranged to make an award from 'Secret Service' which was sent to his widow. Would it not be possible to deal with the case of Captain Cromie's wife and mother on the same lines? This would avoid any comparison in public between the treatment of this case and that of Officers killed in action.

Believe Me,
Yours sincerely,
O.A.R. Murray

Whether Gwladys got her 'Secret Service' grant remains unclear, but there are two hand-written notes at the bottom of Murray's letter, one from Lord Hardinge suggesting 'It seems rather a special case' and another, unsigned, to Balfour: 'Would you agree to a special grant of £500?'

Perhaps Cromie would have been better off as a stubborn, high-profile explorer. After all, all he had to contend with in the Baltic was a war, a mutiny, a revolution, espionage, becoming a diplomat, becoming a financier, saving civilians, and sinking ships single-handed. Much easier to have frozen to death in a tent after discovering the Norwegians had beaten you to the Pole, and probably more beneficial, though tragic, for the relatives. Even if Gwladys did get her Secret Service gratuity, the 'extras' she would have received amount to a measly £1,303 – probably less than Sir George Buchanan's embassy wine bill for 1917. Anthea's allowance worked out at about 9 shillings per week, with the widow's pension coming in at just under £4 weekly. As wages went in post-Great War Britain, it was not a pauper's income, but compared to Messrs Beatty's, Jellicoe's and Keyes' handouts it looks like an insult. But Francis Cromie had served his purpose. He had run the embassy.

The evidence sadly points to the fact that, despite all his manoeuvrings with his plots with the Letts, the White Guards and others, and his efforts to get fleets and forces ready to assist the Allied advance, not many people were taking much notice towards the end. One of his final telegrams, to Admiral Hall in August 1918, shows how frustrated he had become:[8]

I am endeavouring to make three large anti-Bolshevik organisations who are asking for help and advice, but due to strict control of money is extremely difficult and dangerous to obtain in large amounts and good advice impossible since I have never received any definite news or idea of General Plan from Poole other than to send 1,000 men to Vologda by August 8th which has been done by the military Mission and these men are now being arrested. During the whole time since the arrival of General Poole at Murmansk we have received absolutely no communication except for one already mentioned, we have repeatedly asked for details as we have the whole Onega Flotilla at our disposal . . . I request you inform us outline of plans and policy of Northern Expedition as we are in a position to assist largely with Naval and Military forces . . . The Danish and Dutch Ambassadors express some surprise at diplomatic negotiations being continued when they have been asked to look after French and English interests respectively. Difficulties were further increased by a lack of complete understanding between Ambassadors mentioned . . . it is essential that we be given call sign and wavelengths of ships at Murmansk or Archangel and stations in the North with least possible delay. All cyphers have been destroyed. .01 is the only cypher now available in Petrograd. Ends. Cromie. In view of great importance of issues involved I would suggest communication to Foreign Office.

The Allied intervention was ultimately a washout. The world was weary of war, yet as if the generals had not had enough, in Russia there was an opportunity for another two years of bloodshed. Although after 1918 the White forces, assisted by the French in the Ukraine, and elsewhere in Russia by the Japanese and other assorted Allied forces, made sporadically impressive advances, the Russians had rekindled their fighting spirit and the Red Army had become a force to be reckoned with. There was a White Russian coalition in Omsk, but this collapsed when Admiral Kolchak, the man who had thrown his sword into the Black Sea, lost everyone's respect by his brutality and declared his own dictatorship. The years after Cromie's death saw a civil war which need not have happened, with an estimated death toll of 12 million. It can be argued that the Allied intervention was the catalyst for the Red Terror and the worst excesses of the Bolsheviks. It turned Trotsky into a military leader. It can be speculated whether, without intervention, Russia would have ended up with Stalin and his 'socialism in one country' idea. One thing is certain – Lenin was well aware of Stalin's threatening nature even on his death bed.

The Royal Navy, which under Cromie had striven hard to retain a fighting relationship with its Russian counterpart, became the new Soviet Navy's deadly enemy. The Russian ships Cromie had come to know so well between 1915 and 1918, such as the *Petropavlosk* and the *Andrei Perzovany*, were to be the victims of British torpedoes. In the summer of 1919, the submariners' old home, the *Pamyat Azova*, was sunk by the British in Kronstadt.

Some of the Russian liaison officers who served on Cromie's submarines went on to embrace the revolution, such as Aksel Ivanovitch Berg, who became a Hero of Soviet Labour, and from 1927 was Chairman of the Soviet Navy's Radio and

Communications Committee. Between 1943 and 1944 he was Deputy People's Commissar for the electrical industry and continued up the ladder to be the USSR's Deputy Minister of Defence. Boris Miller became one of Churchill's interpreters. Some, without doubt, stripped of Cromie's well-crafted protection after 1918, met a dubious fate.

Sonia Gagarin, no doubt heartbroken by Cromie's death, struggled on trying to help run Holomki as a convalescence centre for those poets and artists approved by the revolution, but in 1927 gave up. She emigrated to the USA, married a Russian émigré called Rostkovsky and died, childless, in 1979 in Baton Rouge, Louisiana. She never visited Russia again.

Over the next seven decades, the regime which resulted from what Francis Cromie and his men had witnessed from March 1917 onwards was to earn the title, courtesy of a bumbling Hollywood actor in the White House, of 'the Evil Empire'. And all the death, espionage, expense, sorrow and struggle ultimately brought such rewards in the twenty-first century as the free availability of Coca Cola, MTV and Big Macs.

Whilst the knights and lords of the Foreign Office argued over whether Cromie's sacrifice was worth an extra £500, Buckingham Palace had sprung into action and at least one display of proper recognition was forthcoming. On 29 September Gwladys Cromie was invited to an investiture at the Palace, where King George presented her with her husband's posthumous CB. The *London Gazette* of 24 September 1918 announced the details:

> Awarded posthumous honour of Companionship of the Most Honourable Order of the Bath (Military Division) in recognition of his distinguished services in the Allied Cause in Russia and of the devotion to duty which he displayed in remaining at his post as British Naval Attaché in Russia when the British Embassy was withdrawn. This devotion to duty cost him his life.

Apart from keen ex-submariners who know what the job is all about – men like Michael Wilson, Richard Compton-Hall and archivists like Brian Head at the Royal Navy's Submarine Museum – and his family, Francis Newton Allen Cromie CB DSO RN is today largely forgotten. He rarely crops up in the indexes of history books, and figures only in the various works on espionage because of his association with men like Reilly and Boyce. In many respects his trusting nature and political naivety may have been his Achilles heel. He talked too much, perhaps, and often to the wrong people. He lacked the nature of a scoundrel like Sidney Reilly, or the clandestine skills of Ernest Boyce and George Hill.

As to who pulled the trigger and ended his life, that is not clear. It can be assumed, though, that he did manage to get some shots in with Le Page's revolver, but which Bolsheviks he might have killed or wounded is unknown. And there is the mystery of Bucknall's account to Mary Britnieva, who states that Cromie definitely had no gun on him when he was killed. His prolonged stay in Russia was probably, as Admiral Stanley suggested, not so much to 'see the war through' but because of his inability to draw a line under his affair with Sonia

Gagarin. Yet it is obvious that he worked as thoroughly and diligently as any diplomat during 1918.

During my work on this project, various ideas have been laid before me as to what Cromie, the man, was like. My own opinion is that he was neither pro- nor particularly rabidly anti-Bolshevik. He had taken his oath of allegiance to his King and he stuck to it. He was simply obsessed by his fight with the 'Hun'. Another interesting theory is that, in some way, Cromie 'arranged' his own death. He could not return to his former life for many complex reasons. It was known, euphemistically in those days, as 'doing the right thing'. But if Cromie had fallen on his sword, which I doubt, the question is why? It would appear he had everything to live for.

There is a suggestion that he left the safe door open in the embassy so that the Cheka could discover the Allied plans. Of course they were found by the Cheka, and published in the Bolshevik press. Lenin's and Trotsky's suspicions were therefore justified. But even if the safe had been locked, the Bolsheviks had already thrown caution to the wind by taking the embassy – a well-placed grenade would easily have opened the safe. Yet an alternative to this calumny has been put forward – the embassy staff were being paid on 31 August.

This raises another question. George Bucknall senior had originally intended to visit the Embassy that day to withdraw cash from his 'account', according to Mary Britnieva. Vasiuk, the chauffeur, put him off approaching the building by his warning glance across the road. However, at the end of the document on the raid signed by Nathalie Bucknall is attached a list of those present in the Embassy during the raid.[9] Bucknall senior, as well as his son, is on that list, but not arrested, simply listed as 'released'. So it appears that he *was* in the embassy after all. Had he told Mary the truth? This is just one example of the tangled web of duplicity and secrecy which surrounds everything connected to the Petrograd embassy in 1918. If Sidney Reilly could get away with so much colourful invention yet still be regarded by Whitehall as their top man, then perhaps everyone else had to lie their heads off.

In any case, as for passing information to the Cheka, even if Cromie had been a kind of double agent, his task would have been superfluous. There were plenty of dubious characters frequenting the embassy, and with a 'friend' like Moura Budberg, he might as well have given his gossip to *Pravda*. He did his best, under circumstances which would have driven weaker men to desertion. He knew how to handle men and a submarine, but in the murky sea of espionage he was out of his depth.

I have also been bombarded from various quarters with the many complicated conspiracy theories which surround the Russian revolution. These involve Wall Street, suggestions of 'Jewish' plots behind Trotsky and Lenin, outrage that they used German money, and pages of complex detail on the 'Northern Underground' finance/espionage conduit between America, Britain and Russia. This is the territory of extremists who give prominence to all this as part of their 'New World Order' paranoia, so I decided to pass. Cromie's story is complicated enough without sullying it with lightly veiled and anti-Semitic conspiracy theories. If Lenin had not used any available German money he would have been a fool. The fact remains that revolution in Russia was inevitable, with or without Berlin, J.P. Morgan or the Chase National Bank in New York.

None of Francis Cromie's personal correspondence to his family exists. If there was a personal diary, that too has been destroyed. But if he was an adulterer, even in the fullest sense of the word, he was no worse than any other of a thousand military men abroad. He spent his days facing death or imprisonment in a city which, despite the grime of the uprising, is still one of the most beautiful in the world. He met civilised, attractive women, and he was a civilised, attractive man. The two go together. There are few, if any, criticisms of him in the records, apart from an unpleasant little note from Lieutenant R.L. Burridge who served in the Baltic Flotilla from May 1917 to January 1918.[10]

> Cromie was an arrogant, bitter vituperative man. He despised everyone. In the Baltic each E boat had a Russian Officer to help the navigation. They were all Lieutenants in the Imperial Navy. Baron Fersen, Uric Vorgetsky, Berg (a Finn) and Zobellia (a Pole). The only one that Cromie would talk to was Uric Vorgetsky, he had been educated in England and spoke perfect English – and had social clout.
> As for Cromie defending single handed the Embassy, that's a taradiddle. Hayward, an Assistant Paymaster, nowadays Paymaster Lieut. was with Cromie at the end. A deputation came to the Embassy for some quite peaceful reason, Cromie drew his revolver and started shooting. Hayward got away. I ran into him while on leave in London and he told me the facts.

The 'facts' are that Hayward was nowhere near Petrograd in August 1918 – he was many hundreds of miles away on board HMS *Ambrose*. And it would be highly unlikely for him to tell such a yarn; Cromie had sung his praises repeatedly in his reports and certainly helped to advance his career. But a look at Burridge's service record reveals the source of his inventive bitterness. On 31 December 1917 Cromie entered this on Burridge's record: 'Below average. Lacks most of the qualities of an officer. Not recommended for retention in submarines. He might do better under constant supervision in a big ship.'[11] Apart from one mention in his early career concerning a vessel he was commanding not being 'as clean as she could be', the foregoing is just about all the dirt there is on Francis Cromie. Not bad for two decades in the Royal Navy.

I had hoped to find my own final words to sum up Cromie's character and career, but someone had already written them, eight years before his death. They are gung-ho, romantic and emotionally over the top, but in some ways, they seem to fit Cromie, the Great War's jingoism and the revolution. They came in a speech entitled 'Citizen in a Republic' given on 23 April 1910 at the Sorbonne in Paris. The speaker was Theodore Roosevelt.

> It is not the critic who counts, not the one who points out how the strong man stumbled or how the doer of deeds might have done them better.
> The credit belongs to the man who is actually in the arena, whose face is

marred with sweat and dust and blood; who strives valiantly; who errs and comes short again and again; who knows the great enthusiasms, the great devotions, and spends himself in a worthy cause; who, if he wins, knows the triumph of high achievement; and who, if he fails, at least fails while daring greatly, so that his place shall never be with those cold and timid souls who know neither victory nor defeat.

NOTES/SOURCES

Chapter 1

1. WO 76/507/fo.46 PRO, Kew.
2. Army Year Books, PRO, Kew.
3. MS. *Bowen of Roblinston and Camrose*, Record Office, Haverfordwest.
4. Gosden, P.H.J.H. (1969) *How They Were Taught*. Oxford: Blackwell.
5. Regimental Archives, The Hampshire Regiment Museum, Winchester.
6. Family Records Centre, London, January Quarter 1906, Vol. 1a, p.1086.
7. *Bowen of Roblinston and Camrose*, op. cit.
8. FO367/39 PRO, Kew.
9. Ibid.
10. Ibid.
11. FO367/39/36788/07 PRO, Kew.
12. FO367/39/36457 PRO, Kew.
13. WO339/76016 PRO, Kew and Hampshire Regimental Journal, 1915, 1916, Hampshire Regiment Museum, Winchester.

Chapter 2

1. Anon. *Life On Board HMS* Britannia. I am indebted to Mr Robert Gieve, the current Vice-Chairman of Gieves & Hawkes of Savile Row, for the loan of this sole existing copy of a 94-page sales booklet issued by the company in 1904, which was distributed to the parents of potential naval cadets. Gieves have supplied military uniforms to officers for well over two centuries. Sadly, according to Mr Robert Gieve, during the Blitz in the Second World War the bulk of their archive, which, apart from Cromie's accounts, included those of Nelson and Hardy, were destroyed.
2. Hill, J.R. and Ranft, B. (Eds) (1995) *Oxford Illustrated History of The Royal Navy*. Oxford: OUP.
3. ADM 196/47 PRO.
4. Field, Harold C. (Ed.) (1972) *The British Empire* BBC TV/TIME-LIFE Vol. 4.
5. Seymour, Adm. E.H. (1999) *My Naval Career and Travels* quoted in Brooks, Richard, *The Long Arm of Empire*. London: Constable.
6. Brooks, Richard, (1999) *The Long Arm of Empire – Naval Brigades from the Crimea to the Boxer Rebellion*. London: Constable. The make-up of the international naval force varies by a few men depending on sources, but Mr Brooks's work offers the latest research at the time of writing, and he quotes the *Army & Navy Gazette*, September 1900, page 884, Capt. McCalla, USN.
7. von Trapp, Maria (1967) *The Trapp Family Singers*. London: Fontana.
8. ADM 196/47 PRO, Kew.

Chapter 3

1. Admiral Wilson won his VC in a land battle as Captain Wilson RN of HMS *Hecla*. The Battle of El Teb, Sudan, 29 February 1884, involved the Naval Brigade.
2. Lewis, Michael (1948) *The Navy of Britain*. London: Allen & Unwin.
3. Ibid.
4. Humble, Richard (1981) *Submarines – The Illustrated History*. London: Connoisseur Books.
5. Macksey, Kenneth and Woodhouse, William (1991) *Penguin Encyclopedia of Warfare*. London: Viking.
6. Humble, Richard, op. cit. Holland's great achievement was using the internal combustion engine for surface propulsion and electric storage batteries when submerged. Others had used steam and electric batteries, or simply batteries. Other sources:
   Domville-Fife, Charles Charles (1919) *Submarines and Sea Power*. London: Bell
   'Klaxon' (1914) *The Story of Our Submarines*. London: Blackwood
   Compton-Hall, Richard (1991) *Submarines and the War at Sea 1914–18* London: Macmillan.
   Oxford Illustrated History of the Royal Navy
   van der Vat, Dan (1995) *Stealth at Sea*. London: Orion Books.
   Noble, Christine (Ed.) (1999) *Forging The Modern Age 1900–1914*. London: Reader's Digest.

Chapter 4

1. Cromie's Service Record ADM196/47 RNSM Gosport.
2. Compton-Hall, Richard (1991) *Submarines and the War at Sea 1914–18*. London: Macmillan.
3. Durston was proved tragically right. A spark from the electrical system ignited the heavily petrol-vapoured atmosphere on submarine *A5,* injuring twelve of her crew and killing the remaining five.
4. *Pembrokeshire Telegraph*, 8 February 1906.

Chapter 5

1. Lord Charles Beresford at the Admiralty at one time referred to submarines as 'Fisher's Toys'.
2. Fisher's 'retirement' was to be a short one, as Winston Churchill would call him back into the Navy in 1914. Although he resigned again in 1915 over the Dardanelles campaign, he did see out the rest of the war in a characteristically progressive position as Chairman of the Admiralty Invention Board.
3. Kerr, Commander C.L., RN (1939) *All in a Day's Work*. London: Rich & Cowan.
4. Head, Brian, *The Baltic Campaign*, RNSM. Fenner served under Cromie for a year in the Baltic, after relieving Laurence on the *E1*. He died in HMS *K4* in the battle of May Island, in January 1918, shortly after returning from Russia. The so-called Battle of May Island took place in the Firth of Forth and was the greatest of all submarine disasters. (See Everitt, Don (1999) *K Boats* Airlife). Codrington was a submarine commander throughout the war and died of influenza in 1918. Godfrey Herbert DSO was always associated with the Baralong Incident.
5. Fenner, Athelstan, *Amazing Adventure* Appendix 1, memoir, RNSM, Gosport.

Chapter 6

1. Humble, Richard (1981) *Submarines – The Illustrated History*. London: Connoisseur Books.
2. *The Navy List*, September 1914. RNSM, Gosport.
3. Ben Benson's diary, unpublished MS. RNSM, Gosport.
4. Otto Wedigen survived less than six months after sinking the three cruisers. The end of *U-29* and Wedigen's crew was the result of uncanny justice – crushed by the keel of Fisher's 18,000-ton pride and joy, *Dreadnought*.
5. van der Vat, Dan (1995) *Stealth at Sea*. London: Orion Books.
6. Hough, R. (1983) *The Great War at Sea*, London.
7. Although, according to his service record (RNSM Gosport), Cromie took command of HMS *E19* on 21 April she was not actually launched until 13 May and commissioned on 12 July. She was built in the record time of eight months.
8. Corbett, Sir Julian. *The Official History of The War – Naval Operations*. Corbett, novelist, travel writer and historian, eventually became a lecturer at the Royal Naval War College, Greenwich. See also his *Some Principles of Maritime Strategy* (1911).
9. Not to be confused, as she often is, with the SS *Vidar* which had a tragic association with submarines when she was accidentally involved in the sinking of HMS *M1* in 1922. This was a different vessel.
10. Wilson, Michael (1985) *Baltic Assignment*. London: Leo Cooper.

Chapter 7

1. Maylunas, Andrei and Mironenko, Sergei (1996) *A Lifelong Passion – Nicholas & Alexandra, Their Own Story*. London: Weidenfeld & Nicolson.
2. Kerensky, Alexander (1966) *Memoirs – Russia and History's Turning Point*. London: Cassell.
3. These dates are based on the old Russian calendar, which was thirteen days behind the Gregorian.
4. The *Pallada* was sunk the following month by the German submarine *U-26* with the loss of 597 men.
5. Benson, W.L. *Memoirs of an Ancient Submariner*. Unpublished MS, RNSM, Gosport.
6. Diary of Able Seaman Wingrove, RNSM, Gosport. Brian Head of the RNSM also states that Wingrove refers to a replacement 'motor' from Barrow – he would have meant 'armature' because replacing the complete motor would have been a much larger task.
7. 'Josie' was a nickname given to Cromie by his crews. Its origins are lost, but may have been the result of his dark hair and sideburns giving him a vaguely 'Spanish' flair, probably resulting in 'José'. However, it is coincidental that Cromie's mother, Josephine, also signed her letters as 'José', and Cromie's wife Gwladys had Josephine as one of her Christian names.

Chapter 8

1. Benson, W.L. *Memoirs of an Ancient Submariner*. Unpublished MS, RNSM, Gosport.
2. Original Admiralty Papers HS Vol. 1096, ADM 137/1247, PRO.
3. Apart from condensation, and the limited air supply following a long submersion, the fumes from two huge battery systems, each containing 111 cells, soon caused extreme

nausea for a crew, especially during long spells of physical work on repairs. (Longstaff, Robert (1984) *Submarine Command*. London: Robert Hale.)

4. Although a noted pupil of Haverfordwest Grammar School, Cromie's spelling throughout his reports and letters often fell down. (Bruce Lockhart, R.H. (1932) *Memoirs of a British Agent*. London: Macmillan.)

5. They were bombs which had been dropped from a Zeppelin.

6. Commander Max Horton's *E9* had been waiting for the rendezvous with Cromie since 9 September, making good use of his time by stalking a German cruiser.

7. Wilson, Michael (1985) *Baltic Assignment*. London: Leo Cooper.

8. Benson, W.L. *Memoirs of an Ancient Submariner.* Unpublished MS, RNSM, Gosport.

9. Gray, Edwyn (1971) *A Damned Un-English Weapon*. London: Seely, Service & Co.

10. The German captain of the *Svionia* later claimed that Cromie had used a *ruse de guerre* by hoisting a German flag. Cromie made no mention of this in his report, and it seems totally out of character for him to employ such a tactic.

11. Diary of Able Seaman Wingrove, RNSM, Gosport.

12. The crew of the *Walter Leonhardt* were eventually transferred to the German destroyer *S113*, and arrived home safely.

13. Macintyre, Captain Donald, 'A Forgotten Campaign', *Journal of the Royal United Service Institution*, Vol. CVI February–November 1961. The Germans once again claimed Cromie was in neutral waters, but the Swedes disagreed.

14. It was later discovered that Mee and his prize crew were carrying the wrong ammunition for their guns, and had any hostilities ensued their weapons would have been harmless.

15. Able seamen with six years' service earned 2s 3d per day plus 2s submarine pay, which brought their weekly wage up to a princely 29s 9d per week. (*Navy List*, October 1914)

16. Compton-Hall, R. (1991) *Submarines and The War at Sea 1914–18*. London: Macmillan.

17. Cromie, F.N.A., Letters A1990/73 RNSM, Gosport.

Chapter 9

1. Letter from Lt. J.J.R. Peirson, to his family, RNSM, Gosport.

2. Gray, Edwyn (1971) *A Damned Un-English Weapon*. London: Seely, Service & Co.

3. Buchanan, Meriel (1918) *Petrograd (The City of Trouble) 1914–18*. London: Collins.

4. Wilson, Michael (1985) *Baltic Assignment*. London: Leo Cooper.

5. Head, Brian, *Baltic Campaign*, RNSM. Also Blacklock, Lt. R., Memoirs

Chapter 10

1. Diary of Lt. Cecil Mee, RNR, RNSM, Gosport.

2. Rear Admiral R.F. Phillimore, private letters, Imperial War Museum.

3. Nield, Lilian, *My Life in Russia*, unpublished MS, Leeds University Russian Archive and interview with the author.

4. Diaries of Cdr. Goodhart, Imperial War Museum.

5. Privately printed MS *Letters From Captain Cromie, R.N.* RNSM, Gosport.

6. Letter from William Dudley to *Saga* Magazine, 2 June 1999, and subsequent interview at his home.

7. Head, Brian, *Baltic Campaign*, RNSM, Gosport. Samuel Kent made a 'collision head' for torpedo practice which enabled the practice torpedo, after hitting its target, to surface instead of sinking, enabling it to be retrieved and used again.

8. Head, Brian, op. cit.
9. The German destroyer *V100*. Halahan blew her bows off with a well-aimed torpedo, which killed twelve sailors, but she refused to sink and was eventually towed back to Libau for repairs.

Chapter 11

1. Trotsky, Leon (1970), *My Life*. London: Penguin. The quotation is taken from page 256, and was originally part of an article Trotsky wrote for the paper *Nashe Slovo* in 1916.
2. Keegan, John (1998) *The First World War*. London: Hutchinson.
3. Letter from Cromie to Commodore Hall 17 June 1916, RNSM, Gosport.
4. Maylunas, Andrei and Mironenko, Sergei (1996) *A Lifelong Passion – Nicholas & Alexandra, Their Own Story*. London: Weidenfeld & Nicolson.
5. Moynahan, Brian (1992) *Comrades – Russia in Revolution 1917*. London: Hutchinson.
6. See Benson W.L. *Memoirs of an Ancient Submariner*, RNSM, Gosport. The name of the admiral is not mentioned, but Ben writes that his fate during the revolution was to be 'tied to a fountain in Helsingfors and burned alive'; it may have been Admiral Viren.
7. Buchanan, Meriel (1918) *Petrograd (The City of Trouble) 1914–18*. London: Collins.
8. Maylunas, Andrei and Mironenko, Sergei, op. cit.
9. Service, Robert (2000) *Lenin – A Biography*. London: Macmillan.

Chapter 12

1. Staff Surgeon Kenneth Hole's Baltic Flotilla report 1916–18, supplied by Michael J. Northeast RN (Retd), from the Library of the Royal Joint Services Hospital, Gosport, Hants.
2. (1920) *Official German Documents Relating to the World War*. II 1320–1321. Oxford: OUP.
3. Keegan, John (1998) *The First World War*. London: Hutchinson.
4. Trotsky, Leon (1970) *My Life*. London: Penguin.
5. Ibid.
6. Maylunas, Andrei and Mironenko, Sergei (1996) *A Lifelong Passion – Nicholas & Alexandra, Their Own Story*. London: Weidenfeld & Nicolson.
7. Reed, John (1979) *Ten Days That Shook the World*. London: Penguin. Reed compares the work of the *zemstvos* on the Russian front to that of the American YMCA.
8. Moynahan, Brian (1992) *Comrades – Russia in Revolution 1917*. London: Hutchinson.
9. Ibid.
10. Maylunas, Andrei and Mironenko, Sergei, op. cit.

Chapter 13

1. Lieutenant-Commander John Eastman, recording *c.*1958, Australian Broadcasting Corporation, interview on cassette loaned by Mrs Molly Williams of Birmingham, his daughter. He became well known in Australia for his hobby – remarkable for a man with no sight – of rug-making. He was a regular prize-winner in this field and often featured in the Australian media.

2. Letter from Capt. F.N.A. Cromie DSO RN, to Commodore Hall, 14/27 March 1917, RNSM, Gosport.

3. Berberova, Nina (1982) *Zheleznaia Zhenshchina (Iron Woman)*. New York. The work was published in French as *L'Histoire de la Baronne Budberg*, but there is no English translation. Additional information provided by Professor Richard Spence, University of Idaho, to whom the author is grateful.

4. Bruce Lockhart, R.H. (1932) *Memoirs of a British Agent*. London: Putnam.

5. This was outlined to me by Professor Richard Spence of the University of Idaho, who came across it in his research for his forthcoming biography of Sidney Reilly.

6. Lieven, Dominic (1993) *Nicholas II Emperor of All the Russians*. London: Pimlico.

7. Benson, W.L. *Memoirs of an Ancient Submariner*, RNSM, Gosport.

8. Benson, W.L. op. cit.

9. Benson, W.L. op. cit.

10. Ashmore, Vice-Admiral L.H. (2001) *Forgotten Flotilla*, Manuscript Press, Portsmouth. Leslie Ashmore was navigating officer on board *E18*.

11. Moynahan, Brian (1992) *Comrades – Russia in Revolution 1917*. London: Hutchinson.

12. Ashmore, Vice-Admiral L.H. *Forgotten Flotilla* MSS RNSM.

13. Maylunas, Andrei and Mironenko, Sergei *1996 A Lifelong Passion* Weidenfeld & Nicholson, London.

14. Ibid.

15. Paléologue, Maurice (France's Ambassador in Petrograd), Memoirs, quoted in Maylunas, Andrei and Mironenko, Sergei (1996) *A Lifelong Passion – Nicholas & Alexandra, Their Own Story*. London: Weidenfeld & Nicolson.

Chapter 14

1. Letter from Cromie to Rear-Admiral Phillimore 4 May 1917, RNSM, Gosport.

2. Ashmore, Vice-Admiral L.H. (2001) *Forgotten Flotilla* Manuscript Press, Portsmouth.

3. Ibid.

4. Benson, W.L. *Memoirs of an Ancient Submariner*, RNSM, Gosport.

5. Buchanan, Meriel (1919) *Petrograd, (The City of Trouble) 1914–18*. London: Collins.

6. Benson, W.L. op. cit.

7. Letter from Cromie to Commodore Hall 4/17 April 1917, RNSM, Gosport.

8. Head, Brian *Baltic Campaign*, RNSM, Gosport.

9. Wilmott, Ned (1979) *Strategy and Tactics of Sea Warfare*. London: Marshall Cavendish.

10. Farmborough, Florence (1974) *A Nurse at the Russian Front – A Diary 1914–18*. London: Constable.

11. Smith. L. 1994 *Between Mutiny and Obedience: The Case of the French Fifth Infantry Division During World War I*. Princeton.

12. Letter from Cromie to Commodore S. S. Hall 17 April 1917, RNSM, Gosport.

13. Wilson, Edmund (1940) *To the Finland Station*. London: W.H. Allen.

14. Ibid.

15. The notion that Lenin's train was 'sealed' is mistaken. According to Robert Service in *Lenin – A Biography*, there were various points on the trip where members of the party alighted, and the only 'sealed' element involved a line, drawn in chalk across the carriage floor, which separated the German guards from Lenin's party.

Chapter 15

1. Diary of Able Seaman Jefferys, RNSM, Gosport.
2. Ibid.
3. Maylunas, Andrei and Mironenko, Sergei (1996) *A Lifelong Passion – Nicholas and Alexandra, Their Own Story*. London: Weidenfeld & Nicolson. The 'tomb' referred to was that of those who had fallen during the recent uprising. According to Count Benckendorff's memoirs, quoted by Maylunas and Mironenko, on 15 April 'The work of digging a trench near the Chinese Theatre was begun to bury the pretended victims of the revolution at Tsarskoe . . . they were, in reality, six or seven drunkards who had died of drink the day when the wine shops had been looted. There was a great display of troops, red flags, bands playing the *Marseillaise* and other revolutionary tunes.'
4. Letter from Cromie to Admiral Phillimore 4 May 1917, RNSM, Gosport.
5. McGlaughlin, Steve *Biographical Directory of Russian Naval Officers 1850–1918* unpublished MS, contents available on the Internet at WWI The Maritime War *http://raven.cc.ukans.edu/* Mr McGlaughlin is an indispensable source of information and has compiled short biographies of over 2,000 Russian naval officers.
6. Head, Brian *The Baltic Campaign*, RNSM, Gosport.
7. Buchanan, Meriel (1918) *Petrograd (The City of Trouble) 1914–18*. London: Collins.
8. Trotsky, Leon (1970) *My Life*. London: Penguin.
9. Head, Brian *The Baltic Campaign*. Lt. Kershaw achieved great fame after the war as an international fencing champion and an England rugby international. See also, Vice-Admiral L.H. Ashmore's *Forgotten Flotilla* – 'Kershaw . . . became an Olympic fencer and Navy champion-at-arms. He commanded the headquarters ship *Bulolo* at the D-Day landings.'
10. Service, Robert (2000) *Lenin – A Biography*. London: Macmillan.
11. Ibid.
12. Moynahan, Brian (1992) *Comrades – Russia in Revolution 1917*. London: Hutchinson.
13. Keegan, John (1998) *The First World War*. London: Hutchinson.
14. Letter from Cromie to Admiral Phillimore 11 July 1917, RNSM, Gosport.

Chapter 16

1. Wilson, Michael (1985) *Baltic Assignment*. London: Leo Cooper.
2. Ibid.
3. Letter from Cromie to Admiral Phillimore 27 September 1917, RNSM, Gosport.
4. Rear Admiral Victor Stanley, British Naval Liaison Officer in Russia.
5. Letter from Cromie to Commodore Hall 10 October 1917, RNSM, Gosport.
6. Ashmore, Vice-Admiral L.H. *Forgotten Flotilla*, unpublished MSS, RNSM, Gosport.
7. Letter from Cromie to Rear Admiral Phillimore 29 November 1917, RNSM, Gosport.
8. Macintyre, Capt. Donald DSO DSC RN 'A Forgotten Campaign', *Journal of the Royal United Services Institution*, Vol. CVI Feb.–Nov. 1961.
9. Letter from Cromie to Rear Admiral Phillimore 29 November 1917. RNSM, Gosport.
10. Macintyre, Capt. Donald DSO DSC RN *A Forgotten Campaign* RUSI Journal 1961.
11. Service, Robert (2000) *Lenin, A Biography*. Macmillan, London.
12. Ibid.
13. Reed, John (1979) *Ten Days That Shook the World*. Penguin.

Chapter 17

1. 25/26 October by the Julian calendar, which was in use in Russia at the time.
2. Buchanan, Meriel (1918) *Petrograd (The City of Trouble) 1914–18*. London: Collins.
3. Reed, John (1979) *Ten Days That Shook the World*. London: Penguin.
4. Trotsky, Leon (1970) *My Life*. London: Penguin.
5. Ibid.
6. Staff Surgeon Kenneth Hole's Baltic Flotilla report 1916–18 supplied by Michael J. Northeast, RN (Retd.), from the Library of the Royal Joint Services Hospital, Gosport, Hants.
7. Kerensky, Alexander (1996) *Memoirs – Russia and History's Turning Point*. London: Cassell.
8. Bruce Lockhart R.H. (1932) *Memoirs of a British Agent*. London: Putnam.
9. Stanley Jackson (later engineer captain) was a great help to Cromie and the flotilla. Unfortunately, he died as one of the doomed crew on board the submarine HMS *Thetis* when she sank in Liverpool Bay in 1939, where she was undergoing trials.
10. Ashmore, Vice-Admiral L.H. (2001) *Forgotten Flotilla*, Manuscript Press, Portsmouth.
11. Diary of A.B. Jefferys, RNSM, Gosport.
12. Letter from Cromie to Rear Admiral Phillimore 29 November 1917, RNSM, Gosport.
13. Gerrard, British Consul at Reval. (Gerrard was Cromie's spelling; the correct name was Girard.)

Chapter 18

1. Head, Brian *The Baltic Campaign* unpublished MSS RNSM, Gosport.
2. Buchanan, Meriel (1918) *Petrograd (The City of Trouble) 1914–18*. Collins, London.
3. Benson, W.L. *Memoirs of an Ancient Submariner*, inpublished MSS, RNSM, Gosport.
4. Ibid. *'Song of the Asdic Yeoman'*
5. Ibid. The date of this conversation is not clear but the Buchanans did not receive clearance from Trotsky to leave until 8 January.
6. Letter from Cromie to Commodore Hall 2 December 1917, RNSM, Gosport.
7. Letter from Admiral Stanley to Sir Samuel Hoare 5 January 1937 in the Templewood Papers XVIII.3C(110), Cambridge University Library.
8. There were still, however, many thousands of Austrian and German POWs still imprisoned in more remote areas.
9. Ashmore, Vice Admiral L.H. (2001) *Forgotten Flotilla*, Manuscript Press, Portsmouth.
10. Deck cloths: canvas, scrubbed, painted and laid over the deck, rather like a carpet. They helped prevent seawater from splashing down the conning tower and reaching the batteries, and kept the deck reasonably dry and clean.
11. Benson, W.L. op. cit.
12. Buchanan, Meriel op. cit. One of the passengers with the Buchanans was Admiral Stanley, accompanied by Colonel Knox, who had met Cromie off the train the day the revolution began in March 1916.
13. Ashmore, op. cit.
14. Lt. Cdr, John Eastman, recording *c.* 1958 Australian Broadcasting Corporation, interview on cassette loaned by Mrs Molly Williams of Birmingham, his daughter.
15. Benson, W.L. op. cit.
16. Ashmore, op. cit.

Chapter 19

1. Deacon, Richard (1988) *The Silent War; A History of Western Naval Intelligence*. London: Grafton Books.
2. Letter from Cromie to Admiral W.R. Hall 6/19 January 1918, RNSM, Gosport.
3. Porter, Bernard (1989) *Plots and Paranoia – A History of Political Espionage in Britain 1790–1988*. London: Unwin Hyman.
4. Ibid, quoted from Knightley, Philip (1986) *The Second Oldest Profession: The Spy as Bureaucrat, Patriot, Fantasist and Whore*. London: Deutsch.
5. Letter from Cromie to Commodore Hall 19 January 1918, RNSM, Gosport.
6. Letter from Cromie to Admiral Hall 1 February 1918, RNSM, Gosport.
7. Ibid.
8. SS Secret Service. Although Cromie was claiming to stay 'outside political work', the very essence of this paragraph – 'to put our fingers in' – seems to be just that!
9. Staff List MI5 1918–19 KVI/S9 PRO.
10. Trotsky, Leon (1970) *My Life*. London: Penguin.
11. Ibid.
12. Ibid.
13. Keegan, John (1998) *The First World War*. London: Hutchinson.
14. Letter from Cromie to Commodore Hall 19 February 1918, RNSM, Gosport.
15. Gray, Edwyn (1971) *A Damned Un-English Weapon*. London: Seely, Service & Co.
16. Ashmore, Vice-Admiral L.H. (2001) *Forgotten Flotilla*, Manuscript Press, Portsmouth.
17. Lt. Basil Downie's Official Report to Commodore S.S. Hall, 5 May 1918. 368/04912, RNSM, Gosport.
18. Ashmore, op. cit.
19. *The Times*, 17 May 1918.
20. Head, Brian *Baltic Campaign*, RNSM, Gosport. The transport *Huntsend* was formerly the German *Lutzow* (8,718 tons) captured as a prize in Suez in August 1914.
21. Wilson, Michael (1985) *Baltic Assignment*. London: Leo Cooper.
22. Ashmore, op. cit.
23. Note from Commodore S.S. Hall, 3 June 1918, attached to Lt. Downie's report. 368/04912, RNSM, Gosport.
24. Letter from Cromie to Admiral Phillimore 2 May 1918, RNSM, Gosport.

Chapter 20

1. *British Vessels Lost at Sea 1914–18* (1988) London: HMSO/Patrick Stephens and *Lloyd's War Losses WWI* Lloyd's of London.
2. Prof. Theodor Siersdorfer, maritime historian, Essen, writes 'According to Prof. Meyer of Berlin, the *Toledo* is listed in a Russian handbook *Berez'noi* as having been wrecked when taking troops off Dago Island 5.10.17.'
3. Statement on the fate of the SS *Cicero* by Capt. W.H. Pinchon 17 September 1918, Wilson Line Archives, University of Hull.
4. This must have been Lieutenant Downie, as he mentions they 'had all got safely home'.
5. The author is indebted for the *Cicero* story and the suggestions of her final occupation to maritime researcher S. Keith Smith of Cottingham, near Hull.

6. Letter from Cromie to Admiral Phillimore, 2 May 1918, RNSM, Gosport. A fuller picture of everyday prices and inflation can be obtained in Appendix 2 of John Reed's *Ten Days That Shook the World*.
7. Funt: approximate Russian weight equivalent of British pound (avoirdupois).
8. Silverlight, John (1970) *The Victor's Dilemma*. London: Barrie & Jenkins.
9. Noulens, the French Ambassador, and his party had originally attempted to leave Russia on the train with Sir George Buchanan in January 1918, but unlike the British were unable to leave when they became stranded in Finland. They eventually had to go back into Russia, to Vologda. Noulens, apparently, never forgave the British for 'abandoning' him and his party.
10. Silverlight, John op. cit.
11. Bruce Lockhart, R.H. (1932) *Memoirs of a British Agent*. London: Putnam.
12. Bruce Lockhart, R.H. (1973) (Ed. Kenneth Young) *The Diaries of Sir Robert Bruce Lockhart 1915–1938*. London: Macmillan.
13. A pood was roughly equivalent to 36 pounds (avoirdupois).
14. Letter from Cromie to Admiral Phillimore, 2 May 1919, RNSM, Gosport.
15. Letter from Cromie to Admiral Hall 10 May 1918, RNSM, Gosport.
16. Ibid.
17. *Notes on the Origin and Activities of the Russo-English Dockyards and Shipbuilding Company at Murmansk* FO 175/6 PRO, Kew.
18. Letter from Cromie to Admiral Hall 10 May 1918, RNSM, Gosport.
19. FO 371/3329 PRO, Kew.
20. Ibid.
21. Bruce Lockhart, Robin (1981) *Ace of Spies*. London: Macdonald Futura.
22. Swain, Geoffrey (2000) *Russia's Civil War*. Stroud: Tempus Publishing.
23. Figures vary between sources from 32,000 to 50,000 Czechs.
24. FO 371/3286 PRO, Kew.

Chapter 21

1. Letter from Cromie to Admiral Hall 14 August 1918, RNSM, Gosport.
2. Bruce Lockhart, R.H. (1932) *Memoirs of a British Agent*. London: Putnam.
3. Ibid.
4. Silverlight, John (1970) *The Victor's Dilemma – Allied Intervention in the Russian Civil War*. London: Barrie & Jenkins.
5. Bruce Lockhart, R.H. (1932) *Memoirs of a British Agent*. London: Putnam.
6. Deacon, Richard (1969) *A History of the British Secret Service*. London: Muller.
7. Andrew, Christopher and Gordievsky, Oleg (1991) *KGB – The Inside Story of its Foreign Operations From Lenin to Gorbachev*. London: Sceptre.
8. Service, Robert (2000) *Lenin – A Biography*. London: Macmillan.

Chapter 22

1. Bunyan, James (1936) *Intervention, Civil War and Communism in Russia, Documents and Material*. Baltimore: John Hopkins Press. According to Bunyan, and other sources, Chicherin told the American writer Louis Fischer that the Bolsheviks had approached the German Ambassador, Helfferich, with a proposal that the Germans send an army into Russia to oppose the Allied advance from Archangel. Helfferich

was not keen on the idea, and left Moscow on 6 August 1918. (See also Fischer's *The Soviets in World Affairs.*)

2. ADM 223/637 PRO, Kew; this document is a report from an agent, Harold Trevenen Hall, from Stockholm, dated 19 November 1918. Hall claims to have been with Cromie at his death. The C-in-C Baltic Fleet, Admiral Shastny, is referred to in the document as 'CHASTNI'. It has not been possible to decipher who the mysterious 'Mr Dick' was. There is a chance that 'CHASTNI' may not be the Baltic C-in-C, but as Sabir claimed to be a lieutenant, and he was visiting Cromie, whose area of expertise was definitely the Baltic Fleet, it is safe to assume that, allowing for the wide variation of translation of Russian names into English, CHASTNI is Admiral Shastny. Hall is listed in Nathalie Bucknall's report of the Embassy raid as a 'civilian'. What he was doing in the Embassy at such a dangerous juncture, if this is the case, is unknown. If he was a civilian, he certainly seems to have known quite a lot of privileged information about the Allied plans during August.

3. The names 'Steckelmann' and 'Sabir' are spelled as per H.T. Hall's official report. However, Professor Richard Spence, Sidney Reilly's biographer, rightly points out that the correct translation of the names are probably Shteklman and Sapir. My suggestion that 'Steckelmann' *may* have been German is merely speculative.

4. Lockhart makes no mention of this mysterious duo in his diaries or memoirs.

5. FO 371/3307 PRO, Kew.

6. Captain Grigori Chaplin, Russian Navy, had a similar career to Cromie's. He was also a handsome man in his mid-thirties, and spoke flawless English. He went south to help recruitment for the White armies, and met Cromie at the Embassy in Petrograd in the spring of 1918. He was involved in various anti-German sabotage plots, and in May 1918, as 'Commander Thomson', he donned British navy uniform and carried on recruiting officers to join up with Poole in the north. He helped to stage an anti-Bolshevik coup in Archangel, which made things decidedly easier for the Allied landings.

7. Gillespie was attached to the Military Mission at the Embassy in Petrograd – 'Gillespie' is another of Reilly's suspected aliases.

8. Lockhart did say, however, in *Memoirs of a British Agent*, that after his arrest, 'I had only the vaguest idea of what had happened. It was obvious, however, that the Bolsheviks were trying to link us up with the attempt on Lenin's life. This manoeuvre did not disconcert me.'

9. Deacon, Richard (1987) *A History of the Russian Secret Service*. London: Grafton.

10. Spence, Professor Richard, University of Idaho. At the time of writing Prof. Spence's new biography of Sidney Reilly is nearing completion.

11. Bruce Lockhart, R.H. (1932) *Memoirs of a British Agent*. London: Putnam.

12. Britnieva, Mary (1934) *One Woman's Story*. London: Arthur Baker.

13. Farmborough, Florence (1974) *A Nurse at the Russian Front – A Diary 1914–1918*. London: Constable.

14. Statement on the Embassy Raid by Nathalie Bucknall made to Consul Bosanquet 1 September 1918, FO 337/87 PRO, Kew.

15. Britnieva, Mary op. cit.

16. Harold Trevenen Hall may, at this time, have been a businessman working on some opportunist secondment to Cromie. He does appear as an SIS agent in the post-war years operating in Finland and Estonia, where he made the blunder of buying a series of Russian documents which were said to prove that the Soviets were subsidising the IRA. The documents were later revealed to be White Russian forgeries.

17. Report from H.T. Hall, ADM 223/637 PRO, Kew.

18. Britnieva, Mary. op. cit.
19. Ibid.
20. Nathalie Bucknall's statement to Consul Bosanquet 1 September 1918, FO 337/87, PRO, Kew.
21. The spelling 'Hillier' is taken from the translation of the *Pravda* report on the raid which was reproduced in the London *Times*. 'Hillier' was actually Sehem Leonidovich Geller. Professor Richard Spence, Reilly's biographer explained: 'The Russian alphabet has no exact equivalent to the Latin 'H', so the latter usually ends up transliterated as the Cyrillic 'G', i.e., Hitler becomes Gitler, Hippius, Gippius etc. So Geller is actually Hillier in its original form.'

Chapter 23

1. Phil Tomaselli of Swindon, to whom the author owes much gratitude.
2. Knightley, Philip (1986) *The Second Oldest Profession: The Spy as Bureaucrat, Patriot, Fantastist and Whore*. London: Deutsch.
3. *Isvestia* No. 191, 5 September 1918.
4. Nathalie Bucknall's statement to Consul Bosanquet 1 September 1918, FO 337/87, PRO, Kew.
5. ADM 223/637, PRO, Kew.
6. Bruce Lockhart, Robin (1981) *Ace of Spies*. London: Macdonald Futura.
7. Letter from Frances Wagner to Revd B.S. Lombard, FO371/4023 PRO Kew.
8. Boris Savinkov (Savinkoff) had been Minister of War under Kerensky. M. Filonek was a counter-revolutionary said to be plotting with Savinkov. It is not quite clear why Prince Shashkovsky was in the embassy, but as a close friend of Reilly's and ex-Tsarist Minister of Trade and Industry and councillor of the State Bank, he was quite a catch.
9. *Krasnaia Gazeta*, Petrograd, 2 September 1918.
10. Berezhkov, Vasilii *Vnutri I vne Bol'shogo Doma*. I am indebted to Professor Richard Spence for details of both the *Gazeta* and Berezhkov accounts.
11. Professor Spence offers an intriguing angle on Geller: 'Did Geller know Reilly as well? Was Geller picked up by Reilly to eliminate Cromie as "a man who knew too much" – whether Cromie realised that or not?'

Chapter 24

1. *Biografisch Woordenboek Van Nederland* (1979) s'Gravenhage: Martinus Nijhof. I am also grateful to Dr J.M.A. Dané of the Nederlands Institut voor Oorlogsdocumentatie, Amsterdam, for providing details of Oudendijk's life.
2. Oudendijk, William J. (1939) *Ways and Byways in Diplomacy*. London: Peter Davies.
3. Ibid.
4. Letter from Frances Wagner to Revd B.S. Lombard, FO 371/4023, PRO, Kew.
5. Ibid.
6. Ibid.
7. Ibid.
8. Scott, Hew (1926) *Fasti Ecclesiae Scoticanae* Vol. VI, Edinburgh. (Courtesy Mrs Margaret Thompson, United Reformed Church History Society, Cambridge.)
9. Oudendijk William, J. op. cit.

Chapter 25

1. Wingrove, A.B. 'E19's Outward Voyage' from the diary of Able Seaman Wingrove, RNSM, Gosport.
2. Milosevsky, Vladimir Alexeivich (1989) *Yesterday, the day before Yesterday* 2nd Edition. Moscow: Kniga Publishing House. (Originally published in 1979, but the first edition does not include the Gagarin information.) Translation from the Russian by Isobel Hackett, to whom the author is grateful.
3. According to Prince Gagarin, 'Zamiatin never finished his novel *Oaks*, but the drafts were published in the *Novii Journal* issue no. 2, 1993, St Petersburg.'

Chapter 26

1. Letter from Gwladys Cromie to Sir George Buchanan 18 September 1918, FO 371/3342, PRO, Kew.
2. FO 371/3342 Letter from V.W. Baddeley, Admiralty, to Foreign Office, stating, 'Mrs Cromie has expressed a desire that her husband's body should remain at Petrograd.'
3. Horsefield, John (1986) *The Art of Leadership in War – The Royal Navy from the Age of Nelson to the End of World War I*. Westport, Connecticut: Greenwood Press.
4. FO 371/3342, PRO, Kew.
5. Ibid.
6. Ibid.
7. Ibid.
8. FO 371/3286, PRO, Kew.
9. FO 337/87 Nathalie Bucknall's statement to Consul Bosanquet, PRO, Kew.
10. Burridge, Lt. R.L. 'Submarine Reminiscences' part of a letter, undated, RNSM, Gosport.
11. Lt. Burridge's Service Record BDH Ref., 135 RNSM, Gosport.

BIBLIOGRAPHY

Books

Andrew, Christopher and Gordievsky, Oleg (1991) *KGB – The Inside Story of its Foreign Operations From Lenin to Gorbachev*. London: Sceptre.

Barnett, Corelli (1963) *The Sword Bearers – Studies in Supreme Command in WWI*. London: Hodder & Stoughton.

Bennett, Geoffrey (1964) *Cowan's War*. London: Collins.

Bower, Tom (1989) *The Red Web – MI6 and The KGB Master Coup*. London: Aurum Press.

Brooks, Richard (1999) *The Long Arm of Empire – Naval Brigades from the Crimea to the Boxer Rebellion*. London: Constable.

Britnieva, Mary (1932) *One Woman's Story*. London: Arthur Baker.

Bruce Lockhart, R.H. (1973) *The Diaries of Sir Robert Bruce Lockhart 1915–1938* (edited by Kenneth Young). London: Macmillan.

—— (1932) *Memoirs of A British Agent*. London: Putnam.

—— (1934) *Retreat From Glory*. London: Putnam.

Bruce Lockhart, Robin (1981) *Ace of Spies*. London: Macdonald Futura.

Buchanan, Meriel (1918) *Petrograd (The City of Trouble) 1914–18*. London: Collins.

Bunyan, James (1936) *Intervention, Civil War and Communism In Russia, Documents and Materials*. Baltimore: John Hopkins Press.

Carr, Edward Hallett (1953) *The Bolshevik Revolution 1917–1923* Vol. III. London: Macmillan.

Castleden, Rodney (1994) *British History, A Chronological Dictionary of Dates*. London: Parragon.

Clark, Gregory (1981) *Britain's Naval Heritage*. London: HMSO.

Compton-Hall, Richard (1991) *Submarines and the War at Sea 1914–18*. London: Macmillan.

Corbett and Newbolt (1923) *Official History of The War, Naval Operations* Vols. I–V. London: Longman.

Crankshaw, Edward (1976) *The Shadow of The Winter Palace – The Drift to Revolution 1825–1917*. London: Macmillan.

Deacon, Richard (1988) *The Silent War – A History of Western Naval Intelligence*. London: Grafton.

—— (1987) *A History of the Russian Secret Service*. London: Grafton.

Domville-Pit, Charles (1919) *Submarines and Sea Power*. London: Bell & Sons.

Farmborough, Florence (1974) *A Nurse at the Russian Front – A Diary 1914–18*. London: Constable.

Friedman, Norman (1984) *Submarine Design and Development*. London: Conway Maritime.

Gardiner, Juliet (Ed) (2000) *The History Today Who's Who in British History*. London: Collins & Brown.

Gardiner, Juliet and Wenborn, Neil (Eds) (1995) *The History Today Companion to British History* London: Collins & Brown.

Gosden, P.H.J.H. (1969) *How They Were Taught*. Oxford: Blackwell.

Gray, Edwyn (1971) *A Damned Un-English Weapon*. London: Seely, Service & Co.

Hill, Christopher (1971) *Lenin and the Russian Revolution*. London: Pelican.

Hill, J. R. and Ranft, B. (Ed) (1995) *Oxford Illustrated History of The Royal Navy*. Oxford: OUP.

HMSO (1988) *British Vessels Lost At Sea 1914–18*. Wellingborough: Patrick Stephens.

Honan, William H. (1995) *Great Naval Battles of the Twentieth Century*. London: Robson Books.

Horsefield, John (1986) *The Art of Leadership in War – The Royal Navy from the Age of Nelson to the End of World War I*. Westport, Connecticut: Greenwood Press.

Humble, Richard (1981) *Submarines – The Illustrated History*. London: Connoisseur/Basinghall.

Humphreys, Rob and Richardson, Dan (1997) *The Rough Guide to St Petersburg*. London: Rough Guides/Penguin.

Jellicoe, J. (1934) *The Submarine Peril; The Admiralty Policy in 1917*. London: Cassell.

Keegan, John (1998) *The First World War*. London: Hutchinson.

Kemp, Paul (2000) *Submarine Action*. London: Chancellor Press.

Kerensky, Alexander (1965) *Memoirs – Russia and History's Turning Point*. London: Cassell.

Kerr, Commander C.L., RN (1939) *All in a Day's Work*. London: Rich & Cowan.

Kinahan, Coralie (1988) *After The War Came Peace?*. Belfast: Pretani Press.

Kipling, Rudyard (1933) *Rudyard Kipling's Verse Inclusive Edition*. London: Hodder & Stoughton.

'Klaxon' (1919) *The Story of Our Submarines*. London: Blackwood.

Kochan, Lionel (1974) *Lenin*. Hove: Wayland Publishers.

Kuusinen, Oleg (1961) *Fundamentals of Marxism–Leninism*. Moscow: Foreign Languages Publishing House.

Lenin, V. I. (publication date unknown) *State And Revolution*. Re-issued by Lawrence & Wishart as *How To Change The Social Order*

—— (1920) *Left Wing Communism – An Infantile Disorder*. Moscow: Progress Publishers.

Lewis, Michael (1948) *The Navy of Britain*. London: Allen & Unwin.

Lieven, Dominic (1993) *Nicholas II Emperor of All the Russians*. London: John Murray.

Longstaff, Reginald (1984) *Submarine Command – A Pictorial History*. London: Robert Hale.

Luck, Steve (Ed.) (2000) *Philip's World History Encyclopedia*. London: George Philip Ltd.

Macksey, Kenneth and Woodhouse, William (Eds) (1991) *Penguin Encyclopedia of Warfare*. London: Viking.

Mawdsley, Evan (1978) *The Russian Revolution and the Baltic Fleet*. London: Macmillan.

Maylunas, Andrei and Mironenko, Sergei (1996) *A Lifelong Passion – Nicholas and Alexandra, Their Own Story*. London: Weidenfeld & Nicolson.

Moynahan, Brian (1992) *Comrades – Russia in Revolution 1917*. London: Hutchinson.

Noble, Christine (Ed) (1999) *The War to End Wars 1914–18*. London: Reader's Digest.

—— (1999) *Forging the Modern Age 1914–18*.

Oudendijk (Oudendyk), W.J. (1939) *Ways and By-Ways in Diplomacy*. London: Peter Davies.

Payne, Robert (1967) *The Fortress*. London: W.H. Allen.

Porter, Lionel (1989) *Plots and Paranoia – A History of Political Espionage in Britain 1790–1988*. London: Unwin Hyman.

Reed, John (1979) *Ten Days That Shook the World*. London: Penguin.

Reynolds, Clark G. (1976) *Command of the Sea – History and Strategy of Maritime Empires*. London: Robert Hale.

Schapiro, Leonard (1963) *The Communist Party of the Soviet Union*. London: Methuen.

Seaman, L.C.B. (1966) *Post-Victorian Britain, 1902–1951*. London: Methuen.

Service, Robert (2000) *Lenin – A Biography*. London: Macmillan.

Silverlight, John (1970) *The Victor's Dilemma – Allied Intervention in the Russian Civil War*. London: Barrie & Jenkins.

Sutton, Antony G. (1981) *Wall Street and the Bolshevik Revolution*. Morley, Western Australia: Veritas Publishing.

Swain, Geoffrey (2000) *Russia's Civil War*. Stroud, Gloucestershire: Tempus Publishing.

Taylor, A.J.P. (1993) *From Napoleon to the Second International*. London: Hamish Hamilton.

Trotsky, Leon (1970) *My Life – An Attempt at a Biography*. London: Penguin.

—— (1965) *History of the Revolution, Vol. III*. Gollancz, London.

Leon Trotsky Internet Archive *http://www.marxists.org/archive/trotsky*

Ustinov, Sir Peter (1983) *My Russia*. London: Macmillan.

van der Vat, Dan (1995) *Stealth at Sea*. London: Orion Books.

von Trapp, Maria (1967) *The Sound of Music – The Trapp Family Singers*. London: Fontana.

Wilmot, Ned (1979) *Strategy and Tactics of Sea Warfare*. London: Marshall Cavendish.

Wilson, Edmund (1960) *To the Finland Station*. London: Fontana.

Wilson, Michael (1985) *Baltic Assignment*. London: Leo Cooper.

—— (1988) *Destination Dardanelles*. London: Leo Cooper.

Archive Material

Public Record Office, Kew

Admiralty Documents: ADM196/47 137/2067 223/637 137/1247 137/2068

Army Lists 1870–1915 Navy Lists 1914–18

Foreign Office Documents: 175/6 337/87 367/39 371/3286 371/3329 371/3342 371/4023

The Times Index 1914–18

War Office Documents: 76/507/fo.46 339/7606

Staff List, MI5 1918–19 KV1/S9

Cambridge University Library

The Templewood Papers XVIII (Sir Samuel Hoare, later Viscount Templewood)

Royal Navy Submarine Museum, Gosport

Ashmore, Vice-Admiral L.H. and Macintyre, Captain Donald, *Forgotten Flotilla*

Benson, L.W. 'Ben' *Memoirs of an Ancient Submariner*

Burridge Lt. R.L., RN, Service Record BDH Ref. 135

Cromie, Capt. F.N.A., CB, DSO, RN Letters A1990/73

Downie, Lt. B., RN, Report on the Destruction of the Baltic Flotilla 368/04912 1983/59

Hayward, P.U., RN, Paymaster, Service Record BDH Ref. 238
Head, Brian *Baltic Campaign*
Holmes, Leading Stoker George, Diary
Log Book, HMS *E19*
Jefferys, A.C., Able Seaman, Diary
Macintyre, Capt. Donald, DSO RN, 'A Forgotten Campaign',
Journal of the Royal United Services Institution, Vol. CVI Feb–Nov 1961
Mee, Lt. Cecil, RNR *Diary of Lt. Cecil Mee*
Wingrove, Able Seaman, Diary

Miscellaneous

A Collection of Reports on Bolshevism in Russia, HMSO 1919.
Letters and Papers of Commodore S.S. Hall, Imperial War Museum
Archives of the Wilson Line, Hull University
Lloyd's Shipping Registers 1914–18
Nield, Lilian, *My Life in Russia*, Leeds University Russian Library
Hale, Julian 'The Past in A Foreign Country', article on Tina Alexander (Moura
    Budberg's daughter) returning to Estonia *Telegraph Magazine*, January 1997
Cromie, Charles Francis, Service Record, Hampshire Regiment Museum
McGlaughlin, Steve, *Biographical Directory of Russian Naval Officers*, via the internet at
    WWI The Maritime War *http://raven.cc.ukans.edu*
Furst Gagarin, The Gagarin Archives c/o Prince Andrey Gagarin, St Petersburg
Helsingin Sanomat, Helsinki, Finland
Barometern, Kalmar, Sweden

INDEX

The index is arranged alphabetically, except for the subheadings under Captain Francis Cromie which are arranged chronologically. Page numbers in *italics* refer to illustrations.